Revisiting Nuclear India

Revisiting Nuclear India

STRATEGIC CULTURE AND (IN)SECURITY IMAGINARY

Runa Das

www.sagepublications.com
Los Angeles • London • New Delhi • Singapore • Washington DC • Boston

First published in 2015 by

SAGE Publications India Pvt Ltd
B1/I-1 Mohan Cooperative Industrial Area
Mathura Road, New Delhi 110 044, India
www.sagepub.in

SAGE Publications Inc
2455 Teller Road
Thousand Oaks, California 91320, USA

SAGE Publications Ltd
1 Oliver's Yard, 55 City Road
London EC1Y 1SP, United Kingdom

SAGE Publications Asia-Pacific Pte Ltd
3 Church Street
#10-04 Samsung Hub
Singapore 049483

Published by Vivek Mehra for SAGE Publications India Pvt Ltd, typeset at 10/13 pts Berkeley by Diligent Typesetter, Delhi and printed at Chaman Enterprises, New Delhi.

Library of Congress Cataloging-in-Publication Data Available

ISBN: 978-93-515-0122-0 (HB)

The SAGE Team: Rudra Narayan, Neha Sharma, Rajib Chatterjee, and Rajinder Kaur

*Dedicated to my father Late Debi Prasad Ghosh and
my mother Arati Ghosh*

Thank you for choosing a SAGE product! If you have any comment, observation or feedback, I would like to personally hear from you. Please write to me at <u>contactceo@sagepub.in</u>

—Vivek Mehra, Managing Director and CEO,
SAGE Publications India Pvt Ltd, New Delhi

Bulk Sales

SAGE India offers special discounts for purchase of books in bulk. We also make available special imprints and excerpts from our books on demand.

For orders and enquiries, write to us at

Marketing Department
SAGE Publications India Pvt Ltd
B1/I-1, Mohan Cooperative Industrial Area
Mathura Road, Post Bag 7
New Delhi 110044, India
E-mail us at <u>marketing@sagepub.in</u>

Get to know more about SAGE, be invited to SAGE events, get on our mailing list. Write today to <u>marketing@sagepub.in</u>

This book is also available as an e-book.

Contents

Acknowledgments   ix

1   Discourse in International Relations: Situating India   1
2   Nation-making in Colonial India   26
3   Political Idealism and Atomic Science: 1947–1964   57
4   Defense Preparedness and Nuclear Aggressiveness:
    1964–1991   91
5   At the Nuclear Edge: 1991–1998   139
6   Crossing the Nuclear Threshold and the Neoliberal Turn:
    1998–2004   170
7   Neoliberal Strategic Security/Defense Collaborations:
    Post-2004   215
8   Conclusion   265

Bibliography   278
Index   315
About the Author   330

Acknowledgments

I express my gratitude to my numerous colleagues in the United States and India for their intellectual support and feedback on this book. I am also grateful to the editors of SAGE for their patience as I worked through this book.

1

Discourse in International Relations: Situating India

Interrogating the socially constructed nature of a nation's strategic culture to explain its nuclear security policies is not a common practice in the mainstream scholarships in international relations (IR)/strategic culture studies. This is because the ascendance and continued domination of the neorealist/neoliberal paradigms, the relevance of state-centric analysis, and the structural anarchy as given (resulting in a corresponding marginalization of issues of culture, ideology, and identity politics) have not only shaped the field of IR but have also dominated the international and national spheres of strategy-making. Likewise, a survey of three generations of the strategic culture theorists will reveal that their analysis of strategic culture and strategy-making has been realist-based and cognition-oriented. Despite occasional forays by the critical IR, and the third-generation (ideographic) strategic culture theorists who have drawn attention to the power of representation/interpretation in IR/strategic culture studies, it might be appropriate to note that the disciplinary domains of both have not made efforts to explore "… cultural [discursive] processes through which insecurities of states and communities … are produced, reproduced, and transformed" in international politics (Weldes et al., 1999:2). The recent foray of the critical constructivists into IR based on the premise that "*all* social insecurities are culturally produced" (ibid.:1) provides a different vantage for both conventional and critical IR or strategic culture theorists in revisiting the discursive productions of insecurity in international politics.

This book is an effort to orient strategic culture studies in this critical constructivist direction. In doing so, it addresses the relative silence in the discipline of strategic culture studies in conceptualizing a nation's strategic culture, notions of insecurities, and strategy-making as a socially constructed discourse in international politics. Put simplistically, it explores with a case study of India's nuclear trajectory how discursive articulations of a nation's strategic culture, rendered possible by meaning-producing discourses and codes of intelligibilities of its security community,[1] facilitate interpretations of the state's strategic environment, notions of insecurities, and (non)proliferation policy choices.

Before proceeding further with my research query, it might be important to note that conceptual, epistemological, and methodological issues abound in using strategic culture to describe national security policy-making. Although I do not seek to provide an exhaustive or definitive resolution to such issues, I note a few in order to situate my constructivist efforts in revisiting their link. Conceptual issues center around how strategic culture theorists conceptualize strategic cultures, an aspect which also relates to their ontology, that is, what are they studying in trying to define strategic cultures? The existing strategic culture literatures (which I have elaborated in the book) reveal that strategic cultures have been categorized as national types, military organizational types, or ideographic (case-specific) types. Such categorizations have focused on sociocultural characteristics of national cultures, national heritage, experiences of geography, beliefs and customs of domestic organizations, such as the military and the bureaucracy, and the symbolic roles of political rhetoric. In such conceptualizations, strategic cultures are seen as a shared set of meanings that are determined by historical precedents, cultural conditions, and/or contemporary experiences of real and domestic politics. In such endeavors, strategic cultural theorists have epistemologically relied on cognition (i.e., collective behaviors of organizations) and the structural (realist) edifice in knowing the relationship between strategic cultures and strategies, which, seen from the lenses of a detached researcher, locates these links to means–ends relationship—where states consider appropriate security aims and ways to resolve their insecurities. From the perspective of critical IR, such means–ends relationship between strategic cultures and strategy constitute a problem-solving approach to international security.

The purpose of this book is not necessarily to challenge the existing strategic culture approaches and their contributions to strategic culture studies, rather contending that existing strategic culture studies have not paid adequate attention to the social power of discourse in strategy-making. I use the critical social constructivist approach to proffer an alternative angle in understanding the discursive/representational links between strategic culture, insecurity, and strategy-making in international politics. My broader logic in this context is as follows: Every state has a foundational culture made up of its civilizational, moral, and cultural values from which emerge visions of its strategic culture. Thus, every state exists, and is operative, within the crucible of its foundational culture, which to a great extent shapes the nature of its strategic thinking. Nonetheless, I argue that what constitutes a state's strategic culture is not merely an echo of its foundational culture, that is, a state's strategic culture is not simply historically determined or culturally conditioned. Instead, I argue in this book that a state's strategic culture is socially constructed, where the state's security community, as social/discursive agents, draw from the moorings of its foundational culture, which, in interaction with existing aspects of real, domestic, bureaucratic-institutional, and global politics project certain self-understandings of the state's strategic culture, (in)security imaginaries,[2] and its national security policies.

In drawing attention to the power of discourse that serves as meaning-producing tool to attribute meaning to states' strategic cultures and (in)security imaginaries, I admit that there exists a real world of insecurities and to that extent realist IR theories and the realist-based strategic culture theories make a valid point in explaining states' security policies. Yet, arguing that such conventional approaches are ill-equipped to explore those discursive processes "through which insecurities of states and communities ... are produced" (Weldes et al., 1999:2), I pursue an interpretive approach that, via discourse analysis, highlights the meaning-producing roles of political leaders' discourses that construct their strategic cultural thinking and insecurities in IR. In terms of this interpretive logic, neither sources of dangers nor the identities that they threaten (i.e., the state) are permanent, rather they keep changing according to the political, ideological, and discursive milieu within which states operate. This approach is a reflective of temporality and spatiality engaged in certain shifting discourses to reconstruct their notions of strategic cultures and insecurity imaginations. In incorporating this interpretive approach to proffer a constructivist understanding between states' strategic cultures and insecurities, I suggest initiating an alternative generation of strategic culture scholarship that (unlike preceding scholarships of strategic culture and security practices) incorporates the critical constructivist's premise of discourse to retheorize (along discursive lines) the productions of strategic cultures, insecurities, and security practices in IR.

In initiating this line of query, I use India's nuclear security as a case study to argue that the interrelationship between a nation's (in this case India's) strategic culture, its (in)security imaginaries, and its security policies is not simply culturally conditioned, historically determined, socially acquired or inherited (as alluded by the India-specific theorists of strategic culture and security). However, I suggest that India's strategic culture is a socially constructed field, where discursive contestations of meaning productions are played out by its security community to represent India's strategic culture, (in)security imaginaries, and its security policies.

I specifically examine the following "how possible" research puzzles: First, how is India's strategic culture discursively reproduced via discourses and codes of intelligibilities of its security community? Second, how the discursive construction of India's strategic culture, embodied within and projected through the state's meaning-producing discourses, offer the political–ideological space within which are constructed and reinterpreted shifting understandings of India's IR, its nationalist identity, and its (in)security imaginaries? Finally, how the social construction of India's strategic culture and (in)security imaginaries create an ideological cultural space within which are forged and articulated the shifting contours of India's nuclear security developments? In addressing each "how-possible" question, my aim will be to show how the Indian state's discourses as tools of social and ideological power have produced and sustained a mutually constituted and shifting relationship between India's strategic cultural thinking, its strategic identity, its (in)security imaginaries, and its nuclear policy choices.

Three factors such as conceptual, analytical, and practical (which I will further elaborate in the chapter) underlie this book's efforts in revisiting the literature on strategic culture and security policies. First, conceptually, this book argues that the commonly accepted conception of strategic culture as constituting "the sum total of ideals, conditional emotions responses, and patterns of habitual behavior" (Synder, 1977:9) is problematic because it assumes that strategic cultures are culturally conditioned or historically determined. Instead, this book suggests a how-possible approach to strategic culture studies, namely how strategic cultures are socially constructed. Second, in terms of analytical limitations of existing strategic culture studies, this book is of the view that such studies have been operated with certain epistemological assumptions of international politics where states, identities (self/other), and insecurities are given. This limitation of the strategic culture theorists to challenge the realist edifice of international politics precludes them from analyzing the intersubjectively constituted links between a nation's strategic culture, perceptions of identities of self/other, and the nation's (in)security imaginaries. That is, how the discursive interpretation of a nation's strategic culture, productive of certain (in)security imaginaries, explains the nation's security policies? Finally, a constructivist re-examination of how nations redefine their strategic cultures, (in)security imaginaries, and national security policy choices contains policy implications for interstate security relations namely for the future of a nuclear South Asia—given that those who make decisions of going nuclear are also in a position to create conditions for altering their strategic cultural perceptions vis-à-vis identities of self/adversaries, insecurities, and national security policy choices. This practical implication of the book remains significant given that noticeable discursive-ideological shifts in India's strategic cultural thinking and (in)security imaginaries post-9/11 have indeed created the conditions, or the political–ideological space, for altering the state's strategic perceptions vis-à-vis significant issues such as nonalignment, Gandhi–Nehru's notions of nuclear nonviolence, India's traditional Cold War-centric national security orientations, and perceptions of identities of the self/other in IR.

In revisiting reconstructions of strategic culture, (in)security imaginaries, and India's national security policy-making, this book is concerned with the following questions: (1) What constitutes some of the foundational aspects of India's civilization and culture? (2) How do these foundational aspects of culture shape India's strategic culture and how can one identify the basic contours of India's strategic culture (namely during its anticolonial struggles of making a postcolonial India)? (3) While describing India's strategic culture in its postcolonial context, what sorts of ideological lenses or ideational mindsets have interpreted the past and present understandings of India's strategic thinking and culture? (4) Is the task of interpreting India's strategic culture simply a task of reiterating the foundational forms of its strategic thinking and in this sense culturally conditioned or historically determined? Or, is interpretation a discursively guided meaning-producing endeavor that attributes meanings to India's strategic realities? (5) If it is the latter, then what does any given discursive interpretation of India's strategic culture say about self-understandings of India's national histories, nationalist ideologies, religion, culture, and the identity of the self/enemy? (6) What does any given discursive interpretation of India's strategic culture say about self-understandings of its perceptions of danger, conflict, war, the international system, the use of violence, and a nuclear India's logic of institutionalized nuclear deterrence? (7) How do changing manifestations of India's strategic culture interact with (or are influenced by) factors such as domestic bureaucratic institutional politics, economy, history, culture, modernization, and the globalization dynamic to pursue a certain route of nuclear security policy choices (that are increasingly becoming neoliberal/pro-US for a traditionally nonaligned Indian state)? (8) Can reconstructions of India's strategic culture promote or discourage India's propensity to comply with or violate international norms regarding the pursuit of nuclear weapons expansion, aggressiveness, or a free and fair disarmament? (9) Has India's strategic culture evolved when seen in relation to its foundational aspects, and what is the interactive significance of the structural, economic, cultural, and the ideological in facilitating this transformation? (10) Finally, who are the keepers of India's strategic culture maintaining, reinterpreting, and transforming it through meaning-producing discourses and frameworks of interpretation to pursue its changing notions of national insecurity interests and its strategic security choices in a globalized (yet anarchical) world of post-9/11 IR? The nature of these queries necessitates that this book simultaneously addresses the theoretical scholarships both general and India-specific on strategic culture and security studies in IR.

Theoretical Approaches to Security in IR

Proffering a constructivist understanding of security in IR is a challenging task, because certain commonsense understandings of anarchy explain states as unitary actors operating in an anarchical world and the relevance of the material (i.e., observable) has remained the currency of mainstream IR. In ontological terms, the political realists subscribe to this view of security in IR. Carr (1939:3) suggesting that "facts exist independently of what anyone thinks about them," pioneered this genre of a realist/positivist approach to security in IR. Morgenthau (1949) reinvoked Carr's scientific positivism by claiming that individual states/ statesmen are key to understanding political reality which must be judged as "a factual mass of phenomenon that exist[s] independent of the theorist," and Waltz's (1979) structural realism claimed that IR must be analyzed "structurally and systematically." What becomes particularly important for this book (which considers attribution of meanings as critical in the articulation of insecurity) is Waltz's observation that the primary analytical task of an IR theorist is to separate the "essential" from the "ephemeral" factors in world politics.[3] Although scholarships have sought to rehistoricize neorealists' positivism, these trends representing a discursive amalgam of institutionalism and/or utilitarian rational choice approaches have only rekindled a neoclassical economics or a structure-based approach to security politics in IR (Keohane and Nye, 1977; Gilpin, 1987; Dougherty and Pfaltzgraff, 1997; Frey, 2006).

The 1980s and the 1990s saw a critical literature of IR, which inclusive of Marxism, the postgenre scholars (such as the postmodernists, postcolonialists, poststructuralists, feminists), and the constructivists challenged the positivist/problem-solving approaches of conventional IR. Notable in posing this line of challenge is Cox's (1981) "how-possible" approach that rejecting the notion of an independent reality "out there," insists that knowledge of reality is always intrinsically connected to social practice and to the ways human affairs are organized in particular times and places. To this end, the critical IR theorists namely the postmoderns, postcolonials, and the feminists revisit the "taken-for-granted" approaches to anarchy, security, state sovereignty, and identity in IR. The postmoderns through an intertextual reading have deconstructed the notion of state sovereignty, power–knowledge nexus, politics of representation, and the modernist constitutions of identity/ difference in IR (Ashley, 1987; Der Derian and Shapiro, 1989; Enloe, 1990). Additionally, postcolonial IR theorists, following Edward Said's *Orientalism,* interrogate representations of postcolonial identity formations in hegemonic Western narratives of IR at imbrications of race, class, gender, human rights, security, and global capitalism (Said, 1978;

Krishna, 1999; Persaud and Walker, 2001; Ling, 2002; Chowdhry and Nair, 2002). Yet, these postgenre scholars have not considered how discursive practices may lie at the core of the representative ambiguity of IR.

The 1990s witnessed the emergence of a constructivist turn in IR theory and analysis. Representing a collective genre, constructivism, differing over substantial and epistemological issues but sharing some core assumptions vis-à-vis the realist/neorealist conceptions of security (such as facts are social interventions, the notion of agency as vested within individuals, ideas construct realities, and that all agents and structures are mutually constituted) offers a social perspective of IR (Wendt, 1992; Katzenstein, 1996). Despite introducing such intersubjective angles, the constructivists have operated within a structural IR and have not engaged with understanding security as a discursively produced construct in IR that may implicate states' security practices in international affairs.

As South Asian security analyst Abraham (2009:3) argues one aspect of segregating explanations of national security from structural IR requires revisiting security studies as "a fundamental social activity … embedded in and inseparable from social and cultural meanings." To this end, approaches embedded in realism, neoliberalism, domestic, and bureaucratic institutionalism, which have not really provided a decisive modification of structural realism, have explained nuclear dynamics in South Asia/IR (Karnad, 2005; Basrur, 2006; Frey, 2006; Ganguly and Kapur, 2007). More subjective analysts of India's nuclear policies have proffered the nuclear apartheid argument, identity logic, the modernity logic, historicism, and a socially grounded approach (where nuclear politics is fundamentally a social activity) to explain India's nuclear security affairs (Rosen, 1996; Singh, 1998; Abraham, 1999, 2009; Nizamani, 2001; Biswas, 2002; Krishna, 2006; Malik, 2010; and Chacko, 2012). Yet, there remains a lacuna even in these subjective lenses to consider how the social power of discourse may attribute meanings to India's/ South Asia's nuclear security affairs. More recently, Das' (2002, 2005, 2008) critical constructivist efforts to offer a culturally produced understanding of India's nuclear security affairs indicate a forward move toward a more discursively grounded reinterpretation of India's nuclear security affairs. This chapter draws partially from the above theoretical forays to offer a more discursively grounded approach of India's strategic security affairs, namely uncovering a connection between the discursive productions of India's strategic culture, (in)security imaginaries, and its nuclear/strategic security affairs.

Exploring these constructivist linkages between India's strategic culture, strategic thinking, and nuclear policy-making necessitates that I simultaneously address the existing scholarships on strategic culture and strategy-making. Prior to this review, I deflect briefly to introduce the premise of critical social constructivism with attention to the concepts of "security imaginary" and the politics of "meaning-fixing" (or meaning production) which become significant in my endeavor to provide a constructivist reading of India's strategic culture and security affairs.

Critical Social Constructivism, Security Imaginary, and the Politics of Meaning-fixing

Contrary to the problem-solving approach of the conventional security studies that assume the existence of states and insecurities as given in world politics, critical social constructivists follow a "how-possible" approach to security studies to explain a discursive production of (in)securities in international politics (Weldes et al., 1999:10). Following Tomlinson's (1991:7) claim that "... insecurities are cultural in the sense that they are produced in and out of 'the context within which people give meanings to their actions and experiences and make sense of their lives,'" critical constructivists see (in)securities as "cultural" given that they are produced through a "[a] multiplicity of discourses or 'codes of intelligibility' ... through which meaning is produced—including discourses about 'culture' itself" (Weldes et al., 1999:1–2). These meaning-producing roles of discourses through which "meanings" of cultures and insecurities are produced imply the following: First, culture, made up of contested codes and representations, designates "a field on which are fought battles over meanings." Second, "meanings [that] are fundamentally cultural ... provide the categories through which the world is understood." Third, meanings (like discourses) are shifting, transitory, and can be contested (ibid.:1–2, 13). Thus, the critical constructivist proposition that insecurities are social and discursive productions offer the "how-possible" basis to explore those "cultural [discursive] processes through which insecurities of states and communities—and the identities of the subjects through which insecurities have meaning—are produced, reproduced, and transformed" in international politics (Weldes et al., 1999:1–2).

In this context, Muppidi's (1999:123–124) constructivist argument employs the concepts of "security imaginary" to explain the construction of insecurities in India's national security politics. Muppidi (1999:120) defines security imaginary as "a field of meanings and social power." Security imaginary "... as a field of meanings ... provides an organized set of interpretations for making sense of a complex international system ... [and] as a field of social power,... works to produce social relations of power through the production of distinctive social identities." Both operations enabled via discursive acts of agents (such as states and its security community) are simultaneously constitutive of (and reinforce) frameworks of interpretations, social relations, and fields of meanings that are productive of identities and insecurities in international interactions (ibid.:124). This means that while certain social identities and practices are only possible and only make sense within the security imaginary, the security imaginary itself is reproduced through the continued performance of those [discursive–ideological] practices (ibid.:125). "Security imaginary" in this sense is not real, that is, it cannot be empirically scrutinized. Rather, it is "the product of an act of cultural [discursive] creation which is fundamental to any subsequent system of cultural representation" (Tomlinson, 1991:156–157).

As Muppidi (1999) explains, one of the ways in which the "security imaginary" operates to organize and reproduce meanings in distinctive ways is through articulation and interpellation. Articulation is the process through which meanings may be articulated as politically, culturally, and socially perceived through the "codes of intelligibility" of its articulators, such that "subjectivities," i.e., notions of identities and insecurities, could be socially produced from a variety of "subject-object" positions (ibid.:125). In this context, statist discourses become significant in establishing the state as a "particular *kind* of subject, with a specific identity, and ... interests attendant on that identity," and simultaneously as an "'object' facing insecurities" (Weldes et al., 1999:14). In this context, the concept of interpellation also becomes useful, which refers to "the ways in which people, when 'hailed' by discourses, 'recognize' themselves in that hailing" (Althusser, 1971:174 quoted in Muppidi, 1999:125–126). Thus, both acts of articulation and interpellation, which in practice constitute a discursive process of "producing" meanings of identities and insecurities, constructs a commonsense reality, whereby "security imaginaries" are rendered possible, meaningful, and legitimate in international politics (Muppidi, 1999:126).

The critical constructivist concepts of "security imaginaries," articulation, and the role of discourses as tools of "meaning-production" become significant in this study given that I use these concepts to explore how (1) the distinctive representations of India's strategic culture that are operative within and re-enforce a particular construction of an (in)security imaginary defines India's strategic cultural thinking, identity making, insecurity, and national security policy choices; and (2) the political struggles involved in such acts of discursive representations that offer the political–ideological space and serve as meaning producing tools to "fix" meanings to shifting notions of India's strategic cultures, (in)security imaginaries, and its nuclear security choices.

Strategic Culture and Strategy-making in International Politics

Drawing from the anthropological definition of strategic culture as "collectivity," the term strategic culture was coined by Synder (1977:9) who defined it as "the sum total of ideals, conditional emotions responses, and patterns of habitual behavior that members of a national strategic community have acquired through instruction or imitation and share with each other with regard to nuclear strategy." Synder's analysis (that challenged the game theoretic analysis of national security) offered a cognitive explanation of strategic culture and nuclear strategy which explained how sociocultural characteristics of national culture (in his instance, the Russian Bolshevick culture) rooted in recent historical experiences, ideologies, and high politics becomes important in explaining strategy.

Building considerably on Synder's conceptual framing of strategic culture, emerged three generations of strategic culture theorists. The first-generation theorists forwarded their understanding of strategic culture as a form of national-style thinking. Their argument is that certain elements, for instance the nature and geography of the state, the ethnic culture of its people, and their historical circumstances, interact to constitute a nation's strategic culture that provides valuable insights into the nation's self-image and policy motives. Representing the first generation, Gray (1981), Lord (1985), and Kinkade (1990) identified a discernible American strategic culture that—derived from its national historical heritage; experiences of geography, diversity, pluralism; and political philosophy of liberal democracy—explain American strategic thinking that is "unyielding to military reforms." Reflective of this national-style analysis, Jones (1990) assessment of the Soviet national strategic culture argues how macroenvironmental (consisting of geography, history, and ethnocultural characteristics), societal (consisting of social, economic, and political structures of society), and micro (consisting of military institutions and characteristics of civil–military relations) factors influence Russia's "aggressive" strategic thinking. As a consequence of such interactions, individuals are socialized into modes of strategic thinking that places issues of strategy "on the level of culture [and] ... in a state of semi-permanence" rather than one of mere policy (Gray, 1981:21–22).

The first generation's exposition of national-style strategic cultures as acquired through inheritance is deemed by critics as being deterministic (Johnston, 1998). Furthermore, this conceptualization relies on national homogeneity in assuming that national-type strategic cultures will lead to one type of behavior, that there is one national-type culture shared by the strategic decision-making elites, and leaving unexplored the possible existence of more than one strategic cultures in cross-national/temporal variations (which as I will argue is evidenced in the Indian context). More importantly, a point to which I will return later as the theoretical and analytical starting point for this book, the first generation's emphasis on strategic culture as national-type thinking, precludes consideration that what constitutes social ideals, values, beliefs, and habits of a nation's strategic thinking, that is, its strategic culture, may be socially/discursively constructed.

In this context, Booth, himself a first-generation scholar, critiques national-style portrayals of strategic culture. His argument is that "[ethnocentric] cultural thought ways—myths as well as reasons—form the core of societies and play a central role in the affairs of men" (Booth, 1979:14). He draws attention to how interpretive aspects of threat assessments such as notions of "ideological threat[s]," attribution of "symbolic meanings," "implicit enemy imaging," and the "cultural politics" of foreign policy-making may set the "undercurrents, of mood, tone or milieu" that may define states' security policy-making (Booth, 1990a:51–58, 64, 67). Booth's attention to how threat relationships are affected by mindsets that magnify the problems of threat assessment is an important observation given that it orients the study of strategic culture toward the constructivist claim that "strategic realities are ... in part culturally constructed as well as culturally perpetuated" (Booth, 1990b:124). Yet, Booth does not, like the other first-generation strategic culture theorists, engage in exploring what constitutes culture may itself be socially/discursively constructed.

The second generation's point of departure from the first lies in providing a more interpretive/rhetoric-based (as opposed to a national style) explanation of strategic culture and strategy. Their contention is that rhetoric, symbols, images, myths, and stories serve as tools of political hegemony for states in the realm of war and peace to legitimize dominant conventions of states' strategic behavior. This is evidenced in Stuart's (1988:151) exploration of the American myth of limited war, which, rooted in the ideology of Republican nationalism, has interpreted American expansion "as a beneficial act, and rationalize[d] aggression as the human extension of civilization." Likewise, in reference to American nuclear policy, Klein (1988:135–136) points to the significance of declaratory and operational strategies, where strategy-making as cultural practice involves the ways in which "... political ideologies of public discourse ... help define occasions as worthy of military involvement." These considerations mean that strategic culture of a country and its relations with allies and adversaries have much to do with how such relations are being "interpreted" by the public as well as strategists as comprising the realities of international life. This, in turn, plays a constitutive role in the making of political–military strategy.

The second generation hints at important caveats for the study of strategic culture missing from the first generation. For instance, they go beyond the first generations' assumed fixity of strategic cultures as national styles and define strategic cultures through representations of images, stories, and symbols that legitimize states' strategic policies. Additionally, their interpretive analysis of strategic culture goes beyond the prevailing (realist) standpoint that informs contemporary strategic studies, that is, "military strategy is about a real world that has an existence 'out there' to which responsible leaders must fashion a response" (Klein, 1988:99). Yet, problems remain with the second-generation theorists in assuming that the act of interpretation of realities that occur in a society is "embedded in a looser set of cultural relations" (Klein, 1988:136), thereby, basing their arguments on "cultural relations" as given. I argue that such assumptions result in the reification of society, culture, and politics in explaining strategy-making, and preclude the consideration that strategic cultures may be socially constructed.

The third generation of strategic cultural theorists emerging in the 1990s use culture variously defined as military, organizational, and political–military to target the realist edifice in strategic culture studies and focus on cases where structural definitions of interests cannot explain strategic choices. The underlying theme of their approach is that strategic cultures based on collective beliefs and customs and formed at domestic (organizational) levels offer a cultural analysis of strategic problems and policies. Representative of this generation, Legro (1995) and Kier (1997) study international cooperation between states and argue that organizational cultures (consisting of informal beliefs and customs of military services) interact with formal bureaucratic structures to determine states' strategic behavior. Thus, military doctrines are best understood from a cultural perspective, that is, informal values and cultures of the military. Johnston (1998:20–21), a third-generation theorist, while acknowledging this generation's stride over the previous two, takes issue with their cognitive bias given that their reliance on organizational cultures as influencing strategies precludes an analysis of how "influences of broader and more deeply historical [factors] ..." may explain strategic cultures and choices. Instead, Johnston (1995, 1998) provides a historically grounded interpretive analysis of strategic culture. In this analysis, strategic culture represents "an ideational milieu which limits behavioral choices," where "structural conditions play at best a secondary role in determining strategic preferences of states" (Johnston, 1995:46, 61). Applying this understanding of strategic culture in the Chinese context, Johnston concurs that "realpolitik decisions are cultural" (Johnston, 1998:x).

In the third generation's ideographic approach to strategic culture studies, which dovetailed with the post-positivist approach to IR (i.e., knowledge is not scientific), these theorists see culture as an ideational variable, where ideas were usually domestic and emphasized uniqueness within (rather than similarities across states in the international system). In this context, one cannot deny that Johnston in relation to the others offers a more interpretive analysis of strategic culture and counters "an ahistorical, acultural realist framework for analyzing strategic choices" (Johnston, 1998:2). Yet, for the purpose of this book, which addresses a constructivist lacuna in the field of strategic culture studies, even the third generations' efforts at relying on cognition (i.e., institutional strategic cultures) render them limited in explaining strategy. In fact, even the recent "culturally-based" arguments of Johnson et al. (2009), which explain the influence of strategic cultures on strategy-making remain cognition-based and norm-oriented, that is, how states' domestic norm-adherence policies affect their decisions vis-à-vis weapons of mass destruction. This reliance precludes the third-generation theorists, including Johnston's (1995, 1998) otherwise excellent interpretation of Chinese strategic culture, from considering how strategic cultures may be discursively constructed through discourses by articulating and fixing "meanings" to international realities. Before proceeding to situate my overall critique of the strategic culture literature from a critical constructivist perspective, I briefly situate the India specific scholarships on strategic culture and security.

Strategic Culture and Nuclear Security in the Indian Context

Scholarship on India's strategic culture has generated three interpretations which albeit overlapping may be categorized into the following: First, India's strategic culture as passive; second, there has been a lack in India's strategic thinking; and third, that India has a strong strategic culture. American analyst Tanham (1992:50) supports the claim of passivity in India's strategic culture, and attributes a lacuna in India's strategy-making as derivative of certain factors in India's historical and cultural development. These factors include a lack of political unity and national defense planning in India's history, the "Hindu concept of time," which discourages planning, and the "emotional" Hindu view of life which obstructs planning with any confidence. Prominent Bhartiya Janata Party (BJP) spokesperson and Indian politician Jaswant Singh also sees India's strategic culture as passive given that Indian nationalism, which is non-territorial, emotional, and nonproselytizing, renders a passiveness in India's strategic cultural thinking. Singh (1999:2–9) suggests a "functional" and "assertive" state as essential for India's strategic thought and its evolution (a point to which I will return later in Chapter 6 of this book). A similar view of passivity recently resonates in Jones (2009) who identifies certain "mythological" traits of "sacredness and timelessness" as underpinning the moderation in India's strategic mindset.

The second view on India's strategic culture is represented by Bajpai et al. (1996), who with different explanations, point toward a lack of rigor in India's strategic mindset. Bajpai (1996) identifies a lack in strategic thinking relative to Europe because India's strategic thought as a newly independent nation has taken longer to develop; Mattoo (1996a:206) recognizes an absence in India's strategic thinking, especially with regard to nuclear policy-making, which he attributes not to India's history or culture but "to the regime of secrecy that is in operation"; and Basrur (2001) identifies an incremental progress in Indian's strategic cultural assertiveness. Gordon (1995) is also indicative of such incremental progress in India's strategic culture, which he attributes to the dialogue that is being conducted between India and the global world order. Despite such trends, Gordon (1995:5) also notes that India has "avoid[ed] hard decisions [on strategy] as constituting a politically sophisticated attempt to hedge," which, in the context of India's nuclear decisions, is seen by Ollapally (2001) as one of "non-decision."

Sidhu (1996) however explains the presence of a strong strategic culture in India which has been communicated through an oral tradition but not documented in writing as in the Western sense. He argues that this oral tradition of India's strategic thinking has been ignored in the West given that Western thinkers, relying more on documented traditions, "tend to be uncomfortable with the concept of oral history, especially one that dates back several thousand years" (ibid.:174). Sidhu accounts for the existence of realism, strategic thinking, and strategy-making in

India as documented since the Vedic eras in the Indian epics, Kautilya's *Arthastastra*, in Mahatma Gandhi's approach to nonviolence, as much as in Nehru's idealism.

In this scheme of classification, Latham's (1997) analysis of India's strategic culture remains slightly different given his reference to (but not elaboration of) the constructed relation between India's culture and security affairs. According to him, "culture … and identity … inform India's approaches to security affairs" (Latham defines culture as terms of enduring and widely shared beliefs, traditions, attitudes, and symbols; and defines identity as terms of self-representation of the nation and its proper role in regional and global politics) (ibid.:103). This is because cultural values exercise a profound influence on decision-makers' assumptions based on which they understand security issues and decide methods to deal with them. Latham's proposed link between India's cultural values, identity, and security issues is akin to my interpretive analysis of India's strategic culture and security that I follow in this book. Yet, Latham's analysis (like some of the other India-specific strategic culture theorists) remains embedded in the notion that India's strategic culture is culturally conditioned by India's cultural norms—evidenced in his claim that "culturally-conditioned ideas and images shape contemporary India's security policy" (ibid.:103).

A Critique of Strategic Culture and Security: The Constructivist Puzzle

As evidenced from the above analysis, although the respective generations of strategic culture scholarships, including the India-specific analysts, have provided different understandings of strategic culture and strategy their analyses is based on a commonly accepted understanding of strategic culture as a shared set of meanings which are determined by historical precedents, cultural conditions, and/or contemporary experiences of real and domestic politics. While I agree that the notion of strategic cultures as shared sets of meanings/collectivities is partially correct given that all nations are expressions "imagined communities," I will argue from a critical constructivist angle that the premise of strategic cultures, despite significant historical and cultural influence on their evolutions, are ultimately a matter of social construction.

My starting point of argument is that the commonly accepted conceptual framing of strategic culture as constituting the sum total of ideals conditioned by historical or civilizational norms is devoid of considering how strategic cultures may be socially constructed. I argue that this assumption of strategic culture stems partly from the problem-solving approach that underlies this body of theorists. This means that the strategic culture theorists, with certain exceptions such as Johnston (1995), have, like the conventional IR theorists, operated with certain assumptions of international politics such as states, their identities, and insecurities as given, which explain their problem-solving focus on strategic culture studies, that is, what sorts of strategic cultures will result in what sorts of strategies. In fact, even Johnston's (1995) interpretive analysis of strategic cultures via interpretations of texts, symbols, rhetoric, and myths does not render problematic that strategic cultures may be discursively constituted. In this context, as the critical constructivist efforts of Weldes et al. (1999:16) remind us "to associate the notion of culture, or discourses, or codes of intelligibility with the merely linguistic ....," that is, interpretations of texts and rhetoric, is "misleading." This is because rhetoric, texts, symbols, myths at best serve to interpret a certain representation of reality but discourses and their codes of intelligibilities allocate "meanings" in distinct ways that are productive of various social, political, and cultural "self-understandings" of realities. Accordingly, from a critical constructivist perspective, I reconceptualize strategic cultures as social constructs, which produced through articulators' discourses and codes of intelligibilities, serve as meaning-producing tools to construct commonsense realities in IR.

Conceptualizing strategic cultures as socially constructed leads to certain how-possible questions concerning the productions of identities and insecurities in strategic culture/international security studies. That is, how the socially constructed nature of a nation's strategic cultural thinking offers the political–ideological space within which are constructed shifting notions of the states' self/other identities, (in)security imaginaries, and nuclear security choices. In other words, how a nation's strategic culture inheres in practices and categories through which the world is understood, its meanings molded in discourse, and are productive of certain (in)security imaginaries? This understanding of discursive productions of identities and insecurities in strategic culture/international security studies also implies that insecurities a nation seeks to address rather than being given "... are cultural in the sense that they are produced in and out of 'the context within which people give meanings to their actions and experiences ...'" (Tomlinson, 1991:7).

How meanings are formed, transformed, and who articulates meanings in national security affairs merits attention in a constructivist reading of strategic culture/international security studies. Herein, in contrast to traditional strategic culture studies that assume states and their strategic environments as two distinct entities, the former responding to the latter through its security strategy, I argue following a critical constructivist approach that the two share a mutually constitutive relationship where the state through certain discourses not only constructs its insecurity but the construction of this insecurity (expressive of the state's strategic thinking) reinforces the identity of the (threatened) state requiring a certain security policy. In this sense, states are not given but "cultural" entities, which contingent upon and relational to the nation's strategic cultures are "performatively" constituted (Weldes et al., 1999:11). Needless to say, these complex discursive constructions of state's strategic cultures, their identities, insecurities, and nuclear policies rendered possible through its security community's discourses draws attention to discourses as sites of "social/cultural power," another aspect excluded by traditional strategic cultural/international security studies at the expense of the empirical, structural, and the organizational dynamics of international politics.

Research Query: Strategic Culture, (In)Security Imaginary, and Nuclear India

In rest of the book, I use the above constructivist lines for reapproaching conventional strategic culture/security studies and to unfurl the linkage between the discursive reconstructions of India's strategic culture, (in)security imaginaries, and India's nuclear security choices. In this endeavor, I examine and retheorize the following research puzzles.

First, what constitutes India's strategic culture at any particular temporal and spatial context is a matter of social construction produced by its security community's meaning-producing discourses. In suggesting the socially constructed nature of India's strategic culture, I do not undermine that certain foundational aspects of India's culture and philosophy have influenced the foundations of India's strategic cultural thinking. In fact, my starting point of analyses of the connections between India's strategic culture and its security practices will begin with the claim that certain cultural norms of the Indian society evidenced historically in the Vedas, the *Arthashastra*, the Indian epics, and the tenets of Hinduism have influenced the state's strategic cultural thinking namely with regard to its nationalist identity, beliefs regarding the nature of the international system, and India's moral convictions regarding its proper place and the conduct of its international affairs. Yet, I suggest that this interrelationship between India's foundational culture and strategic thinking, which encapsulates the relation between India's strategic culture and security policies, is not simply a matter of cultural conditioning or historical determinism; rather, it is suggested that the discursive rearticulation of the mainsprings of India's culture as reproduced by the successive generations of post-independent Indian political leaders via their codes of intelligibilities have reproduced India's strategic cultural thinking.

Second, I explore how the socially constructed nature of India's strategic culture sustains a certain political–ideological space within which are articulated shifting understandings of India's IR, its nationalist identity, and its (in)security imaginaries. In this endeavor, I use the term "security imaginary," as denoting a discursive framework of meanings and social relations (Muppidi, 1999), which contingent upon and expressive of the state's strategic cultural visions, attributes meanings to identities and insecurities in India's international politics. In suggesting that India's (in)security imaginary serves as a framework of interpretation to attribute meanings to certain identities and insecurities in India's IR, I am aware of the significance of realist IR, the realist-based strategic culture theories, and the growing real-political challenges faced by the Indian state regionally and globally—which in the contemporary post-9/11 eras have taken the shape of terrorist-proliferation types of dangers facing the Indian state. Despite this significance of the real, I deem it important to explore how the representational power of discourse, working at tandem with India's foundational cultural values, strategic cultural formations, and real politics have attributed shifting meanings to India's (in)security imaginaries. Understanding this discursively constituted relationship between India's strategic culture, (in)security imaginaries, and its nuclear security policy choices would require exploring two related representational practices: First, how the distinctive representations of India's strategic culture that are operative within particular constructions of India's (in)security imaginaries produce self-understandings of India's identity, insecurity, and its national security policy; and second, the political/cultural struggles involved in such acts of representations that render shifting "meanings" of what constitutes India's identity, its insecurities, and its most appropriate nuclear policy choices.

Finally, I retheorize the question as to who articulates these shifting meanings of India's strategic identity and (in)security imaginaries, and how one reconceptualizes the shifting relationships between the articulator's (i.e., the Indian state's) own identity and its notions of (in)security imaginaries? In contrast to the existing strategic culture and security studies scholarship (both general and India specific) that see states' identities as distinct from and facing threats from an anarchical international realm, I argue that the Indian state is a socially/culturally constructed entity, which, contingent upon the socially constructed nature of India's strategic culture and (in)insecurity imaginaries, is constructed by meaning-producing discourses of the state and its security community. In this discursive dynamic, the Indian state is both the "subject" and the "object" of insecurity given these discourses establish the state as a "particular *kind* of subject, with a specific identity, and ... interests attendant on that identity," and simultaneously as an "'object' facing insecurities" (Weldes et al., 1999:14).

Methodology

Given the intersubjective nature of my research query, I use discourse analysis as my methodology. Although the term discourse analysis is an ambiguous one, generally speaking, such analysis refers to the study of the organization of language and its implications beyond words written or spoken as may be evidenced through written texts or conversational exchanges (Stubbs, 1983). As an interpretive framework of inquiry, discourse analysis will ask questions about the ways in which discourse structures (such as power of representation, ideas, and ideological hegemony) may reproduce social, political, and cultural dominance and how such discursive representations will help in the production of commonsense knowledge. This interpretive methodology therefore becomes a pragmatic tool for me to explore those discursive/representational processes through which the "meanings" of India's foundational culture, strategic cultural thinking, nationalist identities, and notions of in securities are produced, reproduced, and transformed to construct a commonsense world of India's nuclear security politics.

I have relied on both primary and secondary sources for my data in this book. Sources of my primary data have included archival materials on foreign policy documents of the Indian government; election manifestos, journals, newspapers, magazines, and pamphlets of the government and India's oppositional political parties; and semistructured open-ended interviews with prominent members of India's security/defense analysts. My secondary sources of data constitute books and scholarly journals on Hinduism, Indian history and politics, India's cultural norms, strategic thoughts, and conventional and critical analyses of India's IR, foreign policy, strategic culture, and its nuclear security developments. Following the recommendations of Fairclough and Wodak (1997) that structures of texts or language are crucial in the discursive legitimization of dominant forms of representations, I have interpreted my data to analyze the discursive links between the constructions of the Indian state's strategic cultural thinking, its (in)security imaginaries, and its nuclear security choices.

Chapter Outlines

Chapter 2 narrates the multiple historical, political, religious, cultural, and colonial influences underpinning the foundations of India's strategic culture since the Vedic eras till the anticolonial struggles of independence. The significance of this chapter is to set the political–historical background of pre-independent India's strategic cultural thinking, which forged out of the cumulative discursive interplays of India's nationalist leaders and colonial administrators and representing a combination of real politics and *dharma* (i.e., India's spiritual morality), have shaped the moorings of post-independent India's strategic cultural mindset. Chapter 3 addresses the interpretive links between India's foundational culture and the constructions of India's strategic culture, (in)security imaginaries, and India's atomic policy under Nehru's government. It delineates how the projection of India's strategic culture as one of political idealism, nonalignment, and Nehru's "charm for science" offered the political–ideological space to construct India's (in)security imaginaries and India's atomic science quest for national development. Chapter 4 explores the reconstructions of India's strategic culture, its (in)security imaginaries, and India's nuclear weapons policy choices under Lal Bahadur Shastri, Indira Gandhi, and Rajiv Gandhi's governments (with the brief interlude of the Morarji Desai and the Charan Singh periods). It explores a discursive–ideological shift in the state's strategic cultural thinking from one of political idealism to an increasing nuclear aggressiveness and some waning of nonalignment, and how these shifting dynamics sustained the political–ideological space to reconstruct India's (in)security imaginaries and its nuclear weapons policies for national defense purposes. Chapter 5 addresses the reconstructions of India's strategic culture, (in)security imaginaries, and its nuclear weapons policy choices after the Cold War era under V.P. Singh, Narasimha Rao, Chandra Shekhar, Deva Gowda, and I.K. Gujral's governments. The chapter narrates how the continuing political–ideological–discursive climate of increasing militarization and nuclear aggressiveness among India's nuclear hawks rendered the country almost at the edge of a nuclear weapons testing by the end of this phase. Chapter 6 explores the reconstructions of India's strategic culture, (in)security imaginaries, and its crossing of the nuclear threshold under Vajpayee's government. The chapter documents a noticeable discursive–ideological shift in India's traditional nonalignment posture to a pro-US orientation, and how this shift offered the political–ideological space within which emerged India's neoliberal strategic security/defense collaborations with the US—as a remarkable aspect of India's post-9/11 nuclear security development. Chapter 7 continues to explore the reconstructions of India's strategic culture, (in)security imaginaries, and the "cautious" balancing of nuclear India's neoliberal strategic security/ defense collaborations with the United States under Manmohan Singh's government. Chapter 8 summarizes the significance of this study as applicable to three major areas: IR theory, theories of strategic culture and strategy-making, and policy-making in South Asia in terms of future nuclear risk reduction and conflict management.

Notes

1. Following Weldes et al. (1999), I define the term security community as a broad section of India's strategic community who have a considerable influence on, and/or are involved in India's strategic/nuclear security policy making. Thus, India's security community will include members of the Indian government at any given point of time, members of India's political spectrum namely oppositional parties, India's bureaucrats, members of India's defense community, the military, its science community, security policy analysts, and influential members of India's academic community. However, as will be documented throughout the book, the official discourse of the Indian government's nuclear weapons policy has not always been consistent with such discourses evidenced within India's broader security community. Thus my usage of the phrase 'the Indian government's official discourses' when used in the book will mean only the government's official voices and will not include the broader spectrum of the security community unless otherwise mentioned. Finally, it must also be mentioned that Indian civilians also possess more informal views on India's nuclear politics as pro or anti-bomb voices, whose views I also document as necessary in the project. For more people-centric views of India's nuclear security discourses, see Ahmed and Cortright (1998), Bidwai and Vanaik (2000), and Krishna (2006).

2. I draw the term "security imaginary" as used in the scholarship of Himadeep Muppidi (1999) to explain the social construction of India's strategic culture, its (in)security imaginary, and nuclear policies from an interpretive angle. Although Muppidi's concept of "security imaginary," which I delineate in the text, focuses on India–US insecurities centering on India's post-colonial identity and does not directly pertain to India's nuclear insecurity, I use his concept of "security imaginary" to understand how this concept, which is an act of cultural–discursive creation, provides "an organized set of interpretations" (or the political–ideological space) for the Indian state to make sense of a complex international system (Muppidi, 1999:129).

3. From this project's interpretive perspective, such "ephemeral" aspects which include the "context and milieu" (such as the ideological mindsets of political leaders, their ideological commitments, questions about the social cultural interactions of states with other states in the international system) are critical in understanding states' nuclear security developments.

2

Nation-making in Colonial India

In keeping with my earlier claim that international relations (IR) and India-specific approaches to strategic culture and nuclear security have ignored constructivist approaches in IR, I explore in this chapter how the foundations of India's culture has influenced the strategic culture, (in)security imaginary, and the nationalist imaginations of India as a colonial state. Exploring this linkage between India's foundational culture, strategic thinking, and nationalist imaginations point to multiple historical, political, religious, and civilizational events in Indian history that include the Indus Valley culture, the Vedic eras, the Turko-Mongol imperial periods, and the recent experiences of British colonization. While indigenous personalities of Indian political history like Kautilya, Mahatma Gandhi, Nehru, and Hindu nationalists like Savarkar, Golwalkar, and others have remained milestones in setting India's strategic culture. British interpretations of native Indian culture as evidenced under administrators like Cornwallis, Wellesley, Hastings, Bentinck, Dalhousie, Curzon, and Churchill are of simultaneous importance in shaping India's strategic culture. Sadly, most mainstream writings on India's strategic culture have remained limited in considering the implications of colonial rule in interpreting India's strategic culture—the legacies of which continue to influence the contours of contemporary India even after almost 65 years since its independence. Keeping in mind this eclectic nature of India's strategic culture, it might be appropriate to claim that the foundations of India's strategic culture have been conditioned both by India's indigenous and colonial interpretations, wherein the contours of India's strategic thoughts have been constructed out of a tension between India's millennia-old civilization and the British dominated political/ideological aspects of colonization.

In this chapter, I narrate these tensions in the evolution of India's strategic culture as they relate to India's nation-making in colonial Indian politics since its Vedic eras until the anti-colonial struggles of India. Following my theoretical premise that India's strategic culture as a social construct sustains discursive articulations of its (in)security imaginaries, I explore how the essence of India's foundational culture—representing a combination of, or a specific notion of militancy, nonviolence, and morality have been rearticulated through indigenous and colonial interpretations to define India's strategic culture, which, in turn, have influenced the visions of nationalist identities and (in)security imaginaries in colonial India. The significance of this discussion is to set the political–historical background of colonial India's strategic cultural thinking, within which has evolved post-independent India's strategic cultural thinking and its institutional, political, scientific, and national security parameters.

This chapter is organized as follows: The following section examines the foundations of India's culture and defines *dharma* (India's spiritual morality) as its essential element. The second section explores how the foundations of India's culture based on *dharma* have influenced the moral–realist foundations of India's strategic culture in ancient and medieval India, and how these moral–realist norms were sustained, enriched, and strengthened in medieval India. The third section explores the evolution of India's strategic culture under the colonial years namely how the discourses of the colonial administration—guided by their political exigencies—have reconstructed India's strategic culture by downplaying the moral–realist foundations of India's strategic mindset. The fourth section explores how these colonial discourses paved the way for alternative discourses among colonial India's political–intellectual elites, wherein they partially imbibed and resisted colonization to reproduce their contesting visions of India's strategic cultural thinking. The fifth section explores how from these contested visions of India's strategic cultural thinking has evolved visions of science and atomic energy in colonial India. I conclude by analyzing how these contending discourses of India's strategic culture by the end of the colonial era paved the ideas of liberal representative institutions and nuclear modernity in postcolonial India.

Foundations of India's Culture

According to Indian historian K.M. Munshi (1962:4), "culture … is the characteristic way of life inspired by fundamental values, in which a people live. It is the sum total of the values expressed through art, religion, literature, social institutions and behavior, the overt acts of individuals and mass action inspired by collective urges." According to Munshi (1964), the first characteristic of culture is continuity, in that it comes from the past, adjusts itself to the present, and moves forward to shape the future (Munshi, 1962:4). In this sense, culture denotes a collectivity or the continuity of a collective life in people and expresses itself in various ways such as common traditions, norms of conduct, institutions, memories of triumphs, and a capacity for collective action. The influence of a vivid memory based on common triumphs in the past—whether mythological, historical, or imaginary—is significant given that they serve to consolidate the collective consciousness and distinctive cultures of the people. However, all cultures need not possess these characteristics in the same degree at the same time. At a particular period of time, one or the other characteristic may be more pronounced than the rest, but most of the characteristics may be present in some form or the other to give vitality to a culture (Munshi, 1964).

The source of India's culture is historically seen as a product of an Indo-Aryan synthesis (1200 BC to 700 BC) where religious practices of the Aryans and the Dravidians were fused (Munshi, 1962). Seen in terms of India's cultural renaissance, this Indo-Aryan synthesis was characterized by an intellectual sweep where wide ranging issues including the meaning and purpose of life was sought to be explained in the four Vedas (authoritative scripts of ancient India) as constituting *dharma*. It is generally accepted that the Vedas established the foundations of Hinduism and other cultural aspects of the early Indian society—elaborated further in the Hindu texts of the time like the *itihasas* (historical event) and the puranas, and in the Indian epics of Ramayana and Mahabharata

(Radhakrishnan and Moore, 1973). These early cultural foundations were encapsulated in the term *dharma,* meaning "a way of life," and, as taught by the *rishis* (holy men of Vedic India), were expected to bring the heterogeneous masses of India into a common fold, thus culling from this heterogeneity the collective essence of India's culture as *dharma* (Munshi, 1962:50). As Indian culture developed in the later Vedic years (700–183 BC), *dharma* remained a significant aspect of Indian society and culture with evolution of social institutions and norms of conduct to enable men to find fulfillment by following *dharma.*[1]

In considering *dharma* as the basis of India's culture, it must be clarified that the connection between the Brahmins as practitioners and propagators of *dharma* has led to the misconception of *dharma* as representing a "Hindu" way of life. Yet, as noted by analysts of India's cultural history, the term *dharma* much like the term Hindu (which itself is a geographical rather than a religious marker) is a plural, all-encompassing, and an ambiguous concept and does not constitute a Hindu way of life (Radhakrishnan, 1989). In this sense, *dharma* does not mean anything religious; rather, a basis of behavior, or a "way of life" seeking to amalgamate the multifarious socio-political, religious, cultural traditions of India that envisages the Indian subcontinent as "a world family," that is, *vasudhaiva kutumbakam* (Munshi, 1962). There are many aspects of *dharma*—political, social, and economic—representing Indian culture, into which I will not enter into a discussion here. Instead, in pursuit of my research query, I proceed to analyze how the foundation of India's culture incorporating the notion of *dharma* has influenced the strategic thinking of ancient and medieval India.

Culture and Strategic Thinking in Ancient and Medieval India

The study of the art of government, warfare, and foreign policy-making in India is very old and is said to have started around 650 BC. The Sanskrit epics of Ramayana and Mahabharata; the successive Greek, Bactrian, Parthian, and Scythian invasions of northern and northwestern India; Alexander's encounter with King Porus at the Battle of the Hydaspes

River; and the able administrations, military incursions, and victories of the Mauryan empire under Chandragupta Maurya and Ashoka, and later Kanishka testify to the art of statecraft and warfare in ancient India. Any analysis of India's real-politics/statecraft must acknowledge the importance of Kautilya's *Arthashastra* (150 AD), a treatise on the art of governance, which documents the relevance of real-politics situated in the context of *dharma*. Instructing practitioners of statecraft, *Arthashastra* upholds three interrelated objectives of a statesman: promotion of the welfare of the subjects, acquisition of wealth, and expanding territory by conquest. These ideas relating to protection are elaborated in the 15 chapters of the *Arthashastra* which depict a rather realist notion in the conduct of ancient India's political affairs reflecting two cardinal principles: First, that no one can be trusted, and second, the king wants to win (Rangarajan, 1992:39, 549). What follows in Chapters 6, 7, 11, and 12 of the *Arthashastra* is an elaboration of these realist protocols, namely the notion of intervention, foreign policy, methods of war, definitions of friends, enemies, conspirators, and traitors in the Indian kingdom. *Arthashastra* also stipulates that the extent to which a king (statesman) can promote his protection function not only depends on the internal constituents of the state such as treasury, army, and the bureaucracy but also "the power that a state/king can bring to bear on promoting its own interests vis-à-vis other states" (ibid.:542). Thus, *Arthashastra* sees the king as encapsulating and protecting all constituents of his state and representing the "national interest ... [that] would nowadays be termed as national interest [of the state]" (ibid.). Evidently, the foreign policy protocols of the *Arthashastra* very much constituted a state-centric document where the Indian state has remained the key entity; the king has remained the key spokesperson; power politics has been defined as physical power; and war, military preparedness, and defense have remained crucial for the state to maintain security of India.

Despite these realist orientations, one can hardly deny that Kautilya, as an IR theorist and a practical advisor, has also nuanced his views on physical power/real politics by clarifying that such power is not a constant over time. This is because intangible factors such as intellectual, moral, and the psychological power of the king also affect the king's decisions on foreign policy and war. In fact, in considering the morality component of ancient India's strategy-making, Kautilya has also situated his realist protocols of India's foreign policy in the context of *dharma* (moral behavior). Situated in terms of IR theory and practice, Kautilya's consideration of the morality component of India's strategy-making, would imply the significance of ideal (or, *dharma* as the morality factor) in a state's strategic affairs.

Despite debates concerning the contemporary relevance of *Arthashastra* in explaining India's real-politics (Rangarajan, 1992), Kautilya's observation on intangible power which considers moral politics and rulers' mindsets as significant in strategy-making is an important observation for this project—given my interpretive efforts at revisiting India's nuclear policy-making as represented through its political leaders' ideologically guided mindsets and discourses.

Yet, as a constructivist IR scholar studying the links between India's strategic culture and its nuclear security policies, I nuance the strategic relevance of *Arthashastra* in India's strategic policy formulations by claiming that *Arthashastra* is relevant for subsequent Indian politics not because of the classical realist assumption that the nature of human beings remains the same or that the sole logic of anarchy guides states' behavior. Rather, my argument will be that the age-long essence of India's strategic thinking as a combination of real politics and *dharma* has retained significance in contemporary political India (although reinterpreted differently at each juncture of India's strategic cultural thinking and nation-making to construct an amalgam of realism and India's morality factor). While I will return later to these linkages between realism, idealism (the moral factor), and their more complex reformulations in contemporary India's strategic culture in the next chapter, I proceed below to trace the evolution of India's strategic culture under its medieval era.

In terms of the evolution of India's culture, the medieval era represented a fusion of India's indigenous Hindu and the foreign Muslim cultures. The era covered the rule of the Guptas, King Harsha, the smaller southern regional kingdoms of the Cholas, Pandyas, and Pallavas, the northwestern Satavahanas, the Turko-Afghan invasions, the Delhi Sultanate, and the Mughals, and is generally noted for the political consolidation, territorial expansion, and the cultural refinement of India. The medieval years were also politically challenging in terms of the foreign invasions faced by India from the Huns of Afghanistan and Central Asia, the Turkish-Afghan invasions of Mahmud of Ghazni, Muhammad of

Ghor, and the Delhi Sultanate under Qutb-ud-din Aibak (although some political stability and cultural enrichment occurred under the Sultanate through the development of Urdu; flourishing of Hinduism, Buddhism, Jainism, and Islam; and other intellectual activities of Hindu and Urdu poetics under the Sultanate rulers) (Ghosal, 1965).[2]

The Mughal era of Indian history established by Babur (1526) began amidst this phase of synergy and adventure, and under Babur's successors Akbar, Shah Jahan, and the brief rule of Sher Shah Suri contributed in unifying the subcontinent by employing both military and diplomatic tactics. What resulted from their efforts of imperial consolidation was the idea of monarchy as a centralized institution which consolidated the foundation of a century-old stable government in India thereafter under the colonial era (Spear, 1965). In addition to their militarism, the Mughals with exception of Auragngzeb followed policies of cultural integration with the Hindus, which led to their greater assimilation in India relative to the earlier Sultanate era (Ali, 1997). Under the Mughal era, the Bhakti Movement spread across northern-central India and under Chaitanya, Kabir, Guru Nanak, and Mira Bai opposed institutionalized religion; discarded caste system; and aimed at the merging Hindu–Muslim consciousness (Thapar, 1966). Under Aurangzeb, there occurred a reversal of this trend, and following his death in 1707 and the defeat of his successors by the Afghan invasions of Nadir Shah and Ahmad Shah Abdali saw a sunset of the Mughal lineage. Politically, India after the battle of Panipat (1757) was "like a swirling sea … divided and lacking direction," and as Spear writes "in the absence of a definite direction western intervention must have come in some form …, because India was too valuable an economic prize to be left to herself …." (Spear, 1965:76–77). Robert Clive, who established British control over Bengal, after Plassey (1757), remarked that "Bengal, an 'inexhaustible fund of riches' would provide all the money needed for the company's trade and army" (Bose and Jalal, 1998:60).

Indian historians provide interesting views to explain the success of these Turkish-Afghan invasions in India which contain some bearings on (how political historians have defined) India's strategic culture. Ghoshal (1965) has explained how a preponderance of the Hindu religion and the rigors of their ceremonies have resulted in the loss of vitality of Hindu culture and was one of the reasons why the Hindu kingdoms of northern India fell prey to foreign powers. Instead, Thapar (1966:234) identifies a lack of organizational skill in the national defense structure of the Hindu kingdoms of the eras and thus their failure to resist foreign invasions. Both views on India's cultural stagnation and its lack of strategic planning should be seen in the light of similar views expressed by the 11th-century Iranian scientist, Alberuni, who traveling through the plains of northern India, noted a lack of perfection in India's scientific thinking and found the Hindus "… in a state of utter confusion, devoid of any logical order, and in the last instance always mixed up with the silly notions of the crowd" (Embree, 1971:22, 25). Alberuni's perceptions on the lack of scientific spirit in India explain his views on the passivity on India's (military) culture. He writes, "Unfortunately the Hindus do not pay much attention to the historical order of things, they are very careless in relating the chronological succession of their kings, and when they are pressed for information are at a loss, not knowing what to say, they invariably take to tale-telling" (ibid.:11). Much later, a host of European and British Indologists such as Francois Bernier, James Mill, and Lord Macaulay also saw India's body politic as deficient. Based on their rationalist philosophies, which I will later elaborate, they alleged that Indian civilization did not possess the strategic stability that flows from the world-ordering rationality of the Western culture.

While such observations denoting the lack of India's systematic strategic thinking dominate current debates of Indian politics, to which I will return later, one must not forget the numerous acts of heroism and wars waged by indigenous Indian clans, such as the Rajputs, Jats, Marathas, Sikhs, and the Gurjars from north-central India, or the roles of other regional Indian kingdoms in Kashmir, Oudh, and Bengal, that have provided numerous oppositions to the Turko-Afghan invaders, the Sultanate, and the Mughals in India. Although there were internecine disputes between India's indigenous clans, which historians argue enabled British victory over India, illustrations of India's indigenous militancy and warfare stand testify to the existence of a realist strategic culture in medieval India. Nonetheless, the common-place approaches to India's strategic culture have danced around assumptions of its homogenized passivity making any scholarly understandings of India's strategic culture a story of its cultural or nonmilitant historical determinism.

On the basis of the above data, I deem it appropriate to make two observations about the nature of India's strategic culture during its ancient and medieval eras: First, with these illustrations of strategy and militarism in India, it is not realistic to approach the question of India's strategic culture in terms of its presence or lack thereof in Indian politics. Rather, it would be more pragmatic to claim that Indian history documents a mixed illustration of militancy and nonmilitancy in India's strategic culture. Second, the above illustrations also serve to counter a religion-based assumption regarding India's strategic culture, that is, the nonviolence of Hinduism supports a passive Indian strategic culture. Such arguments further suggest that militancy in India's strategic thinking has largely been a foreign transplant (referring to the Islamic plunderers of the Indian soil) (Thapar, 1989).

In this context, I will not undermine the fact that from the 11th century onwards, Islamic invaders as for instance, Sultan Mahmud of Ghazni, and their subsequent regimes have used military brutality in establishing their control in India. Furthermore, the militancy of these foreign invaders when contrasted to the moral–spiritual aspects of Indian civilization (i.e., *dharma*), tend to support a homogenization of the passivity of Indian culture. Not to undermine the significance of *dharma* on India's culture, I nonetheless deem it important to take a balanced approach to these religiocentric observations on India's strategic culture. Accordingly, I suggest that India's strategic culture illustrates an indigenous militancy and in this sense is not passive and has evolved further under the influence of, and in interaction with, the military culture of its foreign invaders to represent an amalgamated nature of India's strategic culture. The moral aspects of *dharma* and simultaneous elements of realism (enriched and consolidated further through military strategies, warfare, and statecraft over the years) underscore a more balanced understanding of India's strategic culture, which also demonstrate the socially constructed nature of India's strategic culture. In the section that follows, I continue to explore this socially constructed nature of India's strategic culture under India's colonial years.

Interpretations of Culture and Strategic Thinking in Colonial India

Comprehending the links between the British interpretation of India's culture and strategic thinking during the colonial years require understanding the perceptions with which the British saw, understood, and colonized India.[3] Accordingly, the section explores how the logic and process of colonization as evidenced via the discourses of British Indologists and administrators have interpreted the culture and strategic thinking of India. In my analysis, I remain akin to the critical analysts of colonization but will add to it a constructivist angle, that is, how pre-colonial India's strategic culture was rearticulated by the British colonial administration under the colonial years. My purpose of this discussion is to show how this rearticulation, in interaction with and resistance from, India's indigenous actors has influenced the strategic visions of nation-making in India.

British Indology on Indian Culture

The British who surveyed the Indian scene in the 18th century were exhilarated and sobered by India's political, economic, and sociocultural landscape (Spear, 1965). Debates followed in Britain that asked "What was to be done with India now that Britain controlled it? ... What was to be done ... for the promotion of whose welfare [the British] Parliament had committed itself in the late nineteenth century ...." (ibid.:120–121)? In the context of these debates, the Conservative, evangelical, and radical utilitarian viewpoints became significant in recommending how to "save" the Indian East (Spear, 1965), which, inscribed in the works of Indologists, danced around the idea of "Oriental despotism" to interpret India's sociopolitical state of affairs (Inden, 1990). Two basic propositions of these Victorian-minded Indologists were that India's civilization and culture was essentially ignorant and traditional, and second, the West, in this case Britain, as the source of enlightenment, must save India as a non-West.[4]

Mill's *The History of British India* (1817), written without visiting India and "without having a complete knowledge of India" (Drew, 1987:70) set the tone for many of the discussions on Britain's colonial policies on India. Mill portrayed Indians as absurd, uncivilized, and ignorant; less grateful to reason; with no idea on the skills of government as in Europe; and possessing "all the vices which characterize the style of rude nations ..." (Mill, 1975:34, 37, 58, 192). "Their laws and institutions are adapted to the very [crude] state of society ... as would ... exist, under ... the rudest and weakest states of the human mind" (ibid.: 230, 233). Mill's notion of India's culture and society also shaped his views on India's art of warfare. He wrote, "In the Hindu armies, ... no idea of discipline existed ... [and] That, in war, the Hindus have always been greatly inferior to the warlike nations in Europe ... seems hardly necessary to assert" (Mill, 1975:245–246). Mill's *History* secured the political blessings of the 18th century Whigs, the emerging radical utilitarians in the British government, and operated alongside the prevailing evangelical mindset of the Christian missionaries such as Charles Grant, William Wilberforce, and Alexander Duff (Stokes, 1959:31) to recommend a radical alteration of the Indian society by calling upon Englishmen to civilize India (Mill, 1975: xxviii). Although there were initial differences between the utilitarians and the evangelicals on whether the Indian society be reformed through Christian education or rational laws and institutions (Stokes, 1959), the two fused by the late 1700s, and as captured in two articles by Charles Grant ("Proposal" and "Observations"), spoke of an evangelical project of anglicizing and commercializing British–Indian relations, which, at its ultimate, advocated the doctrine of assimilation to civilize "India's heathen millions" (Embree, 1962:145, 150; Stokes, 1959:31, 34–35).

Although the Eurocentric degradation of Indian culture was countered by European scholars like Luke Scrafton, John Shore, William Hodges, William Robertson, Max Muller, and the Asiatic Society of William Jones, Charles Wilkins, Jonathan Duncan, and Henry Colebrooke, who found a deep wisdom in Indian culture and called for an understanding of the rationality of the Indian mind (Mukherjee, 1968; Drew, 1987), this pro-Indian stand dissipated as the discourses of Anglicization continued to dominate Britain's imperial official accounts of India under James Mill and Lord Macaulay (Macaulay, 1952:316, 722).

A plethora of scholarships have critically taken to task how Britain's Enlightenment biases and the convergence of utilitarian thought with commercial and colonial objectives have defined colonial narratives on India's identity, and the much needed efforts to reapproach colonial historiography from an subaltern angle (Stokes, 1959; Guha, 1988; Inden, 1990; Sen, 2006). Yet, what remains relatively unexplored in these analyses is how the ideological mindsets of the 19th century Britain, evidenced in sorts of political philosophies as expressed by Grant, Mills, Macaulay, and the like, have not only justified Indian colonization on the premises of Enlightenment but have also in course constructed India's strategic cultural identity as a weak and insecure state—opposed to the superior, Enlightened, masculinist, British self. Accordingly, if one extends the existing critical analyses of British India's colonial historiography, one finds that such utilitarian overtones have also sustained an oriental/communal politics of (mis)constructing India's strategic essence. The next section explores this construction.

Colonial Discourses, India's Strategic Culture, and Identity

A study of the policies and discourses of British Governor Generals with some exception of Warren Hastings (Moon, 1949), reveal that while its Governor Generals have drawn on the assumptions of India's passive culture to implant the liberal English mindset in the Indian context, they have also in the process rendered a construction of the Indian state's and its people's identity and culture as weak, inferior, passive, and traditional. This tide of Anglicization remained evident in its Governor Generals, such as Lords Cornwallis, Wellesley, Bentinck, and Dalhousie, who reflecting the overall Whig-Utilitarianism that "… if it [India] becomes open to a free trade, under one mild, liberal, and effective government, that could protect the … lives and liberties of the subjects …" (Stokes, 1959:38–39), continued Europeanizing India's political institutions. It spilled onto India's sociocultural spheres under Bentinck's administration. Lord Cornwallis drew on India's strategic identity as one of "Asian despotism," where oriental principles of government are fundamentally at fault, to introduce European laws and judicial systems in India (ibid.:4); Lord Wellesley continued Cornwallis' efforts at introducing the British system of public law and independent judiciary in India on the ground that "the British system of public law, administered by an independent judiciary, was the best guarantee of toleration and protection for those … masses of uneducated natives" (ibid.: 8); and when Lord Bentinck banned India's social-cultural evils such as Sati, child marriage, and introduced English as India's official language in 1835, he described these changes as efforts by "benevolent administrators, ruling the country with an eye to the good of the natives" (Hunter, 1882:404).[5]

A group of subordinates of the Company, such as Munro, Malcolm, Elphinstone, and Metcalfe resisted the British policies of anglicizing India's politics and culture (Stokes, 1959). Additionally, from the latter half of the 18th century, a host of Hindu, Brahmo, and Muslim intellectuals, social reformers, and reform movements such as Ram Mohan Roy, Jyotirao Phule, Dayanand Saraswati, the Naqshbandi Sufi order in Delhi, and the Chisti Sufi order in Punjab started efforts at dispelling evil practices from the Indian society (such as Sati, child worship, caste practices); seek common fraternal relations; diffuse knowledge amongst all sections of the society; and in general, reinvigorate indigenous social culture, vernacular languages, and rituals to reassert India's indigenous cultural power—whether Hindu, Brahmo, or, Islamic—before colonial denigration. Yet, colonial discourses revealing amnesia of India's intellectual, moral, and cultural strength (Sen, 2006), harped over India's illiteracy, religious bigotry, cruel rites, political despotism, lack of civil rights, and liberties to sustain a discourse that projected India's strategic culture as weak, emasculated, incapable of self-government, and in need of protection and guidance from the British colonial leaders. Communalizing India's strategic identity was a by-product of this colonial discursive trend.

Communalizing India's Strategic Culture and Identity

Prominent Indian historian Gyanendra Pandey documents how a host of official and unofficial accounts of colonial administrators by the end of 1920 drew up an elaborate list of Hindu–Muslim riots in places like Benares, Bareilly, Delhi, Azamgarh, Ayodhya-Faizabad, and others, and used religious identifiers like "the very serious Muharram riots," "mosques destroyed," "Muslims killed," "Muslim houses in the village burnt" to identify Hindu–Muslim differences as a pathological condition of Indian politics (Pandey, 2006:25). Upfront, one must acknowledge that Hindu–Muslim riots did exist in precolonial India as social conflicts exist between social groups everywhere (Sidhwa, 1991), and such conflicts did occur in colonial India owing to political, economic, and religious reasons (Hunter, 1969; McLane, 1977; Robinson, 1975; Bayle, 1985). Yet, a closer reading of these colonial discourses reveal that the administration took recourse to the following ways of representation to construct a communal identity for the nation: First, these discourses amplified and misrepresented Hindu–Muslim riots to project Hindu–Muslim differences (which also meant demonizing an "aggressive" Muslim community's profile vis-à-vis the "weaker" Hindu identity); second, these discourses repeated past incidents of riots to establish their timeless and national character in depicting a communally ridden Indian state; and third, drew upon available Hindu–Muslim religious metaphors, symbols, and festivities to flare up the sometimes colonially instigated Hindu–Muslim riots (Pandey, 2006:30–31).[6] The colonial discourses on the Hindu–Muslim riot of Lat Bhairava in Benares, October 1809, stand as one of the many illustrations to show colonial discourses constructed a communal identity of Hindu–Muslims in India (ibid.:36, 33–40). Likewise, the 1874 and 1893 riots in Bombay were also described by the Bombay Judicial Department as being started by the Muslims, saying that "the first group to turn to violence were the Muslims;" and the riot in Mubarakpur (1909) was summarized by the *Gazetteer* of the Azamgarh district as being instigated by "the Muhammadans … consist[ing] for the most part of fanatical and clannish Julahas" (ibid.:60, 61).

Furthermore, while colonial discourses projected both Hindus and Muslims as irrational, superstitious, and bigotry ridden, more aggressive terms such as "fanatical and clannish," "disorderly," "communities prone to rioting," "fires of religious animosity" were used to depict the Muslim community's cultural identity (ibid.:64). In contrast, the Hindu community was projected as the weaker and the victimized community, and every riot as a moment of "Hindu humiliation" and "Muslim pride" (ibid.:37). In a religious procession undertaken by the Hindus following the Hindu–Muslim riots of Lat Bhairava (1809), Herber defines the "passive/victimized" role of the Hindu Brahmins, who "went down in melancholy procession, with ashes on their heads, … and sate [sic] there with their hands folded, their heads hanging down, to all appearance inconsolable, and refusing to enter a house or to taste food" (Herber, 1828:325 quoted in Pandey, 2006:37). Likewise, Prinsep (1831) by showing how the demolition of a number of temples in the 1809 riots was followed by the construction of mosques "upon the same foundations [and] with the same materials," underscored the "indignation" that was caused to the Hindus by the Muslims in these same riots (Prinsep, 1831, quoted in Pandey, 2006:37). I suggest that these discourses while communalizing Hindu–Muslim identities as trends of the British divide and rule policy also attributed a sense of emasculation and victimization to the collective Hindu community, which, as I will discuss subsequently, was responsible for the rise a militant, extremist Hindu community in colonial Indian politics.

More problematically, colonial discourses projected the assumption that all riots in India are timeless and national in character. Thus, referring to the riots of 1813, 1842, and 1904, the *Gazetteer* of the Azamgarh district claimed that "the features of all these disturbances are similar, so that a description of what took place in the first occasion will suffice to indicate their character" (Pandey, 2006:61). Not only are these essentialist descriptions of Hindu–Muslim riots misleading but also obliterate colonial involvements in instigating and falsely documenting their causes. An illustration is the April 1891 riot in Benares over the full or partial demolition of a Ram temple (ibid.:53–55). Yet, colonial discourses continued to use antagonistic Hindu–Muslim religious symbols and practices to replay Hindu–Muslim differences as experiences of "convulsions" [and] "religious antagonisms" at a national political scale. In opposition to this Hindu–Muslim lawlessness was the rational, secular, enlightened, and the firm order of the colonial Indian state (ibid.:28, 36). What was further disturbing in these colonial projections of lawlessness was the "right" that these projections gave to the colonial state to intervene through policies in the religious, social, political lives of the Hindus and Muslims: The colonial construction of separate electorates for the Hindu–Muslims; the Age of Consent Bill; the partition of Bengal (1905); and the anti-cow slaughter by-law (although the latter issue had an indigenous Hindu component) became crucial in demonstrating how colonial laws served to re-enforce communal identities.

In analyzing colonial articulations of India's communal identity, liberal colonialists like Irwin (1880) saw the rising communal tensions as eroding the fabric of India's national life. This was an apt observation given that by mid-1930s increasing communal antagonisms between Hindus and the Muslims demonstrated the fruits of the colonial efforts at constructing communalism. Yet, creating unified Hindu-Muslim communities also opened up unexpected fissures within these communities that divided the moderate Hindus from the extremists and the reformist Muslims from their revivalist counterparts. The emergence of these inter/intracommunal groupings especially the Hindu militant community became critical in not only altering the pluralist social fabric and strategic thinking of the Indian society but also in generating exclusionist forms of strategic cultural and nationalist imaginations on what constitutes India's strategic identity. Its ramifications continue to influence current India's national security politics as will be elaborated in Chapter 6. However, for our immediate purpose, I focus on how colonial rearticulations of India's strategic culture gave rise to certain counter discourses from India's nationalist leaders forwarding their interpretations of India's strategic culture.

Nationalist Discourses of India's Strategic Culture

Certain indigenous discourses arose among India's nationalist leaders which partly imbibed and resisted colonial discourses to reproduce their visions of India's strategic culture. Predominantly, these indigenous articulations were represented by two major groups the Indian National Congress (INC) and Hindu Mahasabha. The common issue that held the members of these groups was the question of political freedom from colonial domination, which, agreed by both groups was India's independence. But, beyond this common aim, they differed regarding the ways of achieving political freedom and their strategic visions of nationalist identity for a postcolonial India. Thus, their continued opposition to colonial rule saw the emergence of two alternative discourses, which, finding immense value in and drawing from the rich source of India's cultural history and maintaining common visions of a territorially bounded India, articulated two divergent visions of India's strategic culture. Given that a nation's strategic culture serves as the lenses to interpret its worldviews, both discursive articulations on India's strategic culture became critical in forging nationalist identities and (in)security imaginaries for an independent India. Below I analyze these discourses, their overlaps, and divergences.

The Indian National Congress

Four viewpoints emerged within the Indian National Congress, which, with ideological overlaps and differences, influenced India's strategic cultural thought patterns. The first strand constituted the constitutional moderates with selective pro-Western orientation; the second strand formed of activists/revivalists emphasized the spiritual/religious component in India's strategic culture; the third emphasized the intellectual strengthening of the self, that is, *atmashakti*, in regenerating India's strategic culture; and the fourth, formed by Muslim intellectuals and activists, focused on the ideals of Islamic universalism in defining India's strategic culture.

For the first strand, composed of Jawaharlal Nehru, Surendranath Banerjea, Gopal Krishna Gokhale, Sarvepalli Radhakrishnan, and others, Europe simultaneously represented a source of technological attraction and a symbol of colonial domination. These constitutional moderates opposed the colonial aspects of British domination but did not completely reject the progressive technological aspects of the British industrialization, wherein revealing a dual stance in defining their progressive notions of India's strategic cultural visions. Thus, Nehru, Gokhale (who, however, following the partition of Bengal became a radical in actively supporting the strong anti-British Swadeshi movement), Banerjea, Radhakrishnan, and Ambedkar remained ardent supporters of combining the trends of the old and new in forging India's strategic cultural visions. In their collective discourses, these moderates reminded the Indians of their existence as "an ancient race who had attained a high degree of civilization ..." (Sharma, 2002:187), and yet, must face the world with a "new spirit," which included lessons is western science, technology, and industrialization (Nehru and Gopal, 1980:8). Two things must be noted in this context: first, while accepting the combined dynamics of morality and selective westernization, these moderates were aware of issues of colonization and international hierarchy, and with the outbreak of Cold War between the super powers shaped Nehru's views on disarmament in the post-independent context (as will be discussed in Chapter 3); and second, saw the evolution of a scientific discourse in colonial Indian context regarding the significance of science, technology, and industrialization for India's development (a debate that I will soon address).

The second strand was composed of Mahatma Gandhi, Lala Lajpat Rai, Bal Gangadhar Tilak, and Deshbandhu Das. As revivalists, they shared with the moderates the notions of India's cultural plurality, toleration of spirit, and morality but differed from them by emphasizing the spiritual side of India's culture (Nagar, 1977). This revivalist position of "spiritualizing politics," which held them together despite some intragroup differences (Sharma, 2002), is possibly best demonstrated in Gandhi's *Hind Swaraj*, which as a practical philosophy would enable Indians to "unlearn" what they had learnt under colonial domination, reject British representative political institutions, and learn to live consciously, religiously, morally, and simplistically (Gandhi, 1997: xvii–xviii, 67). Despite Gandhi's rather sentimental approach toward religion and politics, Gandhi (and the others) referred to religion only "to emphasize the religious and spiritual side of the nationalist movement" (Nehru, 1948:21–22, 31), and saw "the Indian nation, such as it is or such as we want to build [it], [to be] neither … exclusively Hindu, Muslim, Sikh, or Christian" (Nagar, 1977:175). Furthermore, in conceptualizing India's strategic identity, the pragmatic in Gandhi was not a pacifist, and considering that the government of a free India was likely to discard nonviolence when questions of defense were concerned, upheld militaristic possibilities for a future India while still pleading to hold the banner of nonviolence in defining India's strategic thinking (Gandhi, 1997).

The third strand was composed of political activists/intellectual scholars/spiritual philosophers like Subhas Chandra Bose, Bipan Chandra Pal, Aurobindo Ghose, Rabindranath Tagore, Swami Vivekananda, Sri Ramkrishna Paramhansa, and others, who through scholarships, philosophical declarations, and their activism propounded their visions of India's strategic thinking. This group bore similarities with the moderates and the revivalists in recognizing the values of internationalism and India's indigenous culture but occupied a unique position in emphasizing the intellectual, self-strengthening aspects of the Indian self in regenerating India's strategic culture. As political activists and India's national freedom fighters, Pal and Ghose drew upon India's precolonial and Europe's post-Enlightenment intellectual traditions for India's social regeneration, which strengthened their struggle for independence. Yet, both Pal and Ghose insisted that India's social regeneration must selectively allow "the admission into India of Occidental ideas, methods, and culture" (Ghose,1958:104), such that a "New India can, ... no more ignore the ancient spiritual treasures of the Hindus, ... the ... elements of Muhammadan culture or the intellectual and moral ideals of modern European civilization" (Bose and Jalal, 1998:99). The blend of this "universal-difference" dynamic was also represented through the scholarships of Tagore (Sen, 2006), while Sri Ramkrishna saw an element of "inner spiritualism" as India's essence.

The INC also incorporated Muslim political activists (composed of reformists and revivalists) who joined hands with the INC's Hindu counterpart in opposing colonization but drew attention to the ideals of Islamic universalism. The reform-oriented moderates within this group were led by Mohammed Ali Jinnah, Sayyid Ahmad Khan, and others, who, like Nehru, urged their coreligionists to accept Western education but not all its ideals. On the question of Hindu–Muslim identity, Jinnah deplored Mahatma Gandhi's mixing of religion and politics and for long tried to forge Hindu–Muslim unity (Jinnah, 1960); and Khan saw India as a "beautiful bride" that had Muslims and the Hindus as her "two eyes" (Khan, 2000). Khan's associate, Maulana Shibli Nomani, was another reformist, although he differed from Khan in issues of Muslim nonparticipation in the INC.[7] The reformists were opposed by the revivalists such as Jamal ad-Din al-Afghani who opposed westernization, called for Hindu–Muslim unity in opposing colonization, but simultaneously articulated Islamic universalism as a part of their broader political agenda to launch their anticolonial struggle. Another political activist, Maualana Mohamed Ali, propagated Muslim communal patriotism wherein he described the privileged political-economic dominance of the Hindus in the colonial context as necessitating the Muslim patriots to organize themselves in "self-defense" (Iqbal, 1987:75–113). Despite intragroup differences, this group forwarded their strategic imaginations for a future India, which, with some ambivalence toward westernization and the perceived Hindu dominance within the INC, articulated a Muslim component of India's strategic cultural visions.

An analysis of the four spectrums of the INC members' ideological orientations reveal that despite inter/intragroup differences, this group sustained a holistic interpretation of India's history and culture from which evolved three distinct imaginations of India's nationalist identity and strategic cultural visions: First, that India as a heterogeneous entity incorporates the strength and values of its rich ancient heritage, while not completely shutting its doors to the merits of internationalism; second, India's nationalist identity born out of anticolonial struggle and the presence of international hierarchy must be alert and militaristically open to the potential needs of a future India's national security and defense requirements; and finally, identifying the presence of the West (as a legacy of colonial aggression) in defining India's strategic cultural and (in)security imaginations. Yet, nuances remain as to what extent the West has constituted a haunting specter for the Indian state given that the Western educated moderates such as Nehru have remained quite open in accepting European notions of political institutionalization, science, and technology for postcolonial India's developmental progress. While these nuances will be addressed in Chapter 3, for now, following Chatterjee's (1993:6) claim that "anti-colonialism creates its own domains of sovereignty within colonial society, [dividing] … the world of social institutions and practices into [separate] domains," I proceed to analyze the rise of a Hindu nationalist movement in the colonial Indian context.

Discourses of the Hindu Nationalists

The rise of alternative visions of India's culture came from a group of Hindu nationalists such as Madan Mohan Malaviya, Veer Savarkar, K.B. Hedgewar, and M.S. Golwalkar, who, interweaving Hindu religion, culture, and history forged their visions of India's strategic culture (Malaviya, 1919; Savarkar, 1967, 1971; Golwalkar, 1947, 1980). The Hindu nationalist movement came to the forefront with the establishment of the Akhil Bharat Hindu Mahasabha (1915) to counter the Muslim League and the secular Indian National Congress. Savarkar (1967, 1971) set the tone of a Hindu-centric, militant conception of India's strategic culture. In his *Six Glorious Epochs*, Savarkar described the first, second, third, and fourth epochs in Indian history as eras of "prowess" and "strength" of the Indian empire—noting some degeneration in India's prowess during the second epoch accountable to the nonviolent principles of Buddhism practiced under emperor Ashoka—with the real challenge to India's "glory and purity" coming from the fifth epoch marking the advent of Muslim struggle in India (Savarkar, 1971:69, 127, 155).

Savarkar consistently used the term Hindutva and Hindudharma as the unifying national bond of India, and as the President of the Hindu Mahasabha projected the organization's duty as "defending Hindudom and Hindusthan" (Savarkar, 1949:1, 4). Savarkar defined a Hindu as someone, "... who regards and claims this Bharatbhoomi ... as his Fatherland and Holyland ..." (ibid.:4), and saw the bond of Hindutva, that is, a common nation, common history, and common culture, as tying Hindudom together (ibid.:5). Indeed, Savarkar's concepts of "Hindu, Hindutva, and Hindudom," which he justified as national and not parochial (ibid.:11–15), was bound to project the Indian Muslims as the offsprings of "the Muslim hordes that invaded India" and constituting threats to India (Savarkar, 1971:9). He characterized the Muslims as "antinational" posing a "grave danger" to India (ibid.:167–181). In contrast, he upheld the "misplaced chivalry" [cowardice] of the Hindus (ibid.:167) resulting in the plight of the Hindus as "a dying race" in India (Datta, 1993).

Savarkar's conception of India as a Hindu nation was echoed by Hedgewar and Golwalkar both of whom were in succession Presidents of the Rashtriya Swayam Sevak (RSS). Despite insisting that the RSS was a cultural organization; would not engage in politics; and was concerned only in the national renewal of strength through character building, it narrated an anti-Muslim/Hindu-centric interpretation of the nation and its culture. Thus, claiming that mere geographical territories do not make a nation, Hedgewar defined "the Hindu culture [as] the breath of Hindusthan," and that "if Hindustan is to be protected, we should first nourish the Hindu culture ..." (Seshadri, 1988:13). Likewise, Golwalkar identified religion (Hinduism) as the center piece of India's identity (Golwalkar, 1980:10). Once again, in this Hindu *rashtra*, the Muslims constituted a disparate group, having in common "... their denial, in some fashion, of one or all of the five components geography, race, religion, culture, language—of the Hindu nation .... From the RSS' point of view, these groups .... [were] not just enemies of the RSS but of India" (Golwalkar, 1947: 23–28). So intense was these Hindu nationalists' fundamentalist focus on the religious component of Indian politics that they justified India's anticolonial struggles as liberation struggles of a Hindu nation against a culturally alien, Western, Christian power (Savarkar, 1940, 1971; Golwalkar, 1947).

The Hindu nationalists' quest for a Hindu nation also spilled over to their strategic notions of a militarized India that supported a Hindu-centric foreign policy to defend the country against "alien forces from outside or by an internal anti-Hindu anarchy..." within India (Savarkar, 1967:5). Savarkar (1940:90, 1949:68) explicitly defended this policy view by saying that, "Our foreign policy ... will be guided from an unspoken and an unalloyed Hindu point of view ... [and] the Hindus should henceforth test all national and international politics and policies through the Hindu point of view ..." (Savarkar, 1967:1). In this context, Savarkar (1940:90) also specified that colonial India's relations with England would also be guided by the "Hindu policy [of] having ... absolute political independence of the Hindu nation in view," which, amongst others, constituted one of the core differences between the Hindu Mahasabha and the moderate INC (given that the Hindu leaders felt that the INC moderates were serving more as laborers than leaders in leading the anticolonial struggle in India (Deendayal Research Institute, 1989:10). Accordingly, Savarkar made a rallying call to the Hindu public to "Hinduise All Politics, and Militarize Hindudom," asking the RSS to take immediate steps to give effect to this "Hinduised political program" (Savarkar, 1967:1). To this effect, Savarkar located passivity in India's military life for which he blamed the Congress under the Gandhian lead, and campaigned extensively to "fan up the martial spirit in the Hindu race" (ibid.:3–5). To this end, he urged them "to intensify their efforts ... for militarizing [the] Hindu race and get[ing] it trained up to an up-to-date military efficiency" (ibid.).

In speaking of India's military strength, it might be important to note the Hindu nationalists' concept of a Hindu Sanghatanist economic policy for India whose economic agenda intersected the military dimensions of India's nation-building.[8] Its aim was to rejuvenate the Hindu nation's economy for the benefit of a militarily strong India (Savarkar, 1940:185). The connection between economy, military, and the Hindu culture underpinning the Sanghatanist economic policy was expressed clearly when Savarkar critiqued "the monomaniac remedy of Gandhiji's spinning wheel," by which, he thought Gandhi "want[ed] to convert the whole world into Ahimsa and make it resort to disarmament," and strongly emphasized the Sanghatanist policy's immediate program for promoting the economic, political, and military advancement "of the Hindu nation alone" (Savarkar, 1940:186). Although the quest for India's atomic science was also being forged by India's political activists (such as Nehru, K.N. Katju) and India's science community members (such as Homi Bhabha, Meghnad Saha, and others), what was problematic about the Hindu nationalists' quest for science and a potential military power was that it was being constructed out of a narrow interpretation of India's nationalist vision. In terms of a potential independent India's foreign policy, Savarakar (1967:1) specified that India should be friendly with nations that were friendly or were likely to be friendly with India; should oppose countries opposed to India or were likely to endanger Hindu interests; and be neutral toward those countries that followed a relation of neutrality with India. Although the Hindu nationalist organization RSS was banned briefly from Indian politics from February 1948 to July 1949, the organization thereafter resurged in Indian politics, albeit in an underground manner, to make a more prominent presence in the mainstream of Indian politics through one of its political successors carrying a significant implication for nuclear India.

An overall analysis of the ideological perspectives of the Indian nationalists (the INC and the Hindu nationalists) reveal that they shared three premises on India's cultural identity: First, that the Indian society was a rich source of cultural existence that constitutes the "inner essence" of India's spiritual morality; second, the process of colonization had belittled India's indigenous culture which necessitated anticolonial struggles to reinstate India's cultural identity, sovereignty, and power; and finally, the notion of territoriality (either political or cultural) as important in defining India's nationalist identity.

Yet, following Sarvepalli and Bhattacharya's (1986:210) claim that, "a nation is a process of becoming ...," one notices that beyond these commonalities the moderates and the Hindu nationalists parted ways as to what constitutes the essence of India's cultural/nationalist identity and the core of its strategic cultural thinking. First, in contrast to the INC's conceptualization of India's culture as a heterogeneous composite entity, the Hindu nationalists interpreted India's culture as encompassing a Hindu-centric entity and rendered their definition of India's strategic identity as a race-based Hindu nation. Second, unlike the INC that saw the presence of colonial power and international hierarchy as critical in defining India's (in)security imaginary, the Hindu nationalists prioritized the religious/anti-Muslim component of Indian's cultural identity, which, played out amongst the outer Christian colonial world to define India's strategic cultural identity and insecurity. Finally, in contrast to the cautious military preparedness of the INC (based on Gandhian nonviolence), the Hindu nationalists' Hindu-centric visions of India's strategic identity and insecurity projected for India a militant foreign policy. The Hindu nationalists' conception of a Hindu India opposed to its Western colonial/Muslim adversaries represented an inner/spiritual and outside/material dichotomy in India's strategic cultural thinking (Chatterjee, 1993). Yet, this dichotomy is not very clear, given that both domains accepted the liberalizing component of Western industrial–scientific progress in defining the economic progress of India—an influence felt acutely in colonial India's discourses of science and atomic energy. The economic liberalizer and modernizer in Savarkar is noted to have asked "the Hindu race to improve their social outlook, get rid of economic unemployment, and improve industrialization … [for] promoting Hindu military-mindedness, spirit and value" (Savarkar, 1967:6; Devare, 2009). Shunning passivity and promoting "Hindu military-mindedness" was a part of modernizer Savarkar's strategic vision. Below I analyze how these Indian nationalists' interpretations of India's strategic culture provided a political–ideological space within which emerged discourses of science and atomic energy in colonial India.

Discourses of Science in Colonial India

There developed a community of scientists, mathematicians, physicists, chemists, biologists, and philanthropists in colonial India, who, in conjunction with the existing discourses of India's political–intellectual elites (that spoke of the selective incorporation of Western science and technology with India's traditional values) offered their visions of science and atomic energy in forging the scientific progress of colonial India. A plethora of scientific activities such as establishing formal scientific research institutions and centers; introducing academic departments and modern science courses in universities; undertaking scientific experiments and innovations; and the publication of science journals marked the scientific tempo of colonial India since mid-1900s. Educated, well-traveled, and with extensive research experiences from abroad, a stellar group of India's science community members included, amongst others, C.V. Raman, Ashutosh Mukherjee, Jagadish Chandra Bose, Satyendranath Bose, Debendra Nath Bose, Prasanta Mahalanobis, Meghnad Saha, S.S. Bhatnagar, and Homi Bhabha and became pivotal for infusing organized science in colonial India. Despite the colonial climate's financial limitations, India's scientific activities (with support of Indian philanthropists and through fellowships from Western universities) spanned since the mid-1900s (Anderson, 2010). To this end, scientists like Debendra Nath Bose conducted research in the areas of cosmic ray, radioactivity, and neutron physics; Jagadish Chandra Bose in the field of microwave optics; Satyendranath Bose in theoretical physics; Meghnad Saha in nuclear physics; and Homi Bhabha in cosmic-ray and elementary particle theory. Although the views of India's early scientists reflected divergent political–ideological views concerning the ends–means relationship between science and India's development (which I will later analyze), for now, I address the scientific views of two of India's most prominent scientists Meghnad Saha and Homi Bhabha given that both their views on science influenced the development of nuclear science in postcolonial India.

Before considering Saha's ideas of the role of science in India's development strategies, it may be important to note Saha's ideological perspectives that shaped his attitude toward science for India's national development and planning. From the age of 12, Saha had declared himself against foreign control of India, and formed his views of national development based upon a complete structural attention to social relationships and political institutions. He saw through the experiences of India's freedom struggle that India's industrial development through industrialists and capitalists could create internal dependencies and distorted concentrations of capital within the Indian economy; nor could it prevent foreign control by external powers over the Indian economy significantly. With this line of thinking, Saha's views on national development advocated national planning, public-sector industrialization, the role of science and technology in India's national development, and proposed the use of power from nuclear reactors for production of energy (ibid.:85). Forging steel, petroleum, chemical, and power/energy nexus became Saha's catch-phrase for the use of atomic energy in India's national development (Anderson, 2010:89; Chatterjee and Chatterjee, 1984:63).[9]

Saha's views on science and national development ran counter with some of India's political elites such as Nehru, whose cooperative stance with the British (as Saha thought) represented retrograde thinking in Indian politics (Anderson, 1975, 2010:100–101). Although Saha and Nehru co-opted in many common political interests since 1933 (such as serving on the Planning Committee of the INC), controversies between Saha and India's political elites such as Nehru, Gandhi, and K.N. Katju (Congress Minister for industry in UP) regarding small-scale versus large-scale industrialization became evidenced in the national planning committee debates (Anderson, 2010:83–87). Saha was critical of the Congress high command in taking an ambiguous view of India's industrialization (Nehru, 1965:143–147), denounced Gandhi's idea of small-scale industrialization, was of the view that India was in need of a forced march to progress, and critiqued Nehru for not taking a clear stand on large-scale industrialization (although at times appraising Nehru's support of scientists and their activities) (Anderson, 1975:26–30).[10]

Between the years 1943 and 1945, Nehru also addressed the contradictions between small-scale and large-scale industrialization for India explicitly supporting the urgency of industrialization and modern technology for India's development. He said,

> It can hardly be challenged that, in the context of the modern world, no country can be politically and economically independent within a framework of international interdependence, unless it is highly industrialized and has developed its power sources to the utmost. Nor can it achieve or maintain high standards of living and liquidate poverty without the aid of modern technology in almost every sphere of life. An industrially backward country will continually upset the world equilibrium and encourage the aggressive tendencies of more developed countries. Even if it retains its political independence, this will be nominal only and economic control will tend to pass to others. (Nehru, 1965:147)

To be noted here is that, the above observation by Nehru other than supporting the need of industrialization and modern technology for India's development implied certain critical issues of international power, hierarchy, Western/industrial powers' potential aggressiveness, and possibilities of their control over smaller countries like India—in case the latter failed to develop economically. This antihierarchical/big power perception became significant in charting India's atomic science/nuclear energy quest in its post-independent context. In this context of great-power perceptions, Nehru's views on India's industrialization and development of modern technology (if possible with Western assistance) signified his insistence on developing India's indigenous industrial and scientific base to maintain India's stature (which became further pronounced in his speeches in post-independent India as prime minister).

In contrast to Saha, Bhabha's vision of science in relation to India's development was shaped by Western European influence. Bhabha was aware of the consequences of foreign domination but growing up in a business community (where it was important to keep out of formal politics and collaborate with foreign firms) accepting foreign influence became for Bhabha a fact of economic life. Thus, knowing fully the political–economic ramifications of colonial rule, Bhabha used his arguments (well understood to be a part of his pragmatic neutrality to moderately express his views about Indian politics) to support foreign collaborations for the nation's scientific development (Anderson, 1975:100–101).

Bhabha's research which remained mainly theoretical emphasized two aspects to this end: First, the need for fundamental research, and second, the need for closer collaboration between British and Indian scientists to support war efforts and India's development (ibid.:32). With regard to the former, Bhabha was of the belief that fundamental research must be supported in India for its potential for developing indigenous nuclear energy for India's future uses, groups of research be built only around suitable scientists, and that government support to this end need not entail governmental control of the same. It led to the establishment of the Tata Institute of Fundamental Research in Bombay in June 1942, and establishment of the Atomic Energy Committee in 1945 (ibid.:33). With regard to the latter, that is, the need for closer collaboration between foreign and Indian scientists, Bhabha actively pursued prospects. As Anderson (2010:108–109) writes, normally colonial viceroys did not pay much attention to issues of science and technology in their colonial countries; but, the ongoing World War II related developments in Asia brought the United States' attention toward India in an anti-British/anticolonial manner that presented for India an unexpected situation where a colonial war economy turned into a "planning season" for the

Indian scientists with British collaboration. As early as in 1942, Bhabha with a small group of scientists has already started cosmic-ray measurements with the US Air Force airplanes stationed in Bangalore for military purposes, and around 1943 saw a much enthusiastic mood among British firms to work in India as partners in scientific collaborations. Thereafter, followed a series of extended discussions, conversations, and reciprocal visits among the Indian and British scientists namely British physiologist Archibald Hill, H. Bhabha, S.S. Bhatnagar, J.C. Ghosh, J.N. Mukherjee, Meghnad Saha, S.S. Bhatnagar, J.C. Ghosh, S.K. Mitra, J.N. Mukherjee, Nazir Ahmed, and S.L. Bhatia with the hope of "doing something for the [Indian] people" (Anderson, 2010:210, 214).

Despite these benevolent gestures and feelings of goodwill, it might be worth noting the "scrutiny" that the five Indian scientists, especially Saha, had to undergo in the United States when visiting the Carnegie Institution at Washington DC. Angry at many discussions and inquiries on nuclear science that Saha made with his counterparts at the Carnegie on the ongoing Manhattan Project (the Indian scientists were unaware of the forbidden nature of these discussions), the visiting Indian scientists were accompanied by security agents throughout the rest of their stay in the United States and Canada—until they left for India in February 1945. These perceptions of Orientalist xenophobia which marked India–US atomic energy-related interactions during these colonial years remain noteworthy, given that these issues of US Orientalism continue in contemporary India–US nuclear security relations. I will continue to address this theme in the rest of this project.

In keeping with my theoretical claim that discursive articulations of a nation's strategic culture facilitate interpretations of the nation's insecurity and its atomic science policies, the above analysis has drawn attention to how colonial India's state-science community's interpretations of the nation's insecurities have influenced their atomic science discourses. Accordingly as documented, India's atomic science discourses reflecting the views of India's INC moderates, the Hindu nationalists, and its science community have drawn on their different interpretations of insecurities and nationalist visions to define their atomic science discourses. While the science community justified India's scientific path on grounds of India's economic/industrial insecurities and the need for fundamental research; the INC's moderates (without explicitly denouncing Gandhian norms of small-scale industrialization) grounded their rationality for science in the context of a technological (in)security and India's needs to overcome the same; and the Hindu nationalists' explicitly called for an industrialized (Hindu) India—with possibilities for atomic weapons—to counter a Hindu-centric insecurity. Despite divergences and overlaps in their interpretations of the nation's insecurity, they collectively advocated strengthening the indigenous capacity of India's atomic power and science.

Conclusion

In keeping with the theoretical claim of this book that the discipline of IR and India-specific approaches to strategic culture and security studies have ignored a constructivist angle, I have explored in this chapter how the essence of India's culture as one of openness, plurality, and selective internationalism has influenced the colonial Indian state's strategic culture, nationalist identity, and (in)security imaginations. In this effort, I have summarized the evolution of India's strategic culture under its Vedic, medieval, and colonial eras and have suggested that the evolution of India's strategic culture, rather than being culturally conditioned or historically determined by India's (native) cultural thinking, has been one of social construction, where ideologically guided discourses and interpretive lens of the British colonizers and the Indian nationalists (both moderates and the Hindu nationalists) have been critical in constructing the multiple contours of India's strategic cultural essence. To this end, as documented, while the self-serving nature of colonial discourses in terms of its rationalism, liberal progress, and cultural superiority have sustained an infantilizing interpretation of India's strategic self, one cannot ignore the strength and vitality of India's indigenous culture, which, rooted in notions of its own civilizational morality, indigenous rationality, pluralism, nonviolence, militancy, and selective openness to internationalism has sustained and further enriched India's strategic cultural essence out of which emerged India's atomic energy quest in relation to its insecurities and national development. In charting this socially constructed nature of colonial India's strategic essence, its (in)security imaginaries, and its atomic science discourses, one also notices the emergence of a certain identity of the state, which, born primarily in opposition to India's colonial history appears hybrid (than totally indigenous), given that, while rejecting colonization, was selectively co-opting Western technology and science for India's national development. To this extent, one finds that the multiple discursive articulations of colonial India's strategic cultural thinking, its (in)security imaginaries, and its nationalist visions partially imbibed and resisted colonization, out of which emerged an identity of the colonial state that was simultaneously secular, Hinduicized, modern, traditional, Gandhian, militant, and aggressive. Out of these multiple "meaning-producing" discourses of colonial India's strategic culture (as documented) emerged post-independent India's strategic culture, insecurities, and its atomic dream. The next chapter addresses these dynamics.

Notes

1. In the later Vedic years (700–183 BC), this collectivity of Indian life emerged as a medley of social, cultural, and political practices as documented in the rise of Jainism under Mahavira, Buddhism under Gautam Buddha, and, the further elaboration of Hinduism through the later Vedic text of the *Upanishads*.
2. However, the Sultanate's religious zeal also rendered the Indian masses unassimilated in the Indian social system and having reached its peak under Md. Bin Tughluq, disintegrated into independent kingdoms under provincial governors (Ghoshal, 1965).
3. For scholarly explanations of British colonization of India, see Bose and Jalal (1998), Spear (1965), Stokes (1959), and Pandey (2006).
4. For a background of how writings of the 18th-century European philosophers like Leibniz and Voltaire provided the ideological climate for the British Indologists' scholarships, see Mukherjee (1968).
5. While Western mainstream discourses greatly applaud and publicize the Bentinck Abolition Sati Act as a great accomplishment of the British administrators, what they do not discuss is that the ban on of Sati (although quite problematically under India's indigenous social-cultural pressure, mostly from the Brahmins) was removed a year later. For these discussions see Mani (1998).
6. It may be important to clarify what the terms communal/communalism mean in Western and non-Western/South Asian usages. In Western analyses, communalism refers to social-political conflicts in the backward areas of the

postcolonial worlds where these conflicts as pathological conditions existed long before colonial infiltration in these societies. Instead, in Indian/South Asian context, the term communalism refers to a condition of fear, suspicion, and hostility between members of different religious communities where these conditions unlike West assumptions are not pathological conditions of Indian society. Instead, Indian nationalists see communalism in India/South Asia as "a problem of recent origin, as the outcome basically of economic and political inequality and conflict, and as the handiwork of a handful of self-interested elite-groups (colonial and native), with the mass of the people remaining largely unaffected" (Pandey, 2006:11).

7. However, with subsequent political developments, it became difficult for even moderates like them to accept the perceived emergence of Hindu religious symbolisms and communitarian interests within the INC and led them to advocate Muslim nonparticipation in the Congress (Jinnah, 2000; Khan, 2006).

8. The concept of Hindu Sanghatanist economic policy for India was developed by Savarakar, as an economic policy to attain national development and self-sufficiency of India, and, was also a practical and a political agenda to safeguard the economic and developmental interests of the Hindus and the Hindu nation "whenever and wherever they … [were] threatened by the economical aggression of the non-Hindus" (Savarkar, 1940:186, 189). Embedded in the context of Hindu nationalism, the policy had the following cultural and military components: First, human history and activities in the Indian context were not only economical but also spiritual and cultural; second, economic questions in India are interwoven with religious, racial, and cultural aspects such that activities of rioters, mobs, and, dacoits were associated with "Moslem fanatics" of the state; and, third, India must follow an economic policy of national coordination of class interests, national production on the greatest possible machine scale, and, coordinating capital and labor to attain national development and self-sufficiency at the greatest level (Savarkar, 1940:185).

9. Yet, Saha was careful not to confuse his opposition to foreign influence over Indian economy with the relationship that his scientific colleagues had with foreign companies where they worked, or, with India shared technological collaborations (Anderson, 1975:100–101).

10. Nehru subsequently in 1939 commented on Saha's misconceptions of Nehru's position on small-scale industrialization (Anderson, 1975:100–101).

3

Political Idealism and Atomic Science: 1947–1964

This chapter explores how the strategic culture of post-independent India under Prime Minister Nehru (often called Nehruvian India) between August 1947 and May 1964 has defined the atomic policy discourses of post-independent India.[1] Unlike the structural/ conventional approaches of international relations (IR) that see a state's international structure and its domestic bureaucratic politics as key in defining a state's/India's atomic policy, the constructivist approach that I pursue in this chapter, while considering the above structural factors, will offer an interpretive approach to analyze the discursive/ ideological connections between the constructions of the nationalist identity, (in)security imaginary, and atomic science policies/discourses of Nehru's India. Building from my earlier claim in Chapter 1, that there exists a discursive/interpretative link between a state's strategic cultural thinking, the production of its (in)security imaginary, and its atomic/ nuclear policy choices, this chapter will draw attention to how certain meaning-producing discourses of the Indian state between August 1947 and May 1964, born out of contested interactions of India's colonial history, Gandhian idealism, India's postcolonial identity, quest for modernity, and nuclear sovereignty have socially constructed the strategic cultural thinking, (in)security imaginary, and the atomic policy discourses of post-independent India.

Accordingly, this chapter addresses the following "how-possible'" questions: First, how has the Indian state's strategic cultural thinking between August 1947 and May 1964, embodied within the philosophical moorings of India's cultural history, colonial history, Gandhian idealism, and India's postcolonial identity as a drive to modernity, and projected through the ideological lenses of its political leadership make sense of India's international politics? Second, how the Indian state's interpretation of its current international politics create an ideological and political space, within which were constructed and articulated shifting images of India's nationalist identity, strategic cultural thinking, and (in)security imaginaries? Finally, how the social construction of India's strategic culture and (in)security imaginary created an ideological and cultural space within which are forged and articulated immediate postcolonial India's ideas and discourses on its atomic science policies? In addressing each of these "how-possible" questions, my aim will be to show how the Indian state's discourses as tools of social and ideological power have interacted with India's cultural and philosophical history, colonial memories, Gandhian idealism, India's postcolonial identity, quest for scientific modernity, and India's regional/global geo-politics—to produce and sustain a mutually constituted relationship between Nehruvian India's strategic cultural thinking, (in)security imaginary, and its atomic science policies.

Before proceeding with my analysis on the discursive construction of Nehruvian India's strategic culture and (in)security imaginary, I must mention that the notion of ideologically guided interpretations and discourses that are attentive to constructions of (in)security imaginaries may, to some conventional IR analysts, appear as postmodern jargons that sacrifice the primacy of "the real" (or real politics) in analyzing India's atomic science policies (and thereafter, India's nuclear weapons development policies). Furthermore, the role of interpretation, discourses, and the production of meanings as subjective aspects may even lead to popular skepticism that such subjective issues may have little to do with India's atomic science/nuclear weapons policy making, which fall within the domain of the real.

Given these two possible challenges to my interpretive approach in this study, I reiterate that my approach to India's nuclear weapons development does not negate the significance of real politics. In fact, real politics, defined as international anarchy, is a vital structural factor within which has unfurled India's atomic science/nuclear weapons discourses and policy choices—namely following India's crushing defeat in India–China war of 1962. Acknowledging this significance of real politics, this chapter and the subsequent ones seek to reapproach the dynamics of India's atomic science/nuclear weapons policy developments through an interpretive angle by teasing out how the social, cultural, and ideological power of the Indian state's discourses, played out within the structural context of India's geo-politics and domestic politics, have made sense of the transitory notions/constructions of India's international affairs, its nationalist identity, shifting (in)security imaginaries, and India's atomic science/nuclear weapons options. Speaking at a theoretical level in international relations, I draw attention to the significance of discourse in the social constructions of India's strategic cultural thinking, its (in)security imaginary, and its atomic science policies.

This chapter is organized as follows: The following section addresses the discourses of postcolonial India's nation-building project under Nehru and other key leaders, which, embodied in historically grounded moorings of India's strategic culture, philosophy, colonial memories, and Gandhian idealism, have produced the contours of India's national security and foreign policy perspectives. The second section addresses how the social construction of India's strategic culture (as a part of its historically and culturally influenced nation-building project) has produced an (in)security imaginary for the state, which, embodied within and projected through the state's political leaders and its security community, made sense of India's IR. The third section addresses the emergence of India's disarmament and atomic science developments, which, articulated by India's state-science community within the socially constructed parameters of India's strategic culture and (in)security imaginaries, have forged India's atomic science in a spirit of "scientific temperament" of the Indian mind (Poulose, 1978:102). I also note the rise of an alternative discourse on India's atomic power after 1962 that subsequently geared India's atomic science policies toward producing/deploying atomic weapons for India's defense purposes.

Moorings of Strategic Culture and Discourses of Nation-building

In keeping with my claim that India's strategic culture is an act of discursive production, "produced in and out of 'the context within which people give meanings to their actions and experiences ...'" (Tomlinson 1991:7), I show in this section how the moorings of the Indian state's strategic cultural discourses (drawing from India's colonial history, its postcolonial state-craft, science, development, and the hierarchical place of the West) have defined India's nation-building project.

Any analysis of India's strategic culture must take into account the historical contours of India's nation-making debates, which, evolving early in India's colonial eras through the visions of Mahatma Gandhi and other constitutional moderates, such as Surendranath Banerjee, B.R. Ambedkar, and Sarvepalli Radhakrishnan (as discussed in Chapter 2), were put together by the political acumen of Nehru at the eve of India's independence.[2] In his *Tryst With Destiny*, Nehru spoke of India's dreams, which were "... dreams for India [and] ... also for the world, for all the nations and the peoples ..." (Nehru, 1961:14) Three interrelated themes echoed in these nation-building discourses: First, defining India's identity as a strong, nationalist, secular, democratic, and a self-assertive state. Second, India missed the first industrial revolution and should not miss the second opportunity to bring about India's scientific and technological development. Third, highlighting India's national sovereignty and territorial security, given India's experience of colonization (ibid.:4–21). These themes found reflection in an enormous growth of India's state-building capacities through its political, economic, military, and public welfare institutions. In keeping with my claim that India's strategic culture is an act of discursive production, "produced in and out of 'the context' within which people give meanings to their actions and experiences ..." (Tomlinson 1991:7), I elaborate some of these state-building discourses of the Indian state, that simultaneously nationalist, indigenous, and Western, articulated India's nation-building project, and in that context also laying the foundations of immediate post-independent India's strategic cultural orientations.

Nehru was a liberal individualist at heart in that he believed in individual rights, freedom, civil liberty, and human progress. From this mindset of Nehru, post-independent Indian nationalism represented a new nationalism that was influenced by the "new liberal thought of the West and [its] industrial progress" (Nehru et al., 2003:62), but also recognized India's "noble heritage," "historical roots," and "cultural potential" as key in shaping India's nationalism (Nehru and Gopal, 1980:200–208; 238–241; 225–229; Nehru, 1989; Nehru et al., 2003:18). What kind of India was Nehru aiming for? In his words, "we aim at a strong, free, and democratic India, where every citizen has an equal place and full opportunity of growth and service, where present-day inequalities in wealth and status have ceased to be, where our vital impulses are directed to creative and cooperative endeavor" (Nehru et al., 2003:46, 47–49). This new India, under a centralized government, was to form a unified state that was to be free of hatred, violence, fear and communalism (Nehru, 1950:7, 13; Nehru et al., 2003:45, 64). In terms of communalism and secularism, Nehru in contrast to the Hindu nationalists as the RSS (Seshadri, 1988), held the view that "… it was for the Hindus to make the larger number of Muslims in India feel at home and not see themselves as second-class citizens, existing on sufferance" (Parthasarathy, 1989:8). Although the prime minister was aware that "[t] here might be a few Muslims who are communal and … [would] have to be dealt with sternly," his overall approach to the Indian Muslims was that "… it serves no purpose to question the loyalty of the entire community" (ibid.:8).

Despite critiques to Nehru's secularism and that even the post-Nehru Indian governments under the prime ministers Indira Gandhi, Rajiv Gandhi, Narasimha Rao, and Vajpayee felt compelled to make official distinctions between Hindu and non-Hindu populations (Varshney, 1993; Kumar 2001; Krishna, 2002), it is overwhelmingly accepted that Nehru's secular tolerance came to denote India's identity at a national level. Despite various interpretations of India's nationalist history, secularism, strategic culture, and nation-building visions (as discussed in Chapter 2), Nehru's ideology became the official ideology of the Indian state and his vision of state-building the official explanation of the Indian past. Implementing this ideological vision of India's nationalism meant that the state was committed to economic, social, and technological developments to promote public good and security of its people, where his quasi-social approach to development based on centralized planning and a mixed economy had a "tremendous emotional appeal for the Indian masses" (Nehru et al., 2003:62). It was based on India's own experience and reading of history, was necessary for India's internal peace and freedom, which, in turn, would lead to a stable foreign policy (Nehru, 1950:201).[3]

That an independent India must "be strong enough to protect herself from outside aggression and invasion" was another pillar of Nehru's new nationalism (Nehru et al., 2003:40). Reiterating India's colonial past and faith in its nationalist strength, he claimed that, "If India is strong enough to gain her freedom from British imperialism, … it seems to follow that she will also be strong enough to resist fresh aggression" (ibid.:40). This required that India "… take all necessary steps to strengthen her defenses and … has the industrial and other resources to do so" (ibid.:41). Nehru's concept of a territorially strong India fused certain cultural attributes of the Indian mindset to explain India's greatness, its objective of world peace, and how that could be attained through the Gandhian principles of truth and Dharma—given that "… ideals and objectives can never be divorced from the methods adopted to realize them …" (Nehru, 1950:7). Nehru's vision of a strong India combining idealism and realism paved the way for India's foreign policies known as nonalignment. While I will return to these issues as reflective of India's strategic cultural thinking, I deflect briefly to discuss Nehru's views on science and technology for India's national development—namely to document how these discourses served as the context for the state to construct its strategic cultural thinking and atomic policy choices.

Born out of an antidote to imperialism, the dominant scientific thinking of the post-independent Indian state was to emphasize its scientific momentum "… to capture and develop pockets of excellence that could aid Indian developmental and security aims" (Kapur, 1994: 223). This scientific momentum, however, was not an entirely new projection of the Indian state but a continuation of the industrial and scientific infrastructure set in place in colonial India (as discussed in Chapter 2). However what changed in these scientific endeavors in the postcolonial period was they being rearticulated in the context of the changed nature of the Indian state, that is, as an independent state that is no longer tied to the logistics of Western colonial domination but to the compulsions of Cold War politics and the emerging domination of Western nations. Three factors underpinned the scientific momentum of the Nehruvian Indian state: First, the rich historical heritage of the Indian scientific mind and that India needs to continue this scientific temper for the purposes of statecraft and national development; second, India's material backwardness necessitated the use of science for its economic development; and third, that India's weak international economic and military position necessitated that its political and scientific elites strengthen the material base of Indian power in its scientific, defense, and foreign affairs (Nehru et al., 2003:18).

Evidenced in the multiple writings of Nehru, the need for a strong, secure, and technologically advanced India was primarily to counter India's "psychology of subservience," that had "limit[ed] the mental outlook and horizon of the people" under colonization (Ibid.:29). This is because the modernizer in Nehru saw science as giving humans limitless power, thereby making "the applications of science inevitable and unavoidable for all countries and peoples today" (Nehru, 1950:130; Nehru et al., 2003:97–98). Despite opposition from the Bombay Club and the prominent antisocialist C. Rajagopalachari, state-controlled application of science for construction of dams, roads, railways, hydroelectric plants, basic key and heavy industries, and other industrial projects became key scientific ventures of the Indian state (Nehru, 1950).

Yet, this age of science was also an age of contradiction, struggle, and crisis. This is because the material base of Western science, which was also being selectively imbibed by the Indian scientific mind (Nehru et al., 2003:93), stood at odds with the principles of Indian philosophy—where progress was not merely India's material progress but represented the "quality" and "depth" of the people. Thus, while asserting that "change is essential," Nehru also asserted that "continuity is also necessary," and India must strive to gain its scientific power without negating "… what India has stood for in the past … and in the present time as exemplified by Gandhiji" (ibid.:61, 64). As he stated, "[t]he methods adopted [for scientific progress] will have to depend upon the background and cultural development of a country or a community" (ibid.:62). This required combining science and technology with the "spirit and the philosophical mindset" of Indian masses that represented a more humanistic vision of the Indian mind. Nehru saw it as representing "some kind of a synthesis between old India and modern trends" (ibid.).

It is in these historically grounded political, ideological, and strategic cultural moorings of the Indian state that emerged India's nation-building discourses that blended India's ancient history, culture, and civilization with the benefits of Western scientific progress to define India's nationalist project. It reflected the emergence of a strategic cultural thinking of the state born out of anticolonial sentiments, which, however, did not discard the West especially its benefits of scientific and industrial progress. Instead, it emphasized the significance of India's culture to selectively draw from and function on a revolutionary [read: Western scientific] plane.[4] In recognizing the influence of colonization on India's strategic thinking, I am cognizant that India's strategic culture is to a great extent historically grounded and is also socially acquired through the norms of India's nonviolence and coexistence. Yet, from a constructivist angle, my analysis underscores that these historical, social, and cultural aspects of India's strategic thinking are not static, and have not remained static in defining India's nation-building discourses. In fact, through the meaning-producing role of discourses, which are fundamental to any system of cultural representation (Tomlinson, 1991), India's historically grounded strategic cultural thinking has been continuously reinterpreted by the state to define notions of India's national security and its foreign policy perception. In the next section, I focus on these discursive connections.

Strategic Culture, National Security, and Foreign Policy

In Chapter 1, I defined India's strategic culture as an interpretive framework through which India views its world of international relations. I have also claimed that India's strategic culture projects a certain (in)security imaginary, which sets the context within which are debated issues of India's national security, foreign policy, and nuclear technology. To examine the above claim, I accept R.C. Dutt's definition that "the foreign policy of India, like that of any other country, is a projection into foreign affairs of the values cherished and the national interests perceived by the country" (Dutt, 1987:60). These values and interests may change with changes in the perceptions of India's political leaders and in the configurations of India's domestic and global forces. When this happens,

India's foreign policy also changes. Yet, the perception of a country's foreign policy is also a matter of ideological reflection, social power, and discursive representation of what constitutes a country's cherished values, interests, and its political reality. Accordingly, this section explores how India's nation-building discourses have served as the framework to interpret India's national security/foreign policy and in relation to such interpretation make sense of India's international relations.

Nehru's idea of national security blended India's cultural philosophical attributes such as Gandhi's idealism with Westphalian notions of India as a strong state. To this end, Nehru commented that, "political changes produce certain results but the essential changes are in the spirit and outlook of a nation" (Nehru, 1950:121). The "spirit" of the Indian nation, for Nehru, was encapsulated in a number of interrelated factors such as India's political history, cultural traditions, ethnic diversity, and civilizational norms and philosophies—which, in interaction with India's geo-political compulsions, reflected India's strategic cultural mindset. In terms of India's national security and foreign relations, this Gandhian ideal meant living in "world cooperation and world peace" with others, which, defined as internationalism, stood for India's policy of friendship with her neighbors and avoiding conflict in interstate relations (ibid.:27–28, 254).

As many analysts argue, what developed as India's internationalism was evident in embryonic forms in the early resolutions of the Indian National Congress, and in this sense "policy inherent ... in the conditioning of the Indian mind during freedom struggle ..." (Khan, 1989:20; Bakaya, 1989; Nehru, 1980). But what crystallized as post-independent India's posture of coexistence was cognition of India's historical and colonial circumstances that India would not align itself with the West and its neocolonialism (Haskar, 1989; Jaipal, 1983). Accepted as Nonaligned Movement, this conception, about which Nehru in subsequent statements appeared ambiguous (Gopal, 1975–1984:64), came to represent a significant norm in India's international affairs. It aimed at world peace, disarmament, and liquidation of the manifestations of imperialism and colonialism in global politics.[5] A corollary of Nehru's nonalignment was his Asian Approach in India's regional affairs (Nehru, 1961:280–281).[6] Its outcome was the five principles of coexistence or Panchsheel and necessitated the bilateral resolution of conflicts among the Asian countries. Nehru cemented close and friendly relations with countries of South Asia, East Asia, the Middle East, and East Africa but ran into political disputes with two of its neighboring states China and Pakistan (Nehru, 1961).

Nonalignment, as critiqued by many, was not India's isolation or passivism in world politics or, antagonism vis-à-vis the super powers (Nehru, 1950:213). Instead, it was a psychology of cooperation among states keeping in mind their historical, colonial, cultural backgrounds and their strategic needs of the day (Nehru and Gopal, 1980:367). In this sense, Nehru was no less a realist, and having claimed even before independence that, "self-interest should drive every nation to the wider cooperation" (Mishra, 1989:45), reasserted as the prime minister that, "we live in an abnormal world, full of wars and aggression" (Nehru, 1942:25). Nehru also conceded that his agenda of a militarily strong India was opportunistic, given that if needed India would get military help from other countries and even side with a great power without sacrificing India's sovereign independence (Nehru, 1950:254). In this context of big-power assistance, it must be noted that Nehru was an ardent, though critical, admirer of the Soviet Union (Bakaya, 1987), and from 1955 to 1956 saw Indo-Soviet relationship scaling to new heights and India supporting the Soviet Union on Cold War issues such as Korea and Indochina. Despite its pro-Soviet orientation, India was aware that economic assistance for India's development would be more readily available from the United States and its allies and not the war-devastated Soviets and retained Commonwealth links with the United States and United Kingdom through military exchanges and conference participations (despite critiques from Dr S.A. Dange who preferred India's pro-Soviet stand). This politically autonomous, realist, and cooperative stand of nonalignment (to which others such as Acharya Kripalani opposed) gave rise to a number of developmental, technological, and military cooperation between India and Western states such as the United States, United Kingdom, Soviet Union, France, and Canada (Nehru and Gopal, 1980:367). In this sense, nonalignment, born out of India's own reading of history, was readjusted considering India's strategic nation-building compulsions of the day. Expressed through Prime Minister Nehru's strategic acumen, it constituted "a new method of struggle and political warfare and a new kind of diplomacy" for India in international relations

(Nehru, 1950:28). This dynamism of India's nonalignment that switched between idealism, anticolonialism, realism, pragmatism, and possibilities of big power alliances to define India's strategic cultural mindset, and its nationalist project, also remained critical in interpreting India's world of international affairs. The next section explores this linkage.

Interpreting India's International Relations

This section addresses how the social construction of India's strategic culture, embodied within and projected through the state's ideological lenses and discourses have interpreted India's international relations vis-à-vis China, Pakistan, and the United States. In this endeavor, I do not focus on the chronological details of their foreign policy relations/ development; instead, I explore how a series of Cold War related military and nuclear developments at the global level and the South Asian level have been ideologically perceived and discursively articulated by the Indian state, where factors such as India's colonial memories, resistance to Cold politics, Cold War-related proxy wars, military pacts, an emerging Western hegemonic dominance in India's vicinity, and an expansionist Chinese threat became key in shaping India's interpretation of its international affairs. While India's initial frame of interpretation of its international affairs was primarily guided (and influenced) by India's strategic experiences of colonization and international idealism, India's defeat in the Sino-Indian war saw burgeoning signs of shifts of India's idealism to one of realism to redefine India's national security, international affairs, and, in that light, a shift in India's atomic science quests toward producing atomic weapons for defense purposes.

Post-independent India's interpretation of international relations (and its discourses on disarmament) occurred in a global context of Cold War where "the ideology and doctrines of extreme pathological dependence on nuclear weapons for a range of goals and objectives, among them security" infused the trend of nuclearism in the global arena (Lifton and Falk, 1982). Particularly, the years 1945–1960, which were dominated by the US posture of maintaining an overwhelming nuclear superiority than the Soviet Union, came to represent a period of "massive retaliation"

(Hammond, 1991:191). Simultaneously, both super powers competed for influence in Asia, Africa, and Latin America. Unable to fight each other directly through conventional military and nuclear exchanges, the super powers started proxy wars in Korea, Vietnam, horn of Africa, and Nicaragua and tried to gain ideological and political influence in the developing countries through developmental aid, humanitarian interventions, and Cold War military alliances (Blackett, 1948; Westad, 2005). Cold War infiltrations in the third world through such proxy wars and alliances also represented an economic and political imperialism in the third world that came close to using nuclear weapons in dealing with their Cold War hostilities in these regions (as for instance in the Soviet-Iranian-Azerbaijan, Korean, French control in Vietnam, the Formosa crises, and, most importantly, in Pakistan, bringing the Cold War's militarizing momentum acutely close to the Indian subcontinent). Then came the Cuban missile crisis creating a nuclear-acute momentum in the global political arena, leading to an arms race of unprecedented proportions between the super powers (Harvard Nuclear Study Group, 1983; Garthoff, 1984; Munton and Welch, 2007). Although super power confrontations over Cuba fell short of war, the climate of military war preparedness, escalation of nuclear weapons, and neocolonial encroachment of Cold War related proxy wars in the third world inaugurated an arms race mentality for the post-World War II generations born out of this Cold War-oriented military preparedness (Blackett, 1948; Brodie, 1973; Gray 1979; Hammond 1991; Kremenyuk, 1994).

The trends of arms escalation between the two super powers also initiated nonproliferation policy efforts and institutional mechanisms to check the spread of nuclear weapons among the nonnuclear/non-Western countries. This has become evident as early as the year 1946, when the United States through the Dean Acheson Plan (1946), the Baruch Plan (1946) and the Atomic Energy Act (1946), though unsuccessfully, sought to implement a nuclear arms control policy to check the spread of nuclear weapons technology to the then nonnuclear states (Ebinger, 1978).[7] However, operating during the days of US–USSR Cold War, transgressions occurred on the part of the United States in maintaining a rigid and neutral arms control agenda vis-à-vis the non-Western states, which became acute when President Eisenhower's Atoms For Peace Program (1953),[8] resulted in spreading nuclear technology to the US allies and to other nonaligned countries with super-power acquiescence (Bargman, 1977). This is because despite the US' broader arms control agenda to be maintained through the International Atomic Energy Agency, the Atoms For Peace Program resulted in many bilateral nuclear supply agreements from 1953 to 1956 between the United States, the Soviet Union, and their allies like South Africa, China, India, Israel, Pakistan and North Korea (Ebinger, 1978). It is against these Cold War-related trends of military preparedness, infused with nuclear arms escalation, and encroaching close to the Indian subcontinent that the Indian state through its nonaligned lenses interpreted its world of international relations, and its atomic science policies and disarmament affairs. I address first, India's interpretation of its international affairs.

India's nonaligned posture did not interfere with American interests in South Asia until 1950s, when India and Pakistan remained at the periphery of the US security interests in South Asia. However, with the outbreak of the US–USSR Cold War, analysis of the US' interests in South Asia by the CIA, the National Security Council (NSC Paper 68), and the State Department underscored the region's geo-strategic importance to the Cold War objectives of the United States (McMahon, 1994:16–17, 69) and started a series of political and military interactions between these countries that impacted relations between India and the United States (and India and Pakistan). Three themes underlined these developments: First, at every step of Cold War, while India retained its stern commitment to nonalignment or took a "wishy-washy" stand, Pakistan took a clear and unequivocal stand in favor of America in the war. The Korean war of 1950 encapsulated this trend (ibid.:86). Second, this pro-US ideological alliance of Pakistan (in contrast to India's) necessitated that the United States use Pakistan for its national strategic interests and vice versa (although mutual uses for self-interest purposes also ran into difficulties); and third, started a series of the US–Pakistan military pacts to contain communism in Asia that were deemed by India as signs of bellicose hostility of the US imperialism and anti-Indian activities in region.

The US–Pakistani military pacts unfurled since the mid-1950s when following the rise of Arab nationalism, the Anglo-Egyptian dispute, and the Israeli–Arab conflict Pakistan's strategic importance to the United States continued to grow since the mid-1950s. A Joint State Defense Working Group in April 1952 under the Eisenhower administration, citing Pakistan's martial tradition, strategic location, and eagerness to cooperate with the West, reported that Pakistan's accession to a regional defense organization "would contribute significantly to the military and political strength of the Organization" (McMahon, 1994:145). Although the idea of regional military arrangement known as the Middle Eastern Defense Organization of which Pakistan would be a part did not materialize, other formal military engagements soon ensued between Pakistan and the United States. In 1954, a regional alliance, known as the northern tier state alliance, was formed between Turkey, Pakistan, Iraq, and Iran to serve as a nucleus for a broader regional grouping with the United States relegated to a behind-the-scene role; the Mutual Defense Assistance Agreement was signed between Pakistan and the United States in May 1954, following which the US military assistance reached the Pakistani state; third, Pakistan participated at the United States convened Manila Conference in July 1954 to discuss collective security arrangements for South East Asia; Pakistan on September 1954 became a member of the South East Asia Treaty Organization; and in 1955, was formed the Central Treaty Organization (also known as the Baghdad Pact) between Iran, Iraq, Pakistan, Turkey, and the United Kingdom, which the United States joined later in 1958. Particularly problematic to India was Article I of the Bagdad Pact, which, following the Eisenhower Doctrine,[9] paved the way for specific military engagements between Pakistan and the United States (Nehru, 1961:474). Although Pakistan's high officials such as its Foreign Secretary, S.A. Baig, gave a wider interpretation of this document saying that Pakistan has been specifically told by the United States that this Agreement cannot be used against India, such assurances did not pacify India (ibid.:476). Even the US' assurances to allay India's concerns about its military alliances with Pakistan as a purely tactical gesture, and also offer prospects of similar security pacts with India did not satisfy the latter. Prime Minister Nehru's nonalignment and anti-Cold War lenses perceived these US–Pak alliances as threats to India's security and as breach of the US neutrality in supporting one of the two parties in a conflict (Nayar, 1976).

In terms of the military build-ups between the United States and Pakistan, these alliances did not mean a continuous détente between the United States and Pakistan.[10] Nor did it signify a constant deterioration in India–US relations, and, in fact, saw pro-US sentiments amongst Indian high officials and diplomats such as Girija Shankar Bajpai, K.M. Munshi,

N.R. Pillai, and pro-Indian sentiments within members of the US administration like Chester Bowles, Loy Henderson, President John F. Kennedy, Phillip Talbott, and Kenneth Galbraith (McMahon, 1994). Nonetheless, India–US interactions represented a Cold War-centric "roller coaster" relation revealing two trends: First, each time the United States and Pakistan entered into military engagements, it annoyed India who drifted toward Soviet Union and China as a strategic counter-gesture to America. Second, whenever, the United States took positive policy initiatives toward India as reflected in the NSC Paper 98/1 on South Asia; NSC Policy Statement 5701 on South Asia; or, its policy shifts under President Eisenhower and Kennedy—it irked Pakistan (ibid.).

United States and Pakistan's Cold War-centric military alliances, not to mention their partition history, rendered India's disputes with Pakistan more complex. Political issues marking their bilateral tensions were the Pakistan-backed raids in the Kashmir valley of India (October 1947); the canal water dispute; evacuee property and devaluation; ill treatment of the minority Hindus in East Pakistan causing their influx to India (1950–1951); and mostly importantly, the military pacts of the CENTO, the SEATO by which considerable US military aid entered Pakistan (Nehru, 1961). Of these, the Kashmir issue and the US–Pakistan Cold War-oriented military pacts, when interpreted through the intensely anti-imperial lenses of Nehru, caused considerable insecurities for India, and constructed a Cold War-centric anti-US/anti-Pakistani (in)security imaginary for the Indian state. What became particularly contentious in the genesis of the Kashmir conflict,[11] were India's allegations that Pakistan had used the US-supplied military in the subsequent 1965 Kashmir crisis—although India was unsure whether this military was a part of the US defense aid equipment to Pakistan, or whether it has been purchased through normal commercial channels.

Speaking of big power insecurities in terms of India's international affairs, China also remained important. Although Nehru expressed concern at the lack of freedom of press or parliamentary democracy in China, he also referred to the greatness of China's ancient cultural civilization; had a tremendous respect for the Chinese Peoples' Revolution by Mao; highlighted many Sino-Indian cultural and religious affinities surrounding Hinduism and Buddhism; and the new revolutionary changes occurring in China as in India symbolizing the "new spirit" of the Asian region (Nehru and Gopal, 1980:371). Yet, antagonistic issues irked India–China relations over Tibet (1949–1954, 1959); the fleeing of Dalai Lama to India (1959); the Khampa rebellion in Tibet (late 1950s) causing refugee influx from Tibet into India; the inclusion of the Aksai Chin area under Chinese maps showing it as falling under Chinese territory; Premier Chou En Lai's "denying and negating" the McMahon Line as a permanent boundary dividing India and China; and China's ill treatment of people of Kashmiri origin from India residing in Tibet (see, Nehru, 1961:302–363). Against counter-allegations from China, Nehru made it clear that India had no territorial or political interests in Tibet (rather its interests were commercial and cultural); that India seeks to preserve the security and integrity of India; maintain friendly relations with China; supported Tibet as an independent country under suzerainty or sovereignty of China (which, however, ran counter to Premier Chou En Lai's claims that "Tibet had been a part of the Chinese state"); and extended India's deep sympathy for the people of Tibet (ibid.:302, 323). Although Nehru's reference to Chinese suzerainty over Tibet displeased some academics and politicians within the Indian spectrum, Nehru's strategic thinking was well aware of the power imbalance between India (as the weaker) and China (as the stronger actor), and sought not to militarily challenge this disequilibrium (ibid.:344). It is within these interpretive frameworks of India's anti-Cold War, nonaligned, and expansionist threat perceptions from its global and regional geo-politics were constructed the strategic cultural discourses and the (in)security imaginary of the Indian state.

Reconstructing Strategic Culture and (In)Security Imaginary

Nonalignment born out of India's colonial history, philosophy of non-violence, pragmatism, and realism constituted India's dominant official ideological thinking and underpinned the construction of its strategic cultural discourses and (in)security imaginaries vis-à-vis the United States, China, and Pakistan. In the immediate post-independent period, India's memories of colonial rule symbolically came to represent the West with references to Britain and the United States (Nehru, 1950:221). Although the United States did not have a direct colonial bearing in India's past, the overriding commonality of Anglo-American ways of thinking about world affairs rendered the United States as symbolically representing and being linked to the oppressive West (McMahon, 1994:12).

An intensely nationalistic Nehru as early in 1940 suspected that America's "great material resources" and "dominant position in the world" (Nehru, 1965:3) would enable it to appear as an imperial state in post-World War eras, and following India's independence continued to suspect that economic motivations underlay many American foreign policy initiatives. Although Nehru voiced these negative US viewpoints in private, a "strong suspicion existed in him that the United States possesses the rapacious tendencies attributed to the British, and that in its foreign policy the United States merely substitutes economic imperialism for the political imperialism so long practiced by the British" (McMahon, 1994:41). Nehru, along with key officials in his administration such as India's Defense Minister, Krishna Menon, felt that "America's fixation with its own economic interests coupled with its exaggeration of the Soviet threat to world peace blinded American leaders to more fundamental factors shaping world affairs ..." (Gopal, 1975–1984:2, 43–44), and others like Bharatan Kumarappa (India's diplomat to the UN) commented that Western imperialism (and not communism) are ideologically antagonistic issues that adversely affected India–US relations (McMahon, 1994:96). Seen from a psychological level, the US Ambassador to India, Loy W. Henderson, recalling his conversations with Nehru noted that the PM's "cynical distrust of the United States and its motives ... harbored [in him] a series of deeply ingrained cultural prejudices against the United States" (ibid.:41). Nehru, as Henderson noted, viewed "... the US [as] an overgrown, blundering, uncultured, and somewhat crass nation ...." (ibid.). This cultural bias nurtured in Nehru a "dislike" about America "... bordering on contempt for American ... way of life, and Americans in general" (ibid.). Needless to say, the US–UK diplomatic activities as for instance through the British Information Services office stationed at New York, also sustained their anti-Indian biases (Muppidi, 1999).

Despite anti-US sentiments, Nehru was an ardent admirer of the US ideals of "human liberty, reason, democracy, and fair play," and its technological innovations and accomplishments, and "look[ed] to America in many ways" (Nehru, 1965:3–4), including the use of the US "scientific imperatives" for India's national technological development (Nehru, 1950:133). Strengthening India's military build-up and availing significant economic, technological, and developmental assistance from the West namely the United States, the Soviet Union, the British Commonwealth, France, and Canada were thus conceived, justified, and indeed achieved, as efforts of nation-building and integration, that is, what was most "advantageous" or "worthy policy" to the country (ibid.:205, 217). In fact, India–US technology cooperation began in December 1950 when the two countries signed a bilateral agreement for Technical Cooperation, which stemming from President Harry Truman's Point Four Program, lead to subsequent US technical assistance to India's civilian nuclear plant at Tarapur in its early stage. In some ways, these discourses of Nehru reflective of the realist, developmentalist, and the modernist in him and denoting India's nonaligned psychology of "work and cooperation," especially with the United States, represented India's civilizational greatness, national sovereignty, and the politically autonomous nature of India's strategic mindset in international affairs. Yet, these discourses of India's "cautious" alliances with big Western powers did not lose sight of India's civilizational norms based on Gandhi's world peace and idealism. Thus, on the one hand, Nehru conceded that India has much to learn from Europe and America but also qualified that the West "… must not allow any wind to sweep us off our feet" (ibid.:241). To this extent, he was prepared to accept financial aid from foreign countries provided there were no "strings" attached (Dutt, 1987:62), and also clarified that India's military build-up was "not to make India militarily strong in the Big Power sense" but for its own self-defense (Nehru, 1950:217).

As mentioned earlier, the genesis of the Kashmir crisis (1947) had started an intractable conflict in India–Pakistan relations, which became subsequently intense with India's allegations that Pakistan had used the US-supplied military in the crisis region. A realist in terms of preserving India's territorial and nationalist integration, Nehru did not hesitate to refer to the 1948 war between India and Pakistan as an "… aggression of a brutal and unforgivable kind, … against the people of Kashmir and against the Indian Union" (ibid.: 37), which invoked two security interests of India in Kashmir: First, ensuring the freedom and the progress of the people in Kashmir; and second, to prevent anything from happening in Kashmir that might endanger the security of the rest of India (Nehru, 1950:84). In the context of the first, Nehru made it clear that India is pledged to help the Kashmiris suffering from this brutal and unprovoked invasion and that ultimately the people of Kashmir will decide on their status (ibid.:77). Regarding the second, Nehru claimed that India "... shall fight it to the utmost, for it involves not only the freedom of Kashmir but also the honor of the Indian people and respect for the law of nations" (ibid.:37). Simultaneously, responding to some rumors amongst Pakistani sectors that India might launch a defensive war against Pakistan to dissect the Pakistani state, Nehru assured Pakistan that incorporating Pakistan within the Indian territory would be a costly and burdensome venture for India, and based on its Gandhian norms, India will not undertake any acts of aggression against Pakistan (ibid.:36). Furthermore, aware that their history of partition along religious lines has made their relation more complex, with "intensive propaganda in Pakistan for jihad against India" (Nehru, 1961:466), Nehru claimed that the Kashmir issue was not a communal but a political conflict (Nehru, 1950:77), and appealed for such "psychological barriers" between the two countries along religious and cultural biases be discarded to "create an atmosphere" within which India and Pakistan can converse to resolve their political differences (Nehru, 1950:247; Nehru, 1961:458, 466).

Furthermore, contrary to the wishes of India's Deputy Prime Minister Sardar Patel, Prime Minister Nehru appealed to the United Nations Security Council for a peaceful settlement of disputes between India and Pakistan on the Kashmir question, which remained unsuccessful in meeting a major UN aim, that is, a demilitarization proposal requiring India and Pakistan to reduce their military presence on both sides of the Azad Kashmir region preceding a plebiscite in Kashmir. Although the UN in this issue succeeded in implementing a UN-initiated ceasefire in January 1949, at another level it complicated the issue by facilitating the United States' involvement in the Kashmir solution (by seeking the help of the US diplomats as mediators), thereby further complicating India–US relations at a time when the Korean War and the US–Pakistan military alliances were dominating Asia's political hot bed (McMahon, 1994). This is because given the United States' Cold War interests in the region, the

United States at times leaned toward Pakistan by entering into military alliances, which was deemed by India as a breach of neutrality by the United States in favoring one of the parties in the Kashmir crisis. This dynamic over the Kashmir crisis from 1949 to 1954 was acutely felt in India–US–Pakistan relations (McMahon, 1994:34–35). Nehru warned that, "the consequences of US' intervention in the affairs of South Asia were bound to be unfortunate," and following the formation of the northern tier alliance, in March 1954 requested the removal of all the US nationals serving as members of the UN observation team in Kashmir (Nayar, 1976). Furthermore, following the Baghdad Pact, Nehru opted out of the bilateral negotiations that occurred in August 1953 between himself and the Pakistani Prime Minister, Bogra, and also expressing fears about the pact, claimed that,

> The wider interpretation given by the Pakistan authorities to the latest agreement is, therefore, a matter of grave concern to us, particularly in the context of our past experience of repeated and increasing aggressive action on the part of Pakistan … it is difficult for us to ignore the possibility of Pakistan utilizing the aid received by it from other countries against India even though those countries have given us clear assurance to the contrary. (Nehru, 1961:476)

In fact, Nehru acknowledging that problems in India–Pakistan relations were from the inevitable consequences of partition, also stated that they were made "considerably worse" by the intrusion of American Cold War in the region, and, that "… the United States defense aid to Pakistan encourages the Pakistan authorities in their aggressiveness and increases tension … between India and Pakistan" (ibid.:47, 472–473). Furthermore, evoking India's colonial memories, Nehru derided the US military interactions in the region as "… a wrong step … which adds to the tensions and fears … [and] the feeling of insecurity in Asia" (ibid.:471). He strongly felt that "… one of the symbols of [India's] freedom has been the withdrawal of foreign armed forces … [and] the return of any armed forces from any European or any American country is a reversal of the history of the countries of Asia, whatever the motive" (ibid.:471–472).

Finally, in terms of India's strategic cultural discourses and (in)security imaginaries vis-à-vis China, the Indian state's strategic thinking was cognizant of the power differentials between India and China in international affairs (Nehru, 1961:344), and Nehru as a pragmatic realist, thus summed up the gravity of the insecurity that India faced from a powerful and expansionist Chinese state. He said, "We realized ... that a strong China is normally an expansionist China ... [and] when she is strong, we realized the danger to India" (ibid.:369). In addition, since 1958, there appeared a number of statements from Chinese high officials saying that China wants to develop its own nuclear weapons and master rocket technology (although this preparation might have begun as early as 1954–1955). To this end, in May 1958, Commander of China's Air Force, Liu-Ya-Lou, said that "China's scientists will certainly be able to make the most up-to-date aircraft and atomic bomb ... [to cope] with the enemies who dare to invade our countries;" in October 1961, Premier Chou En Lai said that "the government had decided to proceed with plans for developing nuclear weapons for the armed forces;" in the summer of 1962, China's Foreign Minister, Chen Yi, reiterated that China "was working to develop an atom bomb of its own;" and again in September 1962, held that "a large organization was engaged in research on nuclear weapons and that so long as there are nuclear powers, we shall try to possess nuclear weapons" (Hsieh, 1963). Thus, the need of the hour required easing this friction, and, despite some occasional verbal statements to the contrary, efforts followed to boost India–Chinese cooperation. These included an agreement of peaceful coexistence between India and China over Tibet (1954); stressing India–Chinese friendship and cooperation as the axis of Asian solidarity; exchange of visits between Indian and Chinese high-level politicians and diplomats (1954); mutual conversations at the Bandung Conference (1955) where China was included at India's insistence. Despite criticism from within and outside India's political spectrum about Nehru's "not so stern" approach with China (which may be explained as Nehru's strategic posture given India–China's military power imbalances), Nehru saw the *Hindi Chini bhai bhai* as the pragmatic dictum of the day in forging a long-term relation between these two countries (Nehru, 1961:372).

As mentioned earlier, (in)security imaginary is not real in the sense that it can be empirically scrutinized. Rather, "it is the product of an act of 'cultural creation,' which is fundamental to any subsequent system of cultural representation" (Tomlinson, 1991:156–157). Seen from this conceptual definition of (in)security imaginary, three contours of (in)security imaginaries were constructed by the Indian state's strategic discourses vis-à-vis Pakistan, China, and the United States. In terms of the United States, India's memories of colonialism and its perception of the United States as a symbolically emerging neo-imperial Western state encroaching India's vicinity with its Cold War interests defined India's (in)security imaginary vis-à-vis the United States. Yet, being an admirer of the US ideals of human liberty, reason, science, technological innovations, and democracy, Nehru sustained a "charm for science" (which was a part of his persona and essential to his internationalism) (Anderson, 2010:266), to engage with the United States for its scientific technical advancements as a newly independent and an industrializing state. In terms of Pakistan, the Indian state's discourses have switched from articulations of the US–Pakistan military pacts, military threats from Pakistan, the issue of Kashmir, psychologies of religious differences between them, and their historical and cultural commonalities to define India's (in)securities vis-à-vis the Pakistani state. Yet, India's strategic perceptions vis-à-vis Pakistan rooted in Gandhi's nonviolence also asserted that India–Pakistan insecurities were made "considerably worse" by the Cold War/American intrusion in the region, and reiterated India–Pakistan's age-long "intimate connections" through historical and cultural bondages (Nehru, 1961:30). In terms of China, fears of military and nuclear expansionism pervaded India's (in)security imaginary vis-à-vis the latter, countering which, as a matter of pragmatic strategy, necessitated diplomacy with China. Through these discursive connections between India's strategic cultural thinking and its (in)security imaginaries was constructed a certain strategic identity for the newly independent state, which interacting with India's colonial memories, resistance to Cold War politics, an emerging Western hegemonic dominance in the South Asian region, an expansionist Chinese threat, India's civilizational greatness, and Nehru's quest for human liberty, reason, science, and technology— constructed India as a modernist, idealist, scientific, and a politically autonomous state imbibed in Gandhi's nonviolence.

However, the defeat of India in the Sino-Indian war (1962) changed the idealist sentiments of the Indian state, when India's official (idealist) line of interpreting its regional politics as well as its official line of atomic science discourse (where national security was not given enough prominence) came under attack from India's opposition party members, scientists, and the Indian military establishment in that India gives up its idealism and face real politics in its regional/global affairs. India's nuclear-centric insecurities from China continued to remain acute as China's Foreign Minister, Chen Yi, in October 1963 once again announced China's determination to carry out nuclear weapons tests "within a year or two" because China could not afford to be ranked with second or third class power (Hsieh, 1963). These shifts in India's strategic inse-curities stimulated an intense debate among the government, India's science community, and the military that shifted the focus of India's ongoing atomic science discourses from one of scientific idealism to a more defensive line geared toward producing atomic weapons for India's defense purposes. I explore below how these interpretive frameworks of India's strategic cultural discourses and (in)security imaginaries offered the political and ideological space within which emerged the discourses of India's atomic science development.

Emergence of India's Atomic Science Debates

As claimed by Poulose (1978:102), "there is no guile" in the fact that India's "nuclear [atomic] policy ... originated from a mind imbued with high idealism, [a] deep sense of history, and a world view and always with a vision of strong and modern India." Seen in the context of this claim, one notices the emergence of two parallel discourses within India that articulated by the government, its atomic science community, and the military simultaneously projected India's disarmament and atomic policy discourses. I address below the ideological, strategic cultural, and the global dimensions that offered the political–ideological space within which were articulated India's disarmament discourses, and discourses of India's atomic science development in the spirit of "scientific idealism."

The Indian State's Discourses on (Dis)Armament

The question of disarmament in post-independent India was not only tied to the Cold War arms race but to India's "... abhorrence of nuclear weapons, and nuclear allergy after the supreme tragedy at Hiroshima and

Nagasaki" (Poulose, 1982:102). What exactly did disarmament mean for the Indian state? In answering this, Nehru clarified that he was "not a pacifist," and that "in today's world people have to protect themselves and prepare for every kind of emergency" (Nehru and Gopal, 1980:438). Yet, given his ideological belief that the idea of states' fending themselves was not one of "... military fending but also [one of] intellectual, moral, and spiritual interconnectedness," defined disarmament as a deeper ideological notion which required that "actual disarmament must be preceded by moral disarmament" (Nehru, 1980:388, 416). For Nehru, the evolution of this "new world order" required ideals of international fairness and big power cooperation and envisaged a "different political and economic system which avoid[ed] conflict" (Nehru and Gopal, 1980:389, 399). Despite controversies with the UN's ability to float a free and fair disarmament regime,[12] Nehru had great faith in the UN to build a world without war based on the cooperation of nations, and agreed with the UNESCO's preamble that, "... war begins in the minds of men ... and ultimately it is necessary to bring about the change in our minds and to remove fears ... hatreds and suspicions" (Nehru, 1961:219).

Accordingly, Nehru's ideological posture toward a free and fair global disarmament found expression within global platforms such as the United Nations and its subgroups (such as the UN Disarmament Commission, the UNESCO); at regional and international conferences;[13] and within the Indian Parliament. To this end, India from 1948 and 1959 individually or jointly submitted eight draft resolutions before the United Nations advocating general and complete disarmament, and several representatives of the Indian government to the UN like Mrs Vijaya Lakshmi Pandit, V.K. Krishna Menon, C.S. Jha, V.C. Trivedi and others echoed India's efforts at disarmament (Singh and Sharma, 2000:xvi). Krishna Menon, India's most vocal representative at the UN, strongly and elaborately addressed the West's ongoing practices of horizontal proliferation and the need for an international atomic energy agency to promote the peaceful use of atomic energy in whose constitution and rule-making counties like India should have a "full say" (Jain, 1974:4012). In addition, both houses of the Indian Parliament provided the domestic arena for the Indian government to articulate its views on disarmament as evidenced in Nehru's statements at the Lok Sabha and the Rajya Sabba between April 1954 and March 1962 (Singh and Sharma, 2000).

Not all efforts toward disarmament were in vain as the UN General Assembly adopted several resolutions on disarmament suspending, pending their banning, experimental explosions of nuclear and thermonuclear bombs.[14] Yet, consequences of hydrogen bombs in possession by the two super powers and the limitations of the United Nations to carry on the unlimited inspection of countries' proper work with fissile materials rendered suspect prospects of free and fair disarmament (Singh and Sharma, 2000:43). As will be elaborated in the next chapter, it resulted in the non-nuclear nations perceiving the US–Soviet nonproliferation efforts "at best, as self-serving attempts to protect the political and/economic interests of the two super powers" (Ebinger, 1978:11). It is against these fundamentally discriminatory, self-servicing, and an increasing nuclear momentum in global politics, were articulated India's atomic science discourses.

Atomic Policy Discourses of the State-Science Community

In contrast to India's colonial years when its science discourses were being forged within its colonial climate, a new framework of state-science relations emerged in post-independent India, which articulated by the inner layer (consisting of those like Homi Bhabha, S.S. Bhatnagar, K.S. Krishnan) and the outer layer of Indian scientists (including those like Meghnad Saha, M.K. Dasgupta, B.D. Nagchaudhuri, and others) charted India's atomic policy developments (Kapur, 1994). As noted in Chapter 2, Saha and Bhabha as contemporaries had differed in their ideological thinking and approaches with regard to Indian science, and in their encounters to become the official governmental spokesperson of India's atomic science victory in post-independent India went to the inner layer, which, sharing political congruence with the Indian government, came to dominate India's science infrastructure.

In terms of collaborating science and national development, the inner group's ideology was to promote public science in support of both public objectives and private industries—which enabled them to remain in the "good looks" of India's political elites and survive the political tensions, that gripped Saha, between the fact of widespread private industrial ownership versus public expectations of nationalized ownership for energy production purposes (Krishna, 1993; Anderson, 2010). Thus, Bhabha and his allies came to dominate India's science infrastructure; occupied top-ranking positions in India's scientific and planning commissions and research laboratories, promoted India's international scientific exchanges and collaborations; and, appointed foreign scientists such George Sachs, J.W. McBain, Patrick Blackwell in India's national science laboratories to enhance their research potentials. Situated in the context of India's colonial history, Bhabha was aware of Western exploitative tendencies over India's natural resources which he believed must be protected (although known for his political neutrality, he rarely expressed his views on such matters in print) (Anderson, 1975:66). Yet, he simultaneously was of the view that foreign collaborations had their advantages provided that one should not permanently depend on them. It culminated in his efforts at enhancing India's indigenous scientific knowledge by learning through collaborations without losing (Bhabha, 1966:545–547).

Following India's independence, Bhabha remained the stalwart of the Government of India in directing India's atomic energy plans. His views on atomic power were definite, and his vision of nuclear power for India (which, with Saha and Nehru, shared the same thinking that U233 be synthesized from thorium of which India had large deposits) went beyond the availability and use of conventional fuels to emphasize the importance of India's nuclear revolution. He raised questions on starting dual-purpose atomic power stations in India, whether the country possessed atomic fuel, and in what quantity? Bhabha's logic that India builds atomic power stations was developmental, and specifically argued that developing countries (given their insufficient natural fuel reserves) must "seek the help of the ATOM," and that a study in this direction will be helpful for the "whole humanity" (Kulakarni, Bhabha, and Sarma, 1969:16, 18). Furthermore, going beyond the immediate economics of nuclear power, Bhabha also envisioned safeguarding power supplies for the future and suggested treating India's indigenous possession of thorium to produce uranium which could then be used to increase India's atomic power. This meant that India's atomic power stations are dual purpose and cost-effective that would also produce plutonium, which, as fissile material, could then be treated in 233-thorium reactors to produce nuclear power (Kulakarni et al., 1969:14).

Despite an ardent supporter of atomic science and nuclear power, Bhabha was also a supporter of disarmament with the view that "it would … be in the interest of every one to see that substantial progress towards general disarmament is made, as soon as possible, before more countries have time to develop into major nuclear power" (Kulakarni et al., 1969:37). This is because he was aware that the rise of atomic energy and atomic power industries had put fissile materials in the hands of many—making the production of atomic bombs and weapons a distinct possibility. In fact, his approach to disarmament (and vice versa, nuclear armament) also contained a global hierarchical element in that "the problem of non-proliferation, [was] … not so much one of stopping more countries from making nuclear weapons but one of reversing what had already taken place" (ibid.: 38). To this extent, despite his international orientation, he was unhappy with the UN and the major powers to voluntarily refrain from following a nuclear path while countries like Canada, Japan, Sweden, and India (which could make nuclear weapons) refrained from doing so (ibid.).

At this point, it might also be worth considering the Indian government's official ideology on atomic policy and the structural realities of India's contemporary international relations that charted India's atomic discourses. As noted earlier, Nehru as admirer of the US' ideals of human liberty, reason, democracy, technological innovations, and accomplishments, sustained a "charm for science," and this ideological disposition enabled him as minister in charge of India's Atomic Energy to avail scientific and technological assistance from the West namely the United States, the Soviet Union, the British Commonwealth, France, and Canada for the promotion of energy for peaceful purposes. Charting India's atomic policies through international contacts and exchanges were thus conceived, justified, and achieved as efforts advantageous to the country's national development purposes (Nehru, 1950:205, 217).

A plethora of governmental discourses as evidenced in various speeches of the prime minister, members of the Indian Parliament, and other foreign service diplomats of the Indian Government at the Lok Sabha; at regional and international conferences (such as the First International Conference on Peaceful Uses of Atomic Energy, August 1955); and through joint statements by third world leaders (the Nehru–Tito–Nasser Joint Statement, July 20, 1956) reveal this ideological position of the Indian government on its atomic quest. Several factors underpinned these discourses: a national development factor; fears of a Cold

War-related escalation of nuclear arms race; a realist fear stemming from the presence of Cold War in the South Asian region bringing Pakistan into this orbit; India's quest for technological modernity; and finally an acknowledgement of the cultural norms of Gandhian idealism, nonviolence, and world peace in India's international relations. Accordingly, addressing the necessity of developing atomic energy in India, Nehru at the Lok Sabha (on July 23, 1957) (and elsewhere as the minister in charge of the Atomic Energy Department) detailed "[the] theoretical and practical necessity of keeping abreast of this new realm of knowledge and discovery ... and that it would be of the utmost importance for us in India to utilize the atomic power for peaceful purpose" (Singh and Sharma, 2000:100–101, 132). Furthermore, the government's atomic energy discourses as evidenced in the Nehru–Tito–Nasser Joint Statement, released July 20, 1956, also referenced Cold War, international hierarchy, militarization trends, and its potential to perpetuate violence, and drew attention to "the division of the world ... into powerful blocs of nations [that] tends to perpetuate fears [in international relations]" (ibid.:76).

This ideological nexus evidenced in India's state-science (security) community, despite some ambiguities and intragroup tensions (Krishna, 1993; Kumar, 1994), culminated in the establishment of a series of atomic power stations through foreign collaborations and indigenous efforts by the state. A new building of the Tata Institute of Fundamental Research (TIFR) was established in South Bombay; the Atomic Energy Establishment with its array of reactors and laboratories was formed at Trombay; a monazite plant with French collaboration was opened at Alwaye (1952); a uranium plant was established at Jaduguda; the first atomic research reactor APSARA designed to provide experimental facilities for atomic research was built by the Trombay scientists in 1955 (except for the enriched uranium fuel elements from the UK); the Canadian-India Reactor (a natural, uranium fuelled, heavy-water moderated, high-flux research reactor used for basic research in physics, chemistry, metallurgy, and reactor technology) became functional in 1960. Notably, Nehru had rendered full support to Bhabha to negotiate the terms of this collaboration with Canada and applauding this achievement commented that, "This close collaboration in a highly complicated field between the scientists and engineers of two countries, ... is a symbol of the manner in which the world has shrunk through modern technology and [is] a token of … peace, understanding, and cooperation …" (Kulakarni et al., 1969:23–24). In addition, there occurred a flurry of exchanges between Indian, the United States, and European scientists which led to nonprofit loans to India from the USAID for developing new research techniques such as the CDC 3600 system computer; for enhancing cosmic ray research at TIFR; developing plastic balloon techniques for their advantage of working in low geo-magnetic attitudes as required in the Indian astronomical area; and Indian scientists took field trips abroad to review Western nuclear power stations. These lead to India accepting foreign bids in constructing its nuclear power stations— a notable (and controversial) one being the Tarapur atomic power plant constructed in 1963 with assistance from a US firm.

These foreign collaborations should not undermine the plethora of indigenously constructed atomic power stations by the state. These included the ZERLINA (Zero Energy Reactors for Lattice Investigations and Neutron Assay, 1961); construction of a power station at Kalpakkam (near Madras); a uranium metal plant in 1959; a heavy-duty reconstruction plant in 1962; a heavy water plant 1962; a fuel element fabrication facility in June 1959; and the opening of a laboratory at the Kolar Gold Fields in 1964 to research the behavior of neutrons underground (which led to collaborations with research groups from universities of Osaka, Durham, and England) (Anderson, 1975:75). In essence, India's atomic discourses and policy developments charted a flexible and dual-use approach to India's atomic science developments. According to a US government estimate in May 1964, "The Indians are now in a position to begin nuclear weapons development if they choose to do so" (Kapur, 1994:221).

This official line of India's atomic science discourse where national security was not given enough prominence came under attack from opposition members, scientists, and the Indian military establishment, following India's crushing defeat in the Indo-China war in 1962. Following this defeat and China's further reiteration in October 1963 of its determination to carry out nuclear weapons tests "within a year or two" (Hsieh, 1963), the Jana Sangh (a branch of the RSS and forerunner of today's BJP) vigorously demanded an Indian nuclear deterrent (Mirchandani, 1968:32). In addition, France declared its intention of going nuclear and Britain, and Israel announced their determination of having independent nuclear forces—not to mention the ongoing Pakistan–US military pacts in the South Asian region. These presented India's science community with a challenging insecurity context where the focus of atomic science was not on national development but shifted to national security. An emergency subcommittee was formed by the prime minister to report directly to his Cabinet on "how to reorganize science and technology institutions and mobilize scientists for defense;" saw members of India's defense establishment question the place of national defense in India's science planning process; and Bhabha lamented that "one does not know, how long … countries, will be able to continue to follow their present polic[ies] [of restrain] if China continues to build up a stockpile of atomic weapons" (Kulakarni et al., 1969:38). Thereafter, followed a number of initiatives through interactions among members of the TIFR, The Council of Scientific and Industrial Research (CSIR), the Defense Ministry, and the Indian Government denoting a more military-oriented defensive posture in rearticulating India's atomic science quests now geared toward producing atomic weapons for defense purposes. To this end, the government sanctioned big increases in India's defense budget (Anderson, 2010:265).

These geo-strategic developments were sufficient for Prime Minister Nehru to change his mind on the peaceful use of India's atomic policy, and India's defense experts too advised the prime minister that India has a stronger base than China to develop nuclear weapons for military purposes. Yet, even at this point Nehru made it clear that "we are not making nuclear weapons," and reiterated that "India did not believe in sinking millions of rupees on producing bomb," and instead wants to progress socially and economically (Singh and Sharma, 2000:xviii).

Conclusion

Following my earlier claim that there exists a discursive and ideological linkage between India's strategic culture, (in)security imaginary, and its atomic policies, this chapter has analyzed how postcolonial India's atomic science policies have emerged as an interpretation of ideological, policy-related preferences, and scientific temperamental factors of the state's security community, which were being articulated within the context of the state's strategic cultural thinking. To this end, the chapter has highlighted how the discourses of India's security community have drawn from India's colonial history, postcolonial identity, existing international hierarchy, global Cold War politics encroaching in India's vicinity, a global arms race, compulsions of its regional politics, a desire for technological modernity, and its norms of cultural nonviolence to offer shifting interpretations of India's nationalist identity, insecurity, the significance of the West, and India's indigenous scientific tenor to define India's atomic science projects. In this context, as Poulose (1978:102) reminds us, "[India's] nuclear decisions were not the outcome of any national debate [per se] but deeply rooted in his [Nehru's] scientific temper." In this context, what is notable in the charting of a strictly nonaligned India's atomic science policy is how the technologically savvy mindset of the state's security community was eager to forge Western technological alliances and blend Western science with its indigenous scientific tenor to chart the atomic policies of the state. Finally, these discursive connections between the constructions of India's strategic cultural thinking and (in)security imaginary have constructed a strategic identity for the state, which, interacting with colonial memories, resistance to Cold War politics, an emerging Western hegemonic dominance in the South Asian region, the US–Pakistan Cold War alliances, and an expansionist Chinese threat—projected (and sustained) India's identity as a realist, modernist, scientific, and a politically autonomous state simultaneously imbibed in Gandhian peace and nonviolence as its civilizational greatness. The dynamism of India's nonalignment, as a new method of struggle, political warfare, and a new kind of diplomacy to engage in its international affairs, marked the identity of the Indian state.

The next chapter analyzes how changes in India's regional and global politics namely China's going nuclear in October 1964 offered the political and ideological space within which were reconstructed India's strategic culture, its concept of nonalignment, (in)security imaginaries, and its nuclear weapons discourses.

Notes

1. Given that immediate post-colonial India's scientific endeavor aimed to develop the power of atomic science for the state's development (and not military) purposes, the quest of atomic science for energy production at that point defined the state's approach to its science project. However, post-1962, the state's quest for atomic science shifted to a military purpose for the nation's defense and incrementally came to be associated with nuclear and missiles weapons development.

2. Although several leaders of the Congress Party government contributed to this process of nation-building, Nehru's ideological tenets have historically been regarded as key in establishing the state's identity and its strategic cultural foundation.

3. However, Nehru could not totally ignore the advocates of free market within his own party. This was evidenced in the compromised outcome of the 1948 Industrial Policy Resolution, where the Nehruvian government compromising to the right wing within the Congress resulted in the government's signing of the Industries Act which established the legal and political blueprint of the Indian economy. Three steps followed setting the stage for India's state-led growth: In 1949, was formulated the Statement of Policy on the future role of foreign capital; in 1950, the Planning Commission was created; followed by the publication of the First Five Year plan.

4. However, Nehru at times revealed mixed sentiments about India's ability or desirability to function on a revolutionary plane (Nehru, Gopal, and Iyenger 2003:27).

5. To support this anti-imperial trend, Nehru called for conferences, took initiatives, forged alliances with Afro-Asian countries, and chaired many neutral commissions to bring ceasefires in military zones of conflicts such as in the Indonesian, Indochinese, Korean, Suez, Algerian, Vietnamese, and, the Turko-Greek crises.

6. The Asian approach was not India-specific but represented a break from the European-centric, American-centric, and, Moscow-centric forms of dominance in prevailing world politics. This is because given the historical circumstances of Asia's colonial experience, Nehru felt that it was time that the countries of Asia broke with past tendencies of being controlled by Western hegemonic powers and as a region decide their own way of life in foreign affairs.

7. Under the Baruch Plan, an International Atomic Development Agency was to be established that would possess complete regulatory authority over all nuclear activities of nations and would have the statutory power to control, license, and inspect their use of nuclear facilities for peaceful purposes. However, owing to Soviet perceptions of the United States' self-interested motives in maintaining its nuclear sovereignty through the proposed

International Atomic Development Agency, the Baruch Plan failed. With the foundering of the Baruch Plan, the US government enacted the Atomic Energy Act (1946), which theoretically designed to limit the world-wide diffusion of nuclear power, in practice, gave the US government sole proprietorship over all nuclear facilities and activities in the United States and imposed secrecy over them (Bargman, 1977; Ebinger, 1978).

8. The Atoms for Peace Program was designed by the United States as an arms control devise vis-à-vis the Soviet Union, and called the United States, the Soviet Union, and other countries with nuclear capabilities to make contributions from their stockpiles of fissionable materials to an international agency, the International Atomic Energy Agency (IAEA), which would be responsible for storing these materials until methods were devised to allocate them to the power-starved areas of the world as needed for energy production (Bargman, 1977; Ebinger, 1978).

9. As explained by Nehru (1961), under the US Constitution, the US armed forces cannot be used to assist any other country without the specific authority of the US Congress. However, the use of the US forces in support of any other country without the specific sanction of the US Congress is possible under the Eisenhower Doctrine for the Middle East passed by the Joint Resolution of the Congress on March 9, 1957. The description of this Doctrine as entailed in Section 2 of this Joint Resolution reads that, "The President is authorized to undertake, in the general area of the Middle East, military assistance programs with any nation or group of nations of that area desiring such assistance" (Nehru, 1961:474).

10. In Pakistan their occurred sporadic public demonstrations against the United States whenever Pakistan perceived that the latter leaned toward India, or, when political regimes felt that their government by revealing acute pro-US stance was hampering its national economic development. Such demonstrations occurred in March 1956 under the coalition Muslim League–United Front government that demanded Pakistan's withdrawal from the SEATO and the Baghdad Pact, and again, in 1962, when extensive US aid to India followed after the Sino-Indian war.

11. The genesis of the Pakistan conflict (1947–1949), which began with the North West Frontier Province's Pathan-armed tribes' invasion of Kashmir on October 22, 1947, started an intractable conflict between India and Pakistan that lapsed into crises situations in 1947, 1965, and 1999.

12. As analysts of proliferation studies claim, the US–USSR nonproliferation strategies have failed because they have denied nonnuclear nations the technological capability to go nuclear while continuing to be the "supermen" themselves. In this context, the UN was also perceived as a part of the US-sponsored discriminatory nonproliferation regime and resulted in some countries becoming "disenchanted with, if not hostile to, the United Nations" (Bargman, 1977; Cheodon, 2010). Thus, by the 1960s, an international scenario emerged in the field of nuclear politics where nuclear have-nots rejected

the notion of superpower strategic nuclear parity as a stabilizing geo-political force; the concept of hierarchical ordering of some states possessing nuclear weapons; the argument that horizontal nuclear proliferation is more a threat to world stability than vertical proliferation; and, asserted the right of all sovereign nations to foster their economic independence and strategic security. I address these discriminatory nonproliferation issues in the next chapter.

13. These platforms included the UN Disarmament Commission, the UNESCO; the Geneva conference 1958; the First International Conference on the Peaceful Uses of Atomic Energy at Geneva 1955; the Asian-African Conference at Bandung 1955; the Nehru–Tito–Nasser Joint Statement July 1956; the First Summit Conference of the Non-Aligned countries at Belgrade, 1961; and, several others.

14. The UN's disarmament efforts were reflected in the UN General Assembly Resolutions adopted between 1946 and 1961. These called for a total dismantling of some high risk bombs, declaration by concerned parties their willingness not to manufacture any atomic weapons, that military budgets in all countries be published, and, no further expansion of military strength followed by possible reduction effective immediately (Singh and Sharma, 2000).

4

Defense Preparedness and Nuclear Aggressiveness: 1964-1991

In keeping with my research puzzle that there exists a discursive link between India's strategic culture, (in)security imaginary, and its nuclear policy choices, this chapter explores how the discursive reconstruction of strategic culture and security imaginary by India's security community defined the emergence of India's nuclear policy choices between 1964 (after Nehru) and 1991 (until the end of Cold War). In keeping with the constructivist premise of this book that reconstructions of India's strategic thinking creates an ideological and political space within which are articulated shifting contours of India's identity, (in)security, and nuclear policies, this chapter explores how significant ideological and discursive shifts within India's security community, working at tandem with concurrent changes in India's bureaucratic and institutional, regional, and global (Cold War) politics, saw the emergence of an increasingly aggressive and militaristic reorientation in India's strategic thinking. By the end of the Rajiv Gandhi administration, which coincided with the fall of the Soviet Union and Cold War (that constituted a major determinant of India's nuclear security dynamics), one notices how growing perceptions of military prowess, nuclear nationalism, flexibly of nonalignment, an economically liberalizing climate, and a pro-US affinity (in terms of scientific and technological collaborations) represented a shift in the strategic cultural thinking of the Indian state. In terms of India's nuclear trajectory, it saw a transition to self-reliance in

India's defense preparedness and the emergence of a proactive, preemptive, and an aggressive support for India's nuclear weapons. Despite these militant shifts throughout this period, India was steadfast on its principled norm and tribute of Gandhian nonviolence and sustained a nuclear ambivalence.

This chapter explores the transitions in India's strategic thinking and nuclear security policies through the following phases corresponding to changes at the global (Cold War related), regional, and, India's domestic levels: First, between May 1964 and January 1966 representing Prime Minister Shastri's administration; Second phase (May 1966 to October 1984) representing the renewal of Cold War and changes in India's domestic politics under the two terms of Prime Minister Indira Gandhi (which in the interim also included the brief interludes of PMs Morarji Deasi and Charan Singh); and finally, between October 1984 and November 1989 under Prime Minister Rajiv Gandhi. With reference to these chronological phases, I explore the following "how-possible" questions of India's nuclear politics: First, how did the Indian state's strategic cultural thinking between 1964 and 1991 projected through the ideological lenses of its security community interpret India's regional and international politics? Second, how did the Indian state's strategic cultural thinking during this time frame construct shifting images of (and relationships between) India's national identity and its (in)security imaginaries? Finally, how did these reconstructions of India's strategic cultural thinking and (in)security imaginaries create an ideological and political space within which were forged and articulated India's nuclear policy choices? In addressing each "how-possible" question, my aim is to show how the Indian state's discourses as tools of social and ideological power have produced and sustained a mutually constituted relationship between India's strategic cultural thinking, (in)security imaginaries, and its nuclear policy choices.

Interpreting India's International Relations under Prime Minister Shastri

Lal Bahadur Shastri (May 1964–January 1966) succeeded Nehru as the prime minister. Shastri, a mild personality, was committed to Gandhian ideology in respect to India's developmental and economic priorities;

initially remained steadfast to India's commitment to nonalignment; and was committed to a self-reliant form of India's defense preparedness (Dixit, 2004:101–103). Yet, regional, global, and domestic developments during this phase resulted in a proactive, preemptive, and militaristic reorientation of India's strategic culture, (in)security imaginary, and its nuclear policies.

Shastri became prime minister under critical times when conventional (military) and nonconventional (nuclear) threats from China and Pakistan added complexities to India's national security. Following its series of nuclear threats since 1958 (as discussed in Chapter 3), China conducted its first nuclear test at Lop Nur in October 1964, following which it ran a series of nuclear weapons tests and acquired missile capabilities exacerbating India's threat perceptions. Although the Indian military services' recommendations assessing China's military implications for Indian security remained top-secret classified documents (Cheema, 2010:114), what became public was the outbreak of an intense debate within the government regarding the nature of the Chinese nuclear threat; whether India should adopt its own nuclear weapons policy or ally with the West to face this threat; and what should be the status of India's nonalignment stature in case of such a Western alliance? Two lines of views (to be detailed subsequently) emerged: The first represented by the Swatantra Party; the Praja Socialist Party; Y.V. Chavan (India's Defense Minister); and some members of the Congress Party (such as Bhagwat Jha Azad and Harish Chandra Mathur) who considered China as a direct nuclear threat to India; and the second view, stemming from some Congress Party members (such as R.K. Khadilkar) held that the Chinese "bomb [was] not directed towards India [but] at the world powers" (Perkovich, 1999:77–78). In the absence of unanimity on the nature of the Chinese threat, it is suggested that the government may have not evaluated China's nuclear tests as an immediate nuclear threat to India (Cheema, 2010: 77).

However, intense debates ensued within India's political spectrum about acquiring nuclear weapons for India. Shastri, as an interim policy to ward off the Chinese, mainly at his own initiative approached the United States, UK, and the USSR for a multilateral nuclear security guarantee to India (Brecher, 1968a:127; Cheema, 2010:76). Although the US State and Defense Department officials were contemplating providing India with the US nuclear weapons, President Johnson and his top officials' decision to follow a policy of strict nonproliferation, resulted in its denial

(Cheema, 2010:77). While the United States' unwillingness to provide formal guarantees to India is understandable in the context of the current Cold War and also came with President Johnson's assurance that "nations that did not seek nuclear weapons could count on 'our strong support' if they were faced with some threat of nuclear blackmail" (Seaborg, 1987:115–116), it was a disappointing rejection for India as was reiterated by India's Minister of External Affairs, Swaran Singh and the Indian prime minister (Cheema, 2010:76–77). While prospects of multilateral nuclear security guarantees were eventually surrendered after the 1971 India–Pakistan war, it had two implications for India's strategic thought patterns: First, signifying a lessening of India's nonalignment stance, and second, providing the political and ideological space to the Indian state for an intense debate in rethinking India's national security and acquiring nuclear weapons for the state.

India's threats from Pakistan under Shastri were military stemming from the United States' Pakistan-centric Cold War interests in South Asian region. These Pakistani-centric military (and some nuclear) insecurities occurring in the background of an already-established Pakistan Atomic Energy Commission included: General Ayub Khan's close relations with the United States; Pakistani Foreign Minister Z.A. Bhutto's strengthening of Sino-Pakistani foreign relations to levels of defense cooperations; seizing the northern and northwestern portions of Jammu and Kashmir to China; Pakistan's intruding in the Indian state of Jammu and Kashmir and in the Ladakhi region; Pakistan's building of its military strength with the US-supplied armaments and weapons like Patton tanks and strike aircrafts between 1963 and 1965 (Dixit, 2004:104–107); and on the nuclear front, Pakistan's establishment of the Space and Upper Atmospheric Research Commission at Karachi. This Commission became core in initiating the production of Pakistan's indigenous missile technology, which, not very successful, pushed Pakistan to purchase foreign missiles and related technology, and became another concern for the Indian state (Dhanda, 2010:153). Pakistan also successfully initiated a number of political, defense, and economic arrangements with Iran, Afghanistan, Turkey, and the countries of the Gulf on the principles of Islamic solidarity that enabled a militarily bold Pakistan posing threats for the Indian state. Speculations whether the US' security guarantees to Pakistan in case of a Communist aggression on Pakistan could also be extended to cover Indo-Pakistan conflicts, were put to test at the Rann of Kutch incident (April 1965) and the India–Pakistan war in Kashmir known as Operation Gibraltar (in September 1965), where, in both situations, Pakistan with the US awareness and acquiescence deployed the US military equipment against India (Dixit, 2004:109–111, 113).[1] The war left India disgruntled with the United States. As the 1965 war came to an end with negotiations at Tashkent, General Ayub came under immense domestic criticism mainly by his Foreign Minister Z.A. Bhutto (Wolpert, 1997:93), who even lobbied for a nuclear weapons option for Pakistan (Kamath, 2009: 82). To the contrary, India's strategic responses of the war demonstrated its political leadership's swift, decisive, strategically perceptive reactions with "high virtue[s] of all military doctrines," and created an "international image of reasonableness" for India (Dixit, 2004:110–112, 115). In essence, it signified a militaristic, offensive, and proactive manifestation of India's strategic mindset.

Parallel to these regional developments were emerging international nuclear nonproliferation efforts by the United States in November 1964 under the United Nations that had a direct impact on India's nuclear security concerns. Although the United States was debating whether it could prevent nuclear proliferation by sharing nuclear control with its allies or would itself pursue a policy of promoting complete nuclear abstinence, the idea of sharing was surrendered in favor of a nonproliferation program. Amidst concerns within the US government, the State Department, and the US Arms Control and Disarmament Agency that China's explosion would stimulate proliferation elsewhere, particularly India, the Gilpatric Committee (assigned to look into the issue) reported to President Johnson (by early 1965) that preventing the spread of nuclear weapons is clearly in the US national interest. Furthermore, the Committee realizing that India's willingness to be a part of this proliferation effort would depend on the principle of equity and disarmament by the nuclear powers recommended that the United States and the Soviet Union reduce their emphasis on nuclear weapons through arms control measures such as a comprehensive test ban treaty and a verifiable treaty to end production of fissile materials for weapons purposes (Gilpatric, 1965). To bring India into its nonproliferation fold, the Committee suggested that the United States offer credible assurances to India including assisting India in scientific programs to help India boost its national prestige and stall the latter from pursuing a nuclear weapons agenda (ibid.). Yet, in each case, the United States stopped short of providing concrete assurances of formal nuclear guarantees to India (Noorani, 1967; Kapur, 1976; Perkovich, 1999).

In this scenario, when nonproliferation rose on the international agenda, the Indian delegate to the UN Commission on Disarmament, B.N. Chakrvarthy, on May 4, 1965 declared five nonproliferation treaty conditions that nuclear weapons power must meet to satisfy India (although forwarded mainly as India's security guarantee against China) (Chakrvarthy, 1965:142–151).[2] Yet, as the nonproliferation issue moved to the Eighteen Nation Disarmament Committee in Geneva, debates in July 1965 revealed discrepancies on "equality, a mutual balance of obligations, and the importance ... of principle in negotiating international agreements" (United States Arms Control and Disarmament Agency, 1965; Kapur, 1976: 99, 115). The Indian Representative at Geneva, V.C. Trivedi (a civil servant and a nuclear energy and disarmament specialist) critiqued the discriminatory biases of the United States and the Soviet Union's proliferation proposals against the nonnuclear states—with similar concerns raised in India's domestic politics by India's Foreign Minister, Swaran Singh (Noorani, 1967). Trivedi (1965: 326–339) proposed a two-step treaty suggesting that nuclear weapons states (NWS) should agree not to transfer weapons or related technology to others, and only then would the nonnuclear weapons states (NNWS) agree not to acquire nuclear weapons.

It is within these contexts of regional and international challenges and unequal nuclear control agreements that concerns arose among the Indian government including its critics who began to believe that the real world demanded a more militarily robust approach to India's national security affairs. This offered a political and ideological space where competing discourses on India's nuclear nationalism, national insecurity, and nuclear apartheid rearticulated India's strategic cultural thinking and (in)security imaginaries in a more defensive manner.

Reconstructing Strategic Culture and Security Imaginary

With his inclinations toward nuclear nonviolence, Shastri like Nehru "acknowledged the normative requirement of moral principles governing international policies," but also asserted that "[India] had become equally conscious that international politics and ... relations were essentially a nonmoral phenomenon rooted in the chemistry of power equations" (Dixit, 2004:104–105). However, India did not immediately abandon its nonaligned policy but shifted its national security orientation from India's idealist pretentions about force/military in the world affairs to pay more attention to national security thorough military strength (a shift that had already after India's crushing defeat by China in the 1962 war). This shift from idealism to militarization was bound to accompany a rethinking of the Gandhian–Nehruvian legacy of nonalignment and nonviolence as India's singular moral approach to international affairs. It became evident as India's security community debated the future viability of nonalignment and nonviolence to interpret the Chinese threat and in that light to seek security guarantees from the West.

Those in the political spectrum who considered China a direct threat to India, supported (albeit with differences) a change in India's strategic cultural thinking in terms of nonalignment and nonviolence: For them, India had two choices, first, to seek a nuclear guarantee from the West or itself counter the Chinese threat. To this end, Congress Party members such as Bhagwat Jha Azad and Harish Chandra Mathur argued that "Chinese intimidation required India to be prepared to 'go all out' to use nuclear power for the defense of the country," and that "India should do whatever was necessary to stand up to China" (Lok Sabha, 1964a: 1280, 1309); the Praja Socialist Party, detesting the idea of turning to the United States for security assistance urged the government to seek nuclear weapons (ibid.:1301); and the Swatantra Party, on the grounds that nuclear China posed a psychological and political threat to India, sought India's alliance with the West to combat Sino-Soviet combination (ibid.:1240). To this extent, the Swatantra Party spokesperson held that nonalignment had become untenable and India's need to be more "strategic" in its approach to its national security affairs (Cheema, 2010: 117). In contrast, India's then Defense Minister, Y.B. Chavan, was not in favor of India abandoning nonalignment and suggested that India rely tacitly on the two superpowers to deter Chinese threats in addition to improving its conventional defenses (The Office of the Historians, 1964; Mirchandani, 1968:99–100; Kapur, 1979). However, Chavan's logic of relying on super powers did not hold currency among the skeptical members who thought that it was unrealistic that either super power would interfere—if China actually used its nuclear power on (or threatened) India.

The prevailing ideological climate and discourses within Indian politics also seemed to support India's strategic cultural orientation in favor of a militaristic India. The orthodox Hindu party, Jana Sangh (that was the sole party before 1964 to voice its call for a more militant India) was now joined by other political parties in calling for a more militant and defense-oriented India and be more flexible about India's nonaligned stature. Nath Pai from the Praja Socialist Party emphasized "the imperative of acquiring self-reliance in India's national security to enhance India's national prestige and great power status," and questioned "the relevance of Gandhian philosophy of nonviolence and demanded a strategic approach" for India (Mirchandani, 1968: 32; Shah, 1968:166–167). Others such as V.C. Trivedi, in a realist fashion argued for India's need for self-defense and that the current trend in world politics demanded that "each nation unto itself" (Lok Sabha, 1964b: 1517). The Communist Party divided between the pro-Soviet and the pro-China factions on the nature of the nuclear threat from China,[3] appeared less vocal than the other political parties in demanding a sharp rise in India's military agenda (Shah, 1986).

It is within this broader framework of shifting ideological orientations and discourses on India's strategic culture was constructed a new (in)security imaginary for India under Shastri's administration. In this emerging (in)security imaginary the following contours became evidenced: First, alliances between China and Pakistan becoming the biggest catalyst at that point in constituting direct challenges to India's national security agenda; second, India's concept of nonalignment though not totally abandoned was readjusted to enable India to position itself as an interim ally with the United States with mutual temporary benefits; and third, a rearticulation of India's identity as an "international image of reasonableness" representing a "strengthening [of] Indian capacity to pursue its 'national interests' which were now seen to be essentially regional in character" (Dixit, 2004:15; Cheema, 2010:77). Although the emerging contours of India's strategic cultural thinking and its (in)security imaginaries were not overtly aggressive or expansionist, these reconstructions boding well for India's then national geo-strategic security interests, "brought the principles of realism and practicality to bear on ... [India's] foreign policy and defense planning process," and "[i]n all, ... projected India as a credible military power capable of safeguarding its national interests ... which were very necessary to protect India's economic and defense interests in the Cold War atmosphere" (Dixit, 2004: 115). In essence, this rearticulation had a qualitative effect on the debates on India's nuclear policies under the Shastri period.

Nuclear Weapons Policy Debates

In contrast to the Nehru phase, when "[India's] nuclear decisions were not the outcome of any national debate [per se] but deeply rooted in his [Nehru's] scientific temper" (Poulose, 1978:102), an extensive debate now followed in the Indian Parliament on India's foreign/nuclear policy. Three alternatives on India's nuclear policy emerged in these debates: One calling for an immediate production of an atom bomb; one for embarking on nuclear-based defense installations in India; and the third, asking for a general reorientation in India's foreign policy in light of the Chinese bomb (Mirchandani, 1968). These debates reflected sharp divisions within and without the government and ranged from moderate to hawkish/realist views, to antinuclear views, to high emotional sentiments equating nuclear India with its glory as a big power (Cheema, 2010:116; Malhotra, 2012).

Antinuclear views were represented by Congress Party members such as Krishna Menon and Morarji Desai. Invoking "the Mahatma's teachings and Nehru's legacy" (Lok Sabha, 1964b: 1534, 1553), they argued against seeking nuclear weapons; stood the ground that the atom bomb was one of mass extermination; and using atomic energy for peaceful purposes only (Brecher, 1968b:228, 313; Malhotra, 2012). Desai joined the prime minister in questioning the Atomic Energy Commission Chairman Homi Bhabha's estimates on the bomb in that it would cause "great hardship to the people" (Malhotra, 2012). In contrast, hawkish views from other political parties including the Congress Party also surfaced in these debates: The Praja Socialist Party saw the acquisition of nuclear weapons as necessary to enhance India's national prestige and great power status (Dandavate, 1968:133–135; Malhotra, 2012). Nath Pai from the party expressed this sentiment in that, "we have been indulging once again in sentimental platitudes, confusing the whole [nuclear] issue and unnecessarily dragging [into the debate] Mahatma Gandhi, Pandit Jawaharlal Nehru, and for good measure, Lord Buddha and Samrat Ashok also ..." (Mirchandani, 1968:32; Shah, 1968:166–167; Malik, 2010:54). He urged that India "actively consider acquiring a nuclear deterrent of its own ... to warn China that we are not so helpless ..." (Lok Sabha, 1964a:1301). Likewise, the Swatantra Party also deemed that a "strategic" India must pursue both nuclear and conventional weapons as matters of violence in its foreign policy-making agenda (Cheema, 2010:117), and the Hindu nationalist, Jana Sangh Party (forerunner of today's BJP) introduced a resolution in the ongoing debate explicitly demanding production of atomic bombs (Malhotra, 2012).

Although some members of the All India Congress Committee namely K.C. Pant, Krishan Kant, and Mehr Chand Khanna favored the making of the atom bomb, the formal stand of the party remained closer to the government's official line (Kochanek, 1968:9; Mirchandani, 1968: 33–35) and managed to defeat the Jana Sangh's resolution.[4] While the prime minister summarized the official Indian nuclear policy by saying that "... morality or India's moral purposefulness [must] be factored into policymaking ... [and] we have some noble traditions ... [that] we cannot give up ..." (*The Hindu*, 1964), the prime minister, aware of his party's pro-nuclear mood and growing assertiveness, also chose to mollify them. The prime minister announced in the Lok Sabha in November that India could produce a nuclear bomb within "two or three years" if necessary, and that "this should entail preparations of peaceful nuclear explosives for purposes such as tunneling through mountains ..." (Lok Sabha, 1964c:2287–2288). In other words, he authorized for India a Subterranean Nuclear Explosion Project.

An open commitment to the development of a nuclear deterrent came from India's Atomic Energy Commission headed by its continuing Chairperson, Homi Bhabha. Following, the US-based reports (on September 29, 1964) that China was expected to conduct a nuclear test in the near future, Bhabha began "a public and behind-the-scenes efforts to push Shastri and the rest of the government to authorize more work to target the military applications of nuclear energy" (Dutt, 1966:5–7). Visiting

London on October 4, 1964, he announced "that India could explode an atom bomb within eighteen months of a decision to do so" (*National Herald*, 1964), and given the economic investment that the government had already made on the nuclear program, the country would have no economic difficulties in developing an arsenal of 50 nuclear weapons and 50 two-megaton hydrogen bombs thereafter (Bhatia, 1979:114–116). Although within India, Bhabha's views proved a minority (Mirchandani, 1968: 103, Cheema, 2010:114–115), Bhabha's hawkish message did not go unheard amongst Pakistani officials who believed that Bhabha was leading the nation on a course to produce nuclear weapons (Sharma, 1964). In this scheme of debates, India's armed forces were not consulted or invited by the government to participate. However, senior military officers such as retired Major-General Som Dutt and retired Major General, Y.S. Paranjpe concluded that nuclear weapons at that point would not be useful for India and instead favored improving India's conventional defense (Dutt, 1966; Mirchandani, 1968:54–55; 99–100).

Yet, evolving strategic changes at India's regional and global levels (as discussed earlier) coupled with challenges faced by the prime minister from members of his own party, the opposition, and with dim possibilities of a global nuclear freeze—made it imperative that India could not justify an absolute rejection of nuclear weapons. A more robust nuclear policy was required (Cheema, 2010:155–156). Significant in facilitating this pro-nuclear orientation was Pakistan's Foreign Minister, Z.A. Bhutto's lobbying for a nuclear weapons option for Pakistan after the war of 1965 (Kamath, 2009:82). As a spillover effect of this remark, there was significant pressure on the prime minister from the political spectrum to follow a proactive bomb policy (Mirchandani, 1968:40). Yet, the prime minister, in retaining an ambiguous nuclear stance, responded to these ongoing demands by saying that "[d]espite the continued threat of aggression from China … [the] Government [has] continued to adhere to the decision not to go in for nuclear weapons but to work for their elimination instead," and in fact, urged China "… to desist from developing nuclear weapons" (ibid.:40–41). On the Pakistan factor, the prime minister added that the conflict with Pakistan provided no basis for altering this policy (Perkovich, 1999:111). However, aware that domestic and international inhibitions could not justify an absolute rejection of nuclear weapons, the prime minister declared in the Parliament (on November 27, 1964) that, "I cannot say that the present policy [of nuclear pacifism] is deep-rooted, that it cannot be set aside and that it would not be changed .... Here situations alter, changes take place, and we have to mould our policies accordingly. If there is a need to amend what we have said today, then we will say—all right, let us go ahead and do so" (Mirchandani, 1968:34). However, the prime minister also reaffirmed the commitment of India's nuclear establishment to peaceful purposes only (Mirchandani, 1968).

In this context, one might argue that the prime minister did not entirely repudiate Bhabha's call for a more open nuclear policy for India. Instead, followed a more nuanced official policy toward the issue that well bode with his authorization of a Subterranean Nuclear Explosion Project—representing the Indian government's first public manifestation of a decisive step toward developing nuclear weapons. Expectedly, it would give India the same technology as a weapons test and provide the Atomic Energy Commission with the latitude to conduct research and development on a bomb design as well as its own nonnuclear components (Cheema, 2010:114). This period also saw the expansion of activities of the Defense Research and Development Organization in building a first-generation anti-tank guided missile (ATGM); developing liquid-fuel rocket engines based on the Soviet SA-2 sustainer motor; and undertaking such projects with the objective of creating scientific expertise and technological infrastructure to build for the long-run modern indigenous missiles for India. In addition, the Atomic Energy Commission under its Chair, Bhabha, sought the blueprint of America's explosive along a Plowshare device for India's nuclear weapons development purposes.

An analysis of India's nuclear debate by the end of the Shastri administration reveals that the debate lacked sophistication, and except for a few cases (where the prime minister approved a Subterranean Nuclear Explosion Project and authorized the Atomic Energy Commission to begin preparations for a peaceful nuclear explosive) was devoid of hard thinking with no indication of a doctrine to govern the deployment of nuclear deterrence. In addition, technical and organizational shortcomings of the Defense Research and Development Organization, opposition from armed services, and weak support from politicians

and civilian bureaucrats in the government resulted in the termination of India's ATGM and its liquid-fuel rocket engine development
projects (Dhanda, 2010:86). Thus, the nuclear debate appeared as a
period of gestation—taking an official stand favoring nuclear nonviolence and the development of nuclear explosives for peaceful purposes.
Yet, through this official position, the debate made two significant contributions in reorientating India's nuclear trajectory: First, like Nehru,
Prime Minister Shastri implicitly acknowledged India's traditional
commitment to nuclear nonviolence and nuclear policy for peaceful
uses; and second, breaking grounds with Nehru, explicitly acknowledged that India's commitment to nuclear energy for nuclear pacifism
was not deep rooted, thus implying a defensive turn in India's nuclear
weapons development.

Strategic Culture, (In)Security Imaginary, and Nuclear Policies under Indira Gandhi

Indira Gandhi (January 24, 1966–March 24, 1977) became the next
prime minister, following Shastri in the midst of domestic political and
economic uncertainty. Almost simultaneously, Dr Vikram Sarabhai
(a Gandhian-minded personality) became the new Chairman of the
Atomic Energy Commission. The start of this phase coincided with and
was followed by ongoing global debates on nonproliferation; increasing trends of nuclear hierarchy; and China's third nuclear explosion on
May 9, 1966. Although the global nonproliferation debates and China's
May 1966 detonation did not immediately entail an official support
for India's nuclear weaponization, these issues coupled with subsequent geo-political developments offered the Indian state a political and
ideological space for reinterpreting India's strategic culture in a more
self-defensive way. Its broader parameters, which I delineate below,
resulted in a convergence between the prime ministerial and the Atomic
Energy Commission's mindsets regarding India's nuclear trajectory in
not signing the Nuclear Non-Proliferation Treaty; conducting the peaceful nuclear explosion (PNE) in 1974; and the state's perusal of a robust
nuclear and missile development project.

Interpreting India's International Relations: United States, China, and Pakistan

The United States' attitude concerning a free and fair global nonproliferation agenda and reluctance to take bold steps in providing a security
guarantee to India became the starting point under Indira Gandhi to
redefine India's strategic culture. Following the 1965 nonproliferation
debates at the Eighteen Nation Disarmament Committee in Geneva, V.C.
Trivedi, once again in February 1966, took up the issues of "equitable,
mutual obligations between the haves and have-nots," arguing that any
arms control treaty obligate both nuclear and nonnuclear states to "forego
further production of nuclear weapons and delivery vehicles designed
to carry those weapons" (United States Arms Control and Disarmament
Agency, 1966a:20). Although the US State Department and the Defense
Department responded to Indian concerns by proffering seven alternatives through which it could stop India from going the nuclear route,
each of these, including the alternative of nuclear sharing, was dismissed
by the State Department, the Defense Department, and the Director
of Arms Control and Disarmament Agency on grounds of its potential
impact on Pakistan, Japan, and other South Asian allies of the United
States (Perkovich, 1999:116–117). This denial impacted debates in the
Indian polity about India's nuclear policy options.

The stimulus to the debate came following China's May 1966 nuclear
explosion. A spectrum of India's political parties not directly mention-
ing China supported India's nuclear weapons: the Communist Party
of India urged the strengthening of India's defense with Indian-made
weapons; the Praja Socialist Party's leader, H.V. Kamath, questioned
the government's "lackadaisical attitude" in developing its nuclear
weapons policy and recommended "harnessing the atom both for
peaceful development as well as for the manufacture of nuclear weapons as a deterrent" (Lok Sabha Debates, 1966: 15714; Mirchandani,
1968: 52–53). Pro-nuclear views also emerged from Indian elites such
as K. Subrahmanyam (1968:6–7) and senior government bureaucrats
like Raj Krishna (1965:122) and Sisir Gupta (1966:60–65). In contrast,
Krishna Menon and Morarji Desai from the Congress Party continued to
oppose building nuclear weapons (Mirchandani, 1968: 52–53), and the
Indian representative to the Eighteen Nation Disarmament Committee,

V.C. Trivedi, reemphasized "the much-needed balanced, mutual obligations among nuclear haves and have-nots" (United States Arms Control and Disarmament Agency, 1966b).

In this fluid scenario concerning India's interpretation of its international nuclear politics and relations vis-à-vis the United States and China (Pakistan at this point being relatively less important), the official Indian view was represented by Indira Gandhi by saying that China's explosion of nuclear weapons did not give "sufficient reason for us to change our policy in this matter," and India did not want to "do anything which will precipitate the [nuclear] crisis and lead to the development of nuclear weapons in many more countries" (Mirchandani, 1968:43). Before this still idealist interpretation of India's international relations, Prime Minister Gandhi's stand (revealing that breaking from her father's ideology was not an easy task) stopped the earlier sanctioned Sub-Nuclear Explosion Project (although simultaneously assuring that "We are building up our atomic power … for peaceful purposes …") (Lok Sabha Debates, 1966:15716). The prime minister's view was also backed by the AEC Chairperson, Sarabhai who on economic grounds opposed nuclear weapons (Jain, Vol. 2:179). In this context, Major General Som Dutt (Director of IDSA) and the then Indian Army Staff, General J.N. Chaudhuri (Ministry of Defense) noting a long-term psychological nuclear threat to India from nuclear China, did not favor diverting India's resources to the production of nuclear weapons (Dutt, 1966; Chaudhuri, 1966:257).

However, owing to a series of domestic, regional, and global developments since 1967, centering on geo-strategic insecurities and hierarchical issues of nonproliferation, this ambivalent strategic thinking of the Indian state was about to change—offering a ideological and political space to reinterpret India's strategic culture, (in)security imaginary, and enable a robust nuclear policy demand for the state.

Reconstructing Strategic Culture and Security Imaginary

A concept of nuclear sovereignty emerged in India's discourses and its strategic cultural thinking after April 1967 (which was also a time of political and economic crisis for Prime Minister Gandhi), as rising trends of international nuclear hierarchy became evidenced with the super powers seeking to uphold a horizontal form of global proliferation through Articles I, II, and III of the NPT.[5] As mentioned earlier, the failure of the treaty by then to meet one of India's major expectations that the NWS commit themselves to a binding provision on nuclear disarmament, made India realize how divergent its goals were from that of the superpowers in terms of a global disarmament (Kamath, 2009:10). What further irked India was President Johnson's downplaying global disarmament; emphasizing the need to stop the spread of nuclear weapons among nonnuclear weapons states; and stating that there was no practical distinction between nuclear weapons and peaceful nuclear explosives (the latter also implying contra to India's wish that it keep its nuclear option open) (Mirchandani, 1968:134; Seaborg, 1987:364–366).

To India, it implied nuclear apartheid, that is, the NPT devised by the Western powers characterizing India "as inequitable and colonial," a sentiment strongly articulated by members of the Indian government such as Raja Ramanna, B.N. Chakrvarthy, and V.C. Trivedi (Ramanna, 1992: 94; Jain, 1974). In a 1967 speech, Trivedi said that, "The civil nuclear powers can tolerate nuclear weapon apartheid but not an atomic apartheid in their economic and peaceful development" (Jain, 1974:192–193). It was therefore imperative that the negotiations respect "the sovereign equality of all nations and the principles of equality and mutual benefit" (ibid.:137). By March 1968, redrafts of the NPT did not address India's concerns and following another failed attempt by Prime Minister Gandhi's envoy, L.K. Jha (in 1967) to acquire security guarantees from Moscow, Paris, Washington, and London, India's official discourses (as evidenced through India's Defense Minister, Swaran Singh; Minister of External Affairs, M.C. Chagla; Home Minister, Y.B. Chavan; physicist Raja Ramanna, and Prime Minister Gandhi) took the stand that India should not be a party to the treaty (Mirchandani, 1968:149; Jain, 1974: 191; Jones, 1985:111–112; Ramanna, 1992:94; Malik, 2010:70).

By mid-1968, perceptions of international discrimination had taken center stage and norms of Gandhi–Nehru's nonviolence became secondary in defining the strategic thinking and (in)security imaginary of the Indian state. On June 12, 1968, the Indian Parliament rejected the NPT and Prime Minister Gandhi justified the rejection as being "based on [India's] enlightened self-interest and the considerations of national security" (Kamath, 2009:31; Malik, 2010). The rejection of the NPT gave India the legal space to begin work in developing nuclear explosives under a small team of scientists at the BARC (to be detailed hereafter), although the prime minister simultaneously assured that "... the government of India does not propose to manufacture nuclear weapons ... [and] we shall continue our efforts for nuclear disarmament ..." (Kamath, 2009:31).

International/regional events that were occurring simultaneously with India's general elections of 1971 and challenges that Prime Minister Gandhi was facing from her opposition, sustained this political and ideological space to further rearticulate India's strategic discourses in support of nuclear weapons. These developments unfolded when China (in April 1970) launched a long-range satellite launching rocket, conducted nuclear weapons tests of Lop Nur (in October 1970 and June 1973), and emphasized developing ballistic missiles with nuclear warheads (Cheema, 2010:132–133); as India and the Soviet Union (on August 9, 1971) signed a Treaty of Friendship and Cooperation (to counter which, the US President Nixon and his National Security Advisor, Henry Kissinger, opened relations with China using Pakistan as an intermediary); as conflicts loomed between India and Pakistan over East Pakistan; Indo–US stresses emerged on antipathies between President Nixon, Kissinger, and Prime Minister Gandhi; India's continued critique of the US war in Vietnam; the United States' resumption of exporting lethal military equipment to Pakistan in October 1970; and shortly thereafter, the 1971 India–Pakistan war over Bangladesh. The war got complicated with the US involvement in it when Henry Kissinger declared India as the aggressor state; in December 1970 suspended military sales and economic assistance to India; and dispatched the US aircraft carrier, *USS Enterprise* with nine supporting warships to the Bay of Bengal during the war.[6] Following the end of the war on December 1971, Z.A. Bhutto, on assuming power as Pakistan's prime minister deliberated with Pakistan's Atomic Energy Commission's Chairman, Munir Ahmad Khan, and nuclear scientists to deliver the "Islamic bomb" (Weissman and Krosney, 1981:44–46), and to build a nuclear weapons program that was developmental, technical, and political (Cheema, 2010:155, 157).

The 1971 war, albeit indirectly, implicated the rearticulation of India's strategic culture in support of its nuclear policy: First, India proved that it could defeat Pakistan; second, the war showed that China did not seek to militarily threaten India's security (in fact, after 1970, China took steps to normalize relations with India); third, India's victory buttressed its regional and hegemonic identity and security; and made the US gunboat diplomacy a significant factor in defining India's subsequent security agenda. In the context of the latter, a nuclear debate arose again the Indian Parliament, when on March 17, 1972 and again on November 1972, and the Parliament questioned the government "whether [it] propose[d] to embark on the manufacture of nuclear bomb" (Lok Sabha, 1972a:130–131).

Excepting the two Communist Parties, India's Minister of Defense Jagjivan Ram, and members of Indian defense such as General K.M. Cariappa who did not favor building nuclear weapons and stressed military preparedness based on conventional weapons, a considerable spectrum in the Parliament, especially the Jana Sangh and the left wing Congress intensely advocated nuclear weapons for boosting India's prestige and national security (Singh, 1971:102; Lok Sabha, 1972a:130–131). At this point, two significant changes supported a defense oriented rearticulation of India's strategic culture: first, the Chairman of the AEC, Dr Sarabhai (namely because of emerging global reliance on nuclear deterrence) became a bomb agnostic; and second, the IDSA came under its new Director, K. Subrahmanyam, a forceful supporter of nuclear bombs. Contrary to the government's position, Subrahmanyam argued that China posed a nuclear threat to India; the Chinese threat was to be countered by developing a survivable nuclear deterrent for India (despite India's then technological and institutional shortcomings in developing sophisticated nuclear arsenal); and that nuclear weapons would serve India's moral purpose by ensuring peace through deterrence (Subrahmanyam, 1970).

An analysis of the Indian state's strategic discourses under Prime Minister Gandhi reveals that a form of strategic cultural rethinking was being articulated through the political-ideological lenses of India's security community, where the defense-oriented moorings of India's strategic thinking (that was already set in place under Prime Minister Shastri) became more consolidated. In these rearticulations of India's strategic cultural thinking, a clear departure was made from the previous Nehru–Shastri eras when seen from the following perspectives: First, explicitly grounding India's national identity and security from a militaristic/defense-oriented perspective; second, a scenario where perceptions of international nuclear hierarchy and discrimination took center stage in shaping India's nuclear agenda (relegating issues of regional insecurity from China as existing but secondary); and third, where India's nuclear policy issues were justified clearly for purposes of its military application and defense and not simply for its economic development—thereby also showing a departure from the norms of Gandhi–Nehru nuclear nonviolence.

Within these ideological and discursive shifts of India's security community emerged India's (in)security imaginary based on the following interconnected premises: First, an acute nuclear apartheid sentiment vis-à-vis the NWS; second, India's political sovereignty (as a postcolonial state) to maintain its nuclear sovereignty vis-à-vis its perceived nuclear apartheid; third, a relative diminishing of issues of regional insecurity from China; and finally, the resurgence (after 1971) of a sense of India's new found regional and hegemonic identity and security adding a sense of militaristic prowess. Although in terms of India's global nuclear scenario, the United States and the USSR in 1972 signed an Anti-Ballistic Missile Treaty to prevent vertical growth of nuclear weapons and agreed to stabilize nuclear arms race through the Strategic Arms Limitations Talks I, these simply regulated super power arms race within limits of leaders' comprehensions and did not resolve apprehensions of global arms race (Kamath, 2009). In this context, one may even claim that India's strategic cultural perceptions and its sustained (in)security imaginary at this juncture of Indian politics made India inflexible (determined) in charting its own nuclear policy options/choices. Although Prime Minister Gandhi still treaded cautiously in this matter and in June 1971 held that, "[W]e have discussed this question deeply and rejected the idea of making a bomb" (Sen Gupta, 1984:5), the logic of India's nuclear sovereignty had developed its own militaristic momentum by 1970s—very different from what was comprehended by Nehru's India—leading to India's peaceful nuclear explosion.

Nuclear Weapons Developments and the Peaceful Nuclear Explosion

As mentioned earlier, although Dr Sarabhai in line with the official thinking opposed developing nuclear weapons, scientists at the AEC after China's May 1966 nuclear testing, continued their work on India's

implosion package by producing and separating weapons-grade plutonium; developing expertise to fabricate metal into explosive cores; and
recruiting scientists and engineers from other departments to sustain
work toward production of India's implosion package (Mirchandani,
1968:48–51). In this, India benefitted from American and Canadian
assistance when India, the United States, and the IAEA (in December
1966) signed a tripartite agreement for the supply of a small amount of
the US plutonium to India for research purposes, and signed an agreement
with Canada to extend Canadian assistance to design and construct a
second power reactor at Rajasthan, RAPS II with stronger international
safeguards on it through the IAEA (Mirchandani, 1968:48–51; Kapur,
1979:196; Pathak, 1980:56). Thereafter, India's rejection of the NPT
in June 1968 provided the Bhabha Atomic Research Center (led by its
Director Homi Sethna, Raja Ramanna, Chidambaram and P.K. Iyengar,
B.D. Nagchaudhuri) the legal space to begin work in developing nuclear
explosives.[7]

As discussed earlier, domestic, regional, and international events
occurring in the latter half of the 1970s and a strong mood within
India's atomic science community provided India the impetus to go
ahead with a PNE. Two major breakthroughs occurred at this point
in India's nuclear program: both the Atomic Energy Commission elites
and the official governmental ideology spoke in conjunction to support India's nuclear weapons technology and Dr Sarabhai made a jump
start on India's Atomic Energy and Space Research for India's national
defense purposes. To this end, Dr Sarabhai launched a 10-year plan for
the development of India's atomic energy and space research (known
as the Sarabhai Profile); called on India to launch its first indigenously
produced satellite with a multistage rocket, the SLV3 (Government of
India, 1970:29–31); and in July 1970 established an interdisciplinary
Program Analysis Group for a cautious appraisal of the costs and benefits
of India's atomic energy and space research designs (Sharma, 1983:90).
This phase also saw the establishment of the Department of Space; the
development and test-firing of Rohini-560 (a two-stage solid propulsion
sounding rocket that could reach an altitude of 334 km with a 100-kg
payload); the Purnima reactor became operational in May 1972; and
the Bhabha Atomic Research Center worked on the fission method for
India's future nuclear explosions (Dhanda, 2010:87). On May 18, 1974,

Indian conducted its PNE. The prime minister described the test as "committed to only peaceful uses" (Simons, 1974:A1).

The PNE provided an immediate political lift to Prime Minister Gandhi domestically (Sen Gupta, 1984; Jones, 1985; Joeck, 1986) but also garnered (understandably) strong reactions from Pakistan and the United States. The United States under the Ford administration rendered India target to a series of the US-led nonproliferation control efforts as the administration following up on the Zangger Committee's (1974) recommendations created the Nuclear Suppliers Group (NSG) as an international nonproliferation cartel to restrict India's further proliferation, and the US Congress in June 1976 enacted the Symington Amendment to the Foreign Assistance Act prohibiting the US economic or military assistance to any country importing enrichment or reprocessing technology unless the country accepted IAEA safeguards on all its facilities.[8] The Act was perceived by India as a US-led "intellectual colonialism" of the nonproliferation regime (Chellaney, 1993:64). On its part, Pakistan's President, Z.A. Bhutto saw the PNE as a "fateful development, … [that] introduced a qualitative change in the situation between the two countries," and embarked on a rapid path to Pakistan's nuclear technology expansion (Khan, 1995; Cheema, 2010:159, 165–167). At this juncture, the return of Dr A.Q. Khan to Pakistan was a strategic benefit to Pakistan only to become critical for the Indian state's insecurity.

An analysis of India's nuclear program under Prime Minister Gandhi thus reveals that with pragmatic adjustments to nonalignment and nuclear nonviolence, the Indian state's strategic cultural thinking made a cautious choice to chart its sovereign nuclear policies leading to the PNE. Yet, such transitions of India's strategic rethinking to test in 1974 did not completely abjure the traditional Nehruvian concept of nonviolence and nonalignment as leading sections of India's governmental elites such as India's Minister of External Affairs, M.C. Chagla continued to claim India's nonaligned status; others such as L.K. Jha; Raj Krishna; Sisir Gupta; and the prime minister herself seemed to stake its compromise for pragmatic reasons by seeking Western security guarantees; others like India's Finance Minister, Morarji Desai; George Fernandes opposed a nuclear policy; and yet, others, like H.V. Kamath, K. Subrahmanyam, Raj Krishna, and Sisir Gupta supported a nuclear policy.

Thus, what emerged from these shifts and tensions between India's traditional nonalignment, its philosophy of nuclear nonviolence, and its resurgence of a defense-oriented strategic thinking was a political and ideological space that enabled the Indian state to show resistance to international power hierarchy; an opposition to the principle of international nuclear inequality; reject the NPT; and with pragmatic adjustments to nonalignment and nuclear nonviolence made a cautious choice to chart its sovereign nuclear weapons policies leading to the PNE. These transitions in India's strategic thinking saw a discursive articulation of a politico-diplomatic-military strategy for approaching India's nuclear weapons policies more forcefully under Prime Minister Gandhi's second term (Cheema, 2010:121). Prior to this intensification of India's nuclear momentum came the brief Janata regime.

The Janata Government

In terms of India's strategic culture, (in)security imaginary, and India's nuclear policy, the brief coalition-led Janata government, headed by Prime Minister Desai (March 24, 1977 to July 28, 1979), brought into key governmental positions the pro-bomb politicians such as, L.K. Advani (Minister of Information and Broadcasting), Atal Behari Vajpayee (Minister of External Affairs), and H.M. Patel (India's Finance Minister) who could have indicated a shift in India's nuclear policy discourses. This shift should have become all the more justifiable considering India's then international scenario, namely the continuing trends of international nuclear hierarchy; China's 22nd nuclear test in September 1977; Pakistan's increasing nuclear technology momentum under its new President Zia-ul-Haq since August 1977; and that some segments of India's political and strategic elites reflected a pro-nuclear strategic orientation (Mirchandani, 1978:66; Cheema, 2010).

However, this pro-nuclear shift in India's official nuclear policy did not occur owing to Prime Minister Desai's faith in Gandhian nuclear nonviolence, his national economic considerations, and the United States' interests in nonproliferation. Of significance with regard to the latter was the United States' nonproliferation policy review under

President Carter to indefinitely defer its commercial reprocessing and recycling of plutonium; embargo exports of equipment or technology useful for uranium enrichment and plutonium reprocessing; and strengthening international nonproliferation safeguards. These seeming efforts at the US disarmament, however, entered into problems as the US Congress (on March 10, 1978) passed the Nuclear Non-Proliferation Act (NNPA).[9] It raised tensions between India and the United States with regard to the ongoing supply of the US fuel to the Tarapur reactor as stipulated by the 1963 India–US nuclear agreement (Malik, 2010:73). While these NNPA related developments simultaneously saw some goodwill gestures in India–US bilateral relations,[10] India–US talks on global disarmament did not go as India desired—given that President Carter (despite his genuine interests toward disarmament), fell hostage to the resurgent Cold War arms race, the ongoing arms control negotiations of SALT II, and could not conclude a test ban treaty as India desired. Instead, in India's perception, the terms of the NNPA added to the existing list of the discriminatory and hierarchical technology denial legislations practiced by the United States to keep India technologically backward. It "stoked" India's "postcolonial sensitivities" for its nuclear independence (Malik, 2010).

In this prevailing (in)security imaginary representing the United States' neocolonial presence in guiding international nonproliferation hierarchy, Prime Minister Desai's strategic cultural thinking (representing a combination of Gandhian nonviolence and his aversion to international nonproliferation hierarchy) accepted the ambiguous strategic cultural parameters already laid by the previous Indian administrations that India would not sign the NPT in the absence of global disarmament and stood fast on India's traditional nonnuclear position (Mirchandani, 1968:65–66). Conveying this theme (on March 1977) the prime minister stated that, "the government did not believe in nuclear weapons, … [and] the necessity of peaceful nuclear explosives" (Mirchandani, 1978:65–66); announced in a "unilateral decision to abjure explosions even for peaceful purposes" (Bunn, 1999:23); in a Special Session on Disarmament in the UNGA (in June 1978) reaffirmed his pledge "not to manufacture or acquire nuclear weapons" (Reiss, 1988:235); and in a statement to the Rajya Sabha (July 1978) stressed that India's nuclear policy should be seen "in the broader perspective of our own traditions, our spiritual and moral values and our passion for [peace]" (Desai, 1986:97). Reacting to grave concerns expressed by India's strategic analysts, leaderships within the Bhabha Atomic Research Center, the Atomic Energy Commission, and parliamentarians (such as L.K. Advani and Atal Behari Vajpayee, who would have preferred a more hawkish approach to India's nuclear weapons), the prime minister said "... I should not make a commitment for all future time .... But, if anything is necessary, we can do it always in consultation with other people, if they are convinced" (Perkovich, 1999:201–203; Paddock, 2009:26). Thus, under Prime Minister Desai, India's military and foreign policy issues remained ancillary, Pakistan's rising nuclear ambition (which American intelligence reports in 1979 indicated was commissioning the Kahuta centrifuge plant and was on its way to produce bomb-grade uranium) was muted, and the Department of Atomic Energy's civilian and military projects stalled (Jaywant, 1980).

While the short-lived Charan Singh government (July 28, 1979 to January 14, 1980) emphasized the Pakistan threat as a part of India's defense policy, decided to keep India's nuclear options open, and claimed that "we might have to reconsider our earlier [nuclear policy] decision if Pakistan goes ahead with the atom bomb" (*Statesman Weekly*, 1979:1), the hawkish mindsets of India's strategic community were able to dominate India's nuclear weapons development only after the Soviet invasion of Afghanistan on December 25, 1979. By the time the Cold War broke out over Afghanistan, pending negotiations on SALT II were withdrawn by President Carter accelerating the momentum in global nuclear politics. It implicated India's (the US–Pakistan-centric) regional insecurity developments and enabled India under Indira Gandhi to address more forcefully India's nuclear weapons development.

Strategic Culture, (In)Security Imaginary, and Nuclear Policies under Indira Gandhi

A week after the Soviets invaded Afghanistan, Indira Gandhi became prime minister for the second term (January 14, 1980–October 31, 1984). In contrast to the preceding Janata government, Prime Minister Gandhi gave prime importance to the nuclear issue, wherein certain evolving geo-strategic factors, which I will discuss hereafter, resulted in a more aggressive rearticulation of India's Cold War-centric strategic culture, (in)security imaginary, and its nuclear weapons agenda.

Interpreting India's International Relations

Under Prime Minister Gandhi, three factors related to the resurging Cold War over Afghanistan became important in defining India's US-centric international affairs with acute regional implications: First, an intense remilitarization program in the United States under President Reagan who assumed Presidency in January 1980; second, President Reagan's selective proliferation approach with regard to allies (Pakistan) and potential nonallies (India); and third, the US Cold War-oriented military interactions with Pakistan.

Under President Reagan, an intense remilitarization program came to the forefront of the US politics as widespread anger was created by conservative US Republicans that the United States had fallen from its strategic superiority vis-à-vis the Soviets. This was matched by strong anti-Communist calls from religious and political leaders of the country advocating a militarily superior America (Kamath, 2009:43). Although the Reagan administration in 1982 began negotiations with the Soviet Union to renew the SALT agreement, an outcome of this otherwise militaristic climate resulted in the Star Wars program (in 1982). It was merited on the US' national security grounds despite violating the Outer Space Treaty (1967) (ibid.:43–44). Furthermore, the Reagan administration that for Cold War interests followed a less activist approach to global nonproliferation, began relaxing export controls and other restrictions vis-à-vis countries that could be the US allies in the Cold War. In this effort, the administration also worked cooperatively with countries like Pakistan and China and took a much tougher stand with others (such as India) (Clausen, 1993:157–158). The United States' selective proliferation approach vis-à-vis Pakistan became a concern for India well revealed as Pakistan emerged as a frontline state for the US' Cold War interests in Afghanistan and the Reagan administration invoking an exemption of the earlier imposed Symington Amendment on Pakistan renewed economic and military aid to Pakistan including an aid package of $3.2 billion in 1981 and a supply of F-16 aircrafts (Malik, 1998; Rajagopalan, 1999; Cheema, 2010). The United States moves to arm Pakistan heightened India's concerns that the Zia government could become more aggressive and that the United States could do little to stop Pakistan's nuclear program. Despite Gandhi's cautious diplomacy vis-à-vis the United States, which I address later, these US–Pakistan issues became a major factor in shaping India's strategic culture.

In terms of India's regional nuclear (in)securities a militarily emboldened Pakistan under the Zia regime with the US economic and military assistance became critical. To make things intense, in 1975, Dr A.Q. Khan returned from Western Europe to Pakistan (Dhanda, 2010:15), and supported by President Zia's nuclear zeal employed an extensive (sometimes clandestine) network of connections with Western Asian Islamic states, Western Europe, the United States, and China to obtain necessary materials and technology for developing uranium enrichment capabilities for Pakistan's nuclear plants (Kamath, 2009:82; Cheema, 2010:167). By the early 1980s, Pakistan began pursuing an active ballistic missile development program, which, by the end of Gandhi's term reflected a strategic effort at building a diversified and survival nuclear deterrent capable of targeting the Indian landmass (Dhanda, 2010:154). By the end of 1983–1984, India's threat perceptions from Pakistan further escalated following an interview by A.Q. Khan claiming that, "by the grace of God we have left India behind by many years in uranium enrichment ...," implying that Pakistan with its enriched uranium could produce a bomb, if "the President were to take this extreme step ..." (Khan and Sreedhar, 1987: 57, 69). Despite claims to the contrary by Pakistan's ex-Chief of Staff, General Aslam Beg) (Kamath, 2009:82), reports simultaneously revealed an expansion of Pakistan's missile development by mid-1980s. With the US and Chinese assistance, these included nuclear-capable combat aircrafts; solid-motor and liquid-engine short-range ballistic missiles; F-16 combat aircrafts; land-based ballistic missiles; and the successful designing of the ballistic missile program, the hatf (Dhanda, 2010: 154–155). It increased pressure on India's nuclear momentum.

Although China declared a no-first use policy of nuclear weapons as its official policy even before its first nuclear test in October 16, 1964, India's nuclear threats from China since remained. In the 1980s, what irked India (in addition to China's growing trends of nuclear and military modernization, culminating in another Chinese nuclear test in June 1980) were the growing signs of Sino-Pakistani proximity with China playing a major role in assisting the development of Pakistan's nuclear weapons technology. These included: helping design Pakistan's Kahuta plant (enriched uranium from whose unsafeguarded reactor was used by Pakistan to develop its nuclear weapons); assisting in developing the Khushab reactor; providing Pakistan with pre-tested atomic bomb design and fissile components; and providing Pakistan (in the early 1980s) with blueprints for a U-235 nuclear implosion device (Dhanda, 2010:163). Although China's Ministry of External Affairs declared that China's 1980 test posed no fresh threat to India; nor should the Sino-Pakistan nuclear and military transactions cause a concern to India; and simultaneously through a proposal in the Second Special Session of the United Nations General Assembly on Disarmament on June 21, 1982 entertained the concept of global disarmament—these China-centric and Sino-Pakistani developments did not allay India's concerns (Kamath, 2009:111). Thus, despite diplomatic efforts and meetings in 1981 to improve Sino-Indian relations in nonpolitical fronts, Chinese insecurities remained for the Indian front with their border dispute remaining unresolved (Malhotra, 1989; Cheema, 2010:168). These geo-strategic compulsions as interpreted through the ideological lenses of India's security community constructed a certain form of strategic cultural thinking and (in)security imaginary under Gandhi's administration.

Reconstructing Strategic Culture and (In)Security Imaginary

India's strategic discourses under Gandhi vis-à-vis India revealed a shift in India's strategic cultural thinking in terms of India's US-centric foreign policy, a China–Pakistan–US trio, regional/global diplomacy, and India's nuclear policy. The following represented India's impending insecurities: With augmenting knowledge that Pakistan was engaged in designing nuclear weapons, Gandhi described the Pakistani nuclear capability as a "qualitatively new phenomenon in [India's] security environment" (Cheema, 2010:168). For India, it was particularly discomforting for two reasons: First, unlike India, whose development of missile-based power projection capabilities were based on both regional and extra-regional

(US-centric) security concerns, for Pakistan, these developments were largely Indo-centric (Dhanda, 2010:154); and second, the United States continued to supply Pakistan with military equipment in the backdrop of the Afghanistan war (Cheema, 2010:168). Gandhi in 1982 openly criticized the US cognizance of Pakistan's nuclear capability by saying that "The knowledge we have gained purely from Western sources, American and otherwise, is that they [Pakistan] are going in for a bomb. Now America has accepted that situation, so far as we can make out" (Gandhi, 1982:9). India felt that its nuclear self-restraint went unnoticed by the Americans while doing little to stop Pakistan's nuclear weapons program. It had three implications in terms of India's strategic cultural rethinking: First, India's foreign policy through the Indira Doctrine in 1983 became assertive;[11] second, India pursued a policy of diplomacy with both Pakistan and the United States (although its diplomacy with Pakistan was stalled with intervening developments);[12] and third, under the specter of the Pakistani threat spurred a number of discourses within India's security community about augmenting its nuclear capability. I discuss below these developments namely, India's cautious diplomacy with the United States as it indirectly set the direction of India's nuclear weapons development under the subsequent Indian administrations.

As mentioned earlier, (in)security imaginary is not real in the sense that it can be empirically scrutinized. Rather, "it is the product of an "act of cultural creation," which is fundamental to any subsequent system of cultural representation" (Tomlinson, 1991:156–157). Seen from this definition of (in)security imaginary, one notices that a rather hybrid form of (in)security imaginary was constructed at that point through India's strategic cultural discourses: First, a potentially nuclear weaponizing Pakistan (aided and abetted by China and the United States), whose threat was now perceived at a much intense scale than any other previous Indian administrations; second, a possible US–Pakistan–China trio against India; third, a subtle shift in India's stand on nonalignment as far as its foreign policy/nuclear technology aspects were concerned; and finally, an emerging cautious diplomacy with the United States seeking military and defense collaboration with the United States which could be applied to India's nuclear weapons development system. In sum, India's (in)security imaginary, caught "betwixt and between" India's desire for a global power status and simultaneously facing Cold

War centric insecurities in its regional/international arena, sustained a political and ideological space within which unfolded India's nuclear discourses at this juncture.

Immediately after her election in 1980, contending debates on India's nuclear policy ensued within India's political spectrum that in contrast to the previous administrations, focused closely on the Pakistani threat and leaned toward a more robust nuclear policy for India. Some parliamentarians called on the government's failure "to understand in depth the problems of defense;" others lamented India's reliance on expensive weapons imports and the indigenous failure to produce modern tanks, aircraft, and other systems; others asked what the Indian government was doing considering Pakistan's progress toward nuclear weapon; and a high-ranking retired general called for the creation of a National Security Council to rationalize India's defense planning system (Lok Sabha, 1984a:337, 343–346, 356, 398). Opposition parties, namely the BJP argued the seriousness of a nuclear danger from Pakistan namely in the context of Dr A.Q. Khan's comments (Khan and Sreedhar, 1987: 57,69), and a prominent media report to this extent claimed that "India should respond openly by declaring its nuclear weapons capabilities and matching Pakistan step-by-step" (Bajpai et al., 1995:143).

As in the previous decade, strong advocacy of India's going nuclear continued from the Director of IDSA, K. Subrahmanyam, who claimed (on grounds of China) that "a nuclear weapon can be deterred only by a nuclear weapon," and the only way "in which India can keep its nuclear option open [is by] … exercise[ing] the nuclear option" (Subrahmanyam, 1981:6). At this stage, army strategists became involved in India's nuclear debate. In 1981, Lt General K. Sundarji (1981) commissioned essays documenting the needs of India's nuclear weapons to counter attack on its traditional forces in an environment where Pakistan and China possessed nuclear weapons, and Indian naval officers, like Vice Admiral, M.R. Schunker referring to the memories of USS Enterprise 1971 noted that super power nuclear threats are not necessarily confined to mutual (superpower) deterrence postures, but "that [the] threat can be directed against us [India] also" (Lal, 1981:2).

To these concerns, members of the government (namely India's Minister of External Affairs, Narasimha Rao; Defense Minister, Venkataraman; and the prime minister herself) responded by keeping in mind India's traditional posture of nuclear ambivalence, although simultaneously clarifying that the "government is vigilant in the matter," "We have a pragmatic approach to the Defense problems;" and that "Indian scientists are keeping abreast of all aspects of research and development connected with modern and relevant technologies" (Lok Sabha, 1984b:398). In this context, even a strategic realist like K. Subrahmanyam acknowledged that his arguments for India's nuclear policy were made in a political and civilizational culture inspired by Mahatma Gandhi and qualified his pro-nuclear call by adding that "Gandhi advised that India must not be helpless but rather be conscious of her strength and power" (Subrahmanyam, 1981:7). Thus, a no-nuclear policy continued as the official stance of the Indian government. Indeed, during her term, the prime minister did not seriously consider a nuclear test, sought to downplay nuclear issues, and in an interview with a US-based media reported that "I believe the threat is one of conventional arms and not of nuclear weapons. I'm very much against war of any kind and nuclear war especially" (Gandhi, 1982:25–26). At this point, the government deemed that its armed forces could increase their capacity in weaponry and other strategic doctrine to fight Pakistan in case of hostilities.

However, Prime Minister Gandhi was determined through cautious diplomacy to improve relations with Washington and other Western capitals—a strategic step that sought to intersect India's foreign policy and nuclear technology decisions. Strategically and politically this required overcoming Cold War suspicion, dispelling impressions of proximity to the USSR, and moving beyond the nonproliferation deadlocks that had constrained relations between India and the United States since India's 1974 test. President Reagan and Prime Minister Gandhi met at a global summit in October 1981 to put economic issues on a smoother front; the United States in its annual invitations to foreign Heads of States (in early 1982) invited Gandhi; and the prime minister visited the United States in July 1982. In contrast to the traditional discourses of Indian moralism and anti-US sentiments, the prime minister charmed the Americans with her diplomatic engagement leading to the two Heads of States formalizing an initiative for science and technology cooperation (that formed the basis of the subsequent Indo-US Memorandum of Understanding). There also occurred a positive outcome on the Tarapur Nuclear plant issue when the Reagan administration managed to bypass the NNPA's requirement for safeguards on all of India's nuclear facilities, and India relaxed its defiant approach—in that an end of the US supply of fuels to Tarapur would not mean an end of all India's obligations to adopt safeguards on the Tarapur plant.

What emerged from these negotiations was a shift in the Indian state's strategic thinking vis-à-vis the United States which impacted India's foreign policy and nuclear technology orientation, that is, India's nuclear technology decisions had to serve its "national security interest and its overall bilateral relations with the US" (Ram, 1982:91). Although several factors such as India's doubting of its long-term reliance on the Soviet Union for its technology advancement, the AEC's dependence on indigenous technology for running its nuclear reactors, and a desire of exploring possibilities of purchasing high technology and military hardware from the United States led to this strategic rethinking of the state, this shift (in a noted departure from India's hitherto followed approach of grievance against the United States) also sustained at that juncture the following (in)security imaginary for the Indian state.

Although at that point, India's (in)security imaginaries focused on a nuclear Pakistan, an urgency to face it, and a demand for a robust nuclear policy, these insecurities were simultaneously countered by the government's traditional no-nuclear policy response. Yet, one also notices from the state's strategic cultural discourses that the government's no-nuclear policy faced a conundrum: This is because, from the governmental perspective, without an internationally recognizable provocation of a Pakistani nuclear explosion, mere words or speculations of Pakistani nuclear capability was not enough to cause a radical change in the government's policy for a further nuclear detonation. At that point, a preemptive strike to destroy Pakistan's nuclear capability remained unpromising; reliance on the United States to constrain Pakistan's nuclear program remained dim; and direct diplomacy with Pakistan to reduce the risk of conflict and escalation to a nuclear arms race remained mostly unsuccessful. On the nuclear front, the least risky strategy was to buy time; avoid provocations; keep India's nuclear option ambiguous; and pursue global disarmament as a matter of principle. It meant doing three things: First, maintaining the dual character of India's nuclear program (i.e., simultaneously enhancing India's military and nuclear weapons production); second, sending out contradictory signals on whether and how India would go nuclear (Gandhi, 1982b); and third, keeping India's nuclear option open by simultaneously invoking calls of disarmament (Paddock, 2009:26; Malik, 2010:81–82).

To this extent, notwithstanding failures between the superpowers to reach any disarmament goal, Prime Minister Gandhi (in 1982) at the UN Special Session on Disarmament proposed a convention on no use or threat of use of nuclear weapons, a freeze on the manufacture of nuclear weapons, a cut-off in the production of fissionable materials for weapons purposes, and proposed a comprehensive test ban treaty. In addition, the then External Affairs Minister, P.V. Narasimha Rao repeated these messages of disarmament in a speech to the General Assembly in October 1982 (Malik, 2010:82); in a speech at the Seventh Non-Aligned Summit at New Delhi (March 1983); the prime minister warned against the increasing lethality of nuclear weapons and its potential destruction of humanity; and in her Six-Nation Five-Continent Appeal (on May 22, 1984) (joined by the leaders of Sweden, Mexico, Tanzania, Argentina, and Greece) called for a freeze on all testing, production, and deployment of nuclear weapons and their delivery systems. The state's discourse on this matter emphasized the matter of "principle" and the rejection of the "legitimization" of the possession of nuclear weapons by a select group of nuclear weapons powers which sanctified the division of the world into nuclear-haves and nuclear have-nots (Paddock, 2009:26; Malik, 2010:81). Yet, these nuclear ambivalent discourses of the government belied the fact that India's nuclear establishment was actively expanding India's nuclear and missile development projects for another nuclear explosion to advance from the 1974 test. Below I discuss these developments.

Nuclear Weapons Developments

In addition to her efforts at global disarmament, Prime Minister Gandhi undertook the modernization of India's military and defense and nuclear establishment—that had not achieved its frequently claimed self-sufficiency given its slack under the Janata government. The period saw the expansion of the Defense Research and Development Organization (DRDO) and its laboratories which pursued an active missile and nuclear weapons development project; Prime Minister Gandhi's appointing of R. Venkataraman as India's Defense Minister (who, a strong supporter for technology, was highly respected by the prime minister, the leaders of the BARC, and the DRDO); and gave directives to India's atomic science establishment to import advanced weapons systems for India's nuclear and missile technology development (which resulted in India's completing of a deal with the Soviet Union for the purchase of T-72 tanks and MiG-25 Foxbat aircrafts (Smith, 1995:111).

At this time, Raja Rammana resumed his position as Director of the Bhabha Atomic Research Center (BARC) and with backing from the prime minister, set the following priorities to strengthen India's nuclear deterrent: complete the stalled progress on the Dhruva (R-5) research and plutonium production reactor at Trombay; push forward with the Fast Breeder Reactor at Kalpakkam; the reprocessing of weapons grade plutonium from the CIRUS spent fuel for weapons production at the unsafeguarded Tarapur plant; upgrade the safeguards-free reactors at the Madras Atomic Power Station-I and II (that could produce plutonium for explosive purposes); and in July 1983, commissioned at Tamil Nadu the Madras I nuclear power plant (Ramanna, 1992:108–109). Furthermore, top scientists at the BARC and the DRDO, knowing that the 1974 nuclear test was a rudimentary one, collaborated as a team to improve the neutron initiator and downsize the high explosive to increase the yield of a nuclear device, and by 1982 produced a design for a device that would weigh much lighter than the 1,000 kg 1974 device. Although Ramanna and Arunachalam made their technological case to the prime minister for testing this device, the Prime Minister Gandhi (after an initial approval) denied it (Sidhu, 1997:129).

In addition, India significantly augmented its military strength: In 1983, the DRDO formally began a comprehensive effort called the Integrated Guided Missile Development Program (IGMDP) to produce ballistic missiles for India's indigenous tactical and strategic weapons; the Defense Research and Development in conjunction with the armed forces expressed considerable interest in the Nag antitank guided missile and two surface-to-air missiles the Trishul and the Akash; proposed the Prithvi tactical surface to surface missile and the longer-range Agni missile; and launched India's first satellite launch vehicle, SLV3 and the 35 kg Rohini Satellite (Dhanda, 2010:87). Considering potential restrictions that might be imposed on India by the nonproliferation regime, V.S. Arunachalam and A.P.J. Abdul Kalam promptly produced and acquired key components to manage India's missile and satellite development projects (Perkovich, 1999:247). Yet, Prime Minister Gandhi justified these developments by claiming that India's nuclear program was an example of its determination to be "self-reliant" (Gandhi, 1983:1). It is against this background of India's missile development and other ongoing compulsions of geo-strategic insecurities that Prime Minister Gandhi was assassinated on October 31, 1984.

Strategic Culture, (In)Security Imaginary, and Nuclear Policies under Rajiv Gandhi

Although the unity of India was Prime Minister Rajiv Gandhi's primary concern and foreign and nuclear policy issues secondary (Gandhi, 1987), the young prime minister's penchant for computer software and technology ushered in the Indian mindset a pro-US strategic thinking in terms of high-tech cooperation that had a significant bearing on India's nuclear policy developments. These transitions of India's strategic thinking operating amidst its geo-politics (which I address below), constructed certain (in)security imaginaries for the state, which, initially soft-peddling on nuclear aggressiveness, after 1988 revealed an active progress toward India's nuclear and missile development (although simultaneously retaining its traditional nuclear ambiguity and pursuit of disarmament). Below I analyze these dynamics out of which emerged India's strategic cultural discourses, (in)security imaginaries, and its nuclear and missile development policies under the Rajiv Gandhi administration.

Interpreting India's International Relations

Continuing Cold War links between the United States and Pakistan became the focal point for India to interpret its international relations vis-à-vis the United States. This sparked when after a temporary suspension of military aid to Pakistan under the Pressler Amendment, such aid continued to be dispatched to Pakistan despite congressional acknowledgement that Pakistan had enriched uranium to more than 5 percent of its nuclear stockpile (Namboodri, 1985). Furthermore, the

United States offered Pakistan AIM-9L missiles in lieu of the F-16 air-crafts (Khan and Sreedhar, 1987:80, 86). What concerned India was that the United States' proliferation policy understandably held hostage to its Cold War interests was soft-peddling Pakistan's moves in produc-ing nuclear weapons and was simply seeking Pakistan's assurance that it would refrain from enriching uranium above 5 percent of its nuclear stockpile.

Despite the US–Pakistan Cold War nexus, Rajiv Gandhi's June 1985 visit to the United States resulted in a positive turn in India–US relations in terms of computer technology and software. Following the Memoran-dum of Understanding on Cooperation in High Technology Transfer, signed in December 1984, there followed exchanges by high-ranking the US–India political, science, and defense community members (such as the US Ambassador Harry Barnes; the US Under Secretary of Defense for Policy Fred Ikle; Indian Foreign Secretary Romesh Bhandari; and DRDO Director Dr A.P.J. Abdul Kalam), and technology cooperation agreements between the US–India's Defense Research and Development Organiza-tions' officials to pursue Indo-American security cooperation. India's pri-orities at that point were to secure American participation in the design and production of the Light Combat Aircraft; importing a state-of-the art Cray supercomputer model XMP-24; and negotiating the purchase of general electric 404 jet engines (Perkovich, 1999:269). Although reports of the US–Pakistan Cold War alliances continued and the delivery of the Cray supercomputer raised controversies between the two (Malik, 2010:80), mutual cooperation in the fields of science, technology, and space continued and reaffirmed by President Reagan and Prime Minis-ter Gandhi in their meeting on October 20, 1987. This positive turn in Indio-US relations also concurred with the United States' nonprolifera-tion measures as President Reagan initiated a Space Command in 1987 to regulate the star wars; in December 1987 with Gorbachev signed the Anti-Ballistic Missile Treaty to eliminate intermediate range nuclear mis-siles from Europe; and expressed hopes that these would lead to the elimination of their nuclear weapons arsenal (Kamath, 2009:44).

It might be worth pondering this sudden change of strategic think-ing of India and the United States vis-à-vis each other? For India, did it imply a shift of nonalignment? Did the United States comprehend the implications of this high-level technology cooperation for a potentially nuclear India? To this end, concerns remained amongst some the US Congressional and State Department members that licensed exports of powerful computer and technology to India, which were dual use, could potentially aid in the production of a nuclear India; others saw these strategic engagements with India as a potential counter to a communist China; others saw these as a pragmatic necessity for opening up relations with India to counter the Soviet Union's efforts after Cold War to strike up a relationship with India; and others through engagement wanted to keep India's nuclear weapons capabilities under control (Ottaway, 1989:A8; Chellaney, 1993:206–280). India, on its part remained wary of America's imperialist intentions, practices, and power but recognizing the superiority of American technology and wanting to reduce India's dependence on the Soviets sought high-tech cooperation with the United States including cooperation in defense areas (Malik, 2010:81). This however was not with the idea of buying complete systems from the United States but for joint development and production in high-tech defense areas (Badhwar and Trehan, 1985:50). Needless to say, high-tech cooperation bore profoundly on India's nuclear policy developments (prominently under the Vajpayee and Singh administrations), although neither side at that point made an explicit connection between the two strategic aspects.

Yet, nonproliferation discontent soon brewed following India's testing of the Agni missile in 1989 when the United States, following the recent passage of the Missile Technology Control Regime by the P-5, cancelled the previously agreed export to India of the Combined Acceleration Vibration Climatic Test System and delayed the selling of the Cray XMP-22 super computer—which India urgently desired (Kux, 1985:410). In addition to the "diplomatic snub inherent in these steps," India viewed the MTCR as a reassertion of "colonialism" to restrict India from advancing and competing with advanced nuclear powers, and further consolidated India's national psyche as one of self-reliance in pursuing its nuclear program (Malik, 2010:80).

India's Pakistan-based insecurities continued with Rajiv Gandhi's accession as American and Indian media reports documented Pakistan's clandestine efforts in early March 1985 to procure bomb components; Pakistan's alleged smuggling between 1977 and 1980 uranium enrichment components; and Pakistan's testing of a nonnuclear triggering package for a nuclear weapon in July 1985 (which became crucial in India's strategic cultural discourse vis-à-vis Pakistan) (Spector and Smith, 1990:332). In addition, Dr A.Q. Khan announced that Pakistan could carry "an atomic explosion in a very short time, if required …" (Khan and Sreedhar, 1987: 80, 86). While each report on Pakistan sparked call for action in India especially by the BJP (*The Times of India*, 1985a; News India, 1987), the strategic thinking of the Indian government refrained from referring to Pakistan's nuclear program on the pretext that India was too embroiled in domestic turmoil to risk any confrontation with Pakistan that was receiving generous military aid packages from the United States (Malik, 2010:87). Instead, Rajiv Gandhi in a US-based interview (in June 1985) ruled out a preemptive military strike on Pakistan's nuclear facilities; at the US insistence (in September and October 1985) took regional initiatives with Pakistan to slow their nuclear competition; pursued diplomatic discussions with President Zia (in December 1985) not to attack each other's nuclear facilities; agreed to exchange their lists of nuclear facilities annually (which was then signed and ratified by Gandhi and Benazir Bhutto in 1991); and embarked (rather unsuccessfully) to normalize relations with Pakistan including confidence building measures and resumption of talks on draft treaties on aggression and peace (Kumar, 1986; Bobb, 1986; Thakur, 1994). Although in 1985, the United States passed the Pressler Amendment to the Foreign Assistance Act, the amendment remained controversial given that the United States continued to annually waive its nonproliferation objections to filter aid to Pakistan (Cheema, 2010:168). Then occurred the Brasstacks crisis in January 1986 under General K. Sundarji (the Indian military's most vocal proponent of nuclear weapons), signifying three shifts in India's nuclear policy: First, India's focus of threat shifted from China to Pakistan; second, affected the subsequent Indian perceptions of the role of nuclear weapons in India–Pakistan relations; and finally, revealed excessive centralization in prime ministerial decision-making in planning India's defense/nuclear policy parameters (Bajpai et al., 1995).

Contrary to expectations that post-Cold War would render Pakistan more susceptible to the US nonproliferation pressures, the end of Cold War did not see any reduction in the US–Pakistan nuclear transactions nor a softening in India–Pakistan's nuclear rhetoric vis-à-vis each other (although both countries were under their new generation leaders Rajiv Gandhi and Benazir Bhutto). Furthermore, Prime Minister Bhutto (inheriting a nuclear program controlled by the army) was unlikely to restrict Pakistan's nuclear program, and despite her claims to the contrary, reports in June 1989 disclosed Pakistan's accumulation of highly enriched uranium, and with Chinese assistance designing nuclear weapons weighing about 400 pounds (Smith, 1988:38). What also irked India was that President H. Bush at the end of Cold War and in a position to take a stricter nonproliferation actions toward Pakistan—then under the Pressler Amendment—did not take a stronger stand vis-à-vis a nuclearizing Pakistan. Although Pakistan considering the implications of the Pressler Act agreed to "freeze" its nuclear program, its nuclear establishment continued its weapons enrichment program (Perkovich, 1999:303). As a testimony, Pakistan (on February 11, 1989) conducted the first test launches of the hatf I and hatf II ballistic missiles (with 80 and 300 km ranges and capable of carrying payloads up to 500 kilograms), which, coming roughly a year after India's first launch of the Prithvi missiles, manifested a Pakistani determination of strategic military competition with India (Spector and Smith, 1990:103). The Pakistani (hatf I and hatf II) and the Indian (Prithvi) missiles tests had implications in terms of the US global nonproliferation measures as well as India–Pakistani nuclear dimension: in terms of the former, the two tests occurred at a time when the United States was leading an international effort through the Missile Technology Control Regime to block missile proliferation and the Indian and Pakistani tests fell far below the limit set by the regime—agonizing the United States; and in terms of India–Pakistani relations, began a more aggressive nuclear competition to become fierce with the outbreak of the Kashmir crisis in the 1990s.

India's relationships with China in 1986–1987 also affected India's nuclear insecurities and policies although in a less tangible way than India–Pakistan's. China made a positive overture toward India at the outset of Rajiv Gandhi's tenure when the leading Chinese newspaper, *People's Daily*, noted that the new prime minister had "made certain adjustments to [India's] foreign policy ... and is making efforts to improve the situation in South Asia" (*Statesman Weekly*, 1985a:6). Although this was disrupted in late 1986 over China providing Pakistan with M-9 and M-11 ballistic missiles and China's support to secessionist groups in the Indian state of Arunachal Pradesh (Hoffman, 1990; Dhanda, 2010:163–164) mutual peace ensued as the border issue was resolved by August 1987; mutual peace talks were held between Sino-Indian state officials in New Delhi in November 1987; and Rajiv Gandhi visited China in 1988 (Ganguly, 1989; Hoffman, 1990; Mansingh, 1994). During this visit, the two sides reaffirmed their principles of peaceful coexistence; agreed that peace and tranquility should be maintained as they work to resolve border disputes; signed bilateral agreements to facilitate cooperation and exchanges in science and technology; and conduct cultural exchanges (Thakur, 1994:78–79). The relaxation of Sino-Soviet conflict with Gorbachev coming to power also provided the backdrop of Sino-Indian smoothening of relations.

Although India had achieved conventional military superiority over the Indo-China border region demonstrated by the 1987 Operation Checkerboard led by General K. Sundarji, it seemed that the Indian government did not want "to provoke" China (Malik, 2010:92). Consequently, India's China-centric strategic thinking did not translate to an active nuclear weapons agenda or proliferation plans for India (Sidhu, 1997). In fact, Prime Minister Gandhi remarked on December 1987, that "We have lived with the Chinese bomb now for several years without feeling that we must produce our own" (Malik, 2010:91). However, Indian strategists like K. Subrahmanyam and K. Sundarji perceived China as the decisive nuclear adversary for India—although Subrahmanyam simultaneously noted China's efforts at avoiding balancing India's nuclear build-ups through "proportional reinforcement" measures (Sundarji, 1995; Frey, 2006:113–114). These China-centric insecurities sighted by India's strategic and military gurus, namely China's deploying of nuclear weapons in Tibet, provided ammunitions to India's nuclear hawks to reinsert their calls to go nuclear. Indeed, India's (in)securities stemming from these above-mentioned dynamics of its ongoing international relations created a political-ideological space that enabled the state to rearticulate its strategic culture and (in)security imaginary resulting, since 1987, in a more robust approach to India's nuclear weapons building agenda.

Representing Strategic Culture and (In)Security Imaginary

Pakistan's testing of its nonnuclear triggering package in July 1985 saw India's security community demanding a robust nuclear program for the state. Supported by all political parties (except for the Communist

Parties) the BJP Executive National Committee in July 1985 issued a resolution calling for "immediate steps" to develop nuclear weapons and that India could no longer afford a "policy of drift and escapism" (*The Times of India*, 1985a). In addition, the former Janata government Finance Minister, H.M. Patel argued that "India must now go nuclear" (Reddy, 1985), and in August, 1985, the Minister of State for External Affairs (Khurshed Alam Khan) asserted that "… if Pakistan goes nuclear we will reply … stone by stone" (*The Times of India*, 1985b). Their calls were also joined by members of India's nuclear science community and the military namely Raja Ramanna (from the Bhabha Atomic Research Center); K. Subrahmanyam (from the IDSA); and Lieutenant General K. Sunderji (*Statesman Weekly*, 1985b; Bobb and Singh, 1987; Ramanna, 1992:115; Sundarji, 1995; Subrahmanyam, 1998a; Malik, 2010:85). Overall, their strategic thoughts, based on the logic of deterrence, addressed India's deterrent requirements to deal with Pakistan and China and suggested a minimal deterrent for India to hold hostage targets they valued vis-à-vis their adversarial neighbors (Sundarji, 1995). To this end, Subrahmanyam (1998a), also confirmed for India his idea of a balanced nuclear deterrent force containing warheads and various kinds of delivery systems such as ballistic missiles, submarines, advanced aircrafts, command and control infrastructures, and so forth. However, these calls were muted given that Prime Minister Gandhi's skepticism about the value of nuclear weapons (Gandhi, 1987:5) was backed by a Congress party parliamentary majority that did not yet shift to an explicit pro-nuclear stand. Thus, the prime minister's no-nuclear line of thinking held that, "… we are looking into various aspects of this [nuclear] question to see what action we should take" (Reddy, 1985).

However, after the Brasstacks crisis (late 1986 to early 1987),[13] a growing number of politicians including the Congress Party urged the government to reconsider India's nuclear program. These voices included President of the BJP L.K. Advani; Cabinet Secretary, B.G. Deshmukh; Defense Minister K.C. Pant; and the opposition members of the Congress Party (Reuters, 1987; Deshmukh, 1994). India's atomic energy and defense scientists believing that India could assemble a deliverable bomb by 1987 were once again eager to move ahead with the nuclear program (Bobb and Singh, 1987), while Ramanna (1992) and K. Subrahmanyam (1998a) invoking perceptions of nuclear racism, the

US power hierarchy, and India's nuclear nationalism supported their calls of nuclear weaponization. Although the issue of self-reliance versus the export of nuclear technology created tensions between the prime minister and like-minded atomic scientists like P.K. Iyengar (who felt that India should import some reactors) versus Ramanna (opposed to importing technology) (Ramanna, 1992:109), their pro-nuclear calls strengthened India's national psyche and its goal of nuclear self-reliance. The prime minister took the Brasstacks incident seriously but tried to calm reactions by declaring that "there was nothing new in Pakistan's claims or capabilities and that India had no intentions of manufacturing nuclear weapons" (although the government did increase India's defense spending by 43 percent for the year beginning April 1, 1987) (Patriot, 1987:5). Furthermore, pursuing India's high moral ground in disarmament, the prime minister in May 1988 launched before the United Nations General Assembly an Action Plan for ushering a nuclear weapon-free world order, and also proposed the same year a scheme for eliminating nuclear weapons from the Asian region (Paddock, 2009:26).

An analysis of the strategic culture of the Indian state under Prime Minister Gandhi reveals that a form of strategic rethinking was being articulated through the political-ideological lenses of the state, wherein, a seemingly contradictory mindset underlined the state's approach to India's nuclear weapons question. This being, the government conflicted between the need to do something in the nuclear front and simultaneously to avoid the escalation of nuclear competition especially with Pakistan. Although the prime minister's strategic dilemma led his government to regularly approach the United States to exert nuclear restraint on Pakistan, yet contrary to the Indian strategic community's belief (Ramanna, 1992; Sundarji, 1995; Subrahmanyam, 1998b) deemed it not pragmatic to pursue a nuclear weapons route for the state. Although the strategic and realist side of the prime minister's dilemma led him to set up a small group of advisors in 1985, including Raja Ramanna and K. Subrahmanyam to make their case for India's defense planning needs, the reports of the committee remained inconsequential. Thus, it appears that the Indian state's strategic thinking at that point mired between its high-moral stand in pursuing nuclear disarmament and also its perceived strategic need to back up its national security needs with an energized nuclear weapons program refrained the state from setting up overt work in nuclear weapons production much less developing an operational doctrine for the state.

Yet, a noticeable development at this time was the government's effort to include some military/defense personnel in planning India's defense, which, becoming significant around India's 1998 detonation, at this time remained mute given that these voices were co-opted by the government's official line on nuclear weapons. This also explains why India's strategic community at that point showed a less proactive approach to India's nuclear development (Singh, 1999; Dhanda, 2010:87). Thus, by 1987, the Indian state's strategic thinking manifested through the prime minister's increasingly personalized ways of conducting the country's defense planning, and aided by the then Defense Science Advisor to the government, Dr. Arunachalam, came to embody India's strategic culture in terms of its nuclear weapons. This strategic thinking (or a sense of strategic autonomy) implied that strengthening of India's technological capacity would initially require international cooperation, and while such cooperation progressed, the AEC and the DRDO would indigenously seek to develop India's technological and organizational modalities for a reliable nuclear deterrence.

It is within this shifting framework of ideological orientations and discourses of the Indian state's strategic cultural thinking (representing a transition from an initial waning of India's nuclear aggressiveness to a more robust nuclear orientation) was constructed a new (in)security imaginary for the Indian state. In this emerging (in)security imaginary the following trends related to its contemporary regional, global, and national dynamics became evidenced: First, an amplification of India's nuclear insecurities from Pakistan, which involving increasing the US–Pakistan and Pakistan–China military alliances and transactions, amplified India's insecurities from Pakistan (to a much greater degree than any previous Indian administrations). Second, a shift in India's (in)security imaginary vis-à-vis the United States, with the latter remaining simultaneously a source of security and insecurity for the Indian state: In terms of India's perceived security, Prime Minister Gandhi's administration revealed in an unprecedented manner than any earlier Indian administrations a pro-US, high-tech based strategic rethinking of India resulting in high-tech cooperation between India and the United States. Yet, India simultaneously faced insecurities from the United States' international power, hierarchy, and discrimination in the field of technology transfer and missiles control regimes toward the state. Finally, within its existing lines of the Gandhi–Arunachalam strategic rethinking and its regional and global insecurities, India desired an indigenous nuclear security which, resulting in the further consolidation of India's nuclear nationalism and technological self-reliance, saw the testing of the Prithvi and the Agni missiles, armed with nuclear warheads, under this administration.

Four interconnected lines of reasoning—nuclear nationalism, self-reliance, political–military, and a symbolic desire for big power status—which the Indian government used to justify the Agni and the Prithvi tests—demonstrate the link between India's strategic cultural thinking, (in)security imaginary, and its nuclear and missile development projects. The prime minister declared in the Parliament that the Prithvi took India into "the select group of four nations which have developed this class of surface-to-surface missiles" (Chengappa, 2000:319); Agni with its nuclear warhead and its 2500 kilometer range qualified as India's first weapons system that could hit targets deep inside China (Bobb and Menon, 1989; Chengappa, 1994a); and India's Defense Minister, K.C. Pant, justified these tests by arguing that "… India just cannot afford to overlook the fact that three major nuclear powers operate in its neighborhood and Pakistan is engaged in a nuclear program. If we are to influence these major powers, then it becomes … necessary for us to reckon with their nuclear deterrence belief concepts" (Sidhu, 1997:223–224). Yet, India's moral, economic, political, and strategic considerations which have also been traditionally important in shaping India's strategic culture prevented a full-scale nuclear test by the government.

Nuclear Policy Developments

Despite the prime minister's nuclear dilemma during the early years of his administration, India's nuclear and defense science establishments had continued to augment India's nuclear weapons capabilities through high-explosive nuclear technology developments—in case the need rose to go nuclear. By 1984, India imported nearly one hundred kilograms of pure beryllium from West Germany (that could increase weapons yield to produce dozens of weapons); commissioned a beryllium plant near Mumbai; and an almost indigenously built fast breeder reactor at Kalpakkam. In addition, India's Department of Atomic Energy declared plans for an inertial confinement fusion process associated with thermo-nuclear explosion of nuclear devices, and Raja Ramanna announced (in mid-1987) a new Department of Atomic Energy 15 year plan to create 10,000 megawatts of nuclear power by 2000 (Foreign Report, 1984; Knapik and Hibbs, 1989; Perkovich, 1999:284). Given that govern-mental approval had not yet come on thermo-nuclear weapons testing, the steps toward developing a military strategy or operational plans for nuclear weapons did not occur at this point.

However, by the end of the Cold War scientists like P.K. Iyengar preferred working with international cooperation to begin meeting growth targets for India's nuclear power. By early 1988, negotiations advanced for the supply of two Soviet 1,000 megawatts pressurized-water reactors to India (with international safeguards); scientists at BARC and the DRDO (under Chidambaram, A.P.J. Abdul Kalam, and K. Santhanam) continued refining nuclear weapons designs to increase their explosive yields and to develop boosted-fission weapon capacity; and with the prime minister's approval took steps to prepare ready-to-assemble devices and authorized scientists to transport weapons compo-nents within the country to advance their capabilities in nuclear weapons production. Although the nuclear and defense science establishments were still not authorized to conduct nuclear tests, the process of pre-paredness implied that devices were made that could be turned into weapons if India was attacked, and could be delivered by aircrafts like the French Mirage 2000, Soviet MIG-27, and the British French Jaguar fighter bombers (Perkovich, 1999:294–295). In 1986, Dr. Sivathanu Pillai joined the DRDO to work in the Integrated Missile Development Project under Dr A.P.J. Abdul Kalam's leadership and played a key role in the development of the Agni, Prithhvi, Nag, and Akash missiles. Thereafter, came India's testing of the Prithvi in February 1988 (a sin-gle stage, liquid-fuel missile, with 150 km range, capable of carrying a 1,000 kg payload, and striking a third of the Pakistani territory) and the Agni in May 1989 specifically designed against Pakistan and China. These represented India's efforts at technology empowerment (also to forego the high costs of its imported missiles and that foreign arms suppliers including India's ally the Soviet Union were often reluctant to sell the most advanced missiles demanded by the Indian armed forces) (Dhanda, 2010:88).

Yet, it was also realized that India suffered from missile inaccuracy because India did not possess the precision required of these missiles in hitting target areas; no plans existed as to how India could develop and integrate this technology into a nuclear arsenal with a requisite command and control, reconnaissance, and warning systems to provide a reliable advantage in relation to China; and no timeline existed of how or by when a survival deterrent force vis-à-vis China could be achieved by India. Noting these deficiencies, Air Chief Marshal S.K. Mehra claimed that India should establish a Strategic Air Command that would develop doctrine and operational plans for managing advanced aircraft and prospective missile systems (Sidhu, 1997:332–333), and Minister of Defense, K.C. Pant asked the then Additional Secretary, P.R. Chari, to sketch the establishment and operationalization of a National Security Council for India's strategy planning system. However, the draft when completed saw "institutional and personal resistance" to surrender authority to a new body (Perkovich, 1999:297).

Conclusion

Following my premise that the Indian state's strategic cultural thinking projected through the ideological lenses of its foreign-policy making community, constructs shifting images of India's national identity, (in)security imaginary, and its nuclear policies, this chapter has documented how a series of domestic, regional, and global developments (between 1964 and November 1989) have interacted with the Indian state's security community's shifting ideological lenses to reconstruct and discursively articulate India's strategic culture from one of Prime Minister Shastri's defense-oriented pragmatic realism; to Prime Minister Indira Gandhi's militancy, aggressiveness, and a nuclear prowess; to Prime Minister Rajiv Gandhi's drive (after an initial waning) to expand India's nuclear and missiles arsenal. In doing so, the chapter has summarized how the contours of India's strategic cultural thinking over these years focusing on a China-centric insecurity under the Shatri years, to a Pakistan-centric insecurity under Prime Minister Indira Gandhi and Rajiv Gandhi's years has also drawn from a consolidating sense of India's nuclear nationalism/nuclear apartheid to sustain a ideological and political space that has facilitated explicit calls from its security community to expand India's nuclear arsenal. Seen in the light of this progression, the period 1964 through November 1989 witnessed an overtly aggressive or expansionist transition of India's strategic cultural discourses—bringing in increments "… principles of realism and practicality to bear on … [India's] foreign policy and [nuclear] defense planning process" (Dixit, 2004:115).

Given this increasing aggressiveness in India's strategic thinking, Prime Minister Rajiv Gandhi if interested in testing India's nuclear weapons could have done so. In fact, Pakistani insecurities had provided the Rajiv administration ample reasons for doing nuclear. But, under his strategic thinking (as was also evidenced in the prime minister's between these years), this alternative was unlikely to be pursued by the state which also by 1989 did not have a substantially identifiable pro-bomb lobby in the government (barring some defense/strategic analysts cry for nuclear weapons) (Bobb and Singh, 1987:73). Instead, much like India's traditional nuclear ambiguity, the Indian government and its nuclear scientists during this phase, through strategic maneuvers, reconciled their strains in officially denying India's possession of a nuclear weapons program while advancing its technological know-how and preparedness to retain the nuclear option in case needed to go nuclear. However, the coming of a (non-Congress) government to power in the 1989 elections in a post-Cold War period saw a much aggressive path in India's open quest for nuclear weapons.

Notes

1. As has been substantiated by India's prominent defense analyst K. Subrahmanyam (in an article published in 1977 in *The Times of India*), the United States was aware of Pakistan's intended operations in the state of Jammu and Kashmir that lead to the 1965 war; that the American supplied Patton tanks to Pakistan (as part of their defense assistance) were used by Pakistan against India in the war; and despite being aware

of these developments, did not inform New Delhi about possible Pakistani intentions of deploying American Patton tanks against the Indian state (Dixit, 2004:113).

2. These conditions were: the nuclear powers must undertake not to transfer nuclear weapons or nuclear weapons technology to others; agree not to use nuclear weapons against countries which do not possess them; the United Nations must safeguard the security of countries which may be threatened by nuclear weapons states; progress toward disarmament, including a comprehensive test ban treaty, a complete freeze on the production of nuclear weapons and means of delivery, and substantial reduction in the existing stocks of nuclear weapons; and finally, a treaty committing non-nuclear powers not to acquire or manufacture nuclear weapons (Chakrvarthy, 1965:142–151).

3. The pro-Soviet faction of the Communist Party castigated the Chinese nuclear test and acclaimed the Indian government's restraint for not being driven toward the development of nuclear weapons, and for its overall stance for disarmament; while, the pro-China faction believed that China's nuclear test was meant to enhance its capability against the US imperialism and the Soviet social imperialism, and not against India (Shah, 1968:166–167; 167–169).

4. This is because many bomb advocates did not want to be counted on the side of the Jana Sangh who they considered communal (Malhotra, 2012). Another tacit source of support to the PM's no nuclear policy came from the two communist parties (although separated) who were reluctant to see the country go nuclear, especially the CPM (generally considered pro-China as against the pro-Moscow CPI).

5. The NPT was a two-way street: As per Articles I, II, and II of the treaty, the NWS agreed not to transfer nuclear weapons or other nuclear explosive devices technology to other states; to cap, reduce, and ultimately eliminate their nuclear weapons; and a commitment not to use or threaten to use their nuclear weapons against any NNWS. In turn, the NNWS, in foregoing their sovereign rights to have nuclear weapons, agreed not to manufacture or acquire nuclear weapons (for foregoing which the NNWS were offered access to civilian nuclear technology by the NWS for generation of nuclear energy). To determine the guidelines for the export of civilian nuclear technology to the NNWS, the Zangger Committee was subsequently created (in the 1970s), out of which later, developed the Nuclear Suppliers Group (1974), to coordinate and control by consensus the export of nuclear technology to states that were not signatories to the NPT (Kamath, 2009:30).

6. Although the carrier group was deployed "ostensibly for the evacuation of Americans [in Pakistan]" (Kissinger, 1979: 905), India perceived the "… *USS Enterprise* … with nuclear weapons on board, a helicopter carrier, [and] a missile destroyer …" as a task force "shrouded in mystery [whose] intent was far from friendly" (Cheema, 2010:134).

7. Prime Minister Gandhi apparently was not aware of these developments (given that these projects did not depend on governmental funding) but in her April 24, 1968, statement to the Lok Sabha made her case against India's nuclear power by saying that "Such a course … would not strengthen India's national security" (Jain, 1974, volume 2:201–202).

8. The Symington Amendment was prompted by the fact that the US-supplied heavy water was used by India in the CIRUS reactor that produced the plutonium for India's 1974 test.

9. The Nuclear Non-Proliferation Act, which was greatly prompted by India's PNE, mandated that the US not export any sensitive nuclear technology to any country that does not maintain IAEA safeguards on all its peaceful nuclear activities.

10. India and the US tried to bridge their nuclear differences over the issue of IAEA safeguards on India's nuclear programs; President Carter traveled to India in January 1978 (and not in Pakistan), and highlighted his commitments to human rights and America's respect for India's democracy. This saw the "Carter-Desai" Delhi Declaration reaffirming India–US commitment to democracy, national sovereignty, and a more equitable international economic order. The Indian public, including members of the Janata government, India's Foreign Minister, A.B. Vajpayee, and India's Finance Minister, H.M. Patel, responded to these positive US overtures. Shortly after Carter's visit, the United States increased bilateral aid to India suspended since the 1971 India–Pak war.

11. The Indira Doctrine reflected the traditional Indian conception of the subcontinent as a cultural and geographic unity which would not tolerate the intervention of any external power in the region.

12. India's diplomatic efforts with Pakistan to renounce aggression and promote friendship included the following: In April 1980, Prime Minister Gandhi sent a Special Envoy to Pakistan conveying her desires to President Zia to improve relations; this was reciprocated by the coming of Pakistan's top foreign advisor, Agha Shahi, to India; in June 1980, India's Foreign Minister, Narasimha Rao, traveled to Pakistan emphasizing that India's nuclear policy was only for peaceful purposes; in June 1982, Pakistan–India further conversed on nonaggression; on November 1, 1982, President Zia and Prime Minister Gandhi held their first bilateral meeting in New Delhi resulting in the creation of a joint commission to such further dialogue; and there also followed cultural exchange trips between India and Pakistan (such as Indian and Pakistan cricket and hockey exchange teams).

13. The Brasstacks crisis originated in ambitious plans of the Indian military's exercise in the subcontinent about which India had failed to inform Pakistan lead to a massive defensive reaction from Pakistan. For details, see Bajpai et al. (1995).

5

At the Nuclear Edge: 1991–1998

In keeping with my research puzzle that there exists a discursive linkage between India's strategic culture, (in)security imaginary, and its nuclear policy options/choices, this chapter explores how the discursive reconstruction of strategic culture and security imaginary among India's security community defined the emergence of India's nuclear policy options and choices between 1991 and March 1998 (i.e., since the end of the Cold War until the BJP coming into power). In keeping with my constructivist premise of international relations (IR) that the discursive construction of India's strategic culture rendered possible through the ideological interpretations and meaning-producing discourses of its foreign policy-making community has created an ideological and political space, within which are constructed and articulated the multiple contours of India's identity, (in)security, and its nuclear policy options/choices, this chapter explores how India's strategic cultural thinking during this time frame transitioned from its existing state of militarization, to further nuclear aggressiveness, to the edge of a potential nuclear-testing agenda by the end of March 1998. While several factors, namely the collapse of the Cold War, India's geo-political, economic, domestic, and a scientific and bureaucratic momentum, shaped the transitions of India's strategic culture, (in)security imaginary, and its nuclear trajectory during this period, India throughout this timeframe under its principled norm of Gandhian nonviolence and some of the US' nonproliferation pressure, sustained an ambivalent nuclear policy in its national security context.

This chapter addresses the following "how-possible" questions: First, how did the Indian state's strategic cultural thinking between 1991 and March 1998, projected through the ideological lenses of its security community, interpret and make sense of India's regional and IR? Second, how did the Indian state's strategic cultural thinking during this frame construct shifting images of (and relationships between) India's national identity, insecurities, and its (in)security imaginary? Finally, how did these reconstructions of India's strategic cultural thinking and (in)security imaginaries create an ideological and political space within which were forged and articulated India's nuclear policy options/choices? In addressing each how-possible question, my aim is to show how discourses as meaning-producing tools have constructed and sustained a mutually constituted relationship between India's strategic cultural thinking, (in)security imaginary, and its nuclear policies.

Situating India's National Security and Neoliberal Identity in a Post-Cold War Era

India's post-Cold War nuclear politics opened in the 1990s with domestic, political, communal, and economic turbulence (Weinraub, 1991; Aiyar, 1991; *The Financial Times*, 2001), also witnessing for the first time since its independence four non-Congress Party governments led by prime ministers V.P. Singh, Chandra Shekhar, Deva Gowda, and I.K. Gujral, and only one Congress Party government led by P.V. Narasimha Rao.[1] In this post-Cold War era, India witnessed significant shifts in its international/regional geo-strategic politics as well as a rethinking of its own domestic political culture in terms of its foreign policy approach with the United States, its economic liberalization agenda, and its own national security agenda in the changing context of its pro-US strategic culture (Bajpai, 2002). Although persisting influence of nonalignment and anti-US sentiments from the left-wing prevented a major policy shift for the Indian government, the post-Cold War period made the Indian political leadership realize that the old shibboleths of nonalignment need to be discarded. Accordingly, three major shifts became evident in India's strategic rethinking: First, with the fall of the Soviet Union and considering the US ascension as the leading global power after Cold War, it became a strategic requirement for India to coexist with the United States, also reciprocated by the latter, that further consolidated the pro-US shift in India's strategic thinking that had already begun under Prime Minister Rajiv Gandhi; second, regionally, India saw its future tied more closely with economically booming Asian states, such as South Korea, Malaysia, Singapore—a cognition that manifested itself through a pro-liberalizing economic drive within India; and third, the imperative to stabilize relations with its immediate neighbors China (because China could now be dealt with free from Cold War constraints) and Pakistan (with expectedly a declining Pakistani significance to the United States).

Yet, in this transitioning post-Cold War strategic rethinking of the Indian state, the following proliferation-related tensions/insecurities irked India's relations vis-à-vis the United States, China, and Pakistan: India's rising nuclear trends that agonized the United States and gave rise to the US perceptions of India as a "rogue" state; the US' emerging norms of nonproliferation centering amongst others on the Comprehensive Test Ban Treaty (CTBT); the United States' passing the Hank Brown amendment (1995) resuming military aid to Pakistan (despite the fact that the collapse of Cold War had significantly reduced the strategic significance of Pakistan to the United States); China not putting its nuclear cards on the table nor guaranteeing to stop the transfer of nuclear technology to Pakistan that were occurring with the US acquiescence; an increasingly emboldened nuclear Pakistan throughout the 1990s under nuclear patrons like China and the United States; and, finally, India's own scientific and bureaucratic momentum demanding an open nuclear deterrent for India. In fact, by mid-1990s, India's (in)security imaginary assumed a trio of United States, China, and Pakistan thwarting India's security concerns. I address below these dynamics of India's (in)securities stemming from the United States as a global power-player in India's international affairs.

Interpreting India's International Relations

President Yeltsin's claim in January 1992 that Russia and the United States were no longer potential enemies and their nuclear weapons would no longer aim each other, made the United States in 1994 to rethink its nuclear posture that potentially sought to remove an impediment in Indo-US affairs (Kamath, 2009:112). This rethinking of the super powers coincided with the lessening of nonalignment in India's strategic thinking; its policy makers' pragmatic realization to reevaluate India's relations with the United States on the basis of India's current national interest rather than issues of Cold War, and the need to engage the United States for economic, military, and foreign policy reasons to suit the strategic security imperatives of a post-Cold War India (Dubey, 1993:124). However, as Malik (2010:141) analyzes, the problem lay in "excessive expectations" of the Indian government that the end of the Cold War would automatically bury old antagonisms between India and the United States, allowing the United States to seize the promise of the Indian market and increase economic ties with India. Accordingly, while one notices progressing Indo-American security cooperation in the production, design, and purchase of India's Light Combat Aircrafts, XMP-24 computers, general electric 404 jet engines, and other forms of joint naval and military exercises—a number of political and human rights issues, proliferation control issues, and the emptiness of the United States' declared nuclear posture (Dubey, 1993; Gupta, 1993:38; Moore and Anderson, 1994; Dixit, 1996), which I detail below, irked post–Cold War relations between the United States and India.

In the context of the Warsaw Guidelines (1992) and the January 1992 Bush–Rao meeting on regional nuclear restrains, India's efforts in acquiring nuclear and ballistic missiles capabilities through talks of purchasing highly advanced cryogenic rocket engines from Russia and efforts by the Department of Research and Defense Organization (DRDO) to advance variants of its short, medium, intercontinental range and third-generation missiles as a part of its Integrated Guided Missile Development Program continued to alarm the United States. Sanctions that followed on India by the United States and the Nuclear Supplier Group were perceived by India as "colonial restrictions" on the country's efforts to advance its space technology in the current satellite age (Perkovich, 1999:328; Malik, 2010).[2] Neither did India–US talks in June 1992 on nonproliferation yield results, where the Bush administration during the closing days of his final term requested India to consider agreements not to test nuclear weapons and to cease production of fissile materials for weapons purposes, while itself not contemplating the CTBT as a plausible agenda for global disarmament (Weiss, 1983). However, despite existing nonproliferation issues, the Bush administration, and thereafter under President Clinton, recognizing India as a rising power rationalized building a broader and positive relationship with India beyond proliferation.

United States' approach toward India under President Clinton occurred in the context of the United States' efforts at introducing a Fissile Material Cut-Off Treaty at the UN General Assembly (on September 27, 1993);[3] the United States Nuclear Posture Review (September 1993); the Glenn Amendment Act of 1994 (stipulating greater proliferation restrictions on India and Pakistan); and the indefinite renewal of the NPT in 1995 leading to the CTBT agenda. These furthered proliferation-related irks/insecurities in Indo-US affairs. The major starting point of these contentions was the United States' Nuclear Posture Review under the then US Secretary of Defense, Les Aspin, which initially seeking to limit the role of nuclear weapons in the US national security agenda (by focusing on its deterrent and not war fighting capabilities) ended up maintaining by 1996 (owing to resistance from segments of the US military and its civil-defense bureaucracy) an aggressive force posture that prevailed during the H. Bush administration (Kamath, 2009:116–117).[4] This posture, which did not foreclose any options of reviving what was listed for reduction or elimination of its stockpiled strategic or nonstrategic nuclear weapons, was confirmed in April 1996 by the US' Secretary of Defense, William Perry, in that the United States "would not forswear the possibility" of using nuclear weapons either (ibid.:117).[5] The NPR's aggressive intent was coupled with the United States' indefinite renewal of the Nuclear Non-Proliferation Treaty (NPT) whose "Principles and Objectives for Nuclear Non-Proliferation and Disarmament" recommended the completion by 1996 a Comprehensive Test Ban Treaty.[6]

India joined the United States in cosponsoring the introduction of the CTBT in the UN General Assembly in 1993 making clear its expectations that the CTBT and the Commission of Disarmament address issues of horizontal and vertical proliferation, and that the CTBT be a comprehensive global treaty for disarmament (Ghose, 1997). Problems that arose at the early stages of negotiations on the scope and verification of the treaty, caused further concerns for India when the United States supported by 170 countries managed to get the NPT renewed indefinitely in May 1995; incorporated the entry-into-force clause in the treaty; and China despite signing the treaty retained its rights of low-yield testing. Furthermore, the CTBT's entry-into-force clause not only required that India become a signatory of the treaty before it could come into force but also a provision that those who ratified the treaty could by consensus decide what measures they could take to accelerate the ratification process. For India, it represented an "external legitimization of nuclear weapons and the system of nuclear apartheid" (Paddock, 2009:37; Kamath, 2009:36). After unsuccessful negotiations with delegates of NWS between January and May 1996 reiterating that the treaty articulate commitments by NWS to eliminate in a reasonable span their nuclear arsenal and ban explosive testing for upgrading existing nuclear weapons, India in June 1996 withdrew its support of the CTBT.[7]

A few things need to be noted here about the United States' stance vis-à-vis the CTBT and some of its nonproliferation behavior toward Pakistan and China: First, the United States in 1996 signed but did not ratify the CTBT; second, having signed the treaty the Clinton administration "literally brought support of US nuclear scientists" by allocating an annual budget of $4.6 billion for conducting subcritical tests "to keep nuclear arsenals in perfect usable conditions" (Kamath, 2009:37); and third, in July 1997, conducted a subcritical nuclear weapon test at the Nevada test site. It earned India's indignation calling the CTBT a "charade," allowing the nuclear weapon states (NWS) to make "more sophisticated weapons" (Perkovich, 1999:398). In addition, what also caused India's insecurities from the United States was that while pursuing nonproliferation pressures on India, the United States in October 1993 lifted sanctions that it had imposed on China for the supply of M-11 missile-related technology to Pakistan and through the Brown Amendment in 1995 lifted restrictions on the US arms sales to Pakistan. Although the United States' lifting of sanctions on China came in return for Beijing's promise not to transfer further missile-related technology to Pakistan, India interpreted this act as another instance of American commercial interests in China (also evidenced in the Clinton administration's determination to renew Most Favored Nation trade status to China despite China's ongoing human rights violations) (Goshko, 1994). These developments constructed India's (in)security imaginary (which I address later) advocating a more muscular call for India's nuclear weapons program.

In this hypocritical context, where the United States was retaining its nuclear arsenal, trying to curb proliferation amongst nonnuclear weapons states and turning a blind-eye toward China's abetting of a nuclearizing Pakistan that the Clinton administration redefined the US' policy toward South Asia. This redefinition occurred simultaneously in the context of an emerging "rogue" discourse within the US Department of Defense that after Cold War third world countries' possession of alleged nuclear technology, emerging localized conflicts in the third world, and growing Islamic religious fundamentalism constituted threats to America (Klare, 1995; Tanter, 1998). With testimonies before the Congress that "[t]he arms race between India and Pakistan poses perhaps the most probable prospect for future use of weapons of mass destruction including nuclear weapons," the Clinton administration in April 1993 thus summarized its policy toward South Asia: "Our objective is first to cap, then over time reduce, and finally eliminate the possession of weapons of mass destruction and their means of delivery" (US State Department, 1993:2). Despite some domestic US concerns, the US official thinking "represented an emerging genuine acceptance among key government officials and nongovernmental experts that nuclear weapon capabilities would remain a part of South Asian reality for the foreseeable future" (Perkovich, 1999:335), and saw it as a US foreign policy imperative to engage the two countries to restrict an arms race in South Asia.

Thereafter, followed a number of exchange visits by India–US high-officials in April 1993, May 1994, January 1995, and in November, 1997, where Heads of both states conversed on areas of converging interests and declared mutual intentions to work for nonproliferation of weapons of mass destruction (Mohan, 2006).[8] Of these, Prime Minister Rao's visit to the United States in May 1994, despite occurring amidst domestic controversies and apprehensions within India, was a hit![9] Thereafter, India, under technocrats like Manmohan Singh, Montek Singh Ahluwalia, Ashok Desai, and Shankar Acharya, concentrated on economic liberalization; expressed interest in trade and investment with the United States with hopes of creating a pro-India business lobby in the United States (Burns, 1994); India's then Finance Minister, Manmohan Singh announced in the Parliament in July 1991 that "... the emergence of India as a major economic power in the world happens to be one such idea [of the state]" (Singh, 1991); and at a news conference on May 19, 1994, President

Clinton and Prime Minister Rao highlighted the opportunities of growing business and political ties between the United States and India. Rao also assured Clinton of India's support for a ban on nuclear weapons testing, fissile material production for weapons purposes, and an ultimate elimination of its nuclear weapons (Clinton, 1994).

In January 1995, another benchmark was created in Indo-US relations when the US Defense Secretary William Perry and India's Minister of State for Defense, Mallikarjun signed The Agreed Minutes of Defense Relations—an update of the 1984 Memorandum of Understanding—aiming at expanding Indo-US defense research and cooperation to meet requirements of the post-Cold War age, and sought to involve senior-level officials from the Office of the Secretary of Defense in the United States, the Indian Ministry of Defense, representatives from the US State Department, India's Ministry of External Affairs, and subsequently establish Joint Technical Groups and Defense Policy Groups, whose purpose, among others was to address post-Cold War security planning and policy perspectives of India and the United States. To this end, these groups would promote joint seminars, issue policy guidance, and address strategic issues in South Asia, including terrorism (Malik, 2006:84–85).

Yet, as Malik (2010:144) observes these gestures did not preclude the fact that "[US] pressure would continue" on India on the nonproliferation front—well evidenced through the Shanghai Initiative (1995), the proposed nine-nation conference, and continuing efforts to secure a commitment from India to support the CTBT (Ghose, 1997). This is because the Indian participants would not agree to endorse reciprocal unilateral Indo-Pak cessation of fissile material production if America did not strongly endorse the elimination of nuclear weapons (Perkovich, 1999:357). In addition, differences of perceptions on both sides occurred on the 1995 Minutes of Defense Relations as Perry held that this was simply an agreement to strengthen bilateral cooperation, particularly in the field of defense research and production and not to promote sale of arms or transfer of technology to India from the United States (Malik, 2006:85). These nonproliferation and technology-related tensions/insecurities felt by India vis-à-vis the United States continued to raise issues of international power imbalances, the lack of the principle of equity in implementing proliferation control measures, and the legacy of colonialism in Indo-US nuclear security affairs. However, despite these persisting tensions, the US officials encouraged their pro-India line of thinking (reciprocated by the Indian state), and despite India's rejection of the CTBT in 1996, saw through the US State Department, the US Bilateral Defense Policy Group (established in 1995), and a report by an Independent Task Force on South Asia (created in January 1997 by the Council on Foreign Relations) a positive approach toward the subcontinent. In fact, the Task Force recommending through its South Asia Policy that Washington engage India beyond proliferation issues led to joint military exercises, defense collaborations, and strategic dialogues between India and the United States (Chandran, 1996; *The Hindu*, 1996; Mohan, 1997a). These created a hybrid form of strategic thinking, discourse and an (in)security imaginary within the Indian state's official mindset vis-à-vis the United States—which I later address.

India's post-Cold War relations with Pakistan emerged in the context of President Bush's invoking the Pressler Amendment in October 1990 and cutting off all economic and military aid to Pakistan. While this potentially allayed India's nuclear insecurity from Pakistan, subsequent developments namely Indo-Pakistan crisis over Kashmir (in January–February 1991);[10] Prime Minister Bhutto's promise of a "thousand year war" with India in support of the militants in Pakistan-occupied Kashmir (Hersch, 1993:306–307; Hagerty, 1995/1996:98); Pakistan's Foreign Secretary, Shaharyar Khan's declaration in Washington in 1992 that Pakistan has assembled a nuclear device (Coll, 1992:A23); and Dr A.Q. Khan's proclamation that "Pakistan was not going to abandon its growing reliance on nuclear deterrence" caused concern to India (Perkovich, 1999:324). It gave rise to a series of self-defensive discourses within India's strategic community under the V.P. Singh government, revealing a robust nuclear call for the state (which I will elaborate later).

Furthermore, reports emerged that Pakistan by mid-1990s under the Nawaz Sharif government was investing in producing solid-motor and liquid-engine ballistic missiles programs with assistance from China and North Korea; was pursuing the development of the hatf I and hatf II missiles both of which became operational in mid-1990s; and was planning to further upgrade them to the hatf III and IV missiles. Reportedly, both hatf's occurred with China's aid and resembles China's M-series missiles and all versions of the hatf's were capable of delivering conventional high-explosive warheads (Dhanda, 2010:155, 160, 162).

Moreover, it was believed that in contrast to India, Pakistan's military had achieved or was close to achieving operational capability in mounting nuclear warheads on its ballistic missile fleet (Dhanda, 2010:155), and reports by the US Central Intelligence Agency by the early 1990s documented the active cooperation between China and Pakistan and sales of Chinese M11 ballistic missiles to Pakistan (Chengappa, 1994c:54; Mattoo, 2000:23). Although the Clinton administration's passing of the Glenn Amendment Act in 1994 stipulated greater proliferation restrictions on Pakistan, the Hank Brown Amendment of 1995 partially relieving Pakistan from such sanctions authorized the release of the hitherto withheld 28 F-16 fighters and other defense equipment to Pakistan (Ministry of Defense, 1996–1997). These developments, occurring amidst a remark by the then opposition leader, Nawaz Sharif, in August 23, 1994, that "… Pakistan possesses [the] atomic bomb," and along with it a determination to support Kashmiris of Azad Kashmir for their self-determination irked India (Perkovich, 1999:348–349).

Neither did India–Pakistan's diplomatic negotiations between 1990 and 1997 involving high profile exchanges of Prime Minister's Chandra Shekhar, Nawaz Sharif, Narasimha Rao, I.K. Gujral, and their Foreign Secretaries Shahryar Khan, Salman Haider, Shamshad Ahmad, and Lt. General Satish Nambiar, or, the Gujral Doctrine, help improve India-Pak bilateral ties (Phadnis, 1997; Mahmud, 1997; Manchandani, 1997; Katyal, 1997).[11] Things got further erratic in June 1997, when controversies about India deploying Prithvi missiles to a military site in Jalandhar, eighty miles away from Lahore was interpreted by Pakistan as a "provocative act," and was followed by Dr A.Q. Khan's comment that "by the grace of God, Pakistan has proper and satisfactory arrangements to counter any enemy attack" (Perkovich, 1999:396). Despite some dialogue between India and Pakistan from June and September 1997, the above-mentioned developments provided ample space to India's parliamentarians notably from the BJP to call for a renewed commitment to India's missile programs (Cherian, 1995:329). It put pressure on Prime Minister Gujral to strike a more robust approach in its nuclear and missile development policies (Cherian, 1995).

Following the Cold War, China continued to remain a nuclear threat to India. Despite China's announcement in August 1991 that it would sign the NPT, India's insecurity from China emerged in the light of

China's supply of M-11 missiles to Pakistan, China's bourgeoning nuclear modernization efforts, and a series of nuclear tests through the 1990s. These tests, conducted arguably by taking advantage of the legal space offered in the interim while the CTBT negotiations were being finalized, included a one-megaton nuclear weapons test in May 1992 (occurring more problematically while the Indian President, R. Venkataraman was conducting his first-ever Indian Presidential visit to China); another test in May 1995 (just days before the indefinite extension of the NPT); and another in June 1996 (just after China agreed at the Geneva conventions to drop its insistence on retaining the right to conduct peaceful nuclear explosions under a test ban treaty) (Mohan, 1996a).

However, these tests occurred simultaneously with the Indian and Chinese government's diplomatic interactions between 1991 and 1997 marking the Chinese Premier Li Peng's December 1991 visit to India, Prime Minister Rao's September 1993 visit to China, President Jiang Zemin's November 1996 visit to India, and, other high-level exchanges in February 1994, March 1995, August 1995. During these exchanges, the two sides agreed to institutionalize mechanisms for defusing tension along the border, sought to reduce troops and respect ceasefire lines along their disputed border, to further the withdrawal of forces, and enhance confidence building along their line of Actual Control (Mohan, 1996b). Significant in the context of President Jiang Zemin's 1996 visit was his simultaneous visit to Pakistan—delivering a diplomatically veiled blow to the latter in terms of Kashmir—by calling India and Pakistan to negotiate a settlement on Kashmir. It signified that for China, Kashmir was no longer an international issue requiring international mediation (as Pakistan had desired). China's pro-India gesture, which, boded well with the Indian Foreign Minister I.K. Gujral's Gujral Doctrine, also manifested Beijing's growing recognition of India relative to Pakistan.[12] Furthermore, throughout its nuclear tests, China's commitment to NFU did not change and was reaffirmed on April 5, 1995; China went to great lengths in explaining that its May 1992 tests that coincided with the Indian President's visit was not intended to offend India; China signed the CTBT; and following France's refusal to continue as a supplier of spent fuel to the Tarapur nuclear plant, stepped in as a substitute to supply low-enriched uranium to the plant. Many analysts of India–China nuclear relations see the latter development as a positive one wherein since 1995 China has remained a supplier of low-enriched uranium to the plant.

Yet, these did not allay India's concerns given that India did not obtain any Chinese assurance that it would stop assisting Pakistan's nuclear and missile development program (Chari, 1995; Kamath, 2009:114). While India's defense/security analysts like Brahma Chellaney (1996a) bristled about China's haughtiness, others like Mohan (1996b) and India's defense and foreign policy sectors, possibly owing to the ongoing diplomatic negotiations, chose to mute their criticism of an expanding nuclear China (although exceptions came from K. Subrahmanyam (1996a, 1996b) urging that India end its "vague" nuclear option policy by declaring itself "as an independent global player with a nuclear deterrent" against China. In fact, the Chinese issue, if presented in the Indian media, was in terms of Pakistan's acquisition of missiles and nuclear technology rather than China's breech of the provisions of the MTCR and the NPT. Although the V.P. Singh government (December 1989–November 1990) co-opted some of India's nuclear hawks such as K. Subrahmanyam, General Sundarji, Dr V.S. Arunachalam, and Dr R. Chidambaram in a commission to look into the Chinese nuclear issue, with the fall of the Singh government this group's existence was short-lived (Subrahmanyam, 2000). Thus, no "intolerable pressure" was imposed on the Indian government to "exercise the [nuclear] option" on grounds of China (Chari, 1995:210). However, later in the 1990s, the Chinese nuclear issue drew attention for the Indian government when the Indian Ministry of Defense's Annual Report (April 1997) expressed concerns over China's recent modernization of its nuclear and missile capabilities and its logistical improvements along the India–China border. Yet, in the then ideological mindset of the Indian state under Prime Minister Gujral, the Chinese nuclear threat was couched under the perceived threat stemming from the US-led proliferation control agenda. As claimed by an Indian participant, "Whether our relations improve with China or not is irrelevant, the issue will remain that we are not going to agree to any discriminatory agreement. If several parties are talking and an agreement [needs to be] reached, it should apply to all parties [including China]" (Haniffa, 1993).

It is within these nuclear insecurity concerns stemming from India's regional and international factors and unequal nuclear control agreements, that demands arose among critics of the Indian government who demanded, with variations (to be discussed below), an explicit nuclear testing option for India. It offered a political and ideological space that served to reconstruct along more noticeably robust lines the strategic cultural thinking and the (in)security imaginaries of post-Cold War India.

Constructing Strategic Culture and (In)Security Imaginary

The Pakistani Prime Minister Bhutto's call for a "thousand year war" in March 1990 and rumors in December 1989/January 1990 that Pakistan could detonate a nuclear device (as discussed above) served as the starting point after the Cold War in reconstructing India's strategic rethinking and (in)security imaginaries along more robust, aggressive, pro-nuclear lines. This call however was articulated explicitly not from the Indian government per se but from India's defense community, nuclear scientists, political analysts, and oppositional parties—to be termed as the nuclear hawks of India's security community (Bajpai, 1999).[13] The hawks in their three subdivisions and relying on the "stability through deterrence" logic raised the specter of a nuclear bogey in India (Sundarji, 1990a, 1990b, 1993; Chengappa, 1994a; Singh, 1999; Karnad, 1999; Ramanna, 2003).[14] This hawkish bogey was also joined by India's then opposition members Rajiv Gandhi and S. Krishna Kumar from the Congress and Jaswant Singh from the BJP, who, drawing connections between the supposedly Pakistani-backed insurgencies raging in Kashmir and Punjab, called on the government to address "major change [in] the Indo-Pak nuclear debate" (Malik, 2010:157). Kumar from the Congress remarked "if they [Pakistan] have a nuclear device we shall not hesitate to acquire such a capability and use it ...," and Jaswant Singh called on the government to address the Indo-Pak nuclear debate (ibid.).

India, then under the coalition-led government, headed by Janata Dal leader V.P. Singh (December 1989–November 1990) took an ambiguous stand on the nuclear issue: the prime minister's reasons were financial (India preparing to go to the World Bank for emergency funding); political disturbances in Punjab and Kashmir; and finally, that Pakistan had not yet acquired the bomb (BBC, 2007). Yet, dissatisfied with the "defenselessness" of India's strategic culture, the prime minister also wielded to demands of the strategic community by asking Indians to be "psychologically prepared" for war, and that "if we are confronted with a nuclear threat, I think we will have to take a second look at our policy that we have today. I think we will have no option but to match it ..." (Malik, 2010:157). Thus, Prime Minister Singh called a Commission to look into the nuclear issues; proposed the creation of a National Security Council that would facilitate coordination amongst various ministries and military services to increase India's strategic expertise and clarity in the nuclear policy–making area; and appointed prominent pro-nuclear members such as Raja Ramanna as India's Minister of State for Defense, P.K. Iyengar as the Chair of the AEC, Arunachalam as the Head of the DRDO, and himself held the Defense portfolio—which for many analysts, signified the prime minister's intentions of taking defense issues seriously (Subrahmanyam, 2000). These lines of strategic rethinking were also echoed by then Minister of State for Defense, Raja Ramanna, on May 17, 1990, that India took very seriously the consequence of nuclear fallout and therefore hoped that "good sense would prevail" in Pakistan. However, keeping with India's tribute to nuclear restraint he also added if counseling of restraint went unheeded "we would rise to the occasion" (Subrahmanyam, 1993:182–183).

Under India's next Prime Minister, P.V. Narasimha Rao (June 21, 1991 to May 16, 1996) India's nuclear hawks spanning members of the government, the opposition (namely the BJP), the military, nuclear scientists, and defense/security analysts of the IDSA became further robust. As discussed earlier, this was mainly because of harsh nuclear-centric discourses from Pakistani scientist A.Q. Khan, Pakistani Foreign Secretary Shahryar Khan, and the then Pakistani opposition leader, Nawaz Sharif (Gupta, 1994:6, 26). Despite Rao's focus on India's economic liberalization, its related national defense budget reduction calculus, and his government's stand toward a firmly scheduled, time-bound, universal and nondiscriminatory approach to nuclear disarmament, Indian's nuclear hawks could not resist the space provided by Pakistan's growing nuclear momentum to press the Rao government for a tougher reaction to Pakistan (Narula, 1996a, 1996b). Thus, while the prime minister reiterated before the Army Commanders Conference at New Delhi (April 13, 1994) that India would reject any restrictions on its nuclear option; thereafter on May 3, 1994 reaffirmed that "India would not accept any regional NPT arrangement," and nor were there "any word[s] about capping" (Perkovich, 1999:345–346); India's then Minister of External Affairs Pranab Mukherjee in a speech to the UN General Assembly (1995) linked the CTBT to definite movement toward nuclear disarmament (Narula, 1996a, 1996b); and the opposition party in the Parliament, the BJP, stated that "India must waste no time to go nuclear" (Coll, 1992:A23). Notably, the BJP by then had already created Hindu–Islamic fundamentalist uproars in India over the Ram Janambhoomi Babri Masjid upheaval and had gained momentum in national politics for its more muscular call for nuclear nationalism. The party's then Vice-President, Krishna Lal Sharma simultaneously urged that India acquire nuclear weapons capability to match Pakistan (Perkovich, 1999:324). However, the BJP simultaneously saw merits in the imperatives of concurrent international political economy to continue cooperating with the United States to negotiate global bans on nuclear weapons testing (Goradia, 1991).

At this point, views of members of India's defense community and think-tanks who were traditionally muted became increasingly vocal as important inputs into the government's nuclear security matters (Subrahmanyam, 2005). Excluding few defense community members, such as Lt. General V.R. Raghavan who argued that nuclear arsenal cannot replace the conventional requirements of the Indian military (Raghavan, 1996:26–27), the hawks (responding to dual fears of the Rao government's repercussions of reducing defense budgets and growing the US nonproliferation pressures on the Rao government) took the opportunity to turn the government's rationale of a restrained defense budget to support a nuclear weapons program. Drawing connections between troop reductions, nuclear armament, and Indian security—prominent hawks from India's strategic community such as General Sundarji (Rai, 1994:27), Jasjit Singh (Singh, 1992), Brigadier Vijai Rai (Nair, 1992), and K. Subrahmanyam (2005) generally pointed out that a credible nuclear force was the most strategic option for India before its reducing defense budget (Singh, 1992–1993:33). General Sundarji argued that a nuclear deterrence would allow both India and Pakistan to reduce conventional forces in response to their current economic constraints (Rai, 1994:27); Jasjit Singh (from the of the IDSA) suggested a credible nuclear force as the most strategic option for India before its reducing defense budget (Singh, 1992–1993:33); Brigadier Vijai Rai (retd), based on estimated costs, saw nuclear weapons for India necessary and afford-able given that India already had much of this nuclear infrastructure in place (Nair, 1992); and K. Subrahmanyam (2005) argued that cuts in conventional weapons could be balanced by a minimum deterrence arse-nal not to match China and Pakistan's nuclear capabilities but to ration-alize India's security strategy in an era of resource constraints. To these cost-effective arguments, Chief of Army Staff, General B.C. Joshi, added a military angle noting a revitalized military as offering India a "decisive edge against Pakistan" (Gupta, 1993:38; Sandhu, 1993:50–51). Ideas of India's "self-reliance, excellence, and national honor" were also raised by members of India's nuclear science community such as R. Chidambaram (from the AEC), A.P.J. Abdul Kalam (from the DRDO), and P.K. Iyen-gar (from the AEC) who made "technological cases" for breaking India's nuclear restraint (Iyengar and Balakrishnan, 1991:80, 82, 85).

Although these strategic pro-nuclear voices and signs of impending Pakistani nuclear developments compelled the Rao government to reas-sure the public that "India's reaction would be to make Islamabad bear the burden of suffering for generations," implying nuclear retaliation by India, it was soon followed by another observation that India did not want to "go nuclear" and was "firm in [its] resolve not to manufacture nuclear weapons" (Perkovich, 1999:326–27). Likewise, the Minister of State for External Affairs, Salman Khursheed, elaborated before the opposition demand that "[if] the safety and security of the nation require deployment of conventional and nonconventional weapons on the bor-der, the government will not hesitate to do so" (Gupta, 1994:28), but simultaneously clarified that "the strengths of India lies on morality and not on weapons" (Chari, 1995:90). While analysts agree that the govern-ment officials' veiled submission of India's nuclear weapons program sig-nified that India's nuclear discourse at the governmental level had moved forward in the directions of a more muscular policy yet the robustness of this pro-nuclear discourse did not gain momentum as the Rao govern-ment "quietly meeting US objections" postponed a scheduled test launch of the Prithvi missile weeks before his Washington visit in May 1994 (Chengappa, 2000:45). At this point, the BJP's hawkish thinking once again critiqued the government for "giving up the nuclear option by suc-cumbing to US pressure," with the party leader, Vajpayee, declaring that his party unlike the government would make nuclear weapons if it came to power (Talwar, 1995:9).

Possible reasons why Rao recognizing India's impending nuclear inse-curities chose to mute issues of India's nuclear policy are as follows: First, Rao's focus on regenerating/liberalizing Indian economy with the US assis-tance that necessitated curtailing government expenses including defense budget; second, President Clinton's South Asia policy toward India that rationalized building a positive relationship with India; and third, a cau-tious and pragmatic willingness among Indian officials to reciprocate with the United States in terms of its South Asia policy (despite realizing that beneath this new policy was the foundation for Washington's new non-proliferation policy of ultimately achieving incremental change in India's nuclear policy) (Chengappa, 1994c). To this extent, Rao noted that, "the United States will have to be courted … [and] this friendship will neither be easy nor without cost" (Gupta and Sidhu, 1992:34, 38), and in a joint statement with President Clinton in 1994 supported Indo-US efforts toward "nonproliferation of weapons of mass destruction, their means of delivery, and toward their progressive reduction with the goal of elimination of such weapons" (Paddock, 2009:8–9). The BJP's strategic thinking, otherwise critical of the Rao government's nuclear ambivalence by succumbing to the US pressure, shared the government's view that nonalignment was a dead dogma for India; economics was key to India's destiny; and India should promote international trade and cultivate the several big powers of the new multipolar world (Talwar, 1995:9). Yet, these positive developments, which showed changing strategic cultural reorientations of both India and the United States toward each other occurred amidst nonproliferation contentions (as discussed earlier) and worked in ways that reconstructed India's neoliberally grounded/pro-US strategic thinking but simultaneously consolidated, more defiantly, along lines of anti-Western nuclear racism the (in)security imaginary of India.

The Western/racial focus of India's strategic thinking and (in)security imaginary along with the consolidation of its sense of nuclear nationalism centered around negotiations of the CTBT. Following the adoption of the Principles and Objectives for Nuclear Non-Proliferation and Disarmament in the NPT Review conference of May 1995 and the treaty's "entry-into-force" clause, India's anti-Western discourse against the CTBT was leveled on three grounds: First, the principle of inequality underpinning the treaty's content (language) and intent (evidenced in The Principles and Objectives section) in that it did not bind the nuclear weapon states in a timely commitment toward disarmament the way that the nonnuclear weapon states (NNWS) were bound (Paddock, 2009:30); second, the implications of the treaty if India signed it as relating to the security environment in South Asia; and finally, the prevailing dimensions of Western nuclear hierarchy, consolidation of India's nuclear apartheid, and a strengthening of its postcolonial desire for nuclear power (Paddock, 2009:30; Malik, 2010). Speaking at the Conference on Disarmament in June 1994, India's representative Arundhati Ghose laid down "obligations for all states" toward the treaty, and in the Disarmament Commission in May 1995, urged placing the CTBT in a time-bound program and as a multilaterally negotiated treaty to give effect to the commitment (Paddock, 2009:29, 32). India's apprehension that the treaty was a means for the nuclear weapons states to draw the nonsignatories like India into the NPT, while allowing the continuing expansion and refinement of their own existing nuclear arsenals, was justified when France and China resumed their nuclear testing within weeks of the conclusion of the NPT Review Conference. As the official spokesperson of India's Ministry of External Affairs stated, the fact that "these steps are taken by States which are parties to the NPT, soon after its indefinite extension, highlights the inherent defects of the Treaty" (ibid.: 31).

In terms of India's second line of argument relating to the security environment in South Asia, India's strategic concern was that India by signing the CTBT would forego the right to test nuclear devices and would have limited options as a nonnuclear weapons state in dealing with challenges from Pakistan's nascent nuclear program or its primary nuclear-armed adversary China (that under the treaty could still upgrade its nuclear weapons through subcritical experiments). Pointing to this disparity, an Indian representative to the United Nations General Assembly said in September 1995 that

> [We note that] nuclear weapon states have agreed to a CTBT only after acquiring the know how to develop and refine their nuclear arsenals without the needs of tests .... Developing new warheads or refining existing ones after [the] CTBT is in place, using innovative technologies, would be contrary to the spirit of [the] CTBT. (Paddock, 2009:12)

Finally, in terms of the prevailing dimensions of Western nuclear hierarchy and India's postcolonial desire for nuclear status, the CTBT's "entry-into-force" clause was perceived by India as a discriminatory replication of the imbalance inherent in the NPT and raised the specter of coercive colonial means and "unwelcome foreign duress" on India to enter the treaty so that it would come into force (Dixit, 1996:347; Malik, 2010:133). To India, these perceived discriminatory practices "smacked of duplicity," made India's nuclear nationalism in opposition to the CTBT more defiant (Malik, 2010:178). Serving as the Indian delegation to the UN General Assembly, Vajpayee (1993–1996) in October 1995 stated that the indefinite extension of the NPT had "legitimized for all time ... the division of the world into nuclear haves and have nots ..." (Ministry of External Affairs, 1997:78, 80); the then BJP party spokesperson, K.R. Malkani recalling India's anticolonial struggle and determination to resist the perceived colonialism of the nuclear age commented that "We should go nuclear and sign the NPT as a nuclear weapon state .... We don't want to be blackmailed and be treated as Oriental blackies. Nuclear weapons will give us prestige, power, [and] standing" (Gargan, 1993: A2); and K. Subrahmanyam revealing the "racial sensibility" at the heart of India's resistance to the CTBT, claimed that "the nonproliferation regime represented an attempt by White nations to keep dark-skinned people like Indians from acquiring nuclear weapons" (Perkovich, 1999: 332). However, Subrahmanyam (1995a) also argued that India would still support a global treaty banning fissile material production for weapons purposes only if it was tied to demands that the NWS reduce stocks of weapons, ban the use of nuclear weapons, and provide security assurances to NNWS.

The BJP prominently cashed on the nuclear issue in the election campaigns held in November 1995. Lamenting the lack of India's strategic planning institutions, doctrine, and a command, control, and information system, the BJP critiqued the Congress Party "as a weak, moralizing power, and deferential to outside pressures trying to retard India's nuclear prowess and national strength," and stated that "if elected, ... would act decisively and display India's strength and scientific prowess in ways that would force the international community to give the nation its due" (Perkovich, 1999:360–67). Furthermore, noting that the United States' nonproliferation agenda comes with the "baggage of ... colonialism," the party's Manifesto declared it would it would not agree to the CTBT unless it contained a simultaneous agreement on the time-bound elimination of nuclear weapons; that it would reevaluate India's nuclear policy if it came to power; and would expedite the serial production of the Prithvi missile, make Agni I operational, and would hasten the development of Agni II (Cherian, 1998; Narula et al., 1998). More explicitly, the party's then General Secretary, K.N. Govindacharya, declared that the BJP would test a nuclear weapon if it came to power (Jordan, 1996: A10), and the party's de-facto prime ministerial candidate, Vajpayee, commented, "The BJP alone can undertake the task of leading a reinvigorated, proud India to its rightful place in the comity of nations" (Perkovich, 1999:374). However, the BJP's manifesto at this point was unclear whether its promise to exercise the option to induct nuclear weapons would entail a series of nuclear tests or whether it would just declare India a nuclear weapons power without testing (in which case India could still theoretically be a signatory of the CTBT) (Malik, 2010:189).

Although the BJP's pre-election bomb narrative may be understood as being crafted as an alternative to the government, prominent members of India's strategic community supported a strong nuclear India. Mohan (1996b) claimed that India had "whined" too long on its nuclear policy; Chellaney (1996b:8) noted that India conduct tests "to perfect technical capabilities and convey a political message to other nuclear armed states" before a test ban went into effect making tests much more politically difficult; K. Subrahmanyam (1996a) focusing on the China factor claimed that India declare itself an independent global player with a nuclear deterrent as a way to "befriend and balance" China; R. Chidambaram referred to "an extraordinary range of knowhow and expertise on all aspects of nuclear technology" to support to India's nuclear program (quoted in Chengappa, 1994c:46); and A.P.J. Abdul Kalam pointed to the "colonial" Missile Technology Control Regime and its "racial prejudice" in urging reduction of the US pressures on India to slow or stop the deployment of the Agni missile program (quoted in Chengappa, 1994d:66). In sum, the indigenousness bespoke the postcolonial sentiment of India's nuclear discourse of the state. Although the military was still wary about allocating their budgets for missiles, it believed that Pakistan's nuclear capabilities required a stronger counter from India with its top official, Air Chief Marshal, S.K. Kaul, claiming that "the missiles real value was nuclear" (quoted in Chengappa, 1994d:69). In addition, the DRDO under Dr A.P.J. Abdul

Kalam sought to integrate the military services into India's missile development program to build a broader institutional coalition in support of India's nuclear program (Chengappa, 1994d).

As mentioned earlier, (in)security imaginary is not real in the sense that it can be empirically scrutinized. Rather, "it is the product of an act of cultural [ideological] creation, which is fundamental to any subsequent system of cultural representation" (Tomlinson, 1991:156–157). Seen from this definition of (in)security imaginary, one notices that a hybrid (in)security imaginary was constructed in India's ongoing strategic cultural discourses under Rao's term that while economically liberalizing and willing to reciprocate with the United States' South Asian agenda (and in this was seeking to gain a more secured footing in Indo-US relations) was in the nuclear sphere developing a strong anti-US (in)security phobia. The following contours (with a strong focus on a US-led international nuclear racism) marked India's (in)security imaginary: First, India's realization by then that a global banning of nuclear testing by the nuclear weapons states as an essential step toward global disarmament was irreversible and almost impractical within a specific time frame; second, that the nuclear weapons states' hypocritical attitude toward free and fair global disarmament made regional approaches of disarmament unrealistic and not very prudent; third, that despite rising Asian regional nuclear trends in China and Pakistan, substantial nuclear threats continue to exist from the nuclear weapons states (Cherian, 1995; Paddock, 2009). In fact, this emerging (in)security taking shape just before India's forthcoming May 1996 elections saw the rise of an emboldened strategic discourse amongst India's nuclear hawks, which marked by strong anti-US nuclear apartheid underpinnings and demands for international nuclear equality did not focus on China or Pakistan (exceptions being K. Subrahmanyam, Mohan, and Brahma Chellaney), but on the United States' discriminatory CTBT regime, the United States tilt toward Pakistan, and called on the government to conduct nuclear explosive tests (Sundarji, 1990, 1993a, 1993b; Chengappa, 1994a; Karnad, 1999; Ramanna, 2003). Politics, pride, and principle now prevailed over pragmatism in defining India's nuclear weapons quest in its post-Cold War strategic thinking and culture.

However, the Rao government, preoccupied with political and economic issues, retained a firm anti-CTBT/ambiguous stand on India's nuclear option. This ambiguity was revealed in the prime minister's nuclear jitter as he called off another nuclear test scheduled in December 1995 by noting that India's national interest at that point required restraint (although the prime minister tried to make up for it by authorizing the testing of the Prithvi missile on January 27, 1996 to demonstrate national prowess, strength, and the pride of the nation) (Perkovich, 1999:365, 370, 371). Jaswant Singh (1999), Mohan (1995), K. Subrahmanyam (1995b), and others severely denounced the US factor that possibly inhibited the prime minister's decisions on the 1995 nuclear tests; urged India's defiance of the US' nonproliferation pressures; and called for conducting open nuclear tests.

Under the United Front government of Prime Minister Gowda (June 1996–April 1997), India's official discourse on the CTBT adhered to its stand of nationalist pride, resistance to the US hypocrisy, and India's demand for international nuclear equality. Accordingly, India's major political parties the Congress, the Left, and the BJP, albeit for different reasons, united in their opposition to the CTBT: The Left rejected the CTBT citing nuclear discrimination, the Congress Party because of its strong principled position on complete disarmament; and the BJP on grounds of national security (although a few intellectuals and antinuclear activists such as Praful Bidwai and Achin Vanaik argued signing the treaty as an important, although flawed measure to augment nuclear disarmament) (Chellaney, 1996a, 1996b; Mattoo, 1996a; Narula, 1996b; Dubey, 2000; Malik, 2010:190). By the time India officially rejected the CTBT in June 1996, India's strategic discourse as evidenced within its state officials and science community members signaled a breakthrough from the state's traditional reliance on moral arguments in terms of India's nuclear affairs and explicitly invoked the national security factor in explaining this rejection. India's Ambassador at Geneva Arundhati Ghose (1996) forwarded India's national security considerations as a key factor in India's decision making regarding the CTBT (Ghose, 1996); India's ex-Foreign Secretary, Muchkund Dubey (2000) explained India's rejection of the CTBT to enable India to maintain the option to test nuclear weapons in response to regional nuclear developments; and Rakesh Sood (from the Ministry of External Affairs); I.K. Gujral (India's then Minister of External Affairs), and R. Chidambaram (from the AEC) followed a similar hard-line thinking and rhetoric in that the United States and others would pay more attention to India's nuclear sovereign arguments in terms of proliferation (Narula, 1996b; Dubey, 2000; Malik, 2010). As stated in Gujral's parliamentary speeches to the Parliament in July and August 1996 on the CTBT,

> Our nuclear policy, as expressed in the CTBT negotiations, is intimately linked with our national security concerns. We have never accepted the notion that it can be considered legitimate for some countries to rely on nuclear weapons for their security while denying this right to others. (Malik, 2010:183)

However, not all influences of India's moral tradition was lost in these discourses as Gujral in a September 11, 1996 parliamentary address further asserted that "… our position for the last 40 years has been to abolish and destroy both nuclear tests and nuclear weapons … we shall sustain the glorious path led by Gandhi and Nehru" (Paddock, 2009: 44). Not surprisingly, on December 5, 1996, came an announcement from India's Ministry of Defense that the Gowda government would not produce the Agni missiles unless India's security was threatened.

The political space offered following India's rejection of the CTBT in June 1996 saw the emergence of two options summarizing the kinds of nuclear and missile delivery system capabilities and doctrines the state needed: The first represented by Raja Ramanna, K. Sundarji, K. Subrahmanyam preferred that India maintain a minimum deterrence posture, and a more aggressive line suggested by the BJP that India conduct a high-explosive thermo-nuclear test based on fission weapons. The group supporting a minimum deterrence posture collectively argued that given that a plutonium bomb was "sufficient enough" to act as a deterrent and India possessed that capability, India did not at that point need thermonuclear tests (Rammana quoted in Anbarasan, 1996; Sundarji, 1996b; Subrahmanyam, 1996b). Although Subrahmanyam (1996b) clarified that explosive tests would be necessitated only in case a war-fighting scenario was envisaged with an identified enemy (meaning China), he rejected the idea of India's thermo-nuclear weapons as a China-centric deterrence as he viewed nuclear war-fighting as immoral and unwinnable on the subcontinent. For him, an improved Agni that could reach cities in southern China would suffice as deterrence. In contrast, the more aggressive line of thinking proffered by Dr A.P.J. Abdul

Kalam (in his intense lobbying before the government to speed India's defense research program), the BJP's defense analyst Mohan Guruswamy, BJP's Foreign Affairs spokesperson Brajesh Mishra, and India's foreign policy analyst C. Raja Mohan argued that "we must conduct one or more nuclear tests in order to design nuclear warheads for our missiles" (BJP, 1996b:2). Mohan Guruswamy by October 1996 thus spelt his nuclear preference: "to really be a credible nuclear power we need to develop, both bigger and miniaturized nuclear weapons and an array of delivery vehicles. This means hydrogen bombs and tactical nuclear warheads, ICBM's and cruise missiles, and missiles launching nuclear submarines and long-range bombers" (Guruswamy, 1996).

As Pakistan's nuclear weapons capability became more rampant toward the end of the Gowda term, as the Indian Ministry of Defense's Report in April 1997 expressed concerns over China's continuing nuclear modernization, and the United States in July 1997 conducted a subcritical nuclear weapon test at Nevada—India's strategic enclave continued to pressure the next Prime Minister I.K. Gujral (April 1997– March 1998) to strike a more robust nuclear policy. Thereafter, around mid-1996, sections of India's state officials and political analysts (like K.K. Nayyar) declared that it was "essential to conduct a series of nuclear tests" (*Times of India*, 1996); C. Raja Mohan asserted "[India must] cross the psychological barrier," and like Pakistan, should signal that its "nuclear capability is here to stay" (*The Times of India*, 1996; Mohan, 1997b); Brahma Chellaney (1997:10) noted how India's focus on "nondiscrimination and morality" kept it "illogically" from adopting "rational, self-interest, US-style thinking;" Indian Defense Minister Mulayam Singh Yadav on July 30, 1997, told the Parliament that "it has been decided to accord high priority to the next phase of the Agni program," where efforts will be made to extend the missile's range up to the expected 2,500 kilometers (*The Hindu*, 1997a:1); and Gujral himself commented that India would keep China's assistance to Pakistan "in mind" as "we take care of our preparedness" (Gujral quoted in *Deccan Herald*, 1997). Yet, simultaneously revealing the traditional philosophical perspective on India's national security, the prime minister in a November 13, 1997 speech stated that "India had no desire to manufacture nuclear weapons unless it was forced to do so" (*The Hindu*, 1997b).

It is within these shifting frameworks of ideological orientations and discourses of the post-Cold War Indian state's strategic thinking vis-à-vis the prevailing nuclear politics—was constructed a noticeably anti-Western/US (in)security imaginary of the state, which, surpassing the strategic thinking, nuclear insecurity discourses, and (in)security imaginaries of the previous Indian administrations at this post-Cold War juncture, revealed a noticeably explicit demand from India's nuclear hawks to conduct nuclear tests. While this emerging rethinking and strategic nuclear security discourses of post-Cold War India were not entirely new breakthroughs from the earlier administrations strategic rethinking in terms of India's nuclear options/policies (which, albeit incrementally, had transitioned from Nehru's nuclear idealism; to Shastri's strategic realism; to Indira Gandhi's aggressiveness and militaristic prowess; to Rajiv Gandhi's remarkable shift to a pro-US strategic rethinking to attain technological self-reliance in India's nuclear and missile development projects, yet, these post-Cold War shifts of the Indian state's strategic cultural thinking and (in)security imaginaries remained critical in two ways: First, in revealing the consolidation of a strong racial/anti-US sensibility at the heart of India's resistance to the CTBT, and more importantly, serving as the ideological stepping stones of what was to emerge as a much robust version of India's near-future nuclear policy (under the BJP government).

Accordingly, seen in comparison to the preceding strategic cultural thinking and (in)security imaginaries of the Indian state, the following continuities and discontinuities punctuate the post-Cold War state's ideological and discursive orientations in terms of its nuclear policy: First, a relegation of India's regional nuclear insecurities from China and Pakistan as existing but secondary; second, a deep consolidation and primary relegation of India's perception of nuclear hierarchy stemming from international nuclear politics, that consolidating India's sense of nuclear nationalism, resulted in India's vivid opposition and final rejection of the CTBT; and finally, an explicit and robust strategic call from a vast spectrum of India's political and strategic community members that incorporating voices of India's defense personnel, political and security analysts, the Indian military and the BJP demanded that India conduct a high-explosive thermo-nuclear test based on fission weapons. It came with the BJP's explicit declaration that it would test a nuclear weapon if it came to power. This shifting line of India's strategic rethinking in terms of anti-US nuclear hierarchy and robustness in its nuclear policy also implied the following in terms of India's statist identity: First, a statist identity that was underscored by a strong sense of nuclear nationalism, nuclear sovereignty, and a desire for nuclear power and prestige in the realm of international politics; second, a state, whose pro-US strategic thinking, economically globalizing trends, and simultaneous sentiments of nonalignment revealed a hybrid identity of the Indian state; and finally, a state, whose domestic politics was witnessing the rise of religious fundamentalism/communalism led by the BJP—that was also, as discussed before, carrying the most explicit demands for India's open nuclear policy. Prior to elaborating the linkages between India's strategic culture and nuclear policy developments under the BJP (in the next chapter), I document below the developments of post-Cold War India's nuclear weapons policies.

India's Nuclear Policy

India's nuclear policy developments in the post-Cold War era which began with a stymied progress of India's nuclear and missiles development under Prime Minister V.P. Singh, and an official slack under Prime Minister Rao (June 1991–May 1996), gathered momentum around June 1996 following India's official rejection of the CTBT and witnessed progress in India's Integrated Guided Missile Development Project. However, as documented above, this momentum had garnered only among India's nuclear hawks (i.e., strategic community members from India's defense personnel, political and security analysts, the Indian military, and the opposition party) while the government retained its nuclear ambivalence.

The DRDO, initially under V.S. Arunachalam, and thereafter, since 1992 under Dr A.P.J. Abdul Kalam (a nuclear hawk and an aggressive proponent of India's nuclear and missile development) led efforts at advancing India's nuclear and missile development plans from its mere forays at technology-gathering (such as the Agni TD and Prithvi I) to a full-fledged program to develop and test-fire India's indigenous ballistic missiles and developing infrastructures to advance the Agni and the Prithvi series for India's mission against the Chinese and the Pakistani states. To this end,

India's indigenous nuclear and missile development included the successful test-firing of a series of Prithvi short-range ballistic missiles: SS 250/Prithvi II (a lighter and longer version of the Prithvi I, Prithvi II is a single-stage, liquid fuel, short-range, surface-to-surface missile dedicated to the Indian Air Force, with a range of 250 km, and capable of having a payload of 500–750 kg); SS 350/Prithvi III (a solid-fuel naval service missile, with a 350 km range, and a 1,000 kg payload—which retains high accuracy because of its liquid-fuelled counterparts); developing a medium-range mobile surface to air missile, Akash (with a target capability of 30 kilometers and altitude capability up to 30,000 meters); a short-range surface to air missile, Trishul (with a target capability of 9 kilometers and warhead capability of 5.5 kilograms); and a third-generation Anti-Tank Guided Missile (Nag) (Norris et al., 2002). Noting the short-range limitations of the Prithvi missiles that could not provide India with a delivery system capable of targeting civilian and military points in China, India initiated the further expansion of the Agni TD intermediate-range missile system through the developments of the Agni II IRBM, Agni I SRBM, Agni II AT IRBM, Agni III IRBM, and Agni IV ICBM, which, however, was suspended by Prime Minister Rao on grounds of the US pressure (to be subsequently resumed by the BJP government after 1998). This period also saw Rao's calling off of his previously authorized nuclear tests in December 1995—preparations of which had occurred under the coordination of the DRDO and the BARC teams under the supervision of K. Santhanam (from the DRDO) (Dhanda, 2010:104–106, 365). Reportedly, India was developing with Russian assistance a submarine launched missile with a 300 kilometer range, Sagarika, indicating the DRDO's intention of developing a suite of nuclear delivery systems in the near future (Norris et al., 2002).

Despite such trends, the induction and launch-on-warning operational plans of the missiles remained tardy given that official strategic priorities at that time (in terms of the country's political and economic progress, maintaining India's regional and global standing through diplomacy and most importantly, the issue of sacrificing India's normative and interests by testing nuclear weapons) militated against the tests. Despite this official line of ambiguous restraint, it might be fair to say that India's missile by the end of March 1997 had progressed in tandem with Pakistan's covert nuclear weapons program—with India possessing an extensive and largely indigenous ballistic program including infrastructure for both solid and liquid fuelled missiles to reach target capabilities in Pakistan and China; members of India's nuclear science community like R. Chidambaram and Dr A.P.J. Abdul Kalam started preparing a hydrogen bomb and other weapons for experimental testing; and once again requesting authorization from Deva Gowda to conduct nuclear weapons tests. In this sense, India's nuclear and missile development projects by the end of 1997 did not necessarily acquire the comprehensive, predesignated targeting plans, or launch-on-warning operational plans as pursued by the United States or the Soviet Union. Instead, under the ideological influences of key political leaderships (such as V.P. Singh, Narasimha Rao, and Gowda) who were wedded to the norms of nuclear nonviolence, and a simultaneous robustness of India's nuclear hawks, represented a basic deterrent function of Indian state. These Gandhi/ Nehru notions of nuclear restraint, which in the decades of the 1990s, was aptly reflected in the principles endorsed in the Arunachalam-led committee formed by V.P. Singh in 1990 stood that India should never use nuclear weapons; civilians should exert control over the military in policy and plans; and that, India should not engage in arms racing. It defined the official character and efficacy of India's nuclear policy making decision in the immediate post-Cold War context (Perkovich, 1999:330).

Conclusion

Following my premise that the Indian state's strategic cultural thinking projected through the ideological lenses of its foreign policy making community, constructs shifting images of India's national identity, (in)security imaginary, and its nuclear policies, this chapter has documented how a series of domestic, regional, and global developments between 1991 and March 1998, consolidating acutely around the perceptions of India's US-led nuclear apartheid, has sustained an ideological and political space for India's security community that served to reconstruct along more noticeably robust lines the strategic cultural thinking, nuclear discourses, and the (in)security imaginary of post-Cold War India. To this extent, the chapter has explored how India's strategic cultural thinking during this frame transitioned from its existing state of militarization, to further nuclear aggressiveness, to the edge of a potential nuclear-testing agenda by the end of March 1998. While some nonproliferation irks existed between India and the United States during this period, the chapter has also noted a changing cultural orientation of Indian state toward the United States, which, seeing some progress in Indo-American security cooperation in the production, design, and purchase of India's Light Combat Aircrafts, XMP-24 computers, and such, worked in ways to chart a change in India's identity as an economically liberalizing/pro-US actor. Yet, the chapter has also documented that a long consolidated sense of an anti-US nuclear apartheid has also been the driving force to build a robust call for India's going nuclear. The end of March 1998 thus culminated in a robust demand that India conduct a high-explosive thermo-nuclear test based on fission weapons for potential nuclear deterrence purposes. In this sense, India's nuclear and missile development at the eve of March 1998 (by producing an extensive largely indigenous nuclear and missiles program with the aim of maintaining a basic deterrent function for the state) represented an unprecedented progress in its nuclear weapons development when seen in comparison to any previous Indian administrations but, did not, yet, break the tradition of nuclear nonviolence/restraint held by the state. However, elections of March 15, 1998 that brought the BJP's coalition-led government to power heralded a much aggressive chapter in India's quest for nuclear power, and relatedly, a reconstruction of India's strategic cultural thinking, nationalist identity, and (in)security imaginary. The next chapter documents this shift in India's nuclear trajectory.

Notes

1. The terms of these governments were as follows: V.P. Singh (December 2, 1989–November 10, 1990), Chandra Shekhar Singh (January 10, 1990–June 21, 1991), Deva Gowda (June 1, 1996–April 21, 1997), and I.K Gujral (April 21, 1997–March 19, 1998) leading the Janata Dal headed National Front coalition governments, and the Congress Party led P.V. Narasimha Rao's government (June 21, 1991–May 16, 1996).
2. On May 11, 1992, the Bush administration imposed sanctions for two years on Indian Space Research Organization and the Russian Space Research Organization (Glavkosmos) on grounds that a proposed Indo-Russian deal of the cryogenic rocket engines violated the terms of the MTCR which Russia had pledged to adhere.

3. The Fissile Material Cut-Off Treaty that was introduced by President Clinton at the UN General Assembly (on September 27, 1993) called upon states to negotiate a multilateral treaty banning production of fissile materials for nuclear explosives outside international safeguards.

4. This review, which originally envisioned maintaining the US' strategic forces at warhead levels consistent with START I, coincided with South Africa, Brazil, and Argentina adhering to nonproliferation norms, and also with Russia's efforts at scaling back its nuclear arsenals with eventual elimination of all its land-based multiple re-entry vehicle missiles systems.

5. In sum, the NPR did not actually foreclose any options of reviving what was listed for reduction or elimination of the US' stockpiled strategic or nonstrategic nuclear weapons, left open the US scope to expand strategic computing devices, above-ground sub critical plutonium experiments, and its ability to return to underground testing of nuclear weapons if required; and furthermore, saw new investment proposals by the government of worth $9 billion to extend the life of the US' intercontinental ballistic missiles by 2020, upgrade B-1 and B-2 bombers, and missiles on its Trident submarines.

6. Furthermore, the indefinite extension of the NPT sought immediate commencement and early conclusion of negotiations by the NNWS to ban fissile material production for explosive devices, and their progressive efforts at reducing nuclear weapons with the ultimate goal of eliminating those weapons (through the signing of a CTBT). The nonaligned states, however, wanted the scope of such a proposed CTBT to cover all tests in all environments while the nuclear weapon states including China sought to retain some flexibility over low-yielding nuclear testing.

7. To India's dismay, the nuclear weapons states were neither interested nor receptive to India's proposals nor concerns on the CTBT. The United States appeared to be mainly interested in bringing Russia and China within a control regime through the verification mechanisms; UK and France viewed the CTBT as a pure nonproliferation measure aimed at nonnuclear states while themselves not considering the qualitative capping of their weapons development through the treaty; and Russia remained adamant on the issue of nuclear disarmament. Only China stated that it was in favor of the total destruction of these weapons although not accepting the idea of a time frame.

8. In April 1994, The US Deputy Secretary of State, Strobe Talbott arrived in India to meet Prime Minister Rao. In June 1994 Robert Einhorn, Michael Lemmon (State Department Office of South Asian Regional Affairs, Director), and Norman Wulf (Arms Control and Disarmament Agency Deputy Assistant Director) arrived in India to meet N. Krishnan (an ex-Indian diplomat) and Rakesh Sood. Prime Minister Rao visited President Clinton in Washington DC in January 1995. The US Defense Secretary William Perry visited India and Pakistan in October 1997. The US Under Secretary of State for Political Affairs Thomas Pickering made a trip to India and on November 18 and 19, 1997, the US Secretary of State Madeleine Albright visited India as a part of her South-Asia tour.

9. These controversies and apprehensions centered around the fact that India's economic bankruptcy would cause Prime Minister Rao to cave into the US' proliferation pressures; that the prime minister's vulnerability to the US pressures had led him to postpone a scheduled launching of the Prithvi missile in May 1994; and the prime minister's proposed May 1994 trip was simply creating an illusion of the decades of India–US "reflexive mistrust" (Gupta and Sidhu, 1992; *India Today*, 1994; Dixit, 1996; Chengappa, 2000; Kamath, 2009; Malik, 2010).

10. The Kashmir crisis happened when taking advantage of the Indian government's mishandling of the local situation in Kashmir, prime minister Benazir Bhutto traveled to Pakistan-held portion of Kashmir, and reflecting the anti-Indian mindset of President Ghulam Ishaq Khan, General Aslam Beg (Chief of Army Staff), and Pakistan's Inter-Services Intelligence Directorate (whose enormous power in the Pakistani power structure held the Prime Minister Bhutto hostage) promised a "thousand year war" to support the militants in the Pakistan-held portion of Kashmir.

11. The basic idea of the doctrine was that India as the region's great power would act magnanimously in resolving heretofore contentious issues with smaller parties and create a regional norm or practice of noninterference in others' affairs. This doctrine was applied by Prime Minister Gujral in Bangladesh, Sri Lanka, and Nepal. However, with regard to Pakistan, the doctrine was more guarded.

12. In December 1991, Premier Li Peng visited India (the first Premier since the 1962 war) where the two governments agreed to institutionalize mechanisms for defusing tension along the border and signed agreements to enhance diplomatic representation in each other's country, to further space cooperation, and resume official border trade after a 30 year hiatus. In September 1993, Prime Minister Rao traveled to Beijing where the two governments signed an agreement to reduce troops and respect ceasefire lines along their disputed border, and met again in February 1994, to pursue implementation of the agreements and reductions in troop levels. In March 1995, India and China had completed another meeting to further confidence-building measures along the disputed border including discussion of proposals on prior notification of military exercises and prevention of intrusion into each other's airspace. In August 1995, the two agreed to further troop pullbacks from the eastern sector of their disputed border. The case for diplomacy was augmented by China when on November 28, 1996, President Jiang Zemin visited New Delhi.

13. For details of these two strategic viewpoints see Chopra (1993) and Sundarji (1993a, 1993b).

14. For details of this classification of the hawks, the owls, and the doves see Bajpai (1999) and Vanaik (1995), among others.

6

Crossing the Nuclear Threshold and the Neoliberal Turn: 1998–2004

If changing manifestations of ideology and strategic thinking impact transitions of a state's security policy, then the coming of the coalition-led Hindu nationalist Bharatiya Janata Party (BJP) to power (from April 1998 to March 2004)[1] represented a noteworthy shift in the reconstruction of strategic thinking, nationalist identity, (in)security imaginaries, and finally, the crossing of the nuclear threshold in Indian politics. Following the theoretical premise of this book that there exists an ideological and discursive linkage between the social construction of India's strategic culture, (in)security imaginary, and its nuclear policies, the chapter explores the transition of the Indian state's strategic thinking under the BJP by drawing attention to how the BJP's *Hindutva* ideology, working at tandem with real-politics, has drawn from culturally grounded historical memories to sustain (an initially Hindu-centric) and more aggressive lines of strategic rethinking, (in)security imaginaries, and India's open nuclear policy. Yet, given my claim that a nation's strategic culture is a matter of social and ideological reconstruction in interaction with real politics, I also explore how the BJP government's strategic discourses since its 1998 detonation and after 9/11 (perhaps owing to the structural imperatives and pragmatic necessities of a post-9/11 globalized politics) have revealed a pro-US orientation of India's strategic thinking—signifying a neoliberal turn in India's strategic security/nuclear policies.

Accordingly, this chapter addresses the following "how-possible" questions: First, how the Indian state's strategic cultural thinking between April 1998 and March 2004, projected through the ideological lenses of its security community made sense of India's international politics? Second, how the Indian state's interpretation of its current international politics created an ideological and political space, within which were reconstructed and rearticulated shifting images of India's nationalist identity, strategic cultural thinking, and its (in)security imaginaries? Finally, how within these shifting reconstructions of India's strategic cultural thinking and (in)security imaginaries were forged India's strategic security/nuclear policy developments in relation to the United States. In addressing each how-possible question, my aim is to show how the government's discourses as tools of social and ideological power have (in an unprecedented manner than any previous non-BJP government) produced, reconstructed, and sustained a more militarily aggressive relationship between India's strategic culture, (in)security imaginary, and its nuclear policy choices.

Before proceeding with this analysis, certain historical, political, and analytical qualifiers must be reiterated. First, I remain cognizant that nuclear strategy decisions by states are to a great extent structural, and hence I do not underestimate the significance of realism in analyzing the BJP's nuclear policy choices. Second, I accept that states use ideological manipulation to get support for their national security policies and even pre-BJP governments in India have used India's nationalist ideology in justifying India's nuclear policies, and the BJP did it as well. Furthermore, it is also not unusual for the Indian state under the BJP to have detonated in 1998 given that a robust demand for going nuclear had already existed just before the BJP assumed power, and the BJP's long-standing commitments in its Election Manifestoes of 1996 and 1998 "to re-evaluate the country's nuclear policy and exercise the option to induct nuclear weapons" (Cherian, 1998). In this context, I am also cognizant that the BJP's tests, much like Prime Minister Indira Gandhi's 1974 Peaceful Nuclear Explosive, were conducted on grounds of political/party-based reasons. Given that several scholarships have addressed these why aspects and the pros/cons of these tests (Singh, 1998b; Tellis, 2001; Cohen, 2001; Karnad, 2002; Talbott, 2004; Frey, 2006), this chapter will not address these issues in details. Instead, keeping in mind the critical constructivist focus of this book, this chapter will concentrate on how the BJP's ideology of *Hindutva,* its concept of a Hindu *rashtra* (nation), India's long consolidated sense of nuclear nationalism, the identity of an increasingly nuclear aggressive India, the compulsions of real politics, and the structural and economic necessities of 9/11 facilitated more complex reconstructions of India's strategic culture, (in)security imaginaries, and more neoliberally grounded strategic security/nuclear policy developments for India.

This chapter is organized as follows: The following section begins with a review of the BJP government's nationalist agenda based on *Hindutva* and its linkages in rearticulating the BJP's strategic cultural thinking projecting India as a Hindu rashtra. The second section reviews India's international relations vis-à-vis the United States, China, and Pakistan as interpreted through the ideological lenses of its security community in three phases: At the juncture of the BJP's 1998 detonation; the immediate postdetonation period up to 9/11; and thereafter until the end of BJP era. The third section analyzes the reconstructions of India's strategic culture and (in)security imaginary under the BJP government, namely how the BJP's ideology of *Hindutva* and its drive to recreate a Hindu rashtra has interacted with India's real-politics, nuclear apartheid, and the structural imperatives of 9/11 to redefine a global, neoliberal, and an explicit nuclear aggressive form of strategic rethinking and (in)security imaginary for India. The fourth section analyzes the neoliberal turn of India's strategic security/defense collaborations with the United States.

The BJP: Rebuilding the Nation and Reconstructing India's Strategic Culture

A watershed era in India's nuclear politics began with the coming of the Bharatiya Janata Party (BJP) as a coalition-led government to power in May 1998. Owing its origin to the Hindu fundamentalist organization, the Sangh Parivaar,[2] and allegedly continuing to maintain links with the latter, the rise of the BJP represents the rise of a (modern) Hindu nationalism in the forefront of India (Devare, 2009). In contrast to the Congress Party's claims to so-called secularism (Varshney, 1993;

Krishna, 2002), the BJP's call for reinventing a pan-Indian identity, rooted in the concept of "one nation, one people, one culture," was seen by the party as the unifying factor in the creation of a Hindu rashtra (BJP, 1996:6). Reflecting the legacy of the early 20th-century Hindu nationalist, Veer Savarkar, who, as one of the architects of the Rashtriya Swayam Sevak (RSS), had defined *Hindutva* in a communal manner, *Hindutva*, with its pillars of *pitrabhoomi* (fatherland), *jati* (bloodline), and *Sanskriti* (culture) became a crucial factor for the BJP in establishing the basis of communalism in modern India. This is because the concept implied that only those, whose sacred land—sacred to their religion—lay within their *pitrabhoomi* had the moral basis of claiming citizenship in India (Chowdhry, 2000:97).

Such communal sentiments echo in the writings and campaigns of the BJP, which see *Hindutva* as a unifying force that will create a national identity and ensure social cohesion for India. A prominent espousal of this ideological/communal bias in building a nationalist India is visible in the BJP's Election Manifesto (1996). In its Introduction, the Manifesto declared: "The present millennium began with the subjugation of our ancient land. Let a reinvigorated, proud, and prosperous India herald the next millennium" (BJP, 1996:6). It ended with an appeal to all "patriotic Indians" to assist the BJP in the task of reconstructing a nationalist India (ibid.:80). More communal in implication is the section in the manifesto on "Indian Immigration: A Demographic Invasion," which construed the Muslim immigrant refuges from Bangladesh as threats to Indian democracy. In contrast, the Buddhist immigrant refugees to India from the Chakma district of Bangladesh were not deemed likewise. By the same token, the BJP's espousal of the policy of "justice for all and appeasement for none" has a communal motive to restore a sense of Indianness within the Hindu rashtra (nation) perceived to have been ruptured by the pseudo-secularism of the Nehruvian legacy. As stated by the then BJP President, L.K. Advani "If nationalism is stripped of its Hinduism, it could lose its dynamism" (Malik and Singh, 1996:41).

"[E]very nationalism needs an enemy" (Embree, 1994:625) and certainly for the Hindu nationalism as articulated by the BJP, its enemies, are essential to many of its ideological positions to support a Hindu rashtra. According to *Hindutva*, since the holyland of the Christians and the Muslims lay outside India, this ideological basis of *Hindutva* becomes key for the party to project India's religious minorities, especially the Muslims, as threats to India (Chowdhry, 2000:102). Following the anti-Muslim orientation of the early RSS architect, Savarkar (as discussed in Chapter 2), a part of the BJP's ideology and discourse has been to project "patriots" and "traitors" in terms of their religious affiliations and construct Islam/Indian Muslims as a locus of threat to the Indian nation. For instance, BJP, spokeswoman, Sadhvi Rithambara, supports the Hindus in the Ramjanbhoomi riots (1992) as "a fight for the preservation of a civilization, for Indianness, for national consciousness" (Kakar, 1996:157); BJP spokeswoman, Sushma Swaraj, suspects an alleged treachery of the Muslims against India because "the former rooted for Pakistan during the Indo-Pakistan war" (Chowdhry, 2000:117); and that Indian Muslims, who practice foreign religion and have "extraterritorial loyalties" constitute a "drag" on the nation (BJP, 1998d:1).

It may also be important to note here that the BJP's views on cultural nationalism are not a conspiracy theory against the non-Hindus, especially the Muslims. Instead, these ideological perceptions are well-grounded historically in similar ideological assertions by its predecessor, the Rashtriya Swayam Sevak (Embree, 1994), and also justified by the dilemmas of India's colonial and postcolonial nation-building (as discussed in Chapters 2 and 3). Furthermore, the BJP specifies that *Hindutva* in the context of building a Hindu rashtra is not identical with Hinduism because *Hindutva* is not a Semitic religion or a dogmatic thought system. Rather, it is an assimilative concept that includes all citizens of India. In fact, the BJP, after the 1998 nuclear tests following the trend set by the Rajiv Gandhi and the Rao administrations has accepted a fluid nonaligned stature, the interdependence of globalization, and a pro-US strategic culture (despite prevailing anti-US nuclear contentions and the existence of hardliners within the party structure). Despite these shifts, interpretive aspects such as the party's commitment to *Hindutva*, its interpretation of India's partition history, memories of Hindu–Muslim conflicts, and the notion of a Hindu glory have remained pivotal for the party in shaping India's strategic culture. I analyze in the next section, how *Hindutva* has been mobilized by the BJP to represent a Hinduicized strategic rethinking and a national security agenda for the state.

Reconstructing India's ("Hindu") Strategic Culture and National (In)Security

In terms of its national security agenda, the BJP, like the Congress Party, remains "pledged to defend the unity and integrity of India …" (BJP, n.d.: 10–12). Yet, seen in the context of the party's adherence to *Hindutva,* the party's concept of national integration (in contrast to the Congress') is underpinned by a cultural tone. While affirming its ideal of national integrity, the party mentions that "*Hindutva* is a unifying principle which alone can preserve the unity and integrity of our nation" (BJP, 1996: 15). Referring to Islam, in this context, Jaswant Singh (then Senior Adviser on Defense and Foreign Affairs under the BJP) reiterates that "Professor Samuel Huntington is not wholly wrong in talking about the clash of civilizations. It has always been there in history" (Singh, 1999: xiv). It is in this effort to achieve a Hindu rashtra that the BJP designs its national security agenda in the context of India's (Hindu) strategic culture.

Jaswant Singh reiterates his vision of what he perceives to be India's strategic culture. According to him, to understand India's strategic culture one has to "… examine the very nature of India's nationhood; the very characteristics of its society; and the evolution of its strategic thought over the ages …" (Singh, 1999:2). For him, this evolution of strategic culture represents:

> an intermix of many influences: civilization, culture, evolution, and the functioning of a civil society, etc. It is a by-product of the political culture of a nation and its people; an extension of the functioning of a viable state, [and] more particularly its understanding of, and subscription to, the concept of power … [This] is where history and racial memories influence nation's strategic thought [and] its culture. (ibid.)

Furthermore, representing Rosen's (1996) concept of "mindset" as underlying a country's strategic culture, Singh claims that it is the Hindu civilization/culture that essentially constitute India's strategic culture. In his words:

> above all else, India is Hindu and Hindus think differently from non-Hindus … it is this "ism" [i.e., Hinduism] that has given birth to a culture from which we hope to extract the essence of its [i.e., India's] strategic thought. (Singh, 1999:5)

As expressed from the above quotes, the roots of India's strategic culture is associated with the mindset of the Hindus, their history, and their cultural memories—which by implication links the logistics of the BJPs strategic culture to the ideological underpinnings of *Hindutva*. If the BJPs rearticulation of India's nationalist identity and strategic culture is situated from the perspectives of *Hindutva*, then, can one assume that the BJP may have reinterpreted the secular aspects of the Nehruvian strategic culture, India's nationalist identity, and (in)security along "cultural" lines (as identified with Pakistan) to justify its nuclear agenda? A key in this chapter, therefore, is the necessity to uncover the socially and essentially contestable linkages between the BJP's rearticulation of India's strategic culture, (in) security imaginary, and a nuclear India.

Interpreting India's International Relations

India's international relations under the BJP opened with India ending its record of self-restraint as the government, with an abrupt shift in comparison to the previous non-BJP governments, immediately after coming to power detonated three weapons on May 11, 1998 (a fission device with a yield of about 12 kilotons, a thermonuclear device with a yield of about 43 kilotons, and a sub-kiloton device), and tested two sub-kiloton devices on May 13 (to generate additional data).[3] An acute nuclear momentum that had garnered among India's nuclear hawks (as discussed earlier in Chapter 5) coupled with Pakistan's testing of Ghauri just as the BJP assumed power explains the nuclear testing by India. Other factors, namely technological, electoral, international, regional, cultural, historical, and an acute sense of nuclear apartheid, were ideologically interpreted by the BJP and also rationalized the open path to nuclear India. Thereafter, breaking precedents, the BJP formulated its minimum nuclear doctrine and adopted a No-First-Use posture on the use of nuclear weapons. Although acute realist insecurities at the eve of May 1998 dominated the government's interpretation of its international relations, these perceptions following the tests and post-9/11 transitioned to a more neoliberally grounded and globalized interpretation of India's international affairs. Next, I document these shifts as evidenced in three phases: at the eve of 1998 detonation; the immediate postdetonation period up to 9/11; and from 9/11 to the end of the BJP's term.

India's tests occurred at a point when the Clinton administration's South Asia Policy had initiated steps to develop a strategic dialogue with India, which, between April 14, 1998 and May 1, 1998, saw exchange visits between the US officials and Indian counterparts; the US efforts in pursuing diplomacy with China to pressure the latter to end supplying nuclear technology to Pakistan; and anticipated President Clinton's visit to India in November that year. Understandably, the tests saw a series of comments from the US officials namely the US Secretary of State Albright; Defense Secretary William Cohen; and others condemning the nuclear tests as potentially causing "a chain reaction … [where] other countries [would] see this as an open invitation to try to acquire this technology" (Giacomo, 1998; Perkovich, 1999). In addition, there emerged a series of Orientalist discourses within the United States, which, reflecting the "rogue" doctrine (Klare, 1995; Tanter, 1998), categorized India as a traditional, irresponsible, undemocratic and a "rogue" other (Manning, 1998; Burns, 1998a; Weiner, 1998). Thereafter, the Clinton administration imposed economic sanctions on India (and Pakistan) (Tripathy and Tripathy, 2008:84–85), and mobilized international efforts through the UN Security Council the Group of Eight (G-8) to restrain further nuclear testing by India (and Pakistan). However, in response to positive steps by India individually and through international forums such as the United Nations General Assembly to address the US nonproliferation concerns, post-test sanctions through the Brownback Amendment were removed from India, and saw an unexpected resumption of dialogue between the United States and India.

Post-test dialogue ensued between India and the United States from June 1998 to February 2004, with the US Deputy Secretary of State Strobe Talbott and India's Deputy Chairman of the Planning Commission Jaswant Singh remaining instrumental. As Talbott (2004:3–4) recalls "we met fourteen times at ten locations in seven countries on three continents." Despite differences of opinions within the BJP hardliners (who supported a harder, defiant line with the United States) and the internationalists (who supported a more moderate stand and pragmatic alliance with the United States) and Orientalist fears within American conservatives, both sides rededicated efforts at improving mutual ties.

One of the major goals of these dialogues from the United States side was to get India to sign the CTBT—which the United States well knew was being pursued in a context where "India perceived the CTBT as an [US] effort to pursue P-5 monopoly" (Talbott, 2004:98–99). Amidst these controversial expectations, India–US state officials and the US arms control specialists met on June 1998, July 1998, November 1998, and November, 1998, but with stymied results in getting India to sign the treaty. While India reiterated its rationale for nuclear weapons in view of China and Pakistan, urged the United States to accept India's nuclear weapons status and emphasized the US' receptivity to the BJP's domestic difficulties in signing the treaty—the United States remained headstrong in its nonproliferation expectations, that is, India pledge never to test again by signing the CTBT (ibid.:94–95). To this end, Talbott's demands became vocal at his speech at Brookings Institute in November 1998 spelling the US expectations in preventing an escalation of nuclear and missile competition in the South Asia, strengthening the global nonproliferation regime, and promoting a dialogue between India and Pakistan (Talbott, 1998; Tripathy and Tripathy, 2008: 87–88).

Three additional reasons provided immunity to the Indian state from signing the treaty: First, India's concerns about an "Islamic radicalism" and a nuclear armed Pakistan where the latter was slipping into the group of "failed states" (Shoup and Ganguly, 2006:7); second, the continuing nondiscriminatory environment of an international test ban treaty; and third, that significant sections of India's scientists and military (excluding some like K. Sundarji) felt that India's 1998 tests had not yet exploded a Hydrogen Bomb which was required by India's national security interests and that India not sign the CTBT. Although the pending US–USSR tensions centering on separatist movements of Chechnya and harsh anti-US nuclear rhetoric from President Yeltsin (Kamath, 2009: 113),[4] explains why President Clinton did not foreclose the Nuclear Missiles Defense program nor sign the CTBT,[5] it gave India ample opportunity to assert that the United States stop pestering India for a timetable that required a public commitment to signing the treaty (Talbott, 2004: 94–95). Despite these pending irks, the internationalist components of the BJP government such as Jaswant Singh, Brajesh Mishra, Foreign Secretary, K. Raghunath, and the prime minister himself stressed the need of India–US strategic partnership in their common struggle against an Islamic fundamentalism and sought greater technical assistance from the US nuclear weapons laboratories to enhance India's computer simulation and nuclear experimental/upgrading plans (Talbott, 2004). Although in the immediate post-1998 context, providing such assistance to India was a nonstarter in Washington (to be in violation of the NPT), 9/11 noticeably changed the course of India–US interactions in the areas of nuclear technology/strategic security developments.

9/11 brought a new energy and purpose to the US engagement in South Asia. The Bush administration announced that it would "hunt down the terrorists" suspected to be hiding in Afghanistan (Bush, 2001a, 2001b, 2001c), and in relation the "urgency [to control] ... the spread of dangerous technology to 'rogue states' and their possible use by 'terrorists'" globally and in South Asia (The White House, 2002; National Security Strategy, 2002). In response to India's full support and Pakistan's "indispensable help" in the war on terror, President Bush on September 22, 2001 issued a final determination removing all nuclear related sanctions against India and Pakistan and announced that the United States would "invest time and resources [into] building strong bilateral relations with India..." (National Security Strategy, 2002). Building on this logic of "resource investment," the United States emphasized "strategic partnerships" between India and United States to fight "global terrorism, state sponsors of terrorism, and the proliferation of weapons of mass destruction" (United States Department of Defense, 2003). It finally sparked the much-wanted alliance which India had hoped to build since the 1990s with the United States. What further consolidated India–US' post-9/11 alliance was that in a much noted departure from the prior 9/11 era the US administration now addressed the problem of cross-border terrorism (that had since the 1980s effected the Kashmir valley of India but was ignored by the United States before 9/11 despite its cognizance of the connections between Al Qaeda and Pakistan) (Kamath, 2009). While India became a beneficiary of the US-led drive to free Pakistan from terrorism, it also positively impacted India's relations after 9/11 with Pakistan (to be discussed later).

Yet, United States' antiterror involvement in South Asia was closely linked to the region's nuclear situation where a peace process between India and Pakistan was unlikely to occur. It necessitated that the United States along with resolving the terror question play a major role in setting the stage to thaw the nuclear tension between India and Pakistan (Khan, 2009:148–149; Kronstadt and Pinto, 2013:4). This once again back-fired due to the stagnation of India–Pakistan's collaboration toward a bilateral arms control agenda—which the United States expected would happen in the larger context of the much debated the US' nuclear defense posture. As discussed in the previous chapter, although the United States administration after the Cold War claimed to reform its Cold War nuclear defense posture and on the rhetorical front appeared ready-to-launch nuclear disarmament, President G.W. Bush (backed by his Secretary of Defense, Donald Rumsfeld) since 2000 pushed the United States' Nuclear Missiles Defense program as the single-most urgent defense program of the US government (Ciarrocca, 2002; Kamath, 2009:118). This push came after following the completion of the United States' Nuclear Posture Review in January 2002 (Kamath, 2009:118–120),[6] which, claiming greater flexibility in maintaining a credible deterrence against the new adversaries,[7] in essence, supported for the United States "a nuclear war-winning posture," which could push the United States into a more dangerous security environment than at the height of the Soviet/American Cold War (Hartung, 2000; Ciarrocca, 2002; Krepon, 2003:238–240; Simpson and Nielson, 2004:124; Pincus, 2005). Thus, the fact remained that even after the Cold War, the United States did not surrender the threat of the first use of nuclear weapons; continued to maintain low-yield precision-guided nuclear weapons as tools of counterforce; and did not ratify the CTBT (Kamath, 2009:38, 114). In turn, India and Pakistan, for different reasons,[8] refused to sign the CTBT causing concern to the United States.

Yet, post-9/11 added further momentum in augmenting the ongoing strategic cultural rethinking of India and United States vis-à-vis each other. India's rising significance in terms of information technology, as a nuclear/military power, as a major source of skilled labor, and a bourgeoning market for the US exports necessitated that the George W. Bush administration continue to improve its relations with India (Sibal, 2003). This collaborative sentiment also found expression in India after 9/11 mainly on grounds of geo-strategic interests (Mohan, 2001–2002). As will be discussed later, this strategic cultural reorientation of both led to a number of collaborations between them in counter-terrorism programs, defense military team works, intelligence exchanges, joint naval exercise, flying operations, etc. (Global Security, 2002). In 2004, while both India and the United States were undergoing national elections, they signed (in January 2004) a defense partnership, through the Next Steps in Strategic Partnership (NSSP) Program, which, pending logistical hurdles of implementation, became the foundation for subsequent India–US nuclear cooperation in the post-BJP era (Borman, 2004).[9]

Nuclear developments in Pakistan (as discussed in Chapter 5) crossed a threshold almost as soon as the BJP assumed power with its testing of the nuclear-capable Ghauri missile on April 6, 1998. It gave Pakistan capability to target India's heartland. Although India's Defense Minister, George Fernandes claimed that India "doesn't have reason to feel worried about the Ghauri test … [and] the Prithvi is there, in adequate numbers … [to] take care of our security," the Ghauri surpassed any missile systems that India could deploy vis-à-vis Pakistan (*Statesman*, 1998). As Hoodbhoy (2002) writes, the testing of Ghauri, which created a "euphoric hyper-confidence and a spirit of machoism" within the Pakistani state, was worsened by A.Q. Khan's post-Ghauri comment that Pakistani teams were ready and able to conduct nuclear tests as soon as they could "get permission from the government." India–Pakistan's nuclear aggressiveness that had seen a seeming thaw with Bill Richardson's visit to the subcontinent reversed as India responded to Pakistan's Ghauri with its own nuclear tests on May 11 and 13, 1998.

Despite a range of views in Pakistan's domestic politics namely from Army Chief of Staff Jehangir Karamat, Benazir Bhutto (then in opposition), Pakistan's then Ambassador to the United Nations Akram Munir, and Prime Minister Nawaz Sharif on how to react to India's tests (Sharif, 1998; Bhutto, 1998; Munir, 1998), Pakistan responded with its own tests on May 29 and 30, 1998. Pakistan's security concern further increased, following India's testing of the intercontinental range ballistic missile Agni II IRBM on April 11, 1999. Thereafter, followed a series of test-firing of ballistic missiles by Pakistan: The 1,150 km range Ghauri II missile on April 14, 1999; the 750 km range hatf IV/Shaheen I missile on April 15, 1999; the hatf IA missile in February 2000; the 3,000 km range, North Korean Taepo-based, Ghauri III missile in August 2000; two flight tests of the hatf II versions in May 2002 and March 2003; the haft III/Ghaznavi in October 2003 (inducted into the Army's Strategic Forces Command in February 2002); and finally, the testing of the

1,700–2,500 kms range hatf VI/Shaheen II missile on March 9, 2004 (esteemed to be a two-stage version of the Chinese M-9 or a copy of the Chinese M-18 missile and the most capable ballistic missile of Pakistan) (Sachdeva, 2000:607; Muralidhar, 2002; Dhanda, 2010: 157, 164–166; 171). An India-based insecurity was forwarded by Pakistan's high officials like Ambassador, Munir Akram and Pervez Musharraf as Pakistan's primary concern (Munir, 1998; Bidwai, 2003).

What added to India's Pakistan-centric nuclear insecurity was that Pakistan in the course of expanding its nuclear program did not formulate a nuclear doctrine, rejected India's No-First-Use,[10] and opted in favor of a first-use of nuclear weapons (Sharma, 2005; Kamath, 2009).[11] To this extent, a Press Briefing by Pakistani state officials like General Khalid Kidwai and then Information Minister, Mushahid Hussain stated the "India-specific" criteria for the use of its nuclear weapons (Friedman, 2002; Kamath, 2009:169),[12] and made it abundantly clear that "The direction of our nuclear weapons program will be determined by Indian actions" (Federation of American Scientists, 1999; Kamath, 2009:169). In this context, Pakistan particularly has noted two things: First, that the Indian doctrine speaks of the need to maintain and strengthen Indian conventional military capabilities, and second that India has announced its capability to develop neutron bomb (Kamath, 2009:169). These developments in Pakistan, in addition to China and North Korea's support in strengthening Pakistan's missile development programs (Dhanda, 2010:177–178),[13] consolidated India's (in)securities vis-à-vis Pakistan.

India's interactions with Pakistan between the BJP years were also punctuated by several events namely an immediate postdetonation dialogue,[14] the Kargil crisis (May–July 1999), Pakistan-based terrorist border infiltrations into India-controlled Kashmir (December 2000), 9/11, and post-9/11 diplomacy between India and Pakistan (Khan, 2009:116–117, 120–121). Each remained critical in signifying a transition of the Indian state's interpretation of its international relations and insecurities vis-à-vis Pakistan. In terms of the Agra Summit, as Khan (2009:129–130) writes, although the two governments were unable to reach a verdict on the Kashmir issue, on the Line of Control and on Kashmir's plebiscite, these dialogues which were continuing through secret diplomacy by representatives of both governments were further jeopardized when "[PM] Vajpayee was influenced by [some] hawkish people who did not belief that Nawaz Sharif was to be trusted." From the Pakistani perspective, thus Kargil started disrupting dialogue between the two states (Khan, 2009:130). How Pakistan was desperately lowering its threshold of nuclear tolerance was evidenced during the Kargil when Mushahid Hussain stated that "we will not hesitate to use any weapon in our arsenal to defend our territorial integrity" (Kamath, 2009:178). Although the use of nuclear force was stalled with the US interference, Kargil was an eye-opener for India.

9/11 became critical in defining India's international relations vis-à-vis Pakistan. While 9/11 necessitated that the United States seek Pakistan's strategic alliance to fight the "war on terror" in the region, the United States simultaneously began publicly revealing its grievances against Pakistan's terrorist activities and organizations. Following a number of scholarly and governmental analyses revealing the suspected linkages between Pakistan and its sponsoring of terrorism (Bodansky, 1999; Kamath, 2009:183–184), India's concerns of the same became a reality when India fell prone to a number of Pakistani-backed terrorist attacks: First, an attack on the Legislative Assembly in Srinagar in October 2001; second, an attack by the Pakistani-based Jaish-e-Mohammad on the Indian Parliament on December 13, 2001; and third, a terrorist attack at the Indian army base in Jammu in May 2002 bringing both countries in a close confrontation for several months. The 2002 crisis was a second confirmation (after Kargil) that nuclear weapons on both sides have stabilized nuclear deterrence (although it has occurred in the context of harsh rhetoric, mutual suspicion, distrust, and strategic and military awareness that deterrence may fail).

After the Indian Parliament attack in December 2001, the Bush administration could no longer ignore Pakistan's complicity in terrorism. It launched a two-prong strategy counseling restraint on the part of India and placing Pakistani extremist groups Lashkar-e-Taiba and Jaish-e-Mohammed on the State Department's list of terrorist organizations. Mostly under the US pressure, Musharraf in an address to the nation on January 12, 2002 stated that the Pakistani soil would not be utilized to export terror to any other part of the world and made it his official policy to ban the two terrorist organizations Lashkar-e-Taiba and Jaish-e-Mohammad (Sanger and Eichenwald, 2001). Thereafter, amidst much domestic opposition (although supported by the Pakistani progressives),[15]

Musharraf in a departure from his pre-9/11, in early 2004 called for a *jihad* against the *jihadis* (Khan, 2009:145). Although these policy pronouncements/implementations were not easy and occurred amidst harsh anti-Indian rhetoric of Pakistani leaders (Haqqani, 2002:6; Baruah, 2004; Jones, 2004; Kamath, 2009; Khan, 2009:147), Musharraf's implementation of antiterrorist policies made a difference to the BJP who launched a bold step by 2003 to bring about a qualitative change in India's relation with Pakistan (Budania, 2003). How the Vajpayee government's ideological lenses worked at tandem with real politics to redefine India's strategic cultural thinking and (in)security imaginary vis-à-vis Pakistan after 9/11 will be elaborated in the next section.

India's international relations with China, which had attained some stability in the late 1990s, once again sparked under the BJP with India's 1998 nuclear testing. However, given India's improved relation with China (since their 1993 and 1996 confidence building measures) and the party's culturally akin pro-Chinese/pro-Hindu-Buddhist stand, India's postdetonation strains with China appeared rhetorically milder and less controversial than that with Pakistan (Malik and Singh, 1994; BJP Election Manifesto, 1996:32; Raghavan, 1997). Although India's then Defense Minister George Fernandes identified China as the "No.1" threat to India in justifying India's tests (BJP, 2002a: 23–24) and China was initially critical of the Indian bomb (namely because of the Chinese insecurity pretext within which Indian had justified the bomb), the BJP soon stepped up to rebuild its relations with China—who after the Cold War had also begun perceiving India more as a negotiating partner than a common enemy of China and Pakistan. Thus, despite some prevailing concerns within India immediately after the tests that China's "threatening ambition to be superpower ... [may] make India play second-fiddle to it" (Kamath, 2009:143), there was simultaneously an allaying concern for India that "it [China] is unlikely to use nuclear weapons against India as a rational decision-maker ..." (ibid.). In this context, China's pledging to a No-First-Use in 1964 and reiterating it in 1995 (ibid.:111, 114), offered some consolation to the Indian state's nuclear dilemmas vis-à-vis China. In a congruence of perception, Chinese security experts also commented that China does not "think [that] India will use the nuclear bomb against China" (ibid.:143).

Thus, beginning late April 1998, Sino-Indian dialogue ushered with path-breaking visits of top Chinese military officials including the visit of its Chief of General Staff Fu Quanyou to India (April 1998); recip- rocated by George Fernandes' visit to China, Prime Minister Vajpayee's visit to Beijing in June 2003, and their state officials meeting in January 2004 at the SAARC summit in Islamabad. Vajpayee's June 2003 visit to Beijing became particularly fruitful with the Indian prime minister and the Chinese Premier Wen Jiabao signing a Declaration on Cooperation fully normalizing Sino-Indian relations. At this meeting, both leaders pledged that their countries would work together for regional peace and stability, reaffirmed their commitment to the 1993 and 1996 agreements to maintaining peace and tranquility along the border, and codified the Agreement on the Actual Line of Control. In addition, the Chinese gov- ernment acknowledged that Pakistan faced very little actual threat from India; changed its stance on the Kashmir issue by addressing it as a bilat- eral India-Pakistán problem to be mutually resolved through peaceful negotiations; and the two governments conversed to further pursue bor- der control talks (which, stalled by China prior to India's nuclear tests, were now pushed to the forefront of their political agenda) (Mohan, 2004). Although a political framework for solving the border problem still remained elusive, the fact that the two sides showed a renewed com- mitment to a viable solution to the issue became evidenced as stakes on these talks were raised from the foreign secretary level to the political level with the two sides pledging to exchange high-level emissaries to negotiate the dispute (Shambaugh, 2009:146). Even before the Vajpayee government went out of office in May 2004, four meetings between the Prime Minister Vajpayee's National Security Advisor Brajesh Mishra and his Chinese counterparts were held on this agenda. As a part of their June 2003 meeting, India also reiterated its recognition of Tibet as part of the Chinese territory and made a pact not to support separatist activities by Tibetan exiles in India. China on its part agreed to open a point for border trade in Sikkim, thus indirectly accepting Sikkim's status as part of India.

Yet, it was not all about diplomacy and placating China because after the 1998 tests, India started to show a new confidence in its dealings with China and "the country's strategic analysts began to discuss possible ways to contain China" (Gupta, 2005:34). India's strategy of rethinking containment stemmed from a traditionally existing grievance within

India against China for having provided Pakistan with missile capability (that gave it a credible nuclear delivery system against India), and more recent developments such as Chinese presence in the Indian ocean (particularly using Myanmar as a location for monitoring facilities) and China's development of the port of Gwadar (which potentially enables the Chinese Navy, by using proxies like Pakistan to encircle India). Thus, in addition to diplomacy, India also started building its long-term nuclear and military capabilities against China namely the Su-30 bombers by the India Air Force and the BrahMos supersonic missile by the Indian navy to give the navy a second strike capability use against China. Yet, at the same time, India was also careful not to provoke China with its military/nuclear build-up and repeatedly postponed the testing of the Agni III missile that would give it the capability to hit targets deeper in China (Gupta, 2005:35). Thus, even in a scenario where India believed that "China's intentions may be suspect," India simultaneously by the end of the BJP's term believed that "Beijing is unlikely to attempt to alter dramatically the status quo in the near future" (ibid.:36). In fact, by the end of the BJP's term, India realized that Sino-Indian relations were not necessarily a zero-sum game, and that "business not politics" was a promising alternative to strengthen their relations (*The Indian Express*, 2001). India–China relations could go in three possible directions: coexistence, cooperation, and conflict (Gupta, 2005:35–36) or "coopetition" (Ayres and Mohan, 2009)—which I address in the next chapter.

An analysis of India's interpretation of its international relations vis-à-vis the United States, Pakistan, and China under the BJP reveals that the state's strategic thinking has represented a noticeable transformation of India's perceptions vis-à-vis these actors. As documented above, although acute realist insecurities vis-à-vis the United States, China, and Pakistan at the eve of May 1998 dominated the government's initial interpretations of its international relations (with these interpretations also becoming cultural in the context of Pakistan), following the tests, and after 9/11, these transitioned to a more neoliberal/globalized interpretation of India's world affairs. Thus, despite continuing realist concerns from India's regional dynamics and that India–US' proliferation issues still remained unsettled (with the US Senate rejecting the ratification of the Comprehensive Test Ban Treaty in October 1999), the BJP's term represented a turning point for the Indian state in rethinking its international affairs. The next section analyzes how out of these changing interpretive dynamics of India's international relations were reconstructed India's strategic cultural thinking and its (in)security imaginaries under the BJP years.

Reconstructing India's Strategic Culture and (In)Security Imaginary

India's successive nuclear detonations on May 11 and 13, 1998, followed by Pakistan's on May 29 and 30, 1998, started India's explicit trajectory as a nuclear weapons state reflecting an increasingly aggressive articulation of India's strategic culture and (in)security imaginary under the government. Although the government immediately after the tests declared a unilateral moratorium on any further tests; stated India's doctrine of minimal nuclear deterrence; and India's adherence to no-first-use of nuclear weapons, these detonations changed the nuclear security narratives of the subcontinent. India's security community justified the tests in terms of India's current real-politics, India's perceived nuclear apartheid, expanding India's future nuclear weapons capabilities, and keeping India's nuclear options open (given pending international pressures on India to sign the CTBT) (Cohen, 2001; Biswas, 2002; Karnad, 2005; Frey, 2006). These explanations, while valid, however, do not analyze how the BJP's decision to test and thereafter expand India's nuclear capabilities rendered possible within certain meaning-producing discourses of India's security community (especially by the Hindu Right government) that, in addition to its interpretation of India's current international politics and the post-9/11 compulsions of neoliberal interdependence, have also interacted with the *Hindutva* ideology, the notion of a Hindu India, and India's partition memories to create an ideological and political space within which were reconstructed India's nationalist identity, strategic cultural thinking, and (in)security imaginaries to support India's nuclear deterrence development. In the section below, I address these intersubjectively constructed missing puzzles.

Drawing on the (in)securities articulated by the previous non-BJP governments, the rationales of real-politics (insecurities from China and

Pakistan), technology (that the tests would offer Indian scientists a valuable database for the future design of nuclear weapons); global politics (nuclear hierarchy), and domestic politics (that the tests have established India's parity with the P-5 nations) were resorted to by the government to justify India's detonation (BJP, 1998a, 1998b, 1998c, 1999a, 1999b, 2000a, 2002b; Singh, 1998a). These rationales were thus articulated: India's then Defense Minister, George Fernandes identified China as India's "No.1" threat to justify India's tests (BJP, 2002a:23–24); the BJP's Senior Adviser on Defense and Foreign Affairs, Jaswant Singh pointed to Pakistan's "... using [of] terrorists, [and] infiltrating arms and explosives into the target country [India] ..." to rationalize the detonations (Singh, 1999:xxi); India's then Foreign Secretary K. Raghunath, said that India took "all possible steps to meet its security concerns arising from arms policies in neighboring Pakistan and China, [to ensure that] India would match its neighbors" (Mahapatra, 1998); Prime Minister Vajpayee asserted that "... nuclear weaponization is in self-defense" (Kamath, 2009:150); and India's Home Minister, L.K. Advani, referring to the earlier Congress government's "lackadaisical ambivalence" in responding "to the mounting evidence of Pakistan's nuclear weapons program," asserted that "it is criminally folly to persist with ambiguous policies in this field of critical national interest," and insisted that "India must have its own nuclear deterrent" (BJP, 2000b:65).

Likewise, referring to the lip-service paid by the nuclear powers to India's long-standing calls for disarmament (Sethi, 1998), discourses from government members projected these tests as India's sovereign "right" and "duty" to put an end to India's perceived nuclear apartheid (Burns, 1998b). To this extent, Singh (1998a) lamented the spread of a broad security paradigm from Vancouver to Vladivostok that gave protection to almost all Western states including South Korea, Japan, and Australia leaving South Asia out of any protection, and India's then Ambassador to the United States, Mr. Naresh Chandra, claimed that "to expect a people, who constitute one-sixth of mankind to be outside the network of nuclear guarantees that others have is not acceptable" (Nayar, 2001:52). In showing this anticolonial resistance, Brajesh Mishra (National Security Advisor to Prime Minister Vajpayee) challenged that "who are the Americans to tell us how to take care of our security concerns?" (Khare, 1998:11). The theme of India's nuclear sovereignty, postcolonial pride, and nationalist glory also became clear from these discourses: In a national correspondence after India's tests, Prime Minister Vajpayee said that India's tests should not be cast away as "jingoistic euphoria," but should be seen as a stride toward military self-sufficiency and self-defense "to silence its enemies and show its strength" (Correspondent Sheet, 1998).

However, following the constructivist angle of this book, that a nation's strategic cultural discourses and related (in)security imaginaries are ideologically and discursively constructed by its political leaders, one must also consider how certain cultural factors were also used quite extensively by the Hindu-Right government in its unofficial/informal discourses in justifying India's nuclear tests. This is because in the absence of any clear identifiable danger from Pakistan, not any more than what Pakistan had already posed to India prior to the 1998 detonation (Ahmed and Cortright, 1998) and that several evidences negate any easy calculus of an immediate Chinese threat necessitating at that juncture of Indian politics a nuclear test (Han, 1998; *The Hindustan Times*, September 25, 1999),[16] the Pakistani threat was rendered more intelligible by the BJP through the ideological constructions of an anti-Islamic/Pakistani sentiment in India that viewed Pakistan as a more serious threat to India than China. In fact, as commented by a BJP member in minimizing the potential Chinese threat, "Our preparations to neutralize threats from China are a sure recipe for bankruptcy. In our present state, we just do not have the muscle to engage China in an armed conflict" (*The Hindustan Times*, September 25, 1999). In this context, I suggest that the ideology of *Hindutva*, resting on historical and religious reconstructions of Hindu and Muslim identities, may have been used by the BJP (in addition to real political factors) to recreate and sustain certain communal forms of (in)securities by amplifying Pakistan as a danger to the Hindu India.

Accordingly, as evidenced from party documents such as *BJP Today, Swastika,* and the BJP Election Manifestos, most BJP members (guided by their ideological mindset of *Hindutva*) have identified the religious and cultural history of Indo-Pakistan partition as a factor for India's nuclear concerns from Pakistan. These perceptions rooted in the cultural biases of the two-nation theory have viewed the history of partition as a "living nostalgia," which, despite having occurred 60 years ago, still had the potential to affect the national security of India. Recalling that

India has had a "fractured" past, which began with the "Muslim invasion and destruction of the Hindu-Buddhist cultures" in India, a BJP activist notes, "Buddhism originated in India, so India and China are culturally similar. On the contrary, Pakistan was carved out of India owing to religious animosities" (BJP, 1999c:4–7). Likewise, the *BJP Today* writes: "India is a peace-loving country. We inherit our culture from the principle of *Panchsheel* and Buddhism, which have flourished in this land since time immemorial …. However, India is mainly troubled by … Islamic terrorists … for quarter of a century …" (BJP, 2003:17–20).

Based on such cultural essentials of India–Pakistan history, BJP members apprehended that Pakistan may resort to a "nuclear blackmail" against India to settle the Kashmir issue as a "continuing legacy of the unfinished agenda of partition" (BJP, 1999d: 3, 5). Accordingly, as revealed in the BJP newsmagazine, *Swastika* "… Through its testing of Ghauri, Pakistan has tried symbolically to reinstate history, where Hindu/Indian king, Prithviraj Chauhan was defeated by the Islamic Hindu/Indian king, Muhammad Ghauri to establish Muslim control over India" (BJP, 1998a:8).[17] Furthermore, in culturally and historically rooted interpretation of the Ghauri, the then BJP Vice-President, Bal Thakre, claimed "the testing of Ghauri is not merely an exercise in flexing muscles but is a political message from Islamabad to Delhi, rooted in history" (BJP, 2000b). While from a realist perspective, the Ghauri indeed poses a threat to India, what makes this otherwise acceptable assertion problematic is the party's interweaving of history, culture, and religion to interpret the Ghauri. Such interpretations of the Ghauri in the context of a historical "Islamic" vengeance against a Hindu India not only suggest the workings of a Hinduicized strategic rethinking of the BJP members but also how such rethinking reinterprets issues (in) securities in interstate security affairs. That the BJP's "Hindu" bomb is devised against Pakistan is furthermore evidenced in the May 17, 1998 issue of the BJP's magazine *Organiser* carrying the article "Time to Tame Pakistan" (Karat, 1998).

Although India's prominent military strategist K. Sundarji (as discussed in the previous chapter) had stated that India did not at that point require H bombs for deterrence, India's science community, defense analysts, and the Indian military supported India's tests. Defense analysts and personnel of India's prestigious think-tank, Institute of Defense and Strategic Analysis, published a collective *Nuclear India* immediately following India's tests describing their perspectives and justifications of these tests (Singh, 1998b, 1998c; Beri, 1998; Kumar, 1998; Chittaranjan, 1998; Kartha, 1998). Briefly stated, this collective, with great overlap with the government, justified India's nuclear tests on grounds of India's national security interests, a discriminatory international security regime, the US geo-political power game in South Asia, that the roots of arms race in South Asia were laid by the United States during Cold War, and that the majority of nuclear arsenal is possessed by the nuclear weapons powers thus posing a greater risk in maintaining a global nuclear momentum (Singh, 1998b).

However, despite this mutual overlap between the BJP government and the IDSA analysts concerning their realist perspectives in supporting India's test, most of the IDSA analysts did not justify the tests as a defensive strategy for a Hindu rashtra. Rather, as expressed in the viewpoints of V. Santhanam (then Director, IDSA), Uday Bhaskar (Deputy Director, IDSA), Jasjit Singh (ex-Director, IDSA), and V.K. Shrivastava (then ex-Deputy Director, IDSA), "an external anarchical environment" has necessitated India's detonation, which Bhaskar termed as "multiple point" threats to India (Bhaskar, 2002; Santhanam, 2002a; Shrivastava, 2002; Singh, 2002). The most elegant articulation of these "multiple point" threats to India's national security as referred to collectively by the IDSA informants can be thus summarized, "… that a perceived nuclear apartheid from the nuclear weapons states, including that of China, was a more serious concern for the Indian state than that of Pakistan—where insecurity perceptions from the latter (Pakistan) perhaps becomes narrow/communal when framed from the perspective of India and Pakistan's historical context" (ibid.). Also, neither of the above-mentioned defense analysts recognized any connection between the ideology of *Hindutva,* the BJP's quest for a Hindu rashtra, and that of India's nuclear agenda.

India's science community upheld technological factors as well as the discriminatory nature of the global nonproliferation regime to justify India's tests and its subsequent program of nuclear weapons expansion. Citing technological reasons, Dr A.P.J. Abdul Kalam felt that more tests were necessary to perfect a thermonuclear device (Talbott, 2004), and others like Chidambaram (Chair, Indian Atomic Energy Commission) pointed to India's "nuclear sovereignty" for going ahead with the nuclear tests. He stated, even if India was pressured by the nuclear powers into signing a treaty to end unsafeguarded production of fissile materials, "India's initial explosive experiments with non-weapon-grade plutonium ... [would give India] confidence that this material could be used for bombs ...," and hence equip its scientists to make nuclear weapons of different yields and for different application systems. For him "this would not only add to India's prospective arsenal but also make a fissile-material production cutoff treaty more palatable" (Perkovich, 1999:430). Chidambaram furthermore used the United States and Russian testing experiences to argue the necessity of conducting more nuclear explosions "to increase the database for conducting computer simulations" (ibid.:407).

A significant turn at this point was the involvement of the Indian military in issues of India's strategic deterrence. Following pro-nuclear comments from India's then Chief of the Army Staff, General V.P. Malik and the Former Indian Air Chief Marshal N.C. Suri, that "acquiring a strategic deterrence capability to counter the emerging nuclear and missile challenges" to India's security was "only a responsible act" (Mahapatra, 1998), the Indian army now (at least tried to) become more explicitly involved in issues of India's strategic deterrence. At a five-day army commander's conference, V.P. Malik declared that "a strategic deterrent to counter the emerging nuclear and missile challenges was the need of the hour" and stressed the need of greater financial resources to modernize its forces (Perkovich, 1999:413). Malik hoped that the formation of a National Security Council would give the armed force greater autonomy vis-à-vis the civilian bureaucrats on planning and implementing strategic deterrence, which, as will be discussed, was created by the government's nuclear momentum.

The issue of secrecy aside with regard to the government's decision to detonate, a number of contending political parties outside the BJP (although representing a smaller section) launched a scathing attack on the BJP's tests. Pranab Mukherjee (India's Former External Affairs Minister from the Congress party, the principal opposition party in Parliament), critiqued that "the BJP had gone against the national consensus on the nuclear issue ... which would trigger an arms race in the subcontinent"; Prakash Karat (member, Communist Party of India, Marxist) while cri-tiquing nuclear powers "for not utilizing the opportunities that were available to abolish nuclear weapons after the Cold War period ended," did not support India's weaponization (although simultaneously claiming that the party was in favor of retaining India's nuclear option and that the Agni program should not be frozen); and the Janata Dal and the Communist Party of India (CPI) too opposed the tests or any further induction of nuclear weapons. While the Samajwadi Party, the Rashtriya Janata Dal, and the Akali Dal favored the induction of nuclear weapons "if it [was] absolutely necessary for the defense of the country," the Samajwadi Party held that the BJP was using the nuclear issue as a "political gimmick" (Cherian, 1998). Notably, the BJP's allies in Government who subscribed to the National Democratic Agenda did not evidently devote much attention to the issue (ibid.).

In addition, an array of antinuclear/peace rallies (made up of doctors, engineers, retired military men, environmentalists, media persons, academics, retired military personnel, feminists, social activists, and ordinary civilians) emerged in New Delhi, Mumbai, Calcutta, and at other cities decrying the tests on moral, human, gender, environmental, social, and economic security grounds, with an antibomb/peace organization summing its antibomb slogan by saying "No Food, No Water, No Jobs …. We have the Bomb" (Movement in India for Nuclear Disarmament, 1998). Postdetonation analyses also debated how the BJP's electoral/party-based considerations explain the bomb (ibid.), whether the tests represented a loss of India's moral credibility as a champion of disarmament (Bidwai and Vanaik, 2000), and whether the tests represented a departure from India's traditional strategic culture (Gordon, 1995; Bajpai et al., 1996; Mattoo, 1996; Sidhu, 1996). In the scheme of these debates as Chengappa (cited in Khan, 2009:80) noted although "the Indian decision to acquire nuclear weapons was made in the context of China … [it's] weaponization program was accelerated in the context of Pakistan."

In noting the above analyses of India's 1998 tests and through my own offered in the above section, I must qualify the following points: First, my point in the above analyses was not to contend that the BJP's rise to power constitutes the only explanation for India's nuclear detonation. In fact, the party's decision to detonate is not totally surprising given that the party since the 1980s had been promoting the idea of going nuclear. Furthermore, the tests owed not to one political party, the BJP, under whom the tests were merely conducted but to a string of earlier governments who since the 1950s supported the development of the nuclear option (Cherian, 1998; Narula et al., 1998). Second, my analysis also did not seek to claim that the *Hindutva* ideology has a direct link with the Indian bomb (although the BJP ideologues have since the 1980s spoken of a "Hindu bomb") (Narula et al., 1998). In fact, I am cognizant that the BJP leaders have not explicitly revealed their anti-Pakistani sentiments underlying India's nuclear agenda by saying "nuke Pakistan"; high-ranking leaders of the BJP (although in rare exceptions) have even refused to identify Pakistan as an Islamic danger to India; and only in the more locally available (nonmainstream) journals, pamphlets, and newsletters available at local party offices did the government reveal its "unofficial" concerns about the Pakistani state. Last, but not the least, prominent members of the government namely India's Defense Minster, George Fernandes; National Security Advisor to the Prime Minister, Brajesh Mishra (a strong advocate of the bomb); and India's then Additional Secretary of the United Nations, Dilip Lahiri following the tests reiterated India's pursuit of disarmament (although strongly stressing the "level playing field" within which such disarmament initiatives be taken), and Prime Minister Vajpayee through several speeches on May 18, 21, 27 and 28, 1998, reminded the nation that India would "continue to reflect a commitment to [the] sensibilities and obligations of an ancient civilization, a sense of responsibility and restrain" (Perkovich, 1999:417, 423, 435; Kamath, 2009:142). This comment from a pro-nuclear prime minister, referring to an "ancient [Gandhian] civilization … [of] restrain," is noticeable and may perhaps be seen as the BJP government's continued tribute to India's traditional nuclear restraint.

Despite such qualifiers, what is explicitly evident from the above data is how the BJP's decision to test represented a sharp break from the strategic thinking of the earlier non-BJP governments, and in doing so how the BJP's rearticulations of India's strategic culture has enabled the party to rewrite a Pakistani danger along more communal lines and facilitate its decision to test. Accordingly, in keeping with my theoretical premise that (in)security imaginary "… is the product of an act of cultural creation, which is fundamental to any subsequent system of cultural representation" (Tomlinson, 1991:156–157), I contend here that the eve of India's 1998 detonation witnessed a unique reconstruction of the Indian state's strategic cultural thinking under the BJP, where the BJP's *Hindutva* ideology, its supporting strategic discourses, and an increasingly permissive domestic and external environment that India then faced (from the party's militant factions; an assertive, unpredictable, and rising China; increasing Sino-Pakistani nuclear transactions; and an increasingly nuclear-strong Pakistan under nuclear patrons like China and the United States), worked as meaning-producing tools to create a political and ideological space within which the real-political, cultural, religious, and historical intersected to make a Pakistani-centric (anti-Islamic) (in)security imaginary more real or amplified for the Indian state. These reconstructions of India's strategic cultural discourses and (in)security imaginaries at the eve of its detonation were also rearticulated India's nationalist identity as a nuclear aggressive, militant, robust, muscular, modernizing (Hindu) India—that finally went nuclear.

The emergence of a formal debate within India's government, strategic, and defense sectors immediately after the tests on what India's nuclear strategies, command and control, and delivery systems should be revealed another shift in the Indian state's strategic cultural thinking. This formal debate convened as the Institute of Defense and Strategic Analysis with serving and retired defense officials, academics, foreign-policy officials, and eminent journalists following the tests parlayed to develop a consensus for a coherent strategy for deterring long-term nuclear threats to Indian security (*The Times of India*, 1998). The announcement of India's minimum nuclear doctrine on August 17, 1999 addressed India's urgency to meet a coherent nuclear deterrence posture. Prepared by the National Security Advisory Board and officially adopted by the NDA government on January 4, 2003, the doctrine stipulated the following: First, India's pledge to a No-First-Use doctrine;[18] second, use nuclear weapons only as a second strike to inflict "unacceptable damage" to its aggressor;[19] third, to develop survivability of its nuclear weapons, including developing triads consisting of air force, army, and navy based bombers, missiles, and submarines including missile delivery systems (in which India was at that point far behind Pakistan, not to mention China); fourth, maintain highly effective conventional military capabilities to raise the threshold of the outbreak of conventional military and nuclear wars;[20] and finally, that No-First-Use is only a declaratory policy meaning India's nuclear weapons will not be physically deployed; its nuclear warheads will be maintained in a de-alerted manner; and that nuclear weapons will be maintained by the civilian leadership (i.e., the prime minister and the Indian Atomic Energy Commission) and not the military (Kamath, 2009:131–135).

In addition to institutionalizing an explicit nuclear deterrence posture for India, India's nuclear doctrine also addressed two other strategic issues that were being debated within India's strategic circles: First, "whether India actually possessed hydrogen bombs," and if so, "why its scientists wanted to develop them and what the state proposed to do with them" (a question that also spilled over to the issue of India signing the Comprehensive Test Ban Treaty after going nuclear); and second, the long prevailing area of contention from the military that their views were not being sought by the government in determining India's position on further testing and the signing of the Comprehensive Test Ban Treaty, and whether the government would "continue its long-standing avoidance of allocating nuclear weapons and command-and-control roles to the military" (Perkovich, 1999:431–432). While strategists like Sundarji (1996a) were of the view that India did not need an H-bomb, others such as the AEC Chair Chidambaram, Dr A.P.J. Abdul Kalam, K. Santhanam, the BJP's hawkish nuclear analyst, Mohan Guruswamy, and the military's top-ranking officials supported the testing of H-bombs/ thermo-nuclear devices (Embassy of India, 1998). The proponents of the H-bomb offered a two-fold argument to this end: First, given that India's arch rival, Pakistan, who had rejected India's No-First-Use offer was unlikely even with the assistance of China to develop a H-bomb, acquisition of the latter by India "would put Pakistan it its place;" and second, if a hydrogen bomb was necessary for India's national security and the May 1998 tests were not a success to that end, then a policy driven by India's national security imperatives would call for further nuclear tests and thus would not be in India's national interest to sign the treaty (*The Times of India*, 1998; Perkovich, 1999:431–433). In this scheme of debates, the military's observation that not enough testing had been done by the weaponeers to give the military a reliable and efficient nuclear weapons delivery system paved the way for India to not sign the Comprehensive Test Ban Treaty—which by 1999 had all practical purposes became redundant.

Finally, the minimum nuclear doctrine by stipulating that the military commander will neither use excessive force nor will use it unnecessarily to provoke the enemy (Kamath, 2009), also addressed the long-standing issue of the military's entry into India's strategic policy formulation. This doctrinal resentment of the military's involvement boded well with similar sentiments among sections of the government with the BJP's defense analyst, Mohan Guruswamy stating that nuclear weapons "to avoid competition" should not be transferred to the military services but should remain "under one service" (Cooper, 1998:A22); and India's Defense Minister, George Fernandes, reserving the matter as an issue "to be discussed [subsequently] at great length" (Singh, 1998d). However, there emerged at that point some cooperation among India's military, the government, and India's scientists (with some Indian Air Force officers being trained at the Bhabha Atomic Research Center in weapons manufacturing), wherein prominent members of India's military, Defense (DRDO), and intelligence community such as scientist Dr A.P.J. Abdul Kalam, General Sundarji, IDSA ex-Director Jasjit Singh, Indian RAW's Former Additional Secretary, J.K. Sinha sought to address the operational dilemmas of the Indian nuclear doctrine in what constitutes a sufficient level of India's nuclear doctrine (Kamath, 2009:137), and Dr Kalam continued to assert integrating the military services into India's missile development program to enhance a broader institutional coalition in support of India's nuclear program (Chengappa, 1994).

The issue of India's minimum nuclear doctrine including its No-First-Use posture has been variously debated, including the doctrine's advantages and disadvantages and whether it has represented an erosion of India's strategic thinking? In keeping with Tanham's (1992) claim of "passivity," or Bajpai et al.'s (1996) claim of a lack of strategic thinking in India, Basrur (2001) in his analysis has maintained that India's strategic thinking still remained one of passivity given that the BJP government took almost a year (1999) to announce its minimal nuclear doctrine that was adopted even later in 2003. In this light, Prime Minister Vajpayee's setting up of a National Security Council in November 1998 to undertake India's first-ever strategic defense review not only faced considerable bureaucratic opposition from former Indian Administrative Service officials like D.S. Kamtekar and Madhav Godbole but also failed. In contrast, Bidwai and Vanaik (2000) see the No-First-Use concept as a departure from India's traditional reverence to nonviolence. In this scheme of debate, Kamath (2009:145) suggests that a long history of deterrence (in the sense of restraint) predates India's ancient strategic culture since the ancient days of the *Brihadaranyaka* Upanishad (that teaches restraint or *neti neti*), and seen in this historical context, India's No-First-Use doctrine is logically, morally and philosophically indicative of India's nuclear restraint in its prevailing world order. In this pretext of restraint, India's No-First-Use also has a political and practical value in establishing that India's nuclear weapons are for defense and not for offense, serves as a confidence-building measure in South Asia, and in an ideal scenario may be seen as a step toward the ultimate global emergence of a No-Use of nuclear weapons (Kamath, 2009:142, 147).

As mentioned earlier, (in)security imaginary is not real in the sense that it can be empirically scrutinized. Rather, "it is the product of an act of cultural creation, which is fundamental to any subsequent system of cultural representation" (Tomlinson, 1991:156–157). Seen from this perspective, I contend that the emergence of an institutionalized nuclear deterrence, albeit situated by some scholars in the context of restraint or a strategic necessity for the state, represents a shift to an "institutionalized nuclear militancy" in the strategic mindset of a post-nuclear India—surpassing precedents of a much revered philosophy of Gandhian nonviolence and norms of India's nuclear ambiguity. In the light of this observation, my analysis contends that India's postnuclear strategic cultural thinking and (in)securities that institutionalized the state's nuclear militancy were representative of an urge of a more deserving and expanding nuclear robustness, masculinity, and sophistication of the Indian state to be accepted as a legitimate member of the nuclear club, and to that extent a drive by the state (backed by its security community) to strategize nuclear India's future nuclear policies, operation, command, control, and delivery systems. In this emerging (in)security facing nuclear India after its detonation, India's (Hindu) identity and Pakistan-centric (anti-Islamic) insecurities were muted. In its place was articulated India's identity as a technologically modern, militarizing, and nuclear India paying mere tribute to nonalignment, which, ironically, enabled the state to redefine its nuclear security relations with the United States traditionally deemed by India as a hierarchical player in its international relations. While this trend had already set in motion following India's tests under the internationalist segment of the BJP, 9/11 offered a more accommodative space to both India and the United States (and to

India and Pakistan) for a strategic cultural reorientation in their nuclear security interactions.

As mentioned earlier, 9/11 initiated a US security agenda in search of terror supposedly located in Afghanistan, brought responsible states as the US allies in this hunt, and induced a new mission and energy to the US engagement with India. Although political analysts suggest that countering a rising China was also a motive for the US' engagement with India (Ayres and Mohan, 2009), the US' post-9/11 security discourses with India, unlike its Cold War-oriented discourses now made use of a neoliberal logic of interstate interdependence (as a way of attaining its global security mission) to engage India (United States Department of Defense, 2003). Emblematic in President Bush's comment, "In this moment of opportunity [read: crisis], a common danger is erasing old rivalries. America is working... in ways we have never before to address peace and prosperity .... Together with friends and allies ...we will demonstrate that the forces of terror cannot stop the momentum of freedom" (Bush, 2002). Building on this logic of "resource-investment," the US Ambassador to India, Blackwill, reassured India–US' collaborative gestures by referring to India and the United States as keepers of "enlightened democracies" and "global peace" (Department of State, 2002), and US Under Secretary of Defense for Policy, Douglas Feith in August 2003 noted, "... President Bush and PM Vajpayee have redefined the US-India relationship: democracy, common principles, and shared interest are the foundation of our new strategic partnership" (United States Department of Defense, 2003).

This collaborative sentiment found favorable expression in India mainly on grounds of geo-strategic considerations of 9/11 (Mohan, 2001–2002). In contrast to its traditional anti-US national security conception, there emerged after 9/11 a US-centric national security agenda in India (National Democratic Alliance, 2005), which, with a "we" focus on democratic India and the United States tenuously drew on India's modern, democratic, and global image to maintain mutual security-related missions. Prime Minister Vajpayee immediately after 9/11, stressing democracy as a common political factor between India and the United States, claimed, "I assured President Bush of India's complete support in this [i.e., war on terror]. As multi-religious, pluralist democracies, we should clearly spread the message ... against terrorism ..." (US-India Friendship.net, 2001). To this extent, he continued, "We as democratic states have forwarded our dialogue architecture... of defense collaborations.... The joint working group on counterterrorism has made progress. And we have agreed to launch a joint cyber-terrorism initiative...Both of us agree that synergies and complementarities between our two countries should be ... fully exploited" (ibid.). Likewise, India's then Defense Minister George Fernandes expressed India's solidarity with the United States in its war against terror, conversed on building a strategic framework between India and the United States, and with US Secretary of State Rumsfeld on January 17, 2002, issued joint press statements to the effect that "Today this relationship is qualitatively different from the days of the Cold War, ... [and] we are on a forward movement insofar as strengthening our relations and ... dealing with all the challenges that we are both facing in our respective areas of concern" (United States Department of Defense, 2002).

Thereafter, since 2002 a number of collaborations followed between India–US in the areas of military exercises, counter-terrorist activities, arms sales, cooperation in missile defenses, intelligence exchanges, joint naval exercises, flying operations, etc. (Global Security, 2002; Tellis, 2004). The deepest interaction was in the field of military relations in areas of bilateral exercises, personnel exchanges, military education and training, and officer and unit exchanges to enhance mutual familiarity between armed forces in case the two had to combine arms in future peace and stability missions of the region (Tellis, 2004:8). These defense collaborations were further cemented through the NSSP Initiative (signed between India and the United States in January 2004), which loosened US export restrictions for some items to be exported to India's unsafeguarded nuclear facilities (for nonreactor related uses such as power generation) and became the foundation for subsequent Indo-US nuclear cooperation. In reaffirming the Indian state's neoliberal vision and strategic rethinking in its relationship with the United States, Vajpayee reasserted the "synergies and complementarities" of defense collaborations between India and the United States (US-India Friendship.net, 2001); S.B. Mukherjee (India's Minister of State in the Department of Space), described India–US technology collaborations as "... mutually beneficial cooperation in the area of nuclear power" (Shahin, 2003); and India's Defense Minister, Fernandes, lauded the "technology cooperation[s] between the United States and India" (United States Department of Defense, 2002).

Although India welcomed the Bush administration's plans for a greater Indian role in creating a strategically stable South Asia, tensions remained. For one, the United States' neoliberal discourses with India remained fraught with Orientalist fears given that several members of the Bush administration such as Colin Powell (ex-US Secretary of State under Clinton), cautioned that "the US ... [ought] to balance" its cooperation and trade with India "in its sensitive technology with concern about proliferation and security" (Powell, 2003), and others like Bob Graham and Ed Markey identified India along with Pakistan as "existing axis of proliferation, who were forging ahead in their own rights in building new generations of nuclear proliferation" (Graham, 2003). In addition, revived friendship between the US–Pakistan after 9/11, India–US differences on Kashmir (in that the United States was not doing enough to convince Pakistan to accept the LoC into a formal international border), expectations on nuclear/missile issues, India's growing energy relations with Iran, and Washington's decision to declare Pakistan as a major non-NATO ally (within weeks of the confirmation of news reports that Pakistani scientists had leaked nuclear technology to Iran, Libya, and North Korea) were perceived by India as emblematic of myopic US short-term interests in the region. In this context, there is also concern that Washington is not sufficiently sensitive to India security concerns or its aspirations of being a great power (Mohan, 2006). Accordingly, India too has retained its traditional nuclear apartheid sentiment vis-à-vis the United States evidenced in the defense analysts of the IDSA, academics at the Jawaharlal Nehru University New Delhi, and political parties such as the Communist Party of India (Marxist), suggesting that India follow a cautious approach in its strategic collaborations with the United States (Cheodon, 2010; Mahapatra, 2010). Although Prime Minister Vajpayee has referred to India–US as "natural allies" (Mohan, 2003), the BJP's External Affairs Minister, Yashwant Sinha, has stated that "US interest in our relationship is just that of a friend. They have been talking to us like a friend, and we have also been telling (them) about the developments like a friend .... That is where it stops ..." (Sinha, 2004).

In terms of India's strategic cultural rethinking vis-à-vis Pakistan after 9/11, Musharraf's implementation of Pakistan's antiterrorist policies (as mentioned earlier) made a difference to the BJP government, and even if temporarily, changed the Indian government's strategic thinking vis-à-vis the Pakistani state. Prime Minister Vajpayee, who earlier considered Musharraf to be "untrustworthy," launched a bolder step to bring about a qualitative change in India–Pakistan relations (Haqqani, 2002; Budania, 2003; Khan, 2009:147). Although personal, political, and economic interests may have also underscored these ideological shifts on the part of the Indian prime minister and his government,[21] this change, coming from "the leader of a hawkish Hindu party," carried great significance for Musharraf (Khan, 2009:149), who, by then, had realized that "a conflict simmering endlessly [was] not helping,"[22] and that political and economic imperatives of globalization necessitated that Pakistan accommodate with its rival India in international affairs (Lebow, 1995; Kegley and Raymond, 1999). Despite both Musharraf and Vajpayee's being hostage to their fundamentalist domestic constituencies (Khan, 2009:124–125), both reciprocated with a strong interest through 2003–2004 rapprochement processes to cooperate on multiple levels to achieve common objectives of peace, security, and economic development of both countries (Pattanaik, 2003; Jones, 2004; Baruah, 2004; Khan, 2009:133, 148). Yet, their rapprochement processes remained difficult (Jones, 2004), and Pakistan's implementation of its antiterrorist policies occurred amidst harsh anti-Indian rhetoric, mutual distrust (Bidwai, 2003; Kronstadt, 2004a; Kamath, 2009:179), and replaying hostile forms of Self/Other identity constructions (Khan, 2009:124–125). Yet, on a promising note, one can discern that both Vajpayee and Musharraf's post-9/11 strategic cultural shifts toward each other invested considerable political capital with Musharraf vowing to pursue negotiations with India even at the risk of further assassination attempts (Jones, 2004). India–Pakistan rapprochement processes simultaneously occurred with Sino-Indian high-level diplomacy as discussed earlier.

As mentioned earlier, (in)security imaginary is not real in the sense that it can be empirically scrutinized. Rather, "it is the product of an act of cultural creation, which is fundamental to any subsequent system of cultural representation" (Tomlinson, 1991:156–157). Seen from this definition of (in)security imaginary, one notices the emergence a hybrid form of strategic cultural rethinking and reconstructions of (in)security imaginaries within the post-9/11 Indian state vis-à-vis Pakistan, China, and the United States. Three contours of strategic rethinking and (in)security imaginaries were articulated: Although the previous Indo-American administrations had started this trend, the BJP's term revealed a significant overhaul of the Indian state's strategic thinking and (in)security imaginaries vis-à-vis the United States, which, beginning with India's detonation controversies with the United States, and existing post-9/11 skepticisms, overall shifted to one of a strategic alliance between them after 9/11. Thus, while continued post-9/11 suspicion remained a source of insecurity for the Indian state vis-à-vis its hierarchical Western strategic partner, their burgeoning strategic partnership finally clinched the much-vaunted alliance which India since the 1990s had hoped to build with the United States. In this sense, the latter represented a more secure footing in India–US nuclear relations.

With regard to China, India's (in)security imaginary (although somewhat diluted by their cultural affinity as perceived by the BJP) was no less threatening given India's phobias from a nuclear China, yet, in its postdetonation era, saw India with a "new found" sense of confidence and assertiveness vis-à-vis China—which placed India in a more secure footing vis-à-vis China—and, as speculated, could go in the possible directions of cooperation, coexistence, and competition in their strategic affairs (Gupta, 2005; Ayres, 2009; Ayres and Mohan, 2009; Shambaugh, 2009). However, as will be elaborated in the next chapter, these dynamics of Sino-Indian strategic interactions were to be greatly influenced by the shifting dynamics of the US–India's strategic security relations—which again would depend on the changing contours of the US–Pakistan strategic security affairs.

Finally, the post-9/11 Indian state's strategic thinking and (in)security imaginary vis-à-vis Pakistan also revealed noticeable transitions given that the Hindu-Right government's earlier discursive and ideological interplays of India–Pakistan's partition history, India's *Hindutva* identity, and an Islamic (in)security that foregrounded the government's detonation, post-9/11 shifted to attempts of rapprochement. While proliferation optimists have credited nuclear weapons for introducing deterrence between India–Pakistan (Sundarji, 1990; Hagerty, 1995/1996; Feldman; 1995), and proponents of real, neoliberal, and domestic politics might argue that the BJP's strategic rethinking vis-à-vis Pakistan took place only after Pakistan implemented its antiterrorist policies; owing to the compulsions of globalization (Lebow, 1995; Kegley and Raymond, 1999); and also as a commitment to the BJP's election campaign to improve relations with Pakistan (Jones, 2004), and was not essentially an ideological shift of the government—from the author's perspective remain noticeable—and could not have thus occurred in a still prevailing anarchical world of India–Pakistan affairs. This pro-Pakistani shift, albeit brief, represented at least at the end of the BJP's term, a relatively secure footing than before in India–Pakistan's strategic security affairs.

Finally, in noting these shifts of the Indian state to its pro-US/pro-Pakistani orientations, I suggest that the BJP has been a skilled articulator and interweaver of a Hindu/Indian nationalism, real-politics, its quest for a globalized modernity, and the need of an Indian (Hindu) bomb to redefine the state's identity simultaneously as a Hindu nationalist entity (akin to the early 20th-century Hindu nationalists) and that of a modern, globalized entity in a world of post-9/11 politics. I suggest that these discursive and ideological interplays of the nation, its strategic thinking, and its (in)security imaginaries have worked in meaning-producing ways to create a political and ideological space within which were launched India's nuclear and missile development policies.

Nuclear Developments and Neoliberal Strategic Security Collaborations

India's 1988 tests conducted under the supervision of four lead scientists Dr A.P.J. Abdul Kalam (DRDO), Chidambaram (AEC), K. Santhanam (DRDO), and Anil Kakodkar (BARC) earned them national kudos—namely because the tests had "achieved a second breakthrough ... by providing the effectiveness of deuterium–tritium (DT) neutron initiators to trigger fission explosions" (Perkovich, 1999:431). Reportedly, the scientists and engineers "had been working on such initiators for years to replace the original initiator design that relied on beryllium and polonium" (ibid.). Thereafter, overturning the suspension of India's flight tests (as done by the Rao, the Deva Gowda, and the Gujral governments between 1995 and March 1998), research and development on India's nuclear and missile technology and conducting flight-tests continued unabated

(Chengappa, 2000). Although arms limitations requirements and non-proliferation expectations stemming from the immediate post-1998 India–US diplomacy put some political and diplomatic restraints on the part of the government, the general pro-nuclear climate within India's security community facilitated the weaponeers' agenda to develop and deploy missiles more than twice the range of the original Agni TD/TTB (Technology Demonstrator/Technology Test Bed) missile; build nuclear-powered ballistic-missile submarines; and acquire the most technologically sophisticated "trappings of military-technological power" (Perkovich, 1999:438). Accordingly, between April 1999 and March 2004, the BJP expedited the further development of the Agni series and thereafter carried the successful test firings of the Agni II IRBM, the Agni II AT IRBM, and Agni I SRBM missile systems (Dhanda, 2010:104–106).

Each version of the Agni missiles thereafter produced and flight-tested by the DRDO represented significant sophistications from the Agni TD/TTB in terms of their reentry technologies and their maneuverability as weapons systems. The Agni II IRBM was tested successfully for the first time on April 11, 1999 with a second successful test on January 17, 2001. The missile was developed before the continuous transfer of nuclear technology to Pakistan from China and North Korea, and China's continuous improvements in its nuclear delivery systems. This testing was rebutted by Pakistan through its own testing of the Ghauri II missile on April 14, 1999. A rail/road-mobile, two-stage, solid-propellant system, the Agni II IRBM with a range of 3000 kilometers and a payload capacity of 1,100 kilograms incorporated a global positioning system, and reportedly was in a "ready-to-be-launched" mode within 15 minutes (as compared to almost half a day's preparation needed by the Agni TD). Although the Agni II's global positioning system has been critiqued in comparison to the superiority of the Chinese and North Korean guidance systems that were being used by Pakistan, the missile's simultaneous rail and road mobility, greater flexibility, improved precision in detecting targets, and reduced vulnerability from impending threats—rendered the missile the backbone of India's land-based nuclear deterrence system (*The Hindustan Times*, 1999).

Thereafter came the Agni-IIAT, which was the result of the Continuous Improvement Program of the Agni II, where the DRDO using state-of-the-art technology significantly improved the missile's range to

4,000 kilometers and also adapted it to a newer and lighter ICBM range payload of 1,500 kilograms. After that the DRDO expanding on a crash project that it began in October 1999, test-fired the Agni I missile in January 2002. A single stage version of the Agni II missile, Agni I (with a range between 700 and 890 kilometers and a payload of 1,000 kilograms) was developed after the Kargil crisis when the need for an intermediate range missile became acute to address the range gap between Agni II and Prithvi I/II on the Western front (this need stemmed from the fact that the range of the Prithvi I/II was found too short for strategic use and the range of Agni II was found too long, thus degrading accuracy) (Santhanam, 2002b). With its new guidance and control systems, significant improvements in reentry technology and maneuverability, and ability to carry a 1 ton conventional or nuclear payload—Agni I, without having to be deployed at borders, was capable of reaching most Pakistan-based targets (ibid.). By the end of the BJP's term, India's land-based nuclear deterrent depended heavily on Agni II, Agni I, and the SS 250/Prithvi II SRBMs (the latter already in possession with India by the end of the Gujral government) with an estimated of 18–36 Agni II's; 8–16 Agni I IRBM's; and 150–180 SS 250/Prithvi II SRBM's in India's arsenal (Dhanda, 2010:120).

In addition, the DRDO conducted another field-test of the Nag missile in January 2000 (whose "thermal sight system" was better able to "identify and lock on to a T-55 tank at a range of 5 kms"); in January and March 2001, conducted further tests of the Akash missile (which was a China and Pakistan-specific missile) for operational and evaluation purposes; and in May 2003, test-fired the Astra missile. As a high-end, "state-of-the-art beyond visual range air-to-air missile (BVRAAM)" highly capable of engaging "maneuvering targets"—its goal was to equip the Indian Air Force's MiG29s, Su30MKIs, Light Combat Aircrafts, and Mirage 2000s (ibid.:123–128). Thereafter, the Indian navy also tested its Supersonic cruise missile BrahMos in June 2001 (and again in April 2002 and November 2003 and 2004) to give it a second strike capability use against China (Gupta, 2005:35). Subsequently, the Indian Navy in a 2004 letter of intent with the joint Indo-Russian venture BrahMos Aerospace Limited sought to acquire an undisclosed number of cruise missiles; began deploying the BrahMos missiles on its warship Rajput; and besides the naval version, contemplated the Army and Air Force versions of the BrahMos supersonic missile (Subramanian, 2003). Furthermore, the Indian navy, to be a more active part of India's minimum nuclear deterrence, in 2001 acquired the Akula III (which, based on the Soviet navy's nuclear powered submarine, was an improved version of India's originally acquired Akula I). Once again, this was with a China-specific focus to expand the Indian military's focus from South Asia to a greater role in Asia stretching from the straits of Hormuz to the Straits of Malacca (Gupta, 2005:35).

Additionally, the DRDO contemplated the development of the Surya missile, an upgrade of the Agni series with a greater re-entry speed (although work on this expedited only in 2006 after the production and test-firing of the Agni III missile) (Raghuvanshi, 1999:14), embarked on programs to develop shorter and longer-range versions of Agni II (the Agni-III and Agni-IV), and developed a naval variant of the Prithvi (Dhanush) (*Economic Times*, 2003). Finally, India's Aeronautical Development Establishment with significant engineering assistance in underwater launch technology from Russia continued developing its submarine launched missile, Sagarika, driven mainly by India's long-term goal of achieving a secure, sea-based, second-strike nuclear capability by arming India's nuclear submarine with an Advanced Technology Vessel (Myers, 1998). Although initial developmental work on Sagarika (that had begun in 1992) was delayed, the missile became operational only in 2010.

In addition to these indigenous efforts, there also occurred significant India–US strategic security cooperation since 2002 in the areas of military relationship (involving bilateral personnel exchanges and military unit training and exchanges); economic relationship (with nearly a thousand of American companies doing business in India's rapidly liberalizing economy); counter-terrorist cooperation (involving law enforcement, information sharing, and investigative cooperation between the RAW and the CIA to combat terrorism); military arms sales; missile defense cooperation; and the signing of the NSSP Initiative (Blake, 2004). Accordingly, in September 2003, India–US special forces soldiers held a two-week joint exercise near the India-China border, followed by the Malabar 2003 joint naval exercises off the Indian coast that included an American submarine, and American pilots flew the Russian-built older F-15s (Kronstadt, 2005). Military arms sales also took off, when, in February 2002, the US Congress was notified of the negotiated sale to India of eight counter-battery radar sets (or Fire Finder radars); saw follow-up arrangements in September that year for the sale of four additional sets in a deal worth of $190 million to India (two of which arrived in by July 2003); and witnessed India purchase from the United States various kinds of special force equipments, electronic ground sensors to be used to detect and stem militant infiltrations in Kashmir, and GE-404 engines for its Light Combat Aircraft (Tellis, 2004; Kronstadt, 2005). By the end of the BJP term, the Indian government possessed an extensive list of desired the US weapons including P-3C Orion maritime patrol aircraft (which the US officials described would be equipped with the latest avionics, including sensors and computerized command and control and weapons systems), antimissile systems, electronic warfare systems, and possibly even F-16 fighters (Blake, 2004; Kronstadt, 2005).

Likewise, prospects of India–US' cooperation on missile defense improved greatly following the US' lifting in 2001 of its earlier-imposed sanctions on India (that was imposed following the latter's 1998 tests), and as India defended the US' decision to withdraw from the Anti-Ballistic Missiles Treaty 2001. Following these mutual goodwill gestures, the India–US Defense Policy Group, moribund since the 1998 nuclear testing, was revived in late 2001; India in May 2002 showed willingness to cooperate with the United States on missile defense (reiterated in September 2003); in March 2003 was simulated by the US-India Defense Policy Group a joint missile defense exercise and saw a deepening of India–US dialogue (by early 2004) on a number of strategic issues including missile defense; and resulted in the signing of the NSSP initiative (in January 2004). In March 2003, the two countries held discussions on India joining the US government's Proliferation Security Initiative (PSI) which would give India authority to combat terrorist-proliferation related activities. In addition, India placed before the United States its wish list of acquiring from the latter joint defense research and development items such as the Patriot PAC-3 (or the Israeli Arrow 2 ABM system) electro-optics, encryption, sensors, and jamming technologies—many of which could be potentially used for missile-defense applications. However, at that point, no final decision could be taken by the United States on the PAC-3 transfer, and neither could Israel export the Arrow-2 without prior US approval (Bitzinger, 2005; Kronstadt, 2007:28).

Needless to say, these joint US-India military exercises and arms sales negotiations have caused disquiet in Pakistan in that these developments will strengthen India's position through an appearance that the United States is siding with India (which I elaborate further in the next chapter) (Kronstadt, 2005:10). On its part, although India continued to see the United States its "fickle" partner that may not be relied upon to provide the reciprocity, sensitivity, and high-technology transfers sought by India (given the United States' continued reluctance to license high-leverage military technology to the Indian state) (Tellis, 2004), the ongoing India–US missile defense and hi-tech cooperation, which progressed with caution, represented a happy convergence between the two countries, and signified to a great extent that the political disconnect that in the past had hampered American defense sales to India was relatively smoothened (Blake, 2004).

Conclusion

Following the theoretical premise of this book that there exists a ideological and discursive linkage between the social construction of India's strategic culture, (in)security imaginary, and its nuclear policies, this chapter has explored how the coming of the coalition-led Hindu nationalist Bharatiya Janata Party (BJP) to power from April 1998 to March 2004 has represented a discursive and ideological shift in the reconstruction of India's strategic thinking, (in)security imaginary, and its nuclear policy choices. To this end, the chapter has noted how the BJP government's strategic cultural discourses, as tools of social and ideological power, in an unprecedented manner than any previous non-BJP governments, have at three specific junctures during its term produced, reconstructed, and sustained a mutually constituted and shifting relationship between India's strategic culture, (in)security imaginary, and its nuclear policy choices. In noting this transition, the chapter has noted: First, how at the eve of India's 1998 detonation, the government (backed mostly by its security community) has created a political and ideological space where the real-political, cultural, religious, and the historical have intersected to amplify a Pakistani-centric (anti-Islamic) (in)security imaginary threatening (the Hindu) Indian state. I have also documented how this construction of a Pakistani-centric (in)security have operated among permissive domestic and external threat situations from China and the United States. Second, the chapter has noted how following India's detonation had emerged an institutionalized nuclear militancy in the strategic mindset of the postnuclear Indian state that institutionalized a deterrence posture for India and strategized India's future nuclear policies, operation, command, control, and delivery systems. In this reconstruction, India's (Hindu) identity and Pakistan-centric (anti-Islamic) insecurities were muted, and in its place emerged its identity as a technologically modern, militarizing, and an increasingly globalizing, liberalizing, nuclear India paying mere tribute to nonalignment. Finally, the chapter has documented how post-9/11 has represented a significant overhaul of the Indian state's strategic cultural discourses and (in)security imaginaries in terms of its increasingly noticeable neoliberal and globalizing trends which, ironically, has enabled the state to redefine its nuclear security relations vis-à-vis Pakistan, the United States, and a new element of self-confidence vis-à-vis the Chinese state. Throughout these transitions, the BJP has been the most nuanced articulator and interpreter of meanings and identities (i.e., what constitutes India's strategic cultures, identities, and insecurity imaginaries), and has in an initial replay of a (reactionary) legacy of the early 20th-century Hindu nationalists, and later in the acceptance of globalization, a fluid nonaligned stature, and a vivid pro-US strategic cultural rethinking defined India's nationalist identity from a Hindu state to a globalizing, modern, nuclear state. The next chapter documents how these reconstructions of India's strategic culture continue under India's United Progressive Alliance government.

Notes

1. In the national elections of India held in March 1998, the Bharatiya Janata Party (BJP) came to power as a majority coalition government. In this closely contested election, the BJP earned 26 percent of the popular vote (and with its allies won 250 seats in the Parliament)—leaving the BJP 22 seats short of majority. Although the BJP was without a majority, President K.R. Narayanan

gave the party opportunity to form a government. After almost two weeks of negotiating with regional parties, the BJP (on March 28, 1998) formed a majority coalition government, known as the National Democratic Alliance, with a confidence vote of 275 to 260. Atal Behari Vajpayee was sworn in as Prime Minister leading a fractious coalition of 14 parties.

2. The Jana Sangh (1951) and the Vishwa Hindu Parishad (1964) were formed under the broader umbrella of the Rashtriya Swayam Sevak (RSS). The Jana Sangh, which had formed an alliance with the Janata Dal after the 1977 elections to form a coalition government at the center, broke up from the Janata Party in 1980 and emerged independently in Indian politics as the Bharatiya Janata Party (BJP). Currently, the BJP maintains ideological connections with its master organizations, the RSS and the Vishwa Hindu Parishad, and, are collectively called the Sangh Parivaar. They uphold the Sangh ideology manifested in *Hindutva*.

3. However, controversies ran among Western circles countering that India's tests were not of a thermo-nuclear device but were boosted-fission weapon tests (Moyland and Clark, 1998; Wallace, 1998). In this context, some internal consistencies were also noted among Indian nuclear scientists, given that AEC Chair, Chidambaram, who stated on May 17 that the 43 kiloton blast came from a thermonuclear bomb, a few days later, reversed himself by stating that the tests had set the primary stage of the thermonuclear device (by testing a boosted-fission device whose radiation then detonated the secondary, i.e., the fusion stage) (Perkovich, 1999:416–419, 424).

4. President Yeltsin in December 1999 stated that Russia still "possesses a complete arsenal of nuclear weapons … [and] continues to value nuclear weapons … to overcome … conventional inferiority" (Kamath, 2009:113). To this extent, Russian document 2000 demonstrated Russia's "desire to preserve the freedom of maneuver [including choice of nuclear weapons against the United States] if the military and political situation exacerbates" (ibid.).

5. However, the President did not go ahead with the program on grounds of its uncertain technical feasibility and costs and decided to leave the final authorization for the program to his successor Republicans who were more interested in the system (Kamath, 2009:119).

6. The US' Nuclear Posture Review forwarded three levels of US' insecurities necessitating an aggressive nuclear defense posture: first, US' new enemies such as Iraq, Iran, Libya, North Korea, and Syria (branded by the President as "axis of evil") who could necessitate from the United States immediate or potential nuclear strike capabilities; second, impending threats from various terrorists groups, like Al Qaeda, capable of using weapons of mass destruction (nuclear, biological, and chemical) against the US assets or its allies; and third, China with its course to nuclear modernization as a concern to the United States (Kamath, 2009:118–120).

7. The 2002 Nuclear Posture Review, while proposing to reduce in the next ten years nuclear warheads from 6,000 to 1,700, also stipulated that an

additional 500 warheads on shelf to be readily made available, another 2,200 strategic warheads to be deployed, another 2,400 strategic warheads be maintained in operational condition, and additional strategic warheads in no-operational condition to be retained (Kamath, 2009:119).

8. While India did not sign the CTBT because of hierarchical nondiscriminatory issues of nuclear apartheid from the United States, Pakistan refused to sign the treaty because India did not sign it.

9. The NSSP by undertaking to move India gradually from a country that was on various US export control lists to one that could avail of civilian nuclear, civilian space, dual-use, and eventually ballistic missile defense (BMD) technology was seen as generating a glide path for India's nuclear technology program (Borman, 2004).

10. Pakistan rejected India's NFU by countering that if India was so keen to pursue the NFU, it should "have accepted China's no-first-use offer that would have obviated the need for India's nuclear weapons acquisition, much less for operational deployment." Thus, from the Pakistani perspective, India's NFU was to secure for itself recognition as a NWS (in case any state extended acceptance of its assurance on NFU (Foreign Secretary's Press Briefing, 1999). However, while rejecting India's NFU, Pakistan in May 2003 offered bilateral nuclear disarmament—knowing well that India would not have much strategic interest in the same as India's nuclear program is not Pakistan-specific and included all those who possess nuclear weapons (Kamath, 2009:141–142).

11. Pakistan's reliance over first-use of nuclear weapons arises primarily from military-strategic factors: its inferior status over its conventional force capabilities; its lack of strategic depth to conduct conventional war vis-à-vis India and protect its strategic nuclear assets; and that Pakistan's nuclear weapons concept is rooted in its army's long association with the US armed forces (when the United States and the NATO's reliance on first-use of nuclear weapons were inherited by Pakistan's military elite as a given doctrine) (Sharma, 2005:290; Kamath, 2009:171).

12. These being: if India threatens to conquer parts of Pakistani territory including the Pakistan-occupied Azad Kashmir, if it seeks to destroy Pakistan's army, or economically cripple or politically destabilize the Pakistani territory or governmental entity (Kamath, 2009: 169; Friedman, 2002).

13. As noted by the US intelligence sources, China was not only continuing to actively assist Pakistan through the supply of missile components but also signified the possibility of greater Sino-Pakistani cooperation in assisting the latter to develop intercontinental range ballistic missile systems, land and sea lunched cruise and ballistic missiles, and other means to build ballistic missile systems. The only difference being that, unlike the past when China had transferred complete missile systems, assembly, and production lines to Pakistan, the current pattern of Chinese assistance was apparently restricted

to missile design advice and indirect transmissions to Pakistan through China's ally North Korea (Dhanda, 2010:177–178).

14. The immediate postdetonation dialogues (although unsuccessful in qualitatively improving relations) represented a breakthrough in India–Pakistan's efforts to rebuild their social, political, and cultural ties. These gestures occurred as the Indian–Pakistani leaders met at the 10th SAARC summit at Colombo in July 1998; prime minister Vajpayee in February 1999 inaugurated a bus service between Delhi and Lahore; the two governments that month signed the Lahore Declaration committing to universal nuclear disarmament; and President Musharraf visited India for the Agra Summit in July 2001 (Khan, 2009:116–117; 120–121).

15. Implementations of these policies were not easy given the tremendous domestic pressure that Musharraf faced from people (demonstrated by the three assassinations he escaped) who were bewildered with this drastic policy shift that went against their ideology and doctrine, and for his perceived abandoning the Pakistani militants' cause in support of jihad in Kashmir.

16. While some territorial disputes still existed between India and China over Tibet, and some ongoing cross-border infiltrations were carried out by China in India's North Eastern frontiers, there had been no further evidences of any immediate Chinese hostility or expansionary ambition in the South Asian region just prior to the tests. In fact, Sino-Indian relations were actually improving through the bilateral treaties and peace agreements of 1993 and 1996 (Han, 1998).

17. The reference here is made to the 12th-century Indian history where Shahabuddin Muhammad Ghauri in 1,191 attacked the fortress of Bhatinda in East Punjab. The then Indian ruler, Prithviraj Chauhan, a Hindu, defeated him but spared his life. Ghauri returned a year later, defeated Prithviraj Chauhan, and laid the foundations of the Muslim dynasty in India. The dynasty lasted until the coming of the British in India in the late 17th century.

18. However, after the final document of India's minimal nuclear doctrine was announced, India made a modification to the effect that, if a nonnuclear power uses biological or chemical weapons, India will keep the option open of using nuclear weapons against such a state. This is because India as a signatory to the Chemical and Biological Weapons Treaty has destroyed all its holdings of chemicals and biological weapons.

19. The draft doctrine's original phrase of "assured retaliation" was changed in the final document to "massive response" and the original term "unacceptable damage" to "unaccepted punishment" in its final one (Kamath, 2009:159).

20. The assumption behind this fourth stand was that in the future India will not be able to reduce the size of its armed forces as the threat to Indian security will continue from the low-intensity conflicts with Pakistan.

21. On a personal level, Vajpayee wanted his tenure to leave a mark. On the political level, an India-Pakistan peace initiative would (as a pledge to his 1998 election campaign) expectedly appease India's large Muslim community and bring Vajpayee to power again if the BJP won.
22. In terms of his political and personal considerations, "Musharraf wanted to preserve his military regime by showing that he was interested in peace," and "also wanted to disprove the general belief that military leaders are less inclined to peace." On the economic front, Musharraf was "desperate to have good relations with India because" Pakistan's economy since the end of the cold war was not "doing well" and peace with India could infuse "international economic aid" to Pakistan (Khan, 2009:149).

7

Neoliberal Strategic Security/ Defense Collaborations: Post-2004

The Congress party heading a coalition, known as the United Progressive Alliance (UPA), came to the forefront of Indian politics in May 2004 (and has remained in power following the national elections held in April–May 2009).[1] According to many analysts of Indian politics, the return of the Congress party to power represents—more than any preceding Indian governments—a much stronger vision of India's globalization, and like the previous BJP-led NDA government has recognized the preeminence of the United States and a waning of nonalignment as key factors in India's national security affairs (Bajpai, 2002). Following my theoretical premise of this book that a state's strategic culture is one of social and ideological construction, and that there exists an ideological and discursive linkage between India's strategic culture, (in)security imaginary, and its nuclear policies, this chapter explores how the Congress party-led government's ideological acceptance of the preeminence of the United States and globalization in continuity and disjuncture from the earlier Indian governments has reconstructed India's strategic thinking, nationalist identity, and (in)security imaginary to further consolidate the official Indian mindset's strategic security collaborations with the United States (traditionally perceived by the party's left segments as a hierarchically situated, adversarial, Western player in India's international affairs). Yet, as will be teased out in this chapter, the government's official stand of a neoliberal, globalized, and a pro-US entity had to negotiate with the polity's leftist elements, skepticism from the country's nuclear science community, and its defense analysts to negotiate (and support) a pro-US approach in India's national security affairs. Despite these struggles, official ideological and discursive transformations toward a neoliberal orientation has enabled the government to create a political and ideological space within which were reconstructed and rearticulated the "cautious" neoliberal shifts of India's post-2004 nuclear security affairs. Concomitant to such pro-US changes, the Indian state has also shifted its disarmament stand to an incremental approach of the same in its international affairs.

Accordingly, this chapter addresses the following "how-possible" questions: First, how the Indian state's strategic cultural thinking since May 2004 projected through the ideological lenses of its foreign policy-making community, makes sense of India's international relations? Second, how the Indian state's interpretation of its current international relations created an ideological and political space, within which were reconstructed and rearticulated shifting images of India's nationalist identity, strategic cultural thinking, and its (in)security imaginaries? Finally, how within these shifting reconstructions of India's strategic cultural thinking and (in)security imaginaries were forged India's nuclear policy options/choices, namely balancing cautious neoliberal shifts in its strategic security collaborations with the United States? In addressing each "how-possible" question, my aim will be to show how the state's security community's discourses as tools of social and ideological power have, in an unprecedented manner than any previous Indian governments produced, reconstructed and sustained a more neoliberal understanding of India's strategic culture, (in)security imaginary, and its nuclear/strategic security affairs.

This chapter is organized as follows: The following section begins with an analysis of the coming of the Congress party-led UPA government to power under Prime Minister Manmohan Singh, and its explicit acceptance of a pro-globalization/pro-US stand in India's national security affairs. The second section reviews India's international relations vis-à-vis the United States, China, and Pakistan as interpreted through the ideological lenses of the post-2004 Indian state's security community—where real, domestic, global, and a strong neoliberal sense of globalized interdependence becomes key in reinterpreting India's post-2004 world affairs. The third section analyzes the reconstructions of India's strategic culture and (in)security imaginaries through meaning-producing discourses of the state's security community, wherein complexities and divergences involved in these ideological representations and discourses served to rearticulate a neoliberally embedded sense of strategic autonomy (as identity) of the post-2004 Indian state. The fourth section analyzes the strategic security/defense collaborations of the Indian state as a balance of India's strategic autonomy and neoliberalism.

Return of the Congress Party-led UPA Government: A Neoliberal Nationalist Agenda

In contrast to Nehruvianism under Prime Minister Nehru and the post-Nehru Congress leaders, neoliberalism, despite intraparty differences, represents contemporary India's strategic cultural mindset under the current Congress party-led UPA government. Like Nehruvianism, neoliberalism accepts international relations as anarchical, that coercion plays a significant role in international politics, and war between states is a possibility, but, unlike Nehruvianism, considers the "lure of mutual [economic] gain in any interaction … as a powerful conditioning factor amongst states particularly as they become more independent" (Bajpai, 2002:252). In finding economics as key, most neoliberals redefine international relations by comparing the role of the military and economic power in that economic well-being is vital for national security, and that this economic well-being can primarily come from trade and economic interactions in a free-market economy (Baru, 1998; Gupta, 2001). Thus, neoliberals stress the importance of commerce in reinforcing the web of interdependence in international politics, argue that trade creates material incentives to resolve disputes successfully, and stress that it is the cosmopolitan business elites who benefit from trade and are seen as powerful transnational interest groups with a stake at promoting amicable solutions to festering interstate disagreements (Lebow, 1995; Kegley and Raymond, 1999:246). In other words, "interdependence makes for more pragmatic international policies. States worry not just about war but about trade, investment, and technology" (Baru, 1998:90–91).

This neoliberal approach applied in India's contemporary national security agenda implies the following: First, India must have enough force to defend itself and must be attentive toward its defense needs, but it is the economic power that will eventually make India secure; second, India should overcome old geo-political ways of Cold War, block rivalry, and nonalignment (or its remnants thereof), and instead, should be increasingly perceptive and appreciative of the pragmatic benefits, power, and logic of globalization in reinterpreting its international relations; and finally, that India on the whole focus on India's economic growth, modernization, and its capacity to innovate and integrate into the global economy because that will eventually be the greatest source of India's strength and security in a globalized world economy (Bajpai, 2002:255–256).

Accordingly, an analysis of election campaigns, party manifestoes, and post-2004 speeches of the Congress party testifies to post-2004 India's rise as a global economy and its spillover effect on its defense agenda, national security, and foreign policy. Calling for an appeal to "The Back to Basics," that have formed the essence of India's culture, the impetus to India's independence movement, and the foundations for a modern, self-reliant, and self-confident India, the party's 2004 Election Manifesto referred to a theme of "continuity with change" in India's national-building agenda (Indian National Congress, 2004:2, 6–7). Reiterating to the continuities of an "all-inclusive" nationalism that continue to form the identity of the nation, the Manifesto also called for certain "changes" in India's economic and modernization process, that is, how the party's nation-building focus on a direct attack on poverty in the 1960s–1970s, shifted to a renewed emphasis on science, technology, and modernization of industry in the 1980s, and thereafter shifted to a much "needed bolder economic reform and liberalization and a much larger role for the private sector to accelerate growth and promote India's integration into a rapidly changing world economic system" in the 1990s (ibid.:4, 7). In this context of India's neoliberal agenda, issues of combating terrorism, defense, foreign affairs, and relations were also emphasized as the party sought to "engage the United States in scientific, technological, strategic and commercial cooperation," and also reaffirmed India's traditional bonds with Russia, Japan; improving dialogue with China and Pakistan (including the issue of Jammu and Kashmir); and strengthening ties with the European Union (Indian National Congress, 2004:13).

This theme of a much "needed bolder economic reform and liberalization" formed the crux of postaccession speeches by several pro-globalization members of the UPA government such as Pranab Mukherjee, Shyam Saran, P. Chidambaram, Mani Shankar Aiyar, Ronen Sen, and Prime Minister Singh (Saran, 2005; Sen, 2005; Singh, 2006; Chidambaram, 2007; Embassy of India, 2008b). Situating the Indian economy to the center of its strategic statecraft, and in noting its spillover effects on India's geopolitical grand strategy, Prime Minister Singh's speech in a 2005 address to the Combined Commanders Conference at New Delhi, stated that "Our strategy has to be based on three broad pillars: First, to strengthen ourselves economically and technologically; second, to acquire adequate defense capability to counter and rebut threats to our security; and third, to seek partnerships both on the strategic front and on the economic and technological front to widen our policy and developmental options" (Singh, 2005). In showing these connections between India's economic rise, national security, and its geopolitical grand strategy, the relevance of India's ancient *Arthashastra* did not go unnoticed. Following the moorings of the ancient Indian realist, diplomat, and economist, Kautilya, the prime minister reminded that, "a healthy economy is a sound foundation for well-funded armed forces [and] from the strength of the treasury … the army is born. But, he continued, "it is not only for fiscal reasons that the health of our economy is important for national security. A healthy growing and stable economy in itself enhances security" (ibid.).

Although critics claim that Prime Minister Singh's liberalization process has failed to reform either the economy or the government (Bagchi, 2011), others question if India (despite its economy's growth at an annual average of 3.5 percent from 1950 to 1980, to almost 6 percent from 1980 to 2004, to almost 9 percent since 2004) can still be called a successful welfare state (Baru, 2009:200), and not all in the Congress party have yet fully imbided the consequences of globalization—it is current reality that notions of India's national security and grand strategy are firmly rooted in the foundations of its economic performance—the key to which remains India's continued participation in, and integration with, globalization and a neoliberal economy. This reality as expressed in the words of Prime Minister Singh (2005) is that, "New notions of 'Comprehensive National Power' give high weightage to economic, social, technological, educational, and cultural aspects of power. Military strength alone no longer guarantees a nation's security. Knowledge power and economic capabilities are equally important."

Although phrased in the Congress party's 2009 Election Manifesto as "the middle-path," or a "balance" between building a modern economy and India's traditional industries (Indian National Congress, 2009:5), prominent members of the Congress government, such as Pranab Mukherjee, P. Chidambaram, and the prime minister himself (under the party's second term as coalition-led government since the 2009 elections) have reiterated that "[economic] reform is a continuous process and the UPA government is committed to it" (Mukherjee, 2011; Singh, 2011; Chidambaram, 2013). In fact, Prime Minister Singh, lamenting that "the lack of support from coalition partners and members of his own party [had caused him] to suspend a flagship policy allowing foreign supermarkets [such as Walmart] to open in India," reemphasized the connection between "India's economic growth" and its "national security," and to that extent India undertaking new measures of infrastructural development, including attracting foreign capital into the country (Singh, 2012). Such commitments of the state imply the significance of globalized interdependence through free economy and trade; the need to safeguard an environment of free-market democracy for the state; and also maintaining "more comprehensive visions of national power" that involves knowledge power, military power, economic progress, foreign direct investment, a politically stable state in urgent needs of combating terrorism, and inculcating regional and global powers such as Pakistan, China, Japan, Australia, the European Union, and the United States (Tellis et al., 2009; Singh, 2011). In inculcating this great power relationship, the critical significance of the United States was further reiterated by the prime minister, in that "India needs help from the world community, including the United States, to emerge as a global power" (Goodenough, 2008). It is in this context of the India's "New notions of Comprehensive National Power" that the state reinterpreted its post-2004 international relations.

Interpreting India's International Relations

In the context of post-2004 India's vision of "New notions of [India's] Comprehensive National Power," India's interpretation of its international relations centered on the following objectives: Continuing efforts at strengthening its post-9/11 strategic alliance with the United States; promoting India's peripheral and regional security, which meant continuing dialogue with China and Pakistan to achieve a politically stable South Asia (which also bode well with the United States' post-9/11 political security framework in the region); maintaining Asian power balances; and pursuing its global security interests (which implied its great power vision to be accepted as a legitimate member into the nuclear club and attaining a permanent seat in the UN Security Council) (Kronstadt and Pinto, 2013:21). Below, I discuss these dynamics of India's interpretation of its post-2004 international affairs, which, despite constraints, were primarily contextualized through the ideological lenses and discourses of the Indian state as an economically neoliberal, pro-US, rising power.

9/11, which provided a strong impetus in India–US' strategic cultural reorientation vis-à-vis each other continued under President Bush's second term, and, in fact, was strengthened under Prime Minister Singh, who is seen by political analysts as representing the strongest vision of globalization than any preceding governments in India. In this prevailing neoliberal environment, interweaved with Hobbesian anarchy, India–US congruence continued in advancing trade and exchange of dual-purpose nuclear technology in addition to augmenting India–US military and defense relations, counter-terrorism projects, and other nonmilitary areas of cooperation (Kronstadt, 2005).

These became evidenced as India following the earlier concluded Next Steps in Strategic Partnership (NSSP) signed a High-Technology Trade with the United States on September 17, 2004 marking the conclusion of Phase I of the implementation of the NSSP (the US Department of State, 2004);[2] on October 21, 2004, held talks on Phase II of the NSSP (Malik, 2006:92–93);[3] another round of high-tech trade talks between Indian Foreign Secretary Shyam Saran and the US Under Secretary of Commerce, Kenneth Juster (November 2004) to discuss "practical steps" to remove barriers in high-tech trade (Parasuram, 2004); saw the (somewhat controversial) visit of the US Defense Secretary, Ronald Rumsfeld to India in December 2004 (*Deccan Herald*, 2004);[4] the visit of the US Secretary of State Rice to India in March 2005; reciprocated by Indian Defense Minister Pranab Mukherjee's visit to the United States in June 2005 and signing a new framework for expanding the Indo-US defense relationship for the next 10 years (Text of Indo-US Agreement, 2005; Malik, 2006);[5] the issue of a Joint Statement by President Bush and Prime Minister Singh on July 18, 2005 resolving to establish a global partnership between United States and India (Joint Press Briefing, 2005; *The Hindu*, 2007b);[6] thereafter an announcement by the Bush administration that it sought to cooperate with India on civilian nuclear technology something which had been prohibited for more than 30 years as India had remained outside the Nuclear Non-Proliferation Treaty; a visit by President Bush to India (March 1–3, 2006) initiating discussion on India's Separation Plan and India-specific Safeguards Agreement with the International Atomic Energy Agency on international inspection (International Atomic Energy Agency, 2008);[7] thereafter, numerous conversations between the countries in executing a roadmap to implement such cooperation; the passing of the Hyde Act by the US Congress (December 2006); and the 123 Agreement (July 2007) charting the terms of high-tech cooperation between India and the United States (something that would have been otherwise impermissible under the previous US laws).[8]

As I elaborate later, the passing of the Hyde Act and the 123 Agreement was not an easy task for either country in terms of the operational steps and negotiations required among stakeholders, and was procedurally staled for more than a year to sort out India–US domestic and international obstacles (Ministry of External Affairs, 2004; Sawhney and Wahab, 2004; Text of Indo-US Agreement (2005). The 123 agreement was finally approved by the US Congress and signed by President Bush in October 2008 into a law known as the India–US Civilian Nuclear Accord. The Civilian Nuclear Accord (developed on the basis of the 2005 Joint Statement) marked an enormous victory for the US–India civilian nuclear cooperation but also remained controversial, which I address in the next section.

These developments represented a major policy shift of the US administration toward India (Bitzinger, 2005; Squassoni, 2005; Kronstadt, 2005, 2007; Malik, 2006; Ganguly et al., 2006; Ayres, 2009).[9] There also echoed an array of discourses from both states "blessing" these neoliberal developments. Three themes echoed in these discourses: First, the identity of India and the United States as "enlightened democracies" and as "keepers of global peace" (Department of State, 2002); second, a reminder that the US' search for a 9/11 related terror in South Asia was ultimately the basis of India–US neoliberal nuclear security ventures (although this theme signaled to India of Pakistan's continued importance for the US' South Asian security agenda); and the ultimate objective of a South Asian proliferation control in which India becomes a promoter. To this end, Secretary of State, Rice (2006) supported Indo-US full civilian nuclear energy cooperation by claiming that this represents "shared vision[s] [of] the world's oldest and largest democracies [to] accomplish great things in the new century;" the US Under Secretary of State for Political Affairs, Nicholas Burns (2007) opined that "… the rise of a democratic and increasingly powerful India represent[ed] a singularly positive opportunity to advance [the US'] global interests" in South Asia, and "… there is a tremendous strategic upside to our growing engagement with India …." Furthermore, statements by the US officials such as US Ambassador David Mulford (2005) and the US Secretary of State, Rice (2005) refereed to India's desired great power status in that "It is now official … [that] the policy of the United States [is] to help India to become a major world power in the 21st century" (Mulford, 2005), and that United States' relationship with India is "not just [with] a regional power but as … global power," where the two were entering into "a broader and deeper relationship that [they have] ever had" (Rice, 2005). The nexus of India–US as "enlightened democracies" trying to combat "terrorist-proliferation" types of dangers were also cited by Indian counterparts namely Prime Minister Singh (2006), India's ex-Ambassador to the United States, Ronen Sen (2005), Pranab Mukherjee (Embassy of India, 2008b), and defense analyst K. Subrahmanyam (2010) in supporting India–US nuclear technology momentum (which I will elaborate later as a part of India's strategic culture).

The current Obama administration stands for "change" in the US domestic politics. Related to its global security agenda, this concept of change nonetheless harped on the vulnerability of the US national insecurity, the location of the 9/11 related "enemy" in this agenda, and the need of a comprehensive strategy for the United States that needs to "marshal international support … to defeat an enemy that heeds no borders …"

(Council on Foreign Relations, 2009a). While the Obama administration has shifted to an "Af-Pak" strategy in combating a South Asian terror (D'Souza, 2009), the strategic significance of India remained acute for the United States under Obama. In fact, drawing from the November 2008 terror attacks in Mumbai, President Obama stated that with a "shared belief in democracy, liberty, pluralism, and religious tolerance," India and the United States can work to "... build a future of security and prosperity for all nations...[and] both can help to prevent nuclear proliferation, fight terror ..." (CNN, 2009). Contrary to observations that Democrats have not traditionally been favorable to the Indian state (Thomas, 2010: viii); the United States' Nuclear Posture Review (April 2010);[10] and delays in implementing the 2008 Civilian Nuclear Accord (Loukianova, 2009; Department of Defense, 2010; Kronstadt et al., 2011), the Obama administration, namely during the President and Vice-President Biden's visit to India in November 2010 and July 2013, continued to emphasize India–US' "democratic values," sought to "expand and strengthen India–US global strategic partnership," referred to India as a "great friend and partner to the United States," and sought to advance mutual cooperation in global security, counter-terrorism projects, and other nonmilitary areas of cooperation in green partnerships, economic trade, education, health, and collaborating to politically stabilize South Asia (NDTV, 2010; The White House, 2013a; Sharma, 2013, *The Hindu*, 2013). One of the highlights of President Obama's November 2010 visit to India was the United States' announcement to implement the "export control policy initiative" to expand India–US cooperation in civil space, defense, and other high-technology sectors (Bishoyi, 2011). Following Osama Bin Laden's capture in May 2011, President Obama continues to welcome "India's emergence as a major regional and global power," the US Secretary of State John Kerry continues such dialogue with Indian Minister for External Affairs Salman Khurshid; and the US administration "looks forward to a reformed UN Security Council that includes India as a permanent member" (NDTV, 2010; Tellis, 2013). Under his second term, Prime Minister Singh continues to reciprocate with cautious optimism to these US neoliberal gestures, which unfurl amidst dilemmas over the Afghanistan (requiring the US balancing of India–Pakistan perspectives on the issue) (Blackwill, 2009), and the United States' rebalancing policy in the Asia-Pacific region (Gupta, 2013).

Despite claims that the Bush administration has managed to develop the US–India (and also the US–Pakistan) relations on their own terms (Ayres, 2009; Kronstadt and Pinto, 2013), tensions persist in implementing the 2008 India–US Accord: observance of the US domestic laws; international treaty obligations; and the lack of a liability arrangement and an agreement for monitoring the process for the US nuclear exports to certain Indian nuclear plant facilities delayed the implementation of the Accord (Kronstadt et al., 2011:4). In addition, these transfers had to be politically balanced so as not to fundamentally change the balance of power between India and Pakistan (Ministry of External Affairs, 2004; Sawhney and Wahab, 2004). On the Indian side, its anti-US nuclear skepticism (which I elaborate later) had to ensure that the International Atomic Energy Agency's safeguards that were sought to be imposed on India's nuclear facilitates as a part of the 123 Agreement be cautiously negotiated—so as not to enable the United States as a "global police" to achieve the necessary policy changes through the Nuclear Suppliers Group (NSG) to prevent India from further nuclear testing (Ayres, 2009:7). These critics continued to be skeptical about the extent to which technology-control restrictions will be lifted from India; the reliability of the United States as a supplier of such technology to India; and in essence, that India will acquire only a few substantive items for its space programs (Sekhon and Samuel, 2005). These tensions unfurled with simultaneous US efforts at global nonproliferation, which included the United States presenting in Geneva (in May 2006) a draft global Fissile Material Cutoff Treaty to ban future production of fissile material (which it hoped would be supported by India "as a move … to bolster the US Congressional support for the proposed US–India civil nuclear cooperation" deals) (Kronstadt, 2007:31); President Obama's 2009 Prague Speech stressing global disarmament (Cheodon, 2010); the adoption of a program of work at the Conference of Disarmament (in August 2009) to negotiate through a working group the conclusion of a Fissile Material Cutoff Treaty (Collina and Horner, 2011); and the reopening of CTBT negotiations at the United Nations in May 2010.

In addition, there remained nonproliferation pressures on India, which, reflecting an Orientalist xenophobia of the United States vis-à-vis India, as a postcolonial actor, asserted the United States will "... work cooperatively to ensure that every state with nuclear weapons or weapons-usable materials—even those that remain outside the Non-Proliferation Treaty like India and Pakistan ..., become a part of this global nonproliferation agenda" (Council on Foreign Relations, 2009a). To this end, Nicholas Burns, a supporter of Indo-US nuclear collaborations, referring to the Indo-US global partnership agreements of 2005 claimed to reporters on July 19, 2005 that "this agreement can be verified and will be verified" (Squassoni, 2005), and Strobe Talbott (2006) cautioned that "there remains profound and persistent concerns" about Indo-US global partnership, and that "the consequence of the deal will be to weaken the NPT [Nuclear Non-Proliferation Treaty] which is already under strain. It will do so because, it essentially grants India an exception under the NPT, and there are going to be other countries that will want similar exceptions ...." In fact, by the beginning of the Obama administration, US politics expressed concern that "the world is entering into a "new nuclear era" more dangerous than before, with nuclear know-how proliferation and nonstate terrorist groups seeking to obtain and use weapons of mass destruction" (Inderfurth, 2008). Former US Secretary of State, Henry Kissinger, and other prominent politicians, spoke of the emergence of nuclear terrorism among "rogue" states given that "... the spread of technology—especially peaceful nuclear energy—[among states] ... has multiplied the[ir] feasibility of acquiring a nuclear weapons capability..." (Kissinger, 2009). These discourses when read in the context of the recently concluded Indo-US civilian Nuclear Accord (2008) might well be argued to imply the US' Orientalism vis-à-vis India. These developments have mired political tensions in contemporary India–US nuclear dialogue—which I later elaborate as a part of India's strategic culture.

Furthermore, the United States (reminiscent of its periodic enrollment of Pakistan as a frontline state in its Cold War) continued to cultivate Pakistan as its ally against the war on terror. The United States' proposed sales of F-16 fighters aircrafts and P-3 Orion maritime reconnaissance planes to Pakistan; providing $3 billion economic and military assistance package to Pakistan between 2005 and 2009 (Rubinoff, 2006:53–54); designating Pakistan as a major non-NATO ally of the United States in its war against terror; ignoring Pakistan's illegitimate transfer of nuclear technology to Iraq and Libya; and tolerating the Musharraf administration (which appeared "blatantly hypocritical" in the light of the US' stated interests in combating terrorism) bore evidence of the United States' pro-Pakistani stance in the post-2004 era (Ganguly and Shoup, 2006:5–6;

Hagerty, 2006). Although ex-Secretary of State, Rice (2005), reiterated the US efforts "to de-hyphenate the [US'] relationship with Pakistan," urged Musharraf to modernize and economically liberalize Pakistan, and simultaneously pursued the US missile and defense cooperation with the Indian counterpart—many in India argued that Pakistan has benefitted more than New Delhi from the US' war on terrorism (Rubinoff, 2006:54). Such skeptics have questioned the United States' short-term interests' vis-à-vis India/South Asia (Chari, 2006; Gopalakrishnan, 2006; Ganguly et al., 2006). In turn, the joint US–India military exercises and arms sales negotiations have caused disquiet in Pakistan and has constructed India's nuclear insecurity dilemmas vis-à-vis Pakistan (which I address later as a part of India's interpretation of its international relations with Pakistan) (Kronstadt, 2005:10).

The China factor also created concerns in India–US relations in the post-2004 years (although in a somewhat different manner than the previous years where India was apprehensive of the US–China praxis against India). This is because a steady increase of China's military modernization as evident in the Annual Department of Defense *Report to Congress on the Military Power of the People's Republic of China*, as well as periodic statements by China's administrative officials (which I will elaborate later), simultaneously posed military insecurities for the United States and India, and brought "India–China–US" in a strategic balancing trio in South Asia. In this context, the United States' dual approach to China's military modernization program included monitoring China, and balancing a militarily rising China by building the US defense capabilities in the region, in which India by default remains an active participator. The strategic balancing factor in the "India–China–US" trio became tenuous given that while the United States' principal objective was to strengthen India to limit China's power, it simultaneously drew fears within the United States whether India, in its growing interactions with China, known as coopetition (Ayres, 2009), would draw the United States to counter a militarily strong China (Mohan, 2009:288). Although the debate concerning India's role in this the US' counter-defense policy context has mired in two directions (Mohan, 2009:288; Shambaugh, 2009), what is important to note here is that China, like Pakistan, became a balancing (or bargaining) factor for India to be potentially maneuvered to redefine its interactions with the United States (Gupta, 2005;

Ganguly et al., 2006; Ayres, 2009). In addition, India–Iran's negotiation to construct a gas pipeline from Iranian fields to India's growing markets, India's desire to rise as a great power status (meaning that India be accepted as a dejure member of the nuclear club and get a seat in the UN Security Council), and the United States' recognition of the Line of Control in Kashmir as the international border (and thus freezing territorial status quo in South Asia) continue to strain India–US security affairs.

Normalization of India–Pakistan relations continued under Prime Minister Singh and President Musharraf as official/expert-level talks (as India's Foreign Secretary Shivshankar Menon, the Pakistani counterpart Riaz Khan, Indian Foreign Minister Pranab Mukherjee, the Pakistani counterpart Khurshid Kasuri, Prime Minister Singh, and President Musharraf conversed on June 2004, August 2004, February 2005, January 2006, September 2006, November 2006, January 2007, and October 2007) (Cherian, 2004; Sharma, 2005; Joint Statement, 2005; Treaty Text, 2006; Kronstadt, 2007; Khan, 2009; Behuria, 2011). These conversations, in the areas of deficit trust, security issues, and nuclear confidence building, resulted in the overall improvement of bilateral relations between India and Pakistan.[11] Although Jammu and Kashmir was not discussed until 2006, these goodwill gestures, possibly, accounted for the lowering of the rates of Pakistani-backed infiltration in India in December 2004 (down to some 60 percent from the previous year), and that New Delhi announced the first substantial withdrawal of its forces in Kashmir since the early 1990s (Kronstadt, 2004a:4–5). Yet, this relative ease was strained with concurrent joint military exercises and arms sales negotiation between the United States and India. While Pakistan apprehended that high-tech nuclear and missile defense trade between India and the United States would strengthen India's leverage vis-à-vis an already militarily disadvantaged Pakistan, from the Indian perspective, quite conversely, the US' regular appeasement of Pakistan could potentially disrupt the strategic balance of power between India and Pakistan in the region (Kronstadt, 2005:10). In this fluid context of an India–US/ US–Pakistan post-9/11 strategic alliance, that Pakistan has held on to its traditional Asian ally China (perhaps to offset a US–India alliance)— where Pakistanis have considered having "a fair weather relationship with the United States but an all-weather relationship with China" (Sood, 2009:267).

A number of terrorist incidents—the Varanasi blasts of March 2006 (backed by Pakistan–Bangladesh and some interest of China (Sood, 2009:264–265), the serial bombing of the Bombay commuter trains in July 2006, the explosion on the Indian segment of the Samjhauta [Friendship] Express train linking Lahore with New Delhi on February 18, 2007, and the more threatening terrorist attacks in Mumbai November 2008—brought India and Pakistan in an "eyeball to eyeball confrontation" (Kronstadt, 2007:8; 2009:6; Khan, 2009:136). It carried the potential to (but did not) escalate confrontations between them, and, as stated by India's former Chief of Army Staff, General Shankar Roychowdhury, "Pakistan's threat of nuclear use deterred India from seriously considering conventional military strikes" (Narang, 2010). While Pakistan asserted that these terrorist activities were carried out by nonstate actors (Symonds, 2008), Pakistan's Foreign Minister Shah Mahmood Qureshi (along with Pakistan's then Ambassador to the United States Husain Haqqani) stated that "Pakistan wanted good relations with India and that now was not the time for a blame game" (Dodd, 2008; Rondeaux, 2008). Although India did not publicly reveal any incriminating evidence of the Pakistani government's involvement in the Mumbai attacks (Kronstadt, 2007), there emerged a series of discourses from the Indian state (which I elaborate later) that focusing on India's democracy and antiterrorism struggle, and its lack thereof in Pakistan, constructed India's identity and insecurities vis-à-vis Pakistan (Sen, 2005; Singh, 2006; BBC, 2006; Embassy of India, 2008a; Kronstadt, 2009:4–8). What also frustrated India was the United States' reluctance not to overtly "embarrass" its Pakistani friend, while still deepening India–US counter-terrorism cooperation for the interest of both South Asian states (Kronstadt, 2005:10; 2009:9).

In addition, an unspecified/asymmetrical posture of Pakistan's post-1998 nuclear doctrine implying Pakistan's India-specific nuclear doctrinal stand, its aversion to a no-first-use (NFU), and that its nuclear arsenal continues to remain under the de-facto control of its military pervaded India's nuclear insecurities from Pakistan. This is because Pakistan's nuclear posture (as India perceived it) aims to credibly threaten the first-use of nuclear weapons on Indian ground forces at some unspecified but relatively early threshold level to deter conventional Indian attacks against Pakistan, and continues to purport an "unholy" deterrence/management trade-off posture where Pakistan's military commander with nominal approval from the National Command Authority can release nuclear weapons at a threshold earlier than what the National Command Authority may otherwise enforce (Kronstadt, 2007; Kamath, 2009; Alam, 2012). This asymmetry seen in the more recent post-2004 context gets further complicated given that Pakistan's extremist organizations may create a more permanent crisis footing between India and Pakistan, where Pakistan's exposed nuclear weapons may render such elements to engage in the theft and/or unauthorized or accidental use of such materials (Narang, 2010). While Pakistan has in the recent years taken a number of steps to increase its international confidence in the security of its nuclear arsenal (Hersh, 2009; Kerr and Nikitin, 2013), and official reports from the United States in 2008, 2009, and 2011 have also asserted that "the weapons there are secure," and that Pakistan "has dismantled the nuclear black market," apprehensions still exist of "… those weapons falling into the hands of terrorists and either being proliferated or potentially used" (Kerr and Nikitin, 2013:1, 23). In the context of these developments, analysts have not only found Pakistan's posture of minimum nuclear deterrence questionable, but also explain India's move toward the Cold Start doctrine which envisions prepositioning Indian troops closer to the international border to launch surprise offenses against Pakistan (Narang, 2010).

In addition, Pakistan since 2004 continues to develop its nuclear weapons, expand its nuclear weapons stockpiles based on highly enriched uranium, and advance nuclear warheads and delivery systems, including cruise missiles "which when deployed and added to Islamabad's current ballistic missiles, will enable Pakistan 'to strike a variety of targets at ranges of 200–2,000 kilometers with both conventional and nuclear payloads'" (Kerr and Nikitin, 2013:11). While some analyses hold that it is unclear as to what extent India–US 2008 Nuclear Accord explains Pakistan's current nuclear facilities' expansion (ibid.:17), an array of discourses from Pakistani state officials/media (namely members of Pakistan's National Command Authority; Pakistan's Air Force; military; Pakistan's High Commissioner to the UK; Pakistan's Permanent Representative to the International Atomic Agency; and Pakistan's Foreign Office spokesperson) have explicitly referred to the 2008 Accord as tilting (in Pakistani perceptions) "the South Asian strategic balance between India and Pakistan in favor of the latter;" that the 2008 "agreement could cause an arms race between India and Pakistan;" and that "India's massive conventional military build-up, the India–US nuclear deal," and India's pursuit of missile defense system, has forced Pakistan "to make qualitative and quantitative adjustments" to its nuclear weapons development (Lavoy, 2008; Norris and Kristensen, 2010; Kerr and Nikitin, 2013:7–8).

Thus, "persistent India–Pakistan rivalry" continued to drive Islamabad's efforts at developing its nuclear facility infrastructure, nuclear production facilities, advanced nuclear warheads and delivery systems, which included acquiring F-16s from the United States; contract with the latter to perform the mid-life upgrade on Pakistan's F-16A/B aircrafts; testing the Shaheen-1A missile in April 2012 (described as intermediate range ballistic missile with at least a 3000 kilometer range); progressing work for deploying the solid-fuel nuclear capable hatf VI (test-fired earlier in March 2004); the first successful test-firing of a "newly developed Short Range Surface to Surface Multi Tube Ballistic Missile hatf IX (NASR) with a range of 60 kilometers and capable of carrying nuclear warheads of appropriate yield with high accuracy" (Kerr and Nikitin, 2013:10–11). In addition, Prime Minister Gilani on May 2011 announced that a second nuclear reactor at Chasma with Chinese assistance had become operational with additional ones under construction with assistance from the former (Koreshe, 2011). In the this context, while Pakistan's Foreign Secretary Riaz Mohammad Khan (in October 2007), Pakistan's High Commissioner to the UK (in 2010); and Pakistan Foreign Ministry (in February 2011) asserted that "Pakistan is mindful of the need to avoid arms race with India" (Khan, 2007; Associated Press of Pakistan, 2010; Kerr and Nikitin, 2013:6–7), simultaneous discourses as evidenced from press briefings of Pakistan Foreign Ministry in May 2009 (Kerr and Nikitin, 2013:7); Pakistan's Retired General, Khalid Ahmed Kidwai in April 2011 (ibid.:9); and Pakistan's position at the Conference on Disarmament (in October 2011) to not sign the Fissile Material Cut-Off Treaty (on the grounds that India's fissile material stocks and production capacities were larger than that of Pakistan) (Collina and Horner, 2011)—all allude to the government's position to increase significantly its nuclear arsenal in response to possible Indian plans to do the same.

Yet, Indian and Pakistani leaders continued to converse after the Mumbai blasts, as Prime Minister Singh, President Zardari, Indian External Affairs Minister S.M. Krishna, India's then Minister of External Affairs Pranab Mukherjee, Pakistan's Minister of Foreign Affairs Hina Rabbani Khar, and other high officials conversed on the sidelines of the SCO-BRIC summit in June 2009; the NAM summit on July 16, 2009; at the G-8 Outreach Summit on June 2009; at New Delhi on February 2010 and July 2011; at both Pakistan and New Delhi on September 2011; again in India in April 2012; at New Delhi and Tehran in April and August 2012; and at the United Nations General Assembly meeting at New York in September 2013 (Behuria, 2011; *The Hindu*, 2012a). Resumption of the India–Pakistan cricket match in 2013 (that were stalled following the 2008 Mumbai attacks) also constituted a major aspect of their resumption of bilateral ties. While Prime Minister Singh following the Nehruvian tradition stated that the two countries would cooperate for the welfare of their people and the prosperity of the region (Khan, 2009:136), these good neighborly gestures also asserted that cross-border terrorism must be eliminated before any progress can be made on the security dynamics in the region including Kashmir, and also that India is not in a position to redraw boundaries or engage in territorial adjustments with regard to the latter (Ministry of External Affairs, 2006b).

While controversies continue as to whether Pakistan has done "enough" to control terrorism (Khan, 2009:137–138), analysts with a dose of realism insist that cross-border infiltrations will continue between India and Pakistan's relations (Hagerty, 2006), and others (calling for a mutual trust) assert that domination by hardliners and the military security in Pakistan and complications on the Indian side render it difficult for both sides to resolve the Kashmir issue (Cohen, 2002:223; *The Hindustan Times*, 2006; Khan, 2009:136), India–Pak dialogue continued on such disputed issues—mainly prompted by Pakistan's quest for peace linked to its domestic, economic, and international concerns. Yet, continuing border clashes, harsh rhetoric, and the Afghanistan dilemma continues to cast uncertainty over such dialogue, when Prime Minister Sharif (who in his May 2013 election campaigns had expressed interest to better ties with India), following one of the latest border clash incidents in August 2013, came under pressure from the military to suggest a tougher anti-Indian stand. Pakistan's then Chief of the Army Staff, General Kayani, in a meeting with Prime Minister Sharif, "conveyed the military's reservations over the LoC and border violation by India," and "warned that the recurrence of such incidents was forcing Pakistan's military to respond even harder" (Jayasekera, 2013).

India's interpretation of its international relations with China post-2004 stemmed primarily from the United States' insecurity perceptions from China as a rising military power. The grounds for this was provided when in addition to sporadic statements by Chinese state officials about its rising conventional capabilities, nuclear arsenals, and its ballistic missile inventory (Shambaugh, 2009:156), China's largest official policy document, *China's National Defense* 2004 (issued on December 28, 2004) as its official policy argued for a greater role for military power in China's international affairs. While this policy shift is speculated to be an outcome of China's enhanced confidence about its own increasing military capabilities or efforts to combat post-9/11 terrorism, or as a response to the challenges of the US hegemony and unilateralism (in referring to the US policies leading to the Iraq war), the document's conclusion that "world peace is elusive" and that the "military factor plays a greater role in international configuration and national security" indeed increased the global military disequilibrium in international affairs (Singh, 2009:130). In addition, with a US-specific angle, Chinese Major General, Zhu Chenghu (in 2004), conferred that "if the Americans draw their missile and position guided by ammunition on to the target zone on China's territory, I think we will have to respond with nuclear weapons" (Kamath, 2009:115). India and the United States had a vital stake in this shift in China's military power. While analysts hold that the United States' apprehensions of China's nuclear strength should not be a concern (Kamath, 2009), the US military planners sought to initiate a defense mechanism in Asia to thwart a rising China, in which India became a willing (or, by default) partner (Ayres, 2009).

In this light of these developments, India interpreted its relations vis-à-vis China along three continuums: First, that India (bold and assertive by 2004) must tread cautiously vis-à-vis China as a rising nuclear and military power, that China's economic rise interweaved its economic destiny with India in a globalized era, and China's potential rise to great power status in the near future. While these frames of interpretation were contextualized in the broader context of India–US strategic alliance, which India knew was a US mechanism to offset China (Shambaugh, 2009), yet proactive diplomacy and a mutually beneficial economic engagement formed the crux of India's renewed interactions with China. This proactive diplomacy ensued as high state officials of both countries exchanged mutual visits (as Chinese Premier Wen Jiabao and President Hu Jintao visited India in April 2005 and November 2006 respectively; ruling coalition Chairperson, Sonia Gandhi visited China in November 2007; Prime Minister Singh visited the country in October 2008 and October 2013), and conversed at multiple regional and multilateral meetings (namely at the Asia–Africa Jakarta Summit, 2005; Group of G-8 Summit, 2007; Shanghai Cooperation Organization, 2009; the East Asia Summit, 2013; and the Russia–India–China Trilateral Forum, November 2013). These resulted in mutual agreements on bilateral trade; exchanges in military; negotiations over the boundary; cooperation in industry, agriculture, finance, water, resources, energy, environment, information technology, tourism, education; on issues of regional and global affairs; and a "10-prolonged" strategy for reinforcing their Strategic and Cooperative Partnership (Ministry of External Affairs, 2005; Press Information Bureau, 2006; Limaye, 2010; International Press Center, 2011; Ministry of External Affairs, 2012; Joint Statement, 2013). Simultaneously, on the economic front, there occurred expansions of Indian IT companies into China, China expressed interest in replicating India's success in global services, bilateral trade between them grew exponentially in the past half decade; and there emerged the concept of a "Chindia," where a combined India–China population equal to one-third of the world's population and their economic progress could potentially "shape the new, and yet unsettled" domains of a post-Cold War global affair (Ministry of External Affairs, 2005; *The Hindu*, 2007a; Aiyar, 2008; Baru, 2009). China justified its diplomatic gestures as efforts to counter India's fears of a richer, powerful, and aggressive China, and to ensure China's pursuit of a "peaceful rise/peaceful development" strategy vis-à-vis India/ Asia (Goldstein, 2005).

Yet, their post-2004 interactions, when situated in a historical plateau, where it is commonplace that India and China are ideologically, politically, and militarily different, remained problematic and differences continue to persist between India and China. First, nuclear and military insecurities from China as "a rising power and a non-democratic system" cause concern to India (Subrahmanyam, 2010). Although China continues to adhere to its NFU on grounds that its national priority is economic development; believes that nuclear weapons are usable; and that abandoning the NFU would lead to an arms race and tarnish its image in world affairs, China's escalated expenditures on military modernization; development of space capabilities; and its focus on the development of tactical and short-range nuclear weapons remain a concern for India (Kamath, 2009:114–115; Shambaugh, 2009:156; Singh, 2009:131). This is because militarily, China has the edge in most conventional capabilities (with the largest military in Asia that out sizes any of its immediate neighbors) and 60 percent of its nuclear arsenal and conventional military capabilities have relevance for use only against its neighbors (Shambaugh, 2009:156). Accordingly, Indian defense and policy planners have continued to cite China's combat capable aircrafts; its fourth generation Russia fighters; Chinese navy's surface combatants, destroyers, frigates, submarines; the People's Liberation Army's (PLA) edge in its ground force equipment like battle tanks, towed artillery, and attack helicopters—not to mention the next generation and technological capabilities of these equipment—as "[o]ne of the strategic realities of the present period," in that "the balance of military capabilities between China and India is shifting to our [India's] disadvantage in operational terms … [and] nowhere is this more noticeable than in the air and defense capabilities" (Singh, 2009:131; Shambaugh, 2009:156).

In addition, what also irked India was Chinese assistance (with an India-centric connotation) to strengthen Pakistan's missile equipment. Pakistan is currently developing a fighter aircraft with Chinese assistance; purchasing Chinese naval equipment, including missile boats and submarines that operate very close to India's Northwestern coast. In addition, recent reports indicate that China taking up a number of projects in Pak-occupied Kashmir, a large number of PLA personnel working there, and Chinese construction of port facilities in Gwadar (in Pakistan) add to India's fears of encirclement (Venugopalan, 2011; Mir, 2011). While China's ties with Pakistan are justified in terms of its global ambitions that require containing India and also by its strategic necessity to access the oil-rich Middle Eastern states and the Arabian through Pakistan—for India these developments appear ominous—in that Pakistan is simultaneously gaining from a US–Pakistan military nexus. What also irk India are Chinese efforts at courting its neighbors Bangladesh, Nepal, and Sri Lanka; allegedly arming Maoist rebels in India; establishing its presence in the Indian Ocean; and also looking into engaging Afghanistan well ahead of the NATO's withdrawal from the former (Sood, 2009:261; Kronstadt and Pinto, 2013:23–26). Although in his September 2012 visit to South Asia, China's Defense Minister assured that China is "conducting friendly exchanges and cooperation with its counterparts in the South Asian nations ... and not target[ing] at any third party [India]" (Reuters Canada, 2012), India perceives it an official Chinese policy to restrict India in the Asian subcontinent, and conversely, position itself more prominently in the region.

Thus, controversies remain as to whether India and China's parallel rise in an economic, strategic, and big power sense and their remarkably well diplomatic and commercial relations are making their interests converge? Or, will the two with lingering suspicion and the concept of "Chindia" remain rivals or partners? Or, will China, otherwise, showing an accommodative stance with India on bilateral issues, be willing to give India much maneuverability in the subcontinent (Sood, 2009:147, 159; Shambaugh, 2009:156)? Thus, a prudent part of India's proactive diplomacy has also entailed that India also cultivate cordial relations with East Asian countries threatened by an expansionist China, expand its economic ties and border talks with China, and also continue to build its long-term nuclear and military capabilities against China—which I will elaborate later (Gupta, 2005:35; Limaye, 2010; Kronstadt and Pinto, 2013:29–30). In this context, one must note the increasingly assertive role played by the Indian military, which, backed by the Indian government's increasing attention and money (Kronstadt and Pinto, 2013:8–16), has made China the central focus of its attention, and has also made provocative public statements against the Chinese state. This is evidenced in a number of Sino-Indian border crises, including the most recent one in April–May 2013 (Jayasekera, 2013). In this scheme of affairs, India and the United States' courting of each other to contain China (although both India and the United States have downplayed such assertions) (Kronstadt, 2007:26), and how this courtship is played out within the larger transitioning schemes of India–China–Pakistan–US affairs will remain pivotal in shaping the course of India's international relations vis-à-vis China. It is in these transitional contexts of India's interpretation of its regional and global affairs emerged the reconstructions of India's strategic culture and (in)security imaginary in an anarchical and globalized post-2004 era.

Reconstructing India's Strategic Culture and (In)Security Imaginary

The United States' vested post-9/11 security interests in South Asia, India's desire for global status, and the ongoing neoliberal nuclear technology collaborations with the United States—formed the backdrop against which the Indian state under Prime Minister Singh's government rearticulated India's post-2004 strategic culture, its (in)security imaginary, and its nuclear and missile technology developments. Barring some disproportionately influential leftist sentiments, key political party members, and members of the India's defense and nuclear science community (except for those like K. Subrahmanyam, Rajiv Nayan, occasionally Uday Bhaskar, and Samuel Cherian), who have voiced strong criticisms of (or, at best a nuanced approach to) India–US civil nuclear initiatives, the state's official strategic cultural discourses, unlike the previous decades, in the post-2004 phase contextualized its nuclear security oriented strategic thinking to support India's desired global status; continued nuclear collaboration with the United States; to economically integrate into and benefit from globalization; serve India–US' democratic–security mission to counter terrorist-proliferation types of dangers in the South Asian region; and maintain India's regional security through Asian power balances in the area. This overall pro-US strategic gesture saw India–US congruence in advancing trade and exchange of high-technology dual-purpose nuclear technology related items; India–US military and defense relations; counter-terrorism projects; and other nonmilitary areas of cooperation such as in green partnerships, economic trade, education, health, and collaborating to politically stabilize the South Asian region (Kronstadt, 2005; Global Security, 2006; CNN, 2009).

However, I contend that these strategic cultural discourses of India's security community are not simply neoliberal discourses in support of democratic, economic, technological, and security-related missions between the two countries. Instead, these discourses were also pragmatic maneuvers by the Indian state to simultaneously draw from a "democratic/ we" identity communality between India and the United States to justify India's pro-US nuclear ventures; situate US-India strategic collaborations as a security basis for India to rearticulate its strategic rethinking and (in)security imaginary vis-à-vis the Chinese and the Pakistani states; and finally, revealing a neoliberally embedded sense of strategic autonomy (which I elaborate later) to deal with the American power in its international relations. How ideologically guided discourses of India's security community have served as meaning-producing tools to reconstruct these fluid contours of India's strategic culture and (in)security imaginary—within which continue to unfurl cautious neoliberal dynamics of India–US' strategic security collaborations—will be hereafter addressed.

A plethora of discourses stemming mainly from members of the Indian government noted that "changes in the global economic and political structures and the growing interdependence among nations … offer[s] us [India and United States] a unique opportunity to … establish a strategic partnership of global dimension" (Council on Foreign Relations, 2009b). Accordingly, Prime Minister Singh lauded the Indo-US nuclear collaboration with a neoliberal mindset, in that, such partnerships represent "[a] new India which realizes its destiny in the framework of an open society, … one billion people trying to seek their social and economic salvation in the framework of a democracy, in the framework of an open economy" (Singh, 2006); India's then External Affairs Minister Pranab Mukherjee held that "Globalization today provides opportunities to countries that are willing to draw benefits from it …" (Embassy of India, 2008a); and others like India's Foreign Secretary Shyam Saran; India's Science and Technology Minister Kapil Sibal; and India's Foreign Secretary Shivshankar Menon stressed that India and the United States "build on the momentum...and continue … to focus on … High-tech cooperation …" (Embassy of India, 2008b; Varadarajan, 2007). Simultaneously, India's neoliberal discourses emphasized a "we" concept in India–US' identity as liberal democratic states to engage in neoliberal technology collaborations to fight a terrorist insecurity in the South Asian region. To this end, Prime Minister Singh stated that, "there is a growing convergence in our national interests, both within the bilateral framework and on regional and global issues .... If we are to effectively tackle the multiple [terrorist] challenges that confront the world, India and the United States, ... must work together ..." (Council on Foreign Relations, 2009b). Likewise, India's Ambassador to the United States, Sen (2005:5), claimed

> I see this [i.e., Indo-US cooperation] not only in a bilateral context, but in the context of the world. How do we make the world a safe and a better place? ... We have taken an India-US initiative on democracy, which is to help build capacity in countries in transition to democracy .... It is not only that democracies do not go to war with each other ... [but] also democracy is the ultimate anti-dote to terrorism.

However, almost immediately following the release of the July 18, 2005 Joint Statement and March 2006 Separation Plan, members of Indian political parties, nuclear science community, and defense community voiced criticisms/concerns of the India–US civilian nuclear initiative—so much so that several analysts started expressing increasing doubts about these collaborations (Bitzinger, 2005; Giacomo and Cornwell, 2007; Johnson, 2007). From the political spectrum, two lines of oppositional discourses became evidenced: First, that "by engaging in discussions with, and allegedly acquiescing in the demands made by the United States, we have compromised the independent nature of our foreign policy;" and second (a concern also shared by India's nuclear science community) that the Separation Plan could "... undermine the autonomy of our decision-making, limit the options or compromise the integrity of India's strategic programs; and adversely affect the future of our scientific research and development" (*The Hindu*, 2006a). Furthermore, with an anticolonial/anti-Western skepticism, the oppositional discourse held that the International Atomic Energy Agency's safeguards to be imposed on India's nuclear facilities, in essence, meant the United States serving as the "global police" to achieve the necessary policy changes through the NSG to prevent India from further nuclear testing (Ayres, 2009:7); that the civil nuclear cooperation with India was a cover up for the United States' ulterior motive to curtail India's cooperation with Iran and Central Asian states in areas of defense trade (Varadarajan, 2007); and that the 123 Agreement which has been given a "spin" by its protagonists to "liberate" India from "nuclear apartheid" sentiments would restrict India's political/nuclear sovereignty in international affairs (Sikri, 2007). The Left Front, which remained at the forefront of resistance to India becoming a "junior partner" of the United States through the 123 Agreement, argued that "it represents an attempt on the part of the Indian government to align India's foreign policy more closely with that of US imperialism and gives Washington the means to ensnare India in a dependent nuclear and military leadership" (Kamara and Jones, 2007; Joshi, 2008). The Left pointedly referred to "India's two International Atomic Energy Agency votes on Iran as 'capitulation' to US pressure" which "paved the way for Congressional approval of proposed US–India civil nuclear cooperation" (Kronstadt, 2007:22). In the words of the Communist Party of India (Marxist) General Secretary, Prakash Karat, "the Indo–US treaty cannot be seen as a separate and compartmentalized entity without considering its implications for India's independent foreign policy, strategic autonomy, and the repercussions of the United States quest to make India its reliable ally in Asia" (Kamara and Jones, 2007).

The BJP, then in opposition (which had laid the groundwork for the civil nuclear agreement during its term as government) revealed a relatively flexible approach to the issue (when seen in comparison to the Left) but opposed the Hyde Act and the 123 Agreement in terms of the specifics of the agreement (BJP, 2006). In this scheme of relative flexibility, while Brajesh Mishra (Indian's National Security Advisor under the BJP) supported the 123 Agreement arguing that "the 123 Agreement would not compromise the development of India's nuclear deterrent," other members of the party namely L.K. Advani and Jaswant Singh, opposed the agreement. The party's general stand was that while "a strategic partnership with the United States is actually beneficial, this type of a nuclear deal was not necessarily the best way to achieve this [end] and therefore the [123] agreement should not be negotiated" (Joshi, 2008). Following the US Congress' passing of the Hyde Act (December 2006), the BJP listed numerous objections to the ongoing talks of the India–US agreement calling it "unacceptable" given that it "aimed at capping, rolling back, and eventually eliminating India's nuclear weapons capability" (BJP, 2006); former Prime Minister Vajpayee insisted that "the deal as envisioned would place unreasonable and unduly expansive demands on India, particularly with regard to the separation of nuclear facilities" (Kronstadt, 2007:21); and Jaswant

Singh (then Leader of the Opposition in the Rajya Sabha) lamented that the "[t]he separation plan, ... will result in two-thirds of the nuclear power plants being placed under IAEA safeguards, ... [which] will result in a gap on the fissile material available for weapons purposes, ... [and] India risk[ing] losing its nuclear autonomy by agreeing to place 'two-thirds' of its nuclear power plants under international safeguards" (*The Economic Times*, 2006).

More substantive criticisms of the India–US nuclear initiative came from key members of India's nuclear science community namely former and senior scientists of the Atomic Energy Commission who viewed the 123 Agreement "as being more about nonproliferation and less about energy cooperation" (Kronstadt, 2007:22). This group (whose views are highly credible, who have made the country proud of their indigenous scientific accomplishments, and are sensitive to any signs of "foreign interference" in the country's nuclear industry) opposed the 2005 Joint Statement and the 2006 Separation Plan on grounds of the following technical/political details (some of which are also shared by oppositional political parties to the government): First, India's unilateral moratorium on nuclear tests is potentially being codified into a bilateral obligation through the 2005 Statement (that also would also allow the United States to reclaim any supplied nuclear equipment if India tested a nuclear device); second, India may potentially be denied of nuclear reprocessing technologies warranted under "full-cooperation;" third, India (because of the "termination" clause) has not been given assurances that it will receive unwarranted fuel supplies in perpetuity; fourth, the United States is retaining the right to carry its own intrusive end-use verifications; fifth, a lack of transparency in sequencing the 123 agreement, the IAEA's safeguards agreement, and the NSG's decision-making processes to enable technology transfer to India; and finally, limiting India's foreign policy independence (as evidenced in the framing of language for securing India's assistance) to support the US efforts in preventing Iran from acquiring weapons of mass destruction (Kronstadt, 2007:22–23).

While some senior scientists "did not want to be quoted," others, namely former members of India's nuclear science establishment namely H.N. Sethna, M.R. Srinivasan, P.K. Iyengar, A. Gopalakrishnan, A.L. Prasad vocally opposed India–US nuclear initiative (*The Hindu*, 2006b; Iyengar, 2007; Rajesh, 2007). Noting the "tough conditions and [the] intent of the July 18, 2005 statement [that] are at complete divergences," P.K. Iyengar (2007) noted that unless "the US makes substantial changes in its civil nuclear deal with India, back and forth negotiations on the 123 Agreement are meaningless;" A. Gopalakrishnan (2007), following the signing of the Hyde Act into law, asserted that "the 123 Agreement currently being negotiated must conform in letter and spirit with the provisions of the Act" to ensure there are no violations of the 2005 agreement in restricting India's nuclear sovereignty; and prominent members of the Department of Atomic Energy concurred with such cautious stipulations (although scientist Dr A.P.J. Abdul Kalam also stressed the highly technical theme of energy security in this context) (Subbarao, 2006). On India's independence day of 2006, nine leading scientists, while recognizing the "need" for advanced technology "for the benefit of the nation" and welcoming the historic initiative of the Bush administration's July 2005 Statement, also appealed to the Indian government and its parliamentarians to discuss India's nuclear deal with the United States cautiously, ensure that the implementation of the 123 agreement does not infringe on India's independence in "letter and spirit" to carry on its indigenous research and development in science and technology, does not limit India from holding on to its nuclear option, and does not subject India's significant build-up of its indigenous nuclear technology capability to external control through unfair restrictions (The Hindu, 2006b).

The views of India's defense community between 2004 and 2008 (until the passing of the 2008 Civilian Nuclear Accord) were nuanced in suggesting a "cautious optimism" (Gopalakrishnan, 2006). While these nuanced views expressed through the defense analysts of the Institute of Defense and Strategic Analysis did not completely negate the benefits of India–US collaborations, their perspectives offered concerns in terms of these collaborations. To this end, Bhaskar (2005a, 2005b), as well as Balachandran (2005), while countering many of the potential political and sovereign implications of the 123 Agreement (as articulated by India's political spectrum and its nuclear science community in that the agreement would "cap" India's nuclear sovereignty), instead, focused on the dynamics of the US–Pakistan relations, namely the sale of F-16s to Pakistan; the United States' "support of a military ruler in Islamabad even while being committed to the return of democracy in Pakistan;" and "its willingness to live with the A.Q. Khan iceberg [nuclear transfer scandal] even though addressing nuclear transgression are on top of the Bush priority list."

Others defense analysts expressed anti-US sentiments concerning these collaborations given the "intrinsic impossibility" in the "reciprocity clause" of the 123 Agreement (Chari, 2006), that an antiproliferation motive of the United States through these collaborations was attempting to "freeze the Indian weapon-usable nuclear materials stock at the minimum possible level" (Gopalakrishan, 2006), and India's nonrecognition as de facto nuclear weapons state by the United States would impede the supply of dual-use technology to India from the United States (Nayan, 2005). Thus, Chari (2006) negated the official state discourse that "denied that the India–US nuclear deal would compromise India's strategic requirements;" Gopalakrishan (2006) asserted that India "should retain all the accumulated inventory of such materials ... to maneuver the separation plan to suit its specific objective;" and Nayan (2005), despite being skeptical, also affirmed such progress as "partial victory," given that "no nonnuclear weapon state has been given the privilege of separating civilian and nuclear facilities program by the IAEA."[12]

Although Prime Minister Singh was attentive to some of these controversial aspects of the agreement (*The Hindu*, 2006a), and Shivshankar Menon (India's Foreign Secretary) described these negotiations as "intense, productive, and constructive" (Johnson, 2007), the official stand stood firm on these collaborations on the grounds that "relevant negotiations with the United States have not altered basic Indian policies or affected New Delhi's independence on matters of national interest" (*The Hindu*, 2006a). The government's line of reasoning was that "irrespective of the legally-binding or non-binding nature of certain controversial sections of the agreement, the state has in its ultimate analyses found many of these controversial aspects of the agreement to be either "proscriptive" in ways incompatible with the provisions of the July 2005 and the March 2006 Joint Statements, or "inappropriate to engagements among friends"" (Kronstadt, 2007:23). To this end, the prime minister in numerous explanations at the Parliament on June 29, 2005; February 27, 2006; March 7, 2006; and August 13, 2006 made explicit references to the clauses of the 2005 Joint Statement and the March 2006 Separation Plan (Ministry of External Affairs, 2006a; *The Hindu*, 2006b), and explained that "an unprecedented measure of transparency on our part even in the midst of complex negotiations...has ensured that the autonomy of our strategic program is fully maintained... [and] that the government cannot try to modify the agreement to assuage the objections" of the opponents" (*The Hindu*, 2007b). This government's line was also supported by select defense analysts at the IDSA (Joint Press Briefing, 2005; Bhaskar, 2005a; Nayan, 2005). Yet, this official stand met with little success in allaying the opposition. Forming the most unlikely bed-fellows, the BJP and the Left Front stood the grounds of their opposition; the Left Front supporting the UPA from the outside withdrew its support from the coalition; and only following the UPA's survival (with a vote of confidence from the Samajwadi Party) that the negotiations of the 123 Agreement moved to the global level where a nuclear savvy India, despite its non-NPT status, expressed willingness to separate its civilian nuclear facilities from its military programs and subject 14 civilian thermal power reactors to full-scope safeguards by the IAEA.

The signing of the 2008 nuclear accord did not relieve Indian skepticism given that the flow of dual-use technology to India, which all sectors of the Indian polity considered a litmus test in India–US strategic relations, did not occur smoothly owing to implementation hurdles of the 123 Agreement stemming from the US Export Control Policy; the US Entity List;[13] and India's nonmembership in the four multilateral export control regimes the NSG, the Missile Technology Control Regime (MTCR), the Australia Group, and the Wassenaar Arrangement. Added to these were persisting nuclear apartheid sentiments from Indian skeptics (the lefts and India's defense analysts) who, following President Obama's 2009 Prague Speech and the US' Nuclear Posture Review (April 2010), were not very sanguine about the United States' goal of strategic arsenal reduction versus its insistence on disarmament (Cheodon, 2010; Mahapatra, 2010). Accordingly, defense analyst Nalapat (2010) maintained that President Obama, "wearing postracial preferences" as the previous administrations, maintains selective non-proliferation; leftist sections still deemed the United States a "fickle" partner that may not always be relied upon to provide the reciprocity, sensitivity, and high-technology transfers sought by New Delhi (Kronstadt et al., 2011); and Ozkan (2010) maintained that "with neither side having a clear strategy or blueprint about the future relations, these talks seems to be going nowhere."

However, as Cherian (2010) rightly observes, despite backlog in the transfer of dual-use technology, economic and strategic congruence between India and the United States continued with cooperation expanding in civilian space, defense, and other high-tech sectors. In fact, certain notable developments ensued: In a Joint Statement issued at New Delhi, President Obama during his November 2010 visit to India announced implementing the US export-control policy initiative (which met a long overdue Indian demand that certain Indian defense companies be removed from the US Entity List); following which, the US' Department of Commerce's Bureau of Industry and Security amended the export Administration Regulations removing nine Indian defense and space companies from the US Entity List (Bishoyi, 2011); and on the same visit, the President announced the US support for India's candidacy in the four multilateral export control regimes—the NSG, the Missile Technology Control Regime (MTCR), the Australia Group, and the Wassenaar Arrangement. Interweaving this strategic progress, the global neoliberal momentum, and an existing Hobbesian anarchy, Prime Minister Singh (in 2009) asserted how "the growing interdependence among nations ... offer us [India and the US] a unique opportunity to ... establish a strategic partnership of global dimension" (Council of Foreign Relations, 2009b); "welcomed the deepening relationship between the world's two largest democracies ... [to] promote and secure a stable world" (NDTV, 2010); and recently, expressed satisfaction with progress achieved to date in India–US defense, economic, and trade relations (*The Hindu*, 2013). Yet, this official line of thinking also maintained a sense of strategic autonomy,[14] seen in the state's recent 2011 decision on Medium Multi-Role Combat Aircraft (MMRCA) deal (Rajagopalan, 2011). High-profile members of India's nuclear science community such as Dr Kalam, Anil Kakodkar, and Dr Srikumar Banerjee continue to echo this line of strategic autonomy, which embedded in a neoliberal sense of cautious optimism, explains India–US hi-tech deals on two grounds: First, that nuclear energy remains a nonnegotiable option for India; and second, joint India–US endeavors to build clean space-based solar power satellites for the Indian state (Lele, 2010; Bagchi, 2012; United Press International, 2012).

India–US nuclear security collaborations which offered a security context for India interacted with terrorist insecurities suffered by India (allegedly conducted by Pakistan's nonstate actors) to define the state's strategic cultural discourses and (in)security imaginaries vis-à-vis the Pakistani state. To this end, Prime Minister Singh in 2006 grieved that Musharraf "has not done enough" to control terrorist elements like Lashkar-e-Taiba and Jaish-e-Mohammed who operate out of Pakistan,… [and] it simply means that the General is not inspiring much confidence in New Delhi" (*The Times of India*, 2006); reasserted India's "zero tolerance" policy on rising terrorism in South Asia (BBC, 2006); asked the United States to "isolate and condemn terrorism, wherever they attack, … and whichever country or group provides them sustenance and support" (Singh, 2006); and India's then External Affairs Minister Pranab Mukherjee, while asserting the need to maintain India's economic growth, claimed that "Many of the countries in our region, including Afghanistan, Pakistan … are going through a difficult period of transition [and] it is in our national interest that these countries return to the path of democracy" (Embassy of India, 2008a). In fact, in his mutual concurrence with President Obama in 2010, Prime Minister Singh "condemned terrorism in all its forms," that all terrorist networks, including Lashkar-e-Taiba, must be defeated, and called on Pakistan to bring to justice the perpetrators of the November 2008 Mumbai attacks (NDTV, 2010). In fact, India remains fixated in equating its counter-terrorism cooperation with the United States (such as the July 2010 Counterterrorism Initiative) with exchanging information on terrorist threats emanating from Pakistani extremism (Cherian, 2010).

Furthermore, acutely drawing from the commonalities of India and the United States as "democratic" partners to counter terrorism, Indian discourses constructed its (in)securities from an "antidemocratic" Pakistan (also implicating the latter's identity as antinomy to India's democracy, pluralism, and secularism). Evidenced in the words of India's then Ambassador to the United States, Sen (2005:5), "It is not only that democracies do not go to war with each other … [but] also democracy is the ultimate antidote to terrorism …. All these [i.e., terrorism] are disapproved in India. [The] fact that … we don't have one Indian, … in any international terrorist movement … speaks for itself." In fact, Sen (2005:5) in the rest of his speech mentions how Indo-US joint efforts at nonproliferation, in which "the two are now partners," are in fact related to "the world's biggest [sources] of proliferation, … [which] are in our [India's] immediate neighborhood," and is also linked to "international terrorism." In stressing the "responsible" character of the Indian state, India's then External Affairs Minister Pranab Mukherjee in 2006 explained the government's decision to delay the test-firing of the Agni III missile by saying that "as responsible member of the international community, we want to keep our international commitments on nonproliferation" (although some analysts see this delay in India's testing of the III Agni in the ongoing context of the United States' nonproliferation expectations from the region and their ongoing hi-tech deals) (Kamath, 2009:138).

Furthermore, in noting Pakistan's nuclear and missile defense expansion (as documented earlier), political realists/defense analysts have also deemed it imperative for India's national security to equip itself with minimum nuclear weapons given that "it is not unconceivable that Pakistan's use of nuclear weapons might draw threats of intervention from China, and [that] such a situation [although] unlikely … cannot be denied …. [Thus] India must be minimally armed to counter a threat from China and Pakistan" (Malik, 2009:139). Likewise, Subrahmanyam (2010) cautioned that, "[a] nuclear-armed Pakistan, in a position to exercise nuclear deterrence against any conventional threat, … [and] use terrorism, a derivative of nuclear deterrence, as an instrument of policy" against the Indian state cannot be entirely negated.

From a national security perspective, I do not belittle India's concerns of terrorism and nonproliferation from Pakistan which, in fact, have aggravated since 9/11, and have very little signs of slowing down (Sood, 2009:264). Yet, from a critical constructivist perspective that is attentive to the role of discourses as meaning-producing tools in international politics, it becomes interesting to see how India has taken recourse to certain Orientalist epistemological claims and assumptions about the self (India), its other (Pakistan), and its other's identities, political beliefs, and practices—to justify the politics of identity-making of the Pakistani state. Such assumptions of the Indian state's insecurity discourse ignores the vibrant movements within the Pakistani polity that led by Pakistani progressives and liberals have for long continued to demand a democratic Pakistani state—as also addressed in a recent conversation by India's diplomat/member of Rajya Sabha, Mani Shankar Aiyar and Pakistan's nuclear physicist, Pervez Hoodbhoy (NDTV, 2012).

Yet, India's strategic culture traditions based on Nehruvian *panchsheel* and its territorial security also pervaded the Indian state's strategic discourses vis-à-vis Pakistan given that Indian leaders continue to converse with the latter even after the Mumbai blasts, and Prime Minister Singh, much like the Nehruvian tradition, and in a departure from the history of conflict and mutual recrimination between the two sides, stated that the two countries would cooperate not only for the welfare of the two people but for the prosperity of the South Asian region as a whole (Khan, 2009:136). An underlying sentiment of this cooperation in the prime minister's words is that "You can't choose your neighbors and Pakistan happens to be India's" and given that the "destinies of the two countries are (thus) interlinked, there is no option but to keep this dialogue alive" (ibid.). Yet, in these friendly discussions, the government has firmly stated that India's Pakistan policy short of making adjustments over the *"security territorial element"* (i.e., Kashmir), is primarily seeking to "have an ordinary working relationship with Pakistan on all [other] levels," and willing to do whatever is required to give comfort to people on both sides of the LoC; allow the free movement of people, goods, and ideas; and create opportunities for the celebration of the natural cultural affinity which exists between the people of the two sides (Ministry of External Affairs, 2006b).

In this context, while famous Indian academic S.D. Muni (quoted in Khan, 2009:137–138), and more progressive analysts and politicians of India–Pakistan politics (NDTV, 2012), claim that complications from the Indian side to not compromise on Kashmir complicate the India–Pakistan issue, and India must "go half way" to meet Pakistan on the issue "for the stable peace of the subcontinent," Muni also asserts on a more realist note that India has "... no choice but to consider raising the costs of the terrorist operations, which has not yet happened," and that although "this is not a structural part of India's foreign policy, terrorist operations make it essential for this to be integrated into India's foreign policy" (Khan, 2009:136). In fact, such progressive elements have held that Prime Minister Singh seems to be a rather "lonely" actor in wanting "uninterrupted" dialogue with the Pakistani state (NDTV, 2012). This observation bore well with a more aggressive stand of the Indian army vis-à-vis Pakistan—when following the 2013 August border clash incident with Pakistan, India's official opposition, the BJP, and a group of military and security experts (as India's Defense Minister, A.K. Antony) opposed what they perceived as the government's "soft-peddling" of

Pakistani terrorism. To this end, Defense Minister, Antony asserted that India "will take all possible steps—sometimes strong action—to effectively retaliate against every violation of the Line of Control," and that "such retaliation could include a cross-border raid, action that could easily provoke a rapid escalation" (Jayasekera, 2013). The views of the military have been grounded on the fact that India's strategic alliance with the United States and its economic expansion in the past decade has given India the "geopolitical and economic leverage" to make concessions from Pakistan.

India's interpretation of its international relations with China post-2004 shifted from the previous year's along the following continuum: First, in revealing a shift in India–China's interactions from the regional realist realm of politics to a broader neoliberal globalized realm involving the explicit presence of the United States in the region as a balancer in the region; second, in this neoliberally grounded context, shifting the interpretation of India's (in)securities vis-à-vis China from territorial, military, and nuclear issues to one of economic trade and engagement; and finally, redefining India's (in)securities and interactions vis-à-vis China through cooperation and competition (termed coopetition) as rising Asian powers (Ayres, 2009:4). In this context, as stated by the then Indian Foreign Secretary, Nirupama Rao (2009), "That we strive for a peaceful and stable neighborhood and for building peaceful and mutually beneficial relations with our neighbors goes without saying … since in the absence of such a neighborhood … our unhindered economic development would stand to be affected." Although India's historical line of strategic cultural thinking vis-à-vis China has been to "forge deeper ties with its own neighbors," this thinking took a boost in the post-2004 years, which, as discussed earlier, has resulted in a proactive diplomacy vis-à-vis China not to mention the boost in Sino-Indian trade and economic affairs (Indian Ministry of External Affairs, 2005; Press Information Bureau, 2006; *The Hindu*, 2007a; Aiyar, 2008; Limaye, 2010; International Press Center, 2011; Ministry of External Affairs, 2012; Joint Statement, 2013). Speaking at the end of his first year Prime Minister Singh noted, "Who could have imagined that China would emerge as [India's] second-largest trade partner" (Prime Minister Singh quoted in Sheth, 2008:47)?

However, China's rapid rise of its military power and its emergence as a player of strategic consequences in South Asia, Central Asia, the

Persian Gulf, and the Indian Ocean, not to mention continuing Sino-Pakistani ties (Islamic Republic News Agency, 2013; Pakistan Defense, 2013) have raised the prospect of Beijing's primacy in (South) Asia and has raised concerns for the Indian state. Thus, despite the Indian government's official stand to "forge deeper ties with its own neighbors," as stated by Nirupama Rao (2009), security analysts seriously consider the political–military–nuclear security aspects of China's rise for India. As stated by Jasjit Singh (2009:131),

> There is no question that we must continue to improve our relations with China and reduce the potential for disagreements and potential conflict. It would not be in our [India's] interests to think of China in any adversarial terms. But it would be less than prudent to ignore the changing realities of military power.

Likewise, Mohan (quoted in Kronstadt and Pinto, 2013:38), held that "[T]he increasing influence of China in these regions has compelled India to rethink its own strategy toward its neighboring regions and to recalibrate its ties with the United States." Thus, a prudent part of India's proactive diplomacy has also entailed that India cultivate cordial relations with East Asian countries threatened by an expansionist China (Kronstadt and Pinto, 2013:29–30), and currently witnesses India's engagement with states east of the Malacca Straits and North of the Himalayas (Shambaugh, 2009:146; Limaye, 2010: Kronstadt and Pinto, 2013:29–30).

In this context, one must also consider the increasingly assertive role played by the Indian military in the recent years, which, backed by the Indian government's increasing attention and money, has taken a bellicose public stance and has made provocative public statements against the Chinese state. This is evidenced in a number of Sino-Indian border crises, including the most recent (April–May 2013) one, when the Indian military complained that the Chinese troops had stayed several days in an eastern border area and the Indian Air Force dispatched a C-130J Super Hercules tactical airlift to these mountainous areas potentially to deter Chinese aggression (Jayasekera, 2013). Thus, in addition to diplomacy, India also started building its long-term nuclear and military capabilities against China namely upgrading the Su-30 bombers (through an indigenously assembled Su-30MKI) by the Indian Air Force; the Brah

Mos supersonic missile by the Indian Navy to give the Navy a second strike capability use against China; and testing of the Agni III missile that would give India the capability to hit targets deeper in China (Gupta, 2005:35). In this scheme of things, India's courting of the United States to contain China (and vice versa), and how this courtship is played out within the larger transitioning schemes of India–China–Pakistan–US affairs will remain pivotal in shaping the course India's international relations vis-à-vis China.

In this context of a much speculated India–Pakistan–China–US interactive dilemma and what it might imply for India's strategic cultural thinking and its (in)security, prominent defense analyst, K. Subrahmanyam (2010), has denounced Cold War-centric sentiments that the United States is using India as a "trap" to engage in an anti-China containment policy in South Asia. An optimist of globalized interdependence, Subrahmanyam (2010) claims that "there is nothing odd about "global powers" like the United States, China, and India having an interest in developments around the world," and with extensive interactions/interests through trade investments, the US–China (and India) seem to be sharing a "symbiotic financial relationship" with each other. Yet, on a realist note, he also held cautionary remarks of a China–Pakistan based insecurity for the Indian state. On the China factor he noted that "It is not surprising that China's rise has led to tension with all its neighbors ... [including] India,... and from the early eighties, China ... decided on nuclear proliferation as an instrument of expanding its influence and power." On a more current note, he continues, "The main problem today is that 'rising China' is the only major power which has not accepted democracy. The combination of rising power and a nondemocratic system causes concern to all China's neighbors." Added to this Chinese dynamic, is the insecurity factor from Pakistan, given that "[w]hile there is clear recognition that [a] nuclear-armed Pakistan poses a threat to Indian security, what cannot be overlooked is that Islamabad drives its capability to threaten India from China" (Subrahmanyam, 2010). In this context, he also clarified that "[While] the US has its share of the blame for being permissive of Pakistani proliferation, ... the actual proliferator and continuing supporter of Pakistani nuclear and missile proliferation—and the source of 80 percent of its conventional weapons—is China." Subrahmanyam (2010) thus sums up India's current (in)security imaginary of India, "China and its surrogate, Pakistan, have been attempting to contain India .... China, with its one-party authoritarianism, and Pakistan, its crypto-ally with its *jehadi* expansionism are targeting India. They seek to destabilize India through Islamic terrorism and left-wing violence ...." Before this glaring regional insecurity, Subrahmanyam (2010) suggests that "India needs strategic partnerships with all democratic, pluralistic, and secular powers [such as the United States] to counter the combined threat from an alliance of authoritarianism and monolithic systems allied with *jehadi* forces."

The Indian military recognized the two-way regional insecurity of the Indian state, although, in contrast to the previous years, when Pakistan was the major concern for the military, in the recent years, now focused on China as India's primary (potential) adversary (Kronstadt and Pinto, 2013:8). Accordingly, the attention of the Indian army and its Air Force leaders have been shifting to the "East" (Singh, 2009); India's Defense Minister, A.K. Antony, directed the army to prepare for a "two-front" war (Kronstadt and Pinto, 2013:9); and in May 2012, Antony announced in the Parliament that the government would seek an increase in the slated FY 2012–2013 defense budget to respond to the "new ground realities and the changing security scenario" facing India (*Times of India*, 2012). Furthermore, expanding the ongoing cooperation among the military, the government, and India's scientists (with some Indian Air Force officers being trained at the Bhabha Atomic Research Center in weapons manufacturing), India's strategic and defense planners namely P.R. Chari, Ambassador Leela Ponappa, Major General Dipankar Banerjee, Commodore Uday Bhaskar, and others reassessed the fundamental assumptions behind India's nuclear doctrine in the context of its current security environment and offered a more realist "blueprint" to suit India's strategic insecurity (Institute of Peace and Conflict Studies, 2012). To this extent, they reassessed the fundamental assumptions behind India's nuclear doctrine; accessed the implications of the India–US nuclear accord on China and Pakistan; the impact of a growing China–Pakistan nexus against India; the potential of a growing China–Pakistan "nuclear collusion" vis-à-vis India; accounted for the role of nonstate and sub-state actors in this crisis escalation dynamic; and to this end emphasized the doctrine's force credibility, leadership credibility, and technological credibility to secure India (Institute of

Peace and Conflict Studies, 2012). To this end, the Ministry of Defense's 2011–2012 Annual Reports as well as its 5 Year Defense Plans (covering the years 2012–2022) addressed India's "new ground realities" stemming from China and Pakistan; stressed "ambitions plans to transform the army from a threat based force to a capability-based force to be able to conduct the entire spectrum of war [at both fronts] including counter-insurgency operations (COIN) and nuclear conflict by 2020" (Kronstadt and Pinto, 2013:9); contemplated the Cold Start Doctrine to counter Pakistan; and launched an aggressive move to enhance the trio of land, air, and sea-based intra and inter service networks under the Ministry of Defense, including enhancing nuclear-strike options for India (*The Hindu*, 2012b; *The Times of India*, 2012; Kronstadt and Pinto, 2013:9). As I will elaborate later, this Pakistan–China centric agenda of the Indian military boded well with the Indian state's East Asian Policy of expanding its strategic horizons into the Indian Ocean's Sea Lines of Communications and beyond, and saw the development of a trio of land, air, and sea-based intra and inter service networks under the Ministry of Defense, including enhancing nuclear-strike options for India.

In keeping with my theoretical premise that (in)security imaginary "… is the product of an act of cultural creation, which is fundamental to any subsequent system of cultural representation" (Tomlinson, 1991:156–157), one sees that three interconnected contours of (in)security imaginaries were ideologically and discursively articulated by the Indian state's security community's vis-à-vis China, Pakistan, and the United States: First, a sense of a neoliberally grounded security vis-à-vis the United States in terms of their bourgeoning strategic relations, and yet a continued sense of cautious optimism, and thus, a simultaneous perception of insecurity in implementing their strategic partnership. Second, a growing terrorist-proliferation type of insecurity vis-à-vis the Pakistani state, which supported by the "democratic/we" identity of India and the United States, has enabled India to engage in a politics of identity making vis-à-vis the Pakistani state. Third, a simultaneous form of security/insecurity imaginary vis-à-vis the Chinese state fed by military and economic developments. Yet, each contour of (in)security imaginary of the Indian state is grounded in a neoliberal notion of strategic autonomy of the post-2004 state as its identity, which, different from the Cold War-centric/nonaligned form of autonomy, has constructed a pro-US, globalized image for itself, but, whose simultaneous anti-US skepticism (and at worst a continued sense of nuclear apartheid) has rendered the state to take recourse to an Asian solidarity to deal with the United States in its strategic security affairs. In this current context of the Indian state's identity, the notion of strategic autonomy remains critical given that this autonomy, which conceptually speaking, is a mutation of realism and India's traditional nonalignment (Monsonis, 2009), is also mutually constructed and sustained by the state's meaning-producing discourses, which offered a political and ideological space to forge India's strategic security collaborations with the United States.

What do these dynamics of India's strategic cultural thinking and (in)security imaginaries in the post-2004 period imply in terms of India's traditional stand on a free and fair global disarmament? Unlike the United States, which until the end of the Cold War believed that a limited nuclear war is winnable, nuclear India continues to perceive its nuclear weapons as not for first-use but for ultimate defense, and Prime Minister Singh, after the May 2004 elections, and again, in an interview to the CNN in DC in July 2005, reiterated the government's commitment to the doctrine of minimum nuclear deterrence (Kamath, 2009:152). Yet, one can simultaneously discern a shift in the state's disarmament discourses, which, contrary to the Nehru, Indira Gandhi, and Rajiv Gandhi days when such discourses were defined boldly from an acute anti-US angle, now, are redefined as discourses in partnership with the United States, where both speak with a shared political objective of defining the disarmament goal keeping in mind terrorist-proliferation types of dangers facing the two states. Speaking more authoritatively on the disarmament project as a nuclear weapons state, Prime Minister Singh, in his November 2010 meeting with President Obama "reaffirmed their countries shared commitment to a world without nuclear weapons," which "give[s] them a responsibility to forge a strong partnership to lead global efforts for nonproliferation and universal and nondiscriminatory global nuclear disarmament in the 21st century" (NDTV, 2010). Yet, the government's pursuit of disarmament took a different approach, that is, instead of total disarmament, it now insisted on a "step by step" approach toward the goal of disarmament (Kamath, 2009:142). This incremental approach to disarmament also emphasized, allowing states to legitimately possess nuclear weapons, wherein the prime minister, following India's proposal in the 2010 Nuclear Security Summit to create a Nuclear Energy Center to secure vulnerable nuclear materials by 2014, asserted strengthening "international cooperative activities that will reduce the risk of terrorists acquiring nuclear weapons or material without reducing the rights of nations that play by the rules to harness the power of nuclear energy to advance their security needs" (Nuclear Security Summit, 2010). To this extent, the prime minister reaffirmed the state's "dedication to work together [with the US]" to achieve the incremental goal of disarmament, and "the need for a meaningful dialogue among all states possessing nuclear weapons to build trust and confidence and for reducing the salience of nuclear weapons in international affairs and security doctrines" (NDTV, 2010).

However, not all of India's traditional quest for a global disarmament was lost in the state's strategic thinking, given that in a recent speech at the UN General Assembly (in September 2011), the prime minister stated that "Nuclear proliferation continues to remain a threat to international security. The Action Plan put forward by Prime Minister Rajiv Gandhi for a Nuclear-Weapon-Free and Non-Violent World provides a concrete road map for achieving nuclear disarmament in a time-bound, universal, nondiscriminatory, phased and verifiable manner" (Singh, 2011). In this context, one might rightly argue that "India's historical philosophy of Hinduism and self-righteousness" explains continued reflections of the state's traditional nuclear restraint (Ozkan, 2010). Yet, the fact that the Indian state's disarmament discourses were no longer being contextualized explicitly in the realms of an international nuclear hierarchy/discrimination but rather in the more pragmatic realms of globalized interdependence (where visible economic, financial, political, human insecurity, and international security crises such as terrorism and nonproliferation pervade), was simultaneously evidenced in the prime minister's General Assembly speech on how to strengthen the global nonproliferation effort in the scheme of these global insecurities. To meet the overall nature of these global impediments, the prime minister not only recommended a cooperative approach to world security to be worked out within the framework and spirit of law, but also for global nuclear safety, and to this end, recommended "... international efforts under the aegis of the International Atomic Energy Agency ... [to] enhance levels of [the use of nuclear energy] for safety and security"

(Singh, 2011). In this effort, he asserted India's thorough review of the safety of its nuclear plants for the production and use of nuclear power for meetings the country's energy needs (ibid.). This official line of thinking on India's nuclear energy security continues to be echoed by India's External Affairs Minister, S.K. Krishna (Krishna, 2012), Srikumar Banerjee (current Chair of India's Atomic Energy Commission) (United Press International, 2012), and India's Minister of State, V. Narayanasamy (Yurman, 2012). In this fluid context of the Indian state's disarmament approach, India's nuclear policy stand (in its long term) stipulated taking steps to halt the production of fissile materials and to sign the Fissile Materials Cut-Off Treaty with certain precautions (Kamath, 2009:142).[15] It is within these neoliberally embedded reconstructions of the Indian state's strategic cultural thinking, (in)security imaginary, and identity (as one of strategic autonomy) emerged the post-2004 state's neoliberal (yet cautious) nuclear dynamics.

Strategic Collaborations and Nuclear/Missile Development: Strategic Autonomy and Neoliberal Shifts

Despite the seemingly insurmountable hurdles and increasing doubts among political/security analysts that India–US strategic security partnership would fall through greater bilateral security collaboration and a series of measures to achieve, in fact, continued under the Manmohan Singh government (despite a slow record in the transfer of dual-use technology to the Indian state). Guided by regular high-level meetings of the Indo-US Defense Group, Executive Steering Groups, and Joint Working Group on Counter-Terrorism such collaboration continued to flourish in the areas of military exercises, counter-terrorism activities, arms sales; and defense cooperation (including a potential cooperation in missile defense). In August 2004, a top US diplomat in India said that "Without doubt, military cooperation remains one of the most vibrant, visible, and proactive legs powering the transformation of US–India relations" (quoted in Kronstadt, 2005:9). Accordingly, there flourished a number of joint military exercises since July 2004: An Indian Air Force contingent with US counterparts (in February 2004) participated in the cooperative Cope Thunder Exercises in Alaska; two months later, United

States and Indian Navy held joint exercises in Malabar off the coast of Goa (Kronstadt, 2005:9); in mock air combats (in July 2004) Indian pilots in Russian-built fighters faced American pilots flying the US F-15s; United States and Indian special force soldiers continue to hold joint military exercises; and their naval forces continue to hold joint naval exercises annually at Malabar (with the most recent one held in November 2013 at Bay of Bengal) (Indian Navy, 2013; US Department of Defense, 2011). The objectives of these exercises continued to stress increase of mutual familiarity between the armed forces on both sides in order to advance interoperability, which was deemed essential if the two militaries in the future had to "combine arms" in peace and stability missions in the area (Tellis, 2004; US Department of Defense, 2011). In April 2007, the Commander of the US Pacific Command, Admiral Tim Keating, asserted that the Pentagon intends to "aggressively pursue expanding military-to-military relations with India" (Kronstadt, 2007:26).

Arms deal and defense cooperation constituted the next significant step in India–US strategic security collaborations, which the United States justified in the context of "common principles and shared national interests" of India and the United States (ibid.). In July 2004, the US Congress was notified of a possible sale to India of aircraft "self-protection systems" (worth up to $40 million) to be mounted on the Boeing 737s that carry the Indian Head of the state (ibid.:27); the State Department (in 2004) authorized Israel to sell India the jointly developed the US–Israeli Phalcon airborne early warning system (a long pending Indian request since the Vajpayee administration) an asset that some analysts believe may tilt the regional strategic balance further in India's favor; and between 2006 and 2013, India purchased from the United States the USS Trenton, new fighter jets, and advanced C-130J Hercules military transport aircrafts, along with related equipment, training, and services (Kronstadt, 2007:27; Defense Industry Daily, 2013). In further expanding their defense cooperation, the two countries in June 2005 signed a defense pact, The New Framework for the US–India Defense Relationship, outlining collaboration in multilateral operations, expanding two-way defense trade, increasing opportunities for technology transfers and coproduction, expanding collaboration related to missile defense, and establishing a Bilateral Defense Procurement and Production Group for promoting such collaboration (US Department of Defense, 2011). Thereafter, in early 2006, the two concluded a Maritime Security Cooperation Agreement wherein they committed themselves to "comprehensive cooperation" in protecting the free flow of commerce and addressing a wide range of threats to their maritime security including trafficking of Weapons of Mass Destruction and related materials.

Joint Counter-terrorism cooperation expanded in the areas of law-enforcement, information sharing, and the disruption of terrorist financing, with the two states agreeing that one of the chief threats to their security stems from global *jihadism* (Sibal, 2003). To this end, the June 2005 New Framework for the US–India Defense Relationship listed "defeating terrorism and violent religious extremism" as one of the four key shared security interests between India and the United States, and called for a bolstering of their mutual defense capabilities required for such a goal; the India–US Joint Working Group (in its April 2006 session) reaffirmed determination from both countries to further advance bilateral cooperation and information sharing on areas of common concern such as bioterrorism, aviation security, cybersecurity, WMD terrorism; and following the Counter Terrorism Initiative (signed in July 2010), the two announced a dialogue between India's Ministry of Home Affairs and the US Department of Homeland Security to further deepen operational cooperation, counter-terrorism technology transfers, and counter-terrorism capacity-building (Kronstadt, 2007:29; NDTV, 2010).

Yet, India's strategic autonomy ensured that it was not a passive recipient of such foreign/neoliberal collaborations, and still considering the United States a "fickle partner that may not always be relied upon to provide the reciprocity, sensitivity, and high-technology transfers sought by New Delhi" (Kronstadt, 2005:10), necessitated that the state consolidate the indigenous parameters of its nuclear defense, nuclear energy, and military defense system. To this end, the Indian state in May 2008, test-fired its 3,000 km range surface-to-surface nuclear capable Agni III missile for the second time (designed and optimized to carry lighter 200-kiloton thermo nuclear payload weapons giving the country the capability to hit targets cities in China like Beijing and Shanghai); on 15 November 2011 and 19 September 2012 test-fired the 4,000 km range Agni IV missile; then on 19 April 2012, test-fired the 5,500 km range intercontinental Agni V missile; and is reportedly in the making of the 8,000–10,000 km range intercontinental ballistic missile, Agni VI (Rediff India, 2008; IBN, 2013).

Furthermore, all three services of the Indian military institutionalized reforms to meet India's expanding strategic horizons (in keeping with the China threat, terrorist insurgency threat, and its larger East Asian Policy): The military moved toward intra-and-inter service network centric organizations to enhance interoperability (*The Hindu*, 2012b); the Air Force started building long-term military capabilities against China, namely through Su-30 bombers, constructed new air bases and "Advance Landing Grounds" in the North East, and purchased the Jaguar jet and the French Mirage-2000 (from a European Consortium); and the Navy, continues to play a dominant role in the Indian Ocean's Sea Lines of Communications and beyond by extending its maritime influence as far as the Lakshwadeep, Andaman, and Nicobar Islands—projecting further toward Indonesia, Sumatra, and the Malacca Straits. With this East/China-centric focus, the Navy's expanded its defense base: It inducted the nuclear powered submarines such as BrahMos supersonic missile in 2006 (which gave the Navy a second strike capability); it inducted a miniaturized submarine-launched version of the Agni III (called Agni III SL) in June 2011; launched the submarine launched ballistic missile, Sagarika, in 2010; commissioned its first nuclear powered submarine, Arihant (built indigenously with technical help from Russia) expected to be inducted for sea trials by early 2015 (*The Times of India*, 2014); and bought German HDW submarines for its military arsenal (Rajagopalan, 2011). As rightly pointed by Indian, United States, and independent security analysts, these aggressive expansions point to the Indian state/their defense planners' desire to develop the full group of strategic weapons associated with India becoming a major military power state in world affairs (Kronstatd, 2007; Kamath, 2009; Kronstadt and Pinto, 2013).

Conclusion

Following the theoretical premise of this manuscript that there exists an ideological and discursive linkage between the social construction of India's strategic culture, (in)security imaginary, and its nuclear security policies, this chapter has explored how the return of the Congress Party to power, which, representing a much stronger vision of India's globalization, has, in continuity and disjuncture from the earlier Indian governments, reconstructed the strategic cultural thinking, (in)security imaginary, and a sense of strategic autonomy (as its identity) for India—leading to its strategic security collaboration with the United States traditionally perceived by India as a hierarchically situated, adversarial, and Western player. Yet, as analyzed, the government's official stand of a neoliberal, globalized, and pro-US entity had to negotiate with the polity's leftist elements, skepticism from the country's nuclear science community, and its defense analysts to support a pro-US approach in India's national security affairs. In noting these complexities involved in the reconstructions of India's strategic culture and (in)security imaginaries, the chapter has also documented how the state's official discourses (with some overlap/ divergences with its science, defense, and its extended political community) has served as meaning-producing tools to draw from a "democratic/ we" identity communality between India and the United States to justify India's neoliberal strategic security collaborations; situate the US–India strategic collaborations as a "security basis" for India to rearticulate its strategic rethinking and (in)security imaginaries vis-à-vis the Chinese and the Pakistani states; and finally, with a neoliberally embedded sense of strategic autonomy has dealt with the American power in its strategic security affairs. The chapter's conclusion has observed that unlike the previous years, what is unique at this contemporary juncture of the state's nuclear security affairs is how the state's discourses in pragmatic maneuvers have, in conjunction with its strategic cultural thinking and (in)security imaginaries, constructed a certain sense of strategic autonomy (as identity) of the post-2004 Indian state, which, with an explicit acceptance of globalization; speaking boldly in a pro-US voice (identifying both as strategic partners in terrorist-proliferation related global security missions); and yet, retaining an anti-US skepticism, has consolidated its Asian solidarities to bargain the most with the United States to achieve its great power aspiration and benefit from their ongoing strategic security collaborations.

Notes

1. The United Progressive Alliance (UPA) became the center-left coalition government of India following India's May 2004 national elections, where the Congress party was able to forge a majority of more than 335 members out of the 543 seats in the Lok Sabha with allies as well as external support from the Bahujan Samaj Party, Samajwadi Party, Kerela Congress, and the Left

Front. In the next elections held in April–May 2009, the UPA was once again able to put together a majority of 332 members out of the 543 Lok Sabha seats with external support from the Bahujan Samaj Party, Samajwadi Party, Janata Dal Secular, Rashtriya Janata Dal, and other minor parties.

2. The agreement consistent with the US domestic laws, national and foreign policy objectives, and observance of international laws entailed the removal of the Headquarters of the Indian Space and Research Organization from the US Entity List to ensure the export to India dual-purpose nuclear technology; entailed a presumption of approval for all dual-use items to India (although this excluded the nuclear reactors at Tarapur that come under the restrictions placed by the Nuclear Supplier's Groups); and also agreed to eliminate the need for export licenses for 25 percent of the US items that is imported by India (Borman, 2004). These gestures also required simultaneously that India take strong measures to address proliferation concerns of the United States and ensure compliance with the US export control measures.

3. Following which India reported substantial progress in the areas of biotechnology, nanotechnology, advanced information technology, and defense.

4. Although progress was made in conversations with Rumsfeld in negotiating the procurement of more sophisticated deep-sea submergence rescue vessels, the purchase of Patriot missiles, and in acquiring the advanced PAC-3 version of the Patriot missile system, India also expressed concerned over the United States' proposed sale of F-16 fighter aircrafts and P-3 Orion maritime reconnaissance planes to Pakistan, and made it clear that this sale could have adverse impacts on positive sentiments and goodwill for the United States in India. Rumsfeld stated that he understood Indian concerns but that the United States did not see relations with India and Pakistan as a zero-sum game (*The Deccan Herald*, 2004).

5. This new framework for expanding the Indo-US defense relationship, which, replaced the January 1995 Agreed Minutes of Defense Relations, represented bold initiatives between the two countries to "shed" their past mutual suspicion and chart an active agenda for military cooperation based on shared political objectives to address their current political realities (Text of Indo-US Agreement, 2005).

6. The 2005 Joint Statement enshrined the concept of full civil nuclear cooperation between India and the United States. For details, see *The Hindu* (2007b). In doing so, the Agreement stipulated that such cooperation will include nuclear reactors, aspects of associated nuclear fuel cycle, and technology transfer on an industrial or commercial scale; India has right to reprocess the US origin spent fuel; establish a new national reprocessing facility dedicated to reprocessing foreign nuclear material under the safeguards of the International Atomic Energy Agency; has the right to utilize any fissionable material that may be separated in national facilities under International Atomic Energy Agency safeguards; and that, the United States, that does not historically have a policy of supplying to any country enrichment, reprocessing, and heavy water production facilitates, will through an amendment of

such policy render such technology transfer to India possible. In implementing such full civil nuclear cooperation, the Joint Statement also asserted the principles of reciprocity; certification; safeguard (which was further developed in the March 2006 Separation Plan); the US fuel supply assurances; integrity and reliability of India's strategic program, autonomy of its decision making, and future scientific research and development; and cessation of cooperation by the United States only as an extreme step in the termination of this Agreement.

7. As agreed in the 2006 March Separation Plan, India has accepted only International Atomic Energy Agency safeguards that will be reflected in an India-specific Safeguards Agreement with the International Atomic Energy Agency. For details see, Ministry of External Affairs, 2006a; *The Hindu*, 2007b; International Atomic Energy Agency, 2008.

8. However, even before the 123 Agreement was finalized, the Bush administration obtained a commitment from India to sign the Convention on Supplementary Compensation, designed to limit liabilities facing the US companies supplying nuclear technology with respect to their activities in foreign markets. The argument being that it would help the US companies export nuclear safety technology to foreign markets. India signed the agreement in October 2010, and was expected to ratify it by 2011, which it, yet, has not (Balachandran, 2011).

9. By the end of President Bush's term, the following trends became evidenced as indications of India–US strategic cooperation: First, the Bush administration's positive disposition in supplying India with advanced military equipment, including allowing Lockheed Martin and Boeing to sell F16s and F18s to India and to consider co-production of these platforms in India; second, indications of the US support to India's naval, air force, and the military's requests in areas such as command and control, early-warning, and missile defense systems; third, agreeing to joint Research & Development efforts between the US Department of Defense and India's Defence Research and Development Organisation; fourth, high-level strategic dialogue on India's energy security issues including future cooperation in high technology trade, defense, space, nuclear safety, and in regional issues pertaining to security in South Asia; fifth, integrating India into the global nuclear regime for access to safeguarded nuclear fuel and advanced nuclear reactors; and finally, continued economic dialogue with India in efforts at creating new constituencies in the United States having a stake in India's growing power and prosperity (Tellis, 2005; Malik, 2006; Shoup and Ganguly, 2006; Sood, 2009).

10. The United States' 2010 Nuclear Posture Review, which placed the prevention of nuclear terrorism at the forefront of the United States' national security agenda, described "how the United States will reduce the role and numbers of nuclear weapons" in its national security affairs. To this extent, it asserted that the United States will maintain a "safe, secure, and affective

nuclear arsenal to maintain strategic stability" of the nation and reassure its friends and allies of the United States' security commitment to them. Yet, the Review called for "making much needed investments to rebuild America's aging nuclear infrastructure," and asked for nearly $5 billion to be allotted to the Department of Energy for the next several years to meet this agenda (Department of Defense, 2010).

11. Broadly, these areas of improvement addressed reestablishing/upgrading existing hotlines between India–Pakistan's Foreign Secretaries and Director General of Military Operations to prevent misunderstandings and reduce risks relevant to nuclear issues; conducting an agreement on pre-notifications of flight-testing of missiles (which was completed in the 2006 composite talks); reaffirming their earlier moratorium on further nuclear tests unless their national security was threatened; engaging in multilateral foray on issues related to nonproliferation; conversing toward the implementation of the 1999 Lahore Memorandum of Agreement; opening of the crossing points across the LoC; economic and commercial cooperation; combating terrorism and drug-trafficking; free movement of media products between the countries; restarting bus and rail services; and encouraging people to people contact by issuing more visas between the countries.

12. India's anti-US discourse was being rebutted from the US side, where individuals like Robert Einhorn (proliferation specialist at the Center for Strategic and International Studies) and senators like Jon Kyl (Republican, Arizona) expressed "considerable frustration" over the deal, and those like Senator Joe Biden called for United States "compassion" on the deal (Giacomo and Cornwell, 2007; Johnson, 2007). However, a counter-argument in the US politics also suggested the Bush administration by easing restrictions on the acquisition of dual-use technology and incorporating a state that has already crossed its nuclear threshold is enhancing the sanctity of the non-proliferation regime, and only by allowing India to join the community of the nuclear states can the global nonproliferation objectives may truly be achieved) (Shoup and Ganguly, 2006:4–6).

13. Since Cold War, the US government has relied on two legislative acts (the Export Administration Act, 1979; and the Arms Export Control Act) to regulate the export of defense articles and services to potentially proliferation risky countries (Balachandran, 2011). Since India's detonation of 1998, nine of India's defense and space companies were placed under the Entity List. Since India–US negotiations underway under the Bush–Singh administrations, it has been a long-standing demand that these defense and space companies be removed from the Entity List through export control policy changes so that these companies are treated the same way as any other destination in India for export licensing purposes (Bishoyi, 2011).

14. India's strategic autonomy, which conceptually speaking, is a mutation of realism and India's traditional nonalignment, constitutes a neoliberally grounded notion of the post-2004 Indian state's identity, which, embedded

in a neoliberal sense of cautious optimism, serves as a balancing mechanism to guide India–US strategic partnership (Monsonis, 2009).

15. Two concerns arise of the issue of India's signing of the Fissile Material Cut-Off Treaty: First, Pakistan's insistence in not signing such a treaty stating that India has a much larger stock of fissile materials than does Pakistan, and Pakistan's signing of the treaty will create an imbalance in stockpiles of fissile material in the possession of India and Pakistan, and Pakistan will not accept such an imbalance. It demands that the proposed treaty also cover existing stock of fissile materials (Kamath, 2009:142). Second, India fears that the United States could take India for a ride by pressuring her to stop production of fissile materials even before the treaty is negotiated and signed. This again, could be a ploy on the part of the United States to help Pakistan achieve parity with India in possession of fissile material (ibid.).

8

Conclusion

This book has been an effort to reorient strategic culture and international security studies in a constructivist direction. It narrated India's nuclear security *problematique* to address the relative silence in strategic culture and security studies in conceptualizing strategic cultures, notions of (in)securities, and their nuclear strategy-making as a socially constructed discourse in international relations (IR). To this extent, my discursive narration of India's nuclear trajectory has analyzed how discursive articulations of India's strategic culture rendered possible by meaning-producing discourses and codes of intelligibilities of its security community has facilitated interpretations of the state's strategic environment, its notions of insecurities, and its nuclear security choices.

In proffering an intersubjective framework of analysis that has relied extensively on state's discourses as meaning-producing tools in IR, my analysis has engaged with some limitations of mainstream strategic culture and security studies in grasping the intersubjective dynamics of nuclear security in international affairs. In rendering this discursive approach through a study of India's nuclear security *problematique*, I must admit that—seen through mainstream approaches to strategic culture and security studies—the use of discourses to understand the domain of real politics, such as nuclear policy making, might be seen as postmodern jargon or less systematic attempts in explaining the rigors of nuclear policy making. Likewise, speaking of the relevance of conventional approaches, I remain cognizant in this book about the national, organizational, and ideographic types of explanations in strategic cultural studies (both at the general and at the India-specific level) that have epistemologically relied on cognition (i.e., collective behaviors of organizations) and the structural (realist) edifice in understanding the relationship between strategic cultures and strategy-making. Likewise, the significance of real politics as noted by IR scholars/practitioners like Kautilya (Rangarajan, 1992), Carr (1939), Morgenthau (1949), and others cannot be denied in analyzing nuclear strategy-making. Furthermore, the importance of the neoliberal paradigm's concept of interstate interdependence through low politics, which has become particularly significant in the current eras of globalized interdependence (Keohane and Nye, 1977; Lebow, 1995; Kegley and Raymond, 1999), offers a broader conceptualization of strategy-making involving forms of military/nonmilitary collaborations, and (ideally) seeing a forward move toward a global fissile material cut-off treaty to achieve the idealist goal of reducing state's nuclear arsenal or toward global disarmament.

Despite the partial validity of these explanations, my book is of the view that the overall approach of these mainstream perceptions of strategic culture and security studies, irrespective of occasional forays by some ideographic strategic culture scholars (Johnston, 1995, 1998) and critical IR scholars (Abraham, 1999; Krishna, 1999; Persaud and Walker, 2001), have represented a problem-solving approach to nuclear strategy-making in international affairs, which, rendered from the lenses of detached researchers, locate these studies to one of the means–ends relationship in international affairs—where states identify their appropriate security aims and then consider ways to resolve their insecurities. In other words, these existing approaches have not considered how discursive practices (may interact with other objective issues of real, domestic, and global politics) and may lie at the core of representational ambiguity of nuclear strategy-making in international affairs.

Accordingly, this book has drawn from a "how-possible" (Cox, 1981) approach to international politics to explore a discursive production of strategic cultures, (in)security imaginaries, and nuclear policy choices in India's nuclear security affairs. Therefore, in analyzing the construction of India's nuclear security *problematique,* this book has explored the following research puzzles: First, what constitutes India's strategic culture at any particular temporal and spatial context is a matter of social construction produced by its security community's meaning-producing discourses.

Second, how the socially constructed nature of India's strategic culture (the foundations of which were laid since its ancient Vedic eras and consolidated/reconstructed under its colonial/postcolonial periods) sustains a certain political–ideological space within which are articulated shifting understandings of postcolonial India's IR, its nationalist identity, its (in)security imaginaries, and its nuclear security policy choices. Finally, who articulates these shifting meanings of India's strategic culture, identity and (in)security imaginaries, and how one reconceptualizes the shifting relationships between the articulator's (i.e., the Indian state's) own identity and its notions of (in)security imaginaries?

In deconstructing these "how possible" research puzzles, my chapters have documented the following: Chapter 2 has narrated the multiple historical, political, religious, cultural, and colonial influences that have underpinned the foundations of India's strategic culture, which articulated through the textual/discursive interplays of India's ancient Vedas, Upanishads, the *Arthashasra*, its nationalist leaders, and colonial administrators, have, in a combination of real politics and *dharma* (India's spiritual morality), established postcolonial India's strategic culture. While this chapter by no means suggests that ancient India's cultural norms as evidenced in the Vedas, Upanishads, and the essence of Vedic *dharma* has any "direct" relevance in explaining contemporary India's statecraft or its nuclear strategy-making, the political–historical context of the chapter certainly denotes the existence of an amalgamated (or the socially constructed) nature of ancient/colonial India's strategic cultural thinking—from which were significantly culled postcolonial India's strategic culture. Of particular importance in this historical context is the emergence of a militant Hindu nationalist sentiment through the RSS, one of whose successor branches, the BJP, years later was to become significant in charting India's nuclear weapons development.

Chapter 3 has narrated the discursive construction of India's strategic culture, (in)security imaginaries, and atomic policy choices under Prime Minister Nehru's government. To this extent, the chapter has narrated the ideologically guided reconstructions of postcolonial India's strategic culture by Nehru's government, which, by drawing significantly from the strategic moorings of the colonial Indian state namely elements of real politics as waged though its intense anticolonial struggles, Gandhi's nonviolence, and colonial India's "thirst" for science for national development—has constructed postcolonial India's strategic culture. As documented extensively in this chapter, this discursive reconstruction of Nehruvian India's strategic cultural mindset reflected the emergence of certain strategic visions of the state, which, born out of its anticolonial sentiments did not discard the West especially its benefits for India's scientific and industrial progress. Instead, the Indian state's strategic cultural mindset as rendered through the discourses of Nehru and its security community, in keeping with their anticolonial sentiments bespoke postcolonial India's realist notions of territorial strength, sovereignty (keeping in mind an expansionist Chinese state), political idealism, *panchsheel*, and nonalignment; remained acutely skeptical (and thus insecure) of the possible emergence of a Western/US economic imperialism in world affairs; and remained intensely aware of an increasing Cold War super power rivalry in India's vicinity and a nuclear armaments race. Yet, these (in)securities did not preclude India's ability "to selectively draw from the West and function on a revolutionary [read: western scientific] plane" in terms of its scientific development (Nehru et al., 2003:61). These discursive connections between India's strategic culture and (in)security imaginaries, namely its willingness "to function on a revolutionary [read: western scientific] plane," explain India's atomic science developments for its national development purposes. As documented, the dynamism of India's nonalignment as "a new method of struggle, a political warfare, and a new kind of diplomacy" to engage in its international affairs marked the strategic identity of the Nehruvian Indian state (Nehru, 1950:28).

Chapter 4 has explored the reconstructions of India's strategic culture, its (in)security imaginaries, and India's nuclear weapons policy choices under Shastri, Indira Gandhi, and Rajiv Gandhi's governments (with the brief interlude of the Morarji Desai and the Charan Singh governments). During this phase, the chapter explores a discursive and ideological shift in the Indian security community's strategic cultural thinking from one of political idealism to an increasing nuclear aggressiveness (justified by increasing nuclear threats from India's regional politics and a sense of global nuclear apartheid), and how these shifting discourses sustained the political and ideological space to reconstruct India's (in)security imaginaries and its nuclear weapons policies for national defense purposes. Accordingly, as documented extensively in the chapter, these discursive and ideological shifts in the India state's strategic mindset represented a shift from prime minister Nehru's political idealism, to Prime Minister Shastri's defense-oriented pragmatic realism, to Prime Minister Indira Gandhi's nuclear aggressiveness, to Prime Minister Rajiv Gandhi's drive (after an initial waning) to expand India's nuclear and missiles arsenal. Yet, as documented throughout the chapter, these discursive–ideological shifts of India's strategic thinking did not completely negate "… the normative requirement of moral principles governing international policies," instead, denoting some waning of nonalignment, implied that India had "became conscious that international politics and … relations were essentially a nonmoral phenomenon rooted in the chemistry of power equations" (Dixit, 2004:104–105). This balance between realism and restrain became well evidenced under Rajiv Gandhi, given that his administration on grounds of a nuclear expansionist Pakistan could have tested a nuclear device but refrained. Seen in the light of this progression, the period 1964 through November 1989 witnessed incremental though noticeable shifts of India's strategic cultural and (in)security discourses—bringing in increments "… principles of realism and practicality to bear on … [India's] foreign policy and [nuclear] defense planning process" (ibid.: 115). These shifts in India's strategic culture defined India's identity as a traditionally nuclear ambiguous state where the governments and their nuclear scientists, through strategic maneuvers, reconciled their strains in officially denying India's possession of a nuclear weapons program while advancing its technological know-how to retain the nuclear option in case needed to go nuclear.

Chapter 5 has narrated the reconstructions of India's strategic culture, (in)security imaginaries, and its nuclear weapons policy choices after the Cold War era under V.P. Singh, P.V. Narashima Rao, Chandra Shekhar, Deva Gowda, and I.K. Gujral's governments. The chapter documented how the continuing political–ideological–discursive climate of increasing militarization and nuclear aggressiveness among India's nuclear hawks (although somewhat mellow in its official governmental discourses owing to international pressures of nonproliferation) rendered the country almost at the edge of a nuclear weapons testing by the end of this phase. Following Tomlinson's (1991:7) claim that, "… insecurities are cultural in the sense that they are produced in and out of 'the context within which people give meanings to their actions and experience and make sense of their lives,'" one also notices that its security community's strategic cultural discourses now shifted and consolidated primarily around an acute sense of nuclear apartheid vis-à-vis a hierarchical nonproliferation regime (of which the West/US was a participant) relegating its regional nuclear insecurities as secondary but important. Constructed out of these strategic cultural discourses and notions of (in)security imaginaries were an unprecedented progress of India's nuclear weapons and missiles development when seen in comparison to any previous Indian administrations, but did not yet break the tradition of nuclear nonviolence/restrain by the state. These pro-nuclear shifts in India's strategic thinking and its position of nuclear restrain, occurring amidst an economically liberalizing Indian state under P.V. Narashima Rao's government and waning further in its nonalignment, continued to sustain India's identity as a traditionally nuclear ambiguous state—although a strong nuclear lobby had gained momentum by the end of this phase.

If changing manifestations of ideology and strategic thinking impact transitions of a state's security policy, then the coming of the coalition-led Hindu nationalist Bharatiya Janata Party (BJP) to power (from April 1998 to March 2004) represented a noteworthy shift in the reconstruction of India's strategic thinking, (in)security imaginaries, and finally, the crossing of the nuclear threshold by the state. Chapter 6 narrates these discursive transitions of India's strategic culture, (in)security imaginaries, and its open nuclear detonation under Vajpayee's government. To this end, the chapter has noted how the BJP government's strategic cultural discourses in an unprecedented manner than any previous non-BJP governments have at three specific junctures during its term produced, reconstructed, and sustained a mutually constituted and shifting relationship between India's strategic culture, (in)security imaginaries, and its nuclear policy choices. First, the chapter has documented how at the eve of India's 1998 detonation, the strategic cultural discourses of its security community created a political and ideological space where real-political, cultural, religious, and historical factors have intersected discursively and ideologically to amplify a Pakistani-centric (anti-Islamic) (in)security imaginary threatening (the Hindu) Indian state—constructed among an otherwise permissive domestic and external threat environment. Second, the chapter has noted the emergence of an institutionalized nuclear doctrine for the state following its detonation setting the precedent for formally strategizing India's future nuclear policies, operation, command, control, and delivery systems. Finally, the chapter has documented how post-9/11 has represented a significant overhaul of the Indian state's strategic cultural discourses and (in)security imaginaries in terms of its increasingly noticeable neoliberal and globalizing trends, which, ironically, has enabled the state to redefine its nuclear security relations vis-à-vis Pakistan, the United States, and a new element of self-confidence vis-à-vis the Chinese state. Throughout these discursive articulations of India's strategic culture and (in)security imaginaries, the state in an initial replay of a (reactionary) legacy of the early 20th-century Hindu nationalists, and later in the acceptance of globalization, a fluid nonaligned stature, and a vivid pro-US strategic cultural rethinking has redefined its identity from a Hindu state to a globalizing, modern, nuclear state.

Chapter 7 continued to narrate the reconstructions of India's strategic culture, (in)security imaginaries, and India's neoliberal strategic security/defense collaborations with the United States under Manmohan Singh's government. To this extent, the chapter has documented how the return of the Congress Party to power under Prime Minister Singh represents a much stronger vision of India's globalization, and has, in continuity and disjuncture from the earlier Indian governments, reconstructed India's strategic culture, (in)security imaginaries, which, with an explicit pro-US orientation, has lead to extensive strategic security/defense collaborations with the United States—traditionally perceived by India as a hierarchically situated, adversarial, and Western actor in India's IR. Yet, as has been analyzed, the government's official stand of a neoliberal, globalized, and a pro-US entity had to negotiate with the polity's leftist elements, skepticism from the country's nuclear science community, and its defense analysts to negotiate (and support) a pro-US approach in India's national security affairs. Unlike the previous years, what is unique at this contemporary juncture of India's security community's strategic cultural discourses is how these discourses in pragmatic maneuvers have, in conjunction with its (in)security imaginaries, constructed a certain sense of strategic autonomy (as identity) for the post-2004 Indian state, which—with an explicit acceptance of globalization, speaking boldly in a pro-US voice (identifying both as strategic partners in terrorist-proliferation related global security missions), and yet, retaining an anti-US skepticism—has consolidated its Asian solidarities to bargain the most with the United States to achieve its great power aspiration and benefit from their ongoing strategic security collaborations.

In exploring the socially constructed nature of India's strategic culture, I do not undermine that India's strategic culture has been historically influenced by its norms of cultural civilization, nonviolence, coexistence, India's colonial memories, and memories of India–Pakistan partition. In fact, India's security community has multiple times since the days of Nehru until Singh's contemporary administration continue to refer to the historical themes of Gandhi's peace, nuclear nonviolence, India's continuing quest for global disarmament (although now redefined as an incremental disarmament), India's cultural peace and friendship with Pakistan (barring the territorial dissection of Kashmir to the latter), and on a cautionary note, also refer to India's memories of colonization, anti-Western skepticism, nuclear apartheid sentiments, the United States' ever changing notions of national security interests that sometimes problematically involve the latter in India's regional politics, and the United States' reliability as a strategic partner in current India–US strategic security relations. In fact, India's pro-nuclear defense analyst, K. Subrahmanyam (1981) while calling for India's nuclear weapons program as late as in 1981 acknowledged that his arguments for India's nuclear policy were made in the context of Mahatma Gandhi's inspired civilizational–political culture of the Indian state.

Despite such themes of continuity, my book has contended that such issues of historical influence do not render India's strategic culture and identity as one of static historical determinism as often suggested by the conventional and the more India-specific approaches to strategic culture and security studies (Tanham, 1992; Bajpai et al., 1996; Latham, 1997; Singh, 1999). In fact, as documented India's strategic culture is one of discursive production, which, "… produced in and out of 'the context within which people give meanings to their actions and experiences and make sense of their lives'" (Tomlinson, 1991:7), have switched between political idealism, realism, pragmatism, anticolonialism, possibilities of big/Western power alliances/collaborations, and nuclear apartheid sentiments to define India's world of IR, its (in)security imaginaries, and its nuclear policy choices. As documented, these shifts have been rendered possible through discourses and codes of intelligibilities of India's security community that have allocated "meanings" in distinct ways to reconstruct commonsense realities about India's international affairs.

What does this discursive analysis of the intersubjective links between India's strategic culture, (in)security imaginaries, and nuclear security choices imply in terms of retheorizing understandings and practices of strategic culture and security studies, and in terms of policy-making in South Asia for future nuclear risk reduction and conflict management? In term of IR theory, this study incorporates a critical constructivist analysis of security, that is, how states' (in)securities as cultural/discursive productions articulated by its security community's "meaning producing" discourses serve to construct states' nuclear security policy options/ choices in interstate affairs. In terms of strategic cultural studies and strategy-making, this book has incorporated the critical constructivist premise of discourse to retheorize (along discursive lines) productions of strategic cultures, insecurities, and states' nuclear security practices. This constructivist assumption also contains policy implications on the future of a nuclearized South Asia given that those who make the decisions of going nuclear are also in a position to create conditions for altering their ideational perceptions vis-à-vis identities of adversaries, insecurities, and nuclear brinkmanship.

The question as to how India's shifting notions of strategic culture, strategic identity, and (in)security imaginaries will interact with the current changing dynamics of India's geo-political realities involving primarily Pakistan, China, and the United States will remain critical in denoting the future course of India's strategic culture, security policy formulations, and how the Indian state can create conditions for altering its ideational perceptions vis-à-vis identities of adversaries, insecurities, and nuclear brinkmanship in South Asian affairs. Seen in terms of these future speculations, India's identity as one of its current strategic autonomy remains important, which, an amalgam of real politics, idealism, and some remnants of India's nonalignment, must work as "a dependent control strategy aimed at safeguarding its [India's] independence in foreign policy decision making and protecting [its] strategic assets [both technical and economic] against American pressure [hegemonic interests]" (Monsonis, 2009). In this context, the strong regional character of

Indian state's strategic cultural thinking, which is born out of its "philosophy of Hinduism, self-righteousness, and,...the colonial imprint," as well as "the widespread dominance of a highly calculative and disciplined thinking in the mindsets of Indian policy makers..." (Ozkan, 2010), makes it imperative for the state to keep a sufficient degree of autonomy in its security and military relationship with the United States.

Situated in the context of India's nuclear security *problematique,* which has remained the thematic focus of this book, India's current sense of strategic autonomy can assist India to achieve a modicum of success on nonproliferation issues with the United States while also striking a balance with the latter in terms of their convergences and divergences. In this context, as IDSA analyst Kumar (2008) observes that although for decades "Indians have seen the NPT as discriminatory, so much so that even a rethink of it is now seen as blasphemous," India should also "realize that the driving spirit that motivated it to advocate the NPT and the CTBT are still relevant ...," that is, a world free of nuclear powers, and "its stakes and responsibilities would increase with its nuclear weapons status and greater access to nuclear commerce." This new found identity of India as a nuclear weapons state offers it the political–ideological space to strike a favorable balance between "pragmatism and idealism on issues related to nonproliferation" (ibid.). Striking this balance with the United States is a pragmatic necessity for the Indian state, given its still existing political and nuclear insecurity issues vis-à-vis Pakistan and the China in its current geo-political affairs (Subrahmanyam, 2010). While progressive security analysts in the Indian front hold that Pakistan's "undeniable geographical reality and its irreversible partition history," necessitate that both countries namely Pakistan's military (which controls Pakistan's policy on India and its strategic assets such as nuclear policy making) change their ideological frameworks of interpretation to reproach their historical animosities—indications currently to this end are to the contrary (NDTV, 2012). In contrast, China's potential relation of "coopetition" with India (Ayres, 2009) renders Sino-Indian relations on a relatively secure footing, although not completely devoid of tensions.

With this relative insecurity in its regional front, it has been suggested that India continue to strengthen its strategic alliance and also enhance its big power collaborations. These steps would include India approaching India–US nuclear deal with caution; trade with Russia and France in high-tech and defense materials; draw on its large indigenous supply of thorium; not dwell too much about signing the NPT (given that India is a nuclear power and the CTBT has become irrelevant in nuclear affairs); have a long-term perspective about signing a Fissile Material Cut-Off Treaty depending on regional and global nuclear affairs; work with the United States on their divergences such as gain permanent membership to the UN Security council; gaining access to the four major arms supplies groups the NSG, MTCR, Wassenaar Arrangement, and the Australia Group (joining which will facilitate India's greater access to specialized technologies and recourses and be accepted as a legitimate member of the nuclear club); and strategizing for alternatives to the proposed India–Pakistan–Iran gas pipeline for securing India's energy resources (Kumar, 2008; Ayres, 2009).

Yet, neither is the path of strengthening India–US strategic partnerships (as extensively documented earlier in Chapter 7) an easy task. This is because India and the United States are not equal partners (Sood, 2009:267) and carry baggage of hostilities (Hagerty, 2006:28), made more complicated by the simultaneous strategic balancing activities of the United States, India, China, and Pakistan in the recent post-9/11 politics. Thus, an appropriate question here is can India and the United States create a strategic partnership that will further their mutual security and foreign policy interests in the South Asian region? An ideal answer to this question (which might not always be easy to implement) is that high-tech trade and transfer of technology in areas of energy, aerospace, and nuclear safety—that constitute key pillars of India's long-term strategy of economic and political developments—is "likely to be the fulcrum" around which India–US relations can progress (Shoup and Ganguly, 2006:4–5). On its part, India's pragmatic maneuvers and strategic calculations vis-à-vis the United States can also guide its rise to a great power status and assure its "glide path" to dual-use technology collaborations with the latter. To travel this pragmatic route, India must overcome some if its self-imposed limitations (Shoup and Ganguly, 2006) to cautiously balance its dealing with the United States and China (simultaneously keeping in mind US–Pakistan alliance). Thus, India must also cultivate its relations with China (to offset a growing US–Pakistan alliance but at the same time not offend the United States) and also underplay its growing relations with the United States so as not to adversely impact its ties with China. Talking of strategic acts, India may use China as a balancer to maneuver US–Pakistan's post-9/11 proximity as a "double-edged" sword where India could benefit from greater US' tilt toward Pakistan (Shoup and Ganguly, 2006). In this context, it is also suggested that while the China factor may increasingly draw India and the United States closer, the Pakistan factor may pull them apart (Mohan, 2009).

However, India does not have to be apologetic about its rising ties with the United States (Sood, 2009:267). This is because the United States is still the global super power despite its growing challenges from Russia and China; its domestic economic and energy problems; and international insecurities from Iran and North Korea. Moreover, despite an increasing India–China proximity, neither will be willing to allow a regional (such as a European security community kind of system) or an extra-regional power (such as the United States) to interfere in the security management of the South Asian or the pan-Asian region (Mohan, 2009:288). Furthermore, in contrast to the United States as a "status quo" state, India is a "revisionist" state (which has never been fully comfortable in its dealing with the United States as a Western power players); carries "negative political baggage" vis-à-vis the United States; and, as a "second-tier" power, is wary of the United States' ability to undermine its national interests or complicate its international aspirations (Rubinoff, 2006:54; Hagerty, 2006:28; Mohan, 2009:287). These considerations become pertinent because India despite considering itself a global power still remains a regional power (Rubinoff, 2006). Thus, keeping in mind the rhetoric of an emerging global multipolarity, an Asian solidarity, and India's participation in a so-called strategic triangle (often cited as involving India, China, Russia, or Japan, and as evidence of India's interest in a countervailing coalition against the United States), India must pursue "entente" with the United States and its progress as a great power (Hagerty, 2006; Mohan, 2009). Quite aptly, the issue of dual-use technology transfer (which by 2013 has still not been impressive) will be the "litmus test" by which India–US relations will be measured (Shoup and Ganguly, 2006:4–5).

Yet, how successfully will this "litmus test" be carried out depends on other imperatives such as the American troops potential exit from Afghanistan, the United States' rebalancing policy in the Asia-Pacific region, the India–Pakistan–Iran gas pipeline issue, India's East Policy, the Indian nuclear liability bill (that opens avenues for US companies to invest in India's bourgeoning nuclear industry); and most importantly, the US' stance toward Pakistan in the context of its instability to address India's concerns of terrorism. However, in affirming India–US strategic alliance and simultaneously showing support for the regional security of its long-term ally Pakistan, the United States is indeed walking a "tight-rope" that risks reigniting an arms race in the South Asian region (Rubinoff, 2006:54). In this fluid scenario, how the United States' South Asia policy will deal with India's demonstrated commitment to economic liberalization, its unprecedented economic growth, and its rapid emergence as a high-tech hub with a well-trained IT sector (in contrast to Pakistan's danger of becoming a "failed state") (Shoup and Ganguly, 2006) will be a decisive factor shaping India's strategic thinking, its strategic autonomy, and its (in)security imaginaries at the interconnected levels of its regional and global geo-political affairs. Yet, in keeping with the larger subjective focus of this book, I also suggest that how these empirical factors will ultimately be interpreted and take shape in terms of India's future strategic cultural reorientations will greatly depend on how the ideological and discursive frameworks of its security community will define these changes to socially reconstruct shifting notions of India's strategic cultural thinking and its (in)security imaginaries in its international affairs. India's forthcoming elections this year may project this potential shift in direction.

Bibliography

Abraham, Itty (1999). *The Making of the Indian Atomic Bomb: Science, Secrecy, and the Postcolonial State* (New York: Zed).

———— (2009). *South Asian Cultures of the Bomb: Atomic Publics and the State in India and Pakistan* (Bloomington: Indiana University Press).

Ahmed, Samina and David Cortright (1998). *Pakistan and the Bomb: Public Opinion and Nuclear Option* (Indiana: University of Notre Dame Press).

Aiyar, Pallavi (2008). "India walks a long road to China." *Asia Times*, January 8. Retrieved from http://www.atimes.com/atimes/China/JA09Ad01.html/ (last accessed on November 10, 2014).

Aiyar, Shahnaz Anklesaria (1991). "Interview with Manmohan Singh." *India Today*, July 31.

Alam, Mohammed Badrul (2012). "India and Pakistan's nuclear doctrines: A comparative analysis." April 11. Retrieved from http://www.sspconline.org/opinion/India_Pakistans_NuclearDoctrines_11042012/ (last accessed on November 10, 2014).

Ali, M. (1987). "The communal patriot, February 1912." In Afzal Iqbal, A. (ed.).*Writings and Speeches of Maualana Mohamed Ali* (Lahore: Islamic Book Foundation), 75–113.

Anbarasan, Ethiraj (1996). "No need for further N-test: Ramanna." *The Times of India*. October 29.

Anderson, R.S. (1975). *Building Scientific Institutions in India: Saha and Bhabha* (Center for Developing Area Studies, McGill University, Occasional Papers Series no. 11 (Montreal: McGill University).

———— (2010). *Nucleus and the Nation: Scientists, International Networks, and Power in India* (Chicago: University of Chicago Press).

Ashley, R. (1987). "The geo-politics of geopolitical space: Towards a critical social theory of international relations." *Alternatives*, 12:403–434.

Associated Press of Pakistan (2010). "Pakistan for reducing existing stocks of fissile material: Wajid." October 19. Retrieved from http://app.com.pk/en_/index.php?option=com_content&task=view&id=139030&Itemid=2/ (last accessed on November 10, 2014).

Ayres, Alyssa (2009). "Introduction." In Ayres Alyssa and C. Raja Mohan (eds). *Power Re-alignments in South Asia: China, India, and the United States* (New Delhi: SAGE Publications), 1–19.

Ayres, Alyssa and C. Raja Mohan (eds) (2009). *Power Realignments in Asia: China, India, and the United States* (New Delhi: SAGE Publications).

Badhwar, Inderjit and Madhu Trehan (1985). "A fresh look." *India Today,* July 15.

Bagchi, Indrani (2011). "A tale of two Manmohan Singhs." *Current History,* 110(735):131–134.

———— (2012). "Nuclear energy remains a non-negotiable option for India: Srikumar Banerjee, Former Head, Atomic Energy Commission." May 6. Retrieved from http://articles.economictimes.indiatimes.com/2012-05-06/news/31588223_1_nuclear-reactor-nuclear-energy-nuclear-power/ (last accessed on November 10, 2014).

Bajpai, Kanti (1996). "State, Society, and Strategy." In Kanti Bajpai, Amitabh Mattoo, Rahul Roy Chaudhury, Varun Sahni, and Waheguru Pal Singh Sidhu, (eds). *Securing India: Strategic Thought and Practice* (New Delhi: Manohar), 140–157.

———— (1999). "The great Indian nuclear debate." The *Hindu,* November 12.

———— (2002). "Indian strategic culture." In Michael Chambers (ed.). In *South Asia in 2020: Future Strategic Balances* (Carlisle, Pennsylvania: Strategic Studies Institute), 245–304.

Bajpai, Kanti, Amitabh Mattoo, Rahul Roy Chaudhury, Varun Sahni, and Waheguru Pal Singh Sidhu (eds) (1996). *Securing India: Strategic Thought and Practice* (New Delhi: Manohar).

Bajpai, Kanti, P.R. Chari, Pervaiz Iqbal Cheema, Stephen P. Cohen, and Sumit Ganguly (eds) (1995). *Brasstacks and Beyond: Perception and Management of Crisis in South Asia* (New Delhi: Manohar).

Bakaya, R.M. (1989). "Pre-independence roots of Nehru's foreign policy." In P.N. Haskar (ed.). *Nehru's Vision of Peace and Security in Nuclear Age* (New Delhi: Patriot Publishers), 68–78.

Balachandran, G. (2005). "Indo-US relations: Perception and reality." *Strategic Analysis,* 29(2). April. Retrieved from http://www.idsa.in/strategicanalysis/IndoUSRelationsPerceptionandReality_gbalachandran_0405/ (last accessed on November 10, 2014).

———— (2011). "Should India Give US Nuclear Suppliers a Reprieve from the Indian Nuclear Liability Law?" July 22. Retrieved from http://www.idsa.in/idsacomments/ShouldIndiaGiveUSNuclearSuppliersaReprievefromtheIndianNuclearLiabilityLaw_gbalachandran_220711/ (last accessed on November 10, 2014).

Banerjea, S.N. (1968). *Sir William Jones: A Study of Eighteenth-Century British Attitudes to India* (London: Cambridge University Press).

Bargman, Abraham (1977). "The United Nations, superpowers, and proliferation." In Joseph I. Coffet (ed.). *Nuclear Proliferation: Prospects, Problems, and Proposals* (Philadelphia: American Academy of Political and Social Science), 122–131.

Baru, Sanjaya (1998). "The economic dimensions of India's foreign policy." *World Affairs.* 2(2): April–June.

Baru, Sanjaya (2009). "India: Rising through the slowdown." In Ashley Tellis, Andrew Marbel, and Travis Tanner (eds). *Economic Meltdown and Geopolitical Stability* (Washington, DC: National Bureau of Asian Research), 199–230.

Barua, Amit (2004). "India-Pakistan official-level talks from February 16." The *Hindu*, January 27. Retrieved from http://www.thehindu. com/2004/01/28/stories/2004012807400100.htm (last accessed on November 10, 2014).

Basrur, R. (2001). "Nuclear Weapons and Indian Strategic Culture." *Journal of Peace Research*, 38(2):181–198.

——— (2006). *Minimum Deterrence and India's Nuclear Security* (Stanford: Stanford University Press).

Bayle, C.A. (1985). "The pre-history of 'communalism'? Religious conflict in India, 1700–1860." *Modern Asian Studies*, 19(2):177–203.

BBC (2006). "Bush and Singh in nuclear talks." July 17. Retrieved from http://news.bbc.co.uk/2/hi/south_asia/7496904.stm (last accessed on November 10, 2014).

——— (2007). "Former Indian Prime Minister V.P. Singh." BBC Hard Talk. August 14. Retrieved from http://www.bbc.co.uk/programmes/b007x1mk (last accessed on November 10, 2014).

Behuria, Ashok (2011). "Pakistan-India Relations: An Indian Narrative." Pakistan Institute of Legislative Development and Transparency. January, 1–14.

Beri, Ruchita (1998). "Pakistan's nuclear program." In Jasjit Singh (ed.). *Nuclear India* (New Delhi: Knowledge World), 188–208.

Bhabha, Homi J. (1966). "Science and problems of development." *Science*, February 4:545–547.

Bhaskar, Uday C. (2002). Ex-Deputy Director. Institute of Defense and Strategic Analysis (Personal Interview).

——— (2005a). "India-US ties poised for radical re-orientation." 29(1), January. Retrieved from http://www.idsa.in/strategicanalysis/IndiaUSTiesPoisedforRadicalReorientation_cubhaskar_0105/ (last accessed on November 10, 2014).

——— (2005b). "Good day for India?" July 25. Retrieved from http://www.idsa. in/idsastrategiccomments/GoodDayforIndia_CUBhaskar_250705/ (last accessed on November 10, 2014).

——— (2005c). "F-16s: Can we trust Uncle Sam?" April 5. Retrieved from http://www.idsa.in/idsastrategiccomments/F16sCanwetrustUncleSam_ CUBhaskar_050405/ (last accessed on November 10, 2014).

Bhatia, Shyam (1979). *India's Nuclear Bomb* (New Delhi: Vikas).

Bharatiya Janata Party (BJP) (1996a). *For a Strong and Prosperous India: Election Manifesto, 1996* (New Delhi: Bharatiya Janata Party Central Office).

——— (1996b). "BJP urges government to test, deploy nuclear arms." *Morning Sun* (Dhaka). August 9:2.

——— (1998a). "Testing Ghauri: A signal from Pakistan that it does not want friendship with India." *Swastika*, May 11:5, 9.

Bharatiya Janata Party (BJP) (1998b). "Pokhran II and India's security." *Swastika*, June 29:8, 9.

———— (1998c). "Pakistan-China nuclear transactions." *Swastika*, July 13:9.

———— (1998d). "A dangerous situation for India." *Swastika*, December 7:1.

———— (1999a). "Pakistan's nuclear programs represent an evil design against India." *Swastika*, June 7:1.

———— (1999b). "Pakistan acquires technology to strengthen its nuclear arsenal." *Swastika*, July 9:5, 13.

———— (1999c). "Weak nations don't make history." *BJP Today*, 8(8):4–7.

———— (1999d). "US nuclear hegemony over India." *Swastika*, September 6:3–5.

———— (2000a). "Nuclear bombing over Pakistan is the best and the most worthy response that India can provide." *Swastika*, August, 28:4.

———— (2000b). *President's Addresses: L.K. Advani, 1986–1990, 1993–1998* (New Delhi: Bharatiya Janata Party Office).

———— (2002a). "Pakistan guns silence India's missiles of democracy." *BJP Today*, 11(20):23–24.

———— (2002b). "Pakistan-China's nuclear transactions cause concern to India." *Swastika*, December 4:6.

———— (2003). "Menace of cross-border terrorism: India's view point." *BJP Today*, 12(6):17–20.

———— (2006). "Press statement of the BJP on the India-US nuclear deal." December 10. Retrieved from http://www.bjp.org/ (archive search) (last accessed on November 10, 2014).

———— (n.d.). Bharatiya Janata Party Pamphlet No. 44 (New Delhi: Bharatiya Janata Party Central Office), 1–2.

Bhutto, Benazir (1998). "Punishment: Make it swift, severe…." *Los Angeles Times*, May 18. Retrieved from http://articles.latimes.com/1998/may/17/opinion/op-50669/ (last accessed on November 10, 2014).

Bidwai, Achin and Praful Vanaik (2000). *New Nukes: India, Pakistan, and Global Nuclear Disarmament* (New York: Olive Branch Press).

Bidwai, Praful (2003). "Musharraf's speech raises the nuclear danger." 2 January. Retrieved from http://original.antiwar.com/bidwai/2003/01/02/musharrafs-speech-raises-the-nuclear-danger/ (last accessed on November 10, 2014).

Bishoyi, Saroj (2011). "India-US high technology cooperation: Moving forward." February 16. Retrieved from http://www.idsa.in/idsacomments/IndiaUSHighTechnologyCooperationMovingForward_sbishoyi_160211/ (last accessed on November 10, 2014).

Biswas, Shampa (2002). "'Nuclear apartheid as political position: Race as a post-colonial resource?" *Alternatives: Global, Local, Political*, 26(4):485–522.

Bitzinger, Richard A. (2005). "Asia-Pacific Missile Defense Cooperation and the United States 2004–2005: A mixed bag." Asia-Pacific Center for Security Studies. February:1–7.

Blackett, P.M.S. (1948). *Fear, War, and the Bomb* (New York and Toronto: Whittlesey House).

Blackwill, Robert D. (2009). "The future of US-India relations." South Asian Strategic and Defense Studies. May 5. Retrieved from http://www.rand.org/commentary/2009/05/06/FT.html/ (last accessed on November 10, 2014).

Blake, Robert O. (2004). "India-US relations: The making of a comprehensive relationship." Embassy of India. August 23. Retrieved from http://2001-2009.state.gov/p/sca/rls/rm/35686.htm/ (last accessed on November 10, 2014).

Bobb, Dilip (1986). "The new offensive." India Today. February 15:96.

Bobb, Dilip and Amarnath K. Menon (1989). "Chariot of fire." India Today. June 15:32.

Bobb, Dilip and Raminder Singh (1987). "Pakistan's nuclear bombshell." India Today, March 31:73–76.

Bodansky, Yossef (2001). Bin Laden: Man Who Declared War in America (Rocklin, California: Forum).

Booth, K. (1979). Strategy and Ethnocentrism (New York: Holmes and Meier).

——— (1990a). "U.S. perceptions of Soviet threat: Prudence and paranoia." In Carl G. Jacobsen (ed.). Strategic Power: USA/USSR (New York: St. Martin's Press), 50–70.

——— (1990b). "The concept of strategic culture affirmed." In Carl G. Jacobsen (ed.). Strategic Power: USA/USSR (New York: St. Martin's Press), 121–30.

Borman, Matthew S. (2004). "NSSP: US-India, Interests in Action." The Hindu, October 4. Retrieved from http://www.thehindu.com/2004/10/02/stories/2004100205511100.htm (last accessed on November 10, 2014).

Bose, S. and A. Jalal (eds). (1998). Modern South Asia: History, Culture, Political Economy (London and New York: Routledge).

Brecher, M. (1968a). Nehru's Mantle: The Politics of Succession in India (New York: Praeger).

——— (1968b). India and World Politics: Krishna Menon's View of the World (New York: Praeger).

Brodie, Bernard (1973). Wars and Politics (New York: Macmillan Company).

Budania, Rajpal (2003). "The emerging international security system: Threats, challenges, and opportunities for India." Strategic Analysis, 27(1). Retrieved from http://idsa.in/system/files/strategicanalysis_budania_0303.pdf/ (last accessed on November 10, 2014).

Bunn, George (1999). "The status of norms against nuclear testing." The Non-Proliferation Review (Winter). Retrieved from http://cns.miis.edu/npr/pdfs/bunn62.pdf/ (last accessed on November 10, 2014).

Burns, John F. (1994). "Unlikely reformer coaxes India toward a market economy." The New York Times. May 8. Retrieved from http://www.nytimes.com/1994/05/08/business/unlikely-reformer-coaxes-india-toward-a-market-economy.html?pagewanted=all&src=pm/ (last accessed on November 10, 2014).

——— (1998a). "Nuclear anxiety." The New York Times. May 14. Retrieved from http://www.nytimes.com/1998/05/14/world/nuclear-anxiety-overview-india-carries-2-more-atom-tests-despite-sanctions.html?pagewanted=all&src=pm/ (last assessed November 30, 2013).

Burns, John F. (1998b). "In nuclear India, small stash does not a ready arsenal make." *The New York Times*. July 26. Retrieved from http://www.nytimes. com/1998/07/26/world/in-nuclear-india-small-stash-does-not-a-ready-arsenal-make.html?pagewanted=all&src=pm/ (last assessed November 30, 2013).

Bush, George (2001a). "Remarks at Emma Booker Elementary School." September 11. Retrieved from http://www.americanrhetoric.com/speeches/gwbush-911florida.htm (last assessed November 10, 2014).

————— (2001b). "Remarks at Barksdale Air Force Base." September 11. Retrieved from http://www.americanrhetoric.com/speeches/gwbush911florida.htm (last assessed November 10, 2014).

————— (2001c). "As great people has ben moved to defend a great nation." September 11. Retrieved from http://www.americanrhetoric.com/speeches/ gwbush911florida.htm (last assessed November 10, 2014).

————— (2002). "Text of President Bush's state of the union address." January 29. Retrieved from http://www.americanrhetoric.com/speeches/gwbush-911florida.htm (last assessed November 10, 2014).

Carr, E.H. (1939). *The Twenty Years Crisis: 1919–1939* (New York: Harper).

Chacko, Priya (2012). *Indian Foreign Policy: The Politics of postcolonial identity from 1947 to 2004* (London and New York: Routledge).

Chakrvarthy, B.N. (1965). "Statement by the Indian representative Chakrvarthy." May 4, Documents on Disarmament, 142–151. Retrieved from http://www. un.org/disarmament/publications/documents_on_disarmament/1965/ DoD_1965.pdf/ (last assessed November 10, 2014).

Chandran, Ramesh (1996). "US says India has 'nothing to fear." *The Times of India*. September 13.

Chari, P.R. (1995). *Indo-Pak Nuclear Stand-Off: The Role of the United States* (New Delhi: Manohar).

————— (2006). "Implementing the Indo-US nuclear deal: A pyrrhic struggle." January 5. Retrieved from http://www.idsa.in/idsastrategiccomments/ ImplementingtheIndoUSNuclearDeal_PRChari050106/ (last assessed November 10, 2014).

Chatterjee, P. (1993). *The Nation and Its Fragments: Colonial and Post-Colonial History* (New Jersey: Princeton University Press).

Chatterjee, Santimay and Enakshi Chatterjee (1984). *Meghnad Saha: Scientist with a Vision* (New Delhi: National Book Trust).

Chaudhari, J.N. (1966). *Arms, Aims, and Aspects* (Bombay: Manaktala and Sons Private Limited).

Cheema, Zafar Iqbal (2010). *Indian Nuclear Deterrent: Its Evolution, Development, and Implications for South Asian Security* (New York: Oxford University Press).

Chellaney, Brahma (1993). *Nuclear Proliferation: The United States-Indian Conflict* (New Delhi: Orient Longman).

————— (1996a). "India may balk at ban on nuclear tests: Opposition bipartisan on election eve." *Washington Times*, April 26.

Chellaney, Brahma (1996b). "India must no longer ignore its nuclear imperatives." *Pioneer*. January 17:8.

———— (1997). "Domineering US: Deferential India." *Pioneer*, September 24:10.

Chengappa, Raj (1994a). "Interview with R. Chidambaram." *India Today*, April 30.

———— (1994b). "Interview with A.P.J Abdul Kalam." *India Today*, April 15, [ch 6].

———— (1994c). "Nuclear Dilemma." *India Today*, April 30:53.

———— (1994d). "The Missile Man." *India Today*, April 15:66.

———— (2000). *Weapons of Peace: The Secret Story of India's Quest to be a Nuclear Power* (New Delhi: Harper Collins).

Cheodon, Yeshi (2010). "UN and nuclear disarmament." Paper presented at International Studies Association Conference, New Orleans, February 17.

Cherian, John (1995). "Paying for,complacency." *Frontline*, October 20.

———— (1998). "The BJP and the bomb." *Frontline*, 15(8), April 11–24. Retrieved from http://www.frontline.in/static/html/fl1508/15080040.htm/ (last assessed November 10, 2014).

———— (2004). "Building confidence: India and Pakistan." *Frontline*, 21(14), July 3–16. Retrieved from http://www.frontline.in/static/html/fl2114/stories/20040716001804400.htm/ (last assessed November 10, 2014).

Cherian, Samuel (2007). "Indo-US business relations: Setting new records." *IDSA Comments*. March 8. Retrieved from http://www.idsa.in/idsastrategiccomments/IndoUSBusinessRelations_CSamuel_080307/ (last assessed November 10, 2014).

———— (2010). "Reconciling rhetoric and substance in India-US relations." *IDSA Comments*, December 9. Retrieved from http://www.idsa.in/idsacomments/ReconcilingRhetoricandSubstanceinIndiaUSRelations_csamuel_091210/ (last assessed November 10, 2014).

Chidambaram, P. (2007). "Finance Minister P. Chidambaram: 'India will be an economic power, and nothing will stop us'." October 3. Retrieved from http://knowledge.wharton.upenn.edu/article/finance-minister-p-chidambaram-india-will-be-an-economic-power-and-nothing-will-stop-us/ (last assessed November 10, 2014).

———— (2013). "Chidambaram says financial sectors reforms will take time." *The Hindustan Times.* May 23. Retrieved from http://www.livemint.com/Politics/V8Bv6gkmFA7PhnbAcdDKUI/Chidambaram-says-financial-sectors-reforms-will-take-time.html/ (last assessed November 10, 2014).

Chittaranjan, Kalpana (1998). "Five decades of nuclear weapons." In Jasjit Singh (ed.). *Nuclear India* (New Delhi: Knowledge World), 54–74.

Chopra, Pran (1993). *The Crisis of Foreign Policy* (Allahabad: Wheeler).

Chowdhry, Geeta (2000). "Communalism, Nationalism, and Gender: Bharatiya Janata Party (BJP) and the Hindu Right in India." In Sita Ranchod-Nelson and Mary Ann Tetreault (eds). *Feminist Approaches to Contemporary Debates* (London: Routledge).

Chowdhry, Geeta and Sheila Nair (2002). *Power, Postcolonialism, and International Relations: Reading Race, Gender, and Class* (London, New York: Routledge).

Ciarrocca, Michelle (2002). "The nuclear posture review: Reading between the lines." *Common Dreams*, January, 17. Retrieved from http://www.commondreams.org/views02/0117-10.htm/ (last assessed November 10, 2014).

Clausen, Peter A. (1993). *Nonproliferation and the National Interest* (New York: Harper Collins).

Clinton, Bill (1994). "The President's news conference with prime minister P.V. Narasimha Rao of India." May 19. Retrieved from http://www.presidency. ucsb.edu/ws/?pid=50204/ (last assessed November 10, 2014).

CNN (2009). "Obama says he'll visit India next year." November 24. Retrieved from http://www.edition.conn.com/2009/POLITICS/11/24/us.india. leader/index/html (assessed December 2, 2013).

———— (2011). "Interview with Pervez Musharraf." Piers Morgan Tonight. CNN. May 26. Retrieved from http://transcripts.cnn.com/TRANSCRIPTS/1105/26/ pmt.01.html/ (last assessed November 10, 2014).

Cohen, Stephen (2001). "Moving forward in South Asia." Brookings Policy Brief, No. 81. May. Retrieved from http://www.brookings.edu/~/media/ research/files/papers/2001/5/southasia%20cohen/pb81.pdf/ (last assessed November 10, 2014).

Coll, Steve (1992). "India pressured on the bomb." *Washington Post*, February 15:A23.

Collina, Tom Z. and Daniel Horner (2011). "The South Asian nuclear balance: An interview with Pakistani Ambassador to the CD Zamir Akram." *Arms Control Today*. December. Retrieved from http://www.armscontrol. org/act/2011_12/Interview_With_Pakistani_Ambassador_to_the_CD_ Zamir_Akram/ (last assessed November 10, 2014).

Cooper, Kenneth J. (1998). "Nuclear dilemmas." *Washington Post*. May 25:A22.

Correspondent Sheet (1998). "Vajpayee Nuclear." *Voice of America*. May 20. Retrieved from http://www.fas.org/news/india/1998/05/980520-india. htm/ (last accessed on November 18, 2013).

Council on Foreign Relations (2009a). "Obama's strategy for Afghanistan and Pakistan." Retrieved from http://www.cfr.org/publication/18952/ (last assessed November 10, 2014).

———— (2009b). "A conversation with Prime Minister Dr. Man Mohan Singh." November 23. Retrieved from http://www.cfr.org/india/conversation-prime-minister-dr-manmohan-singh/p20840/ (last assessed November 10, 2014).

Cox, R. (1981). "Social forces, states, and world orders: Beyond international relations theory." *Millennium Journal of International Studies*, 10(2):126–155.

Dandavate, M.R. (1968). "Chinese nuclear challenge to Indian democracy." In A.B. Shah (ed.). *Indian Defense and Foreign Policies* (Bombay: Manaktalas).

Das, Runa (2002). "Post-colonial (in)securities, the BJP, and the politics of *Hindutva*: Broadening security paradigm between the realist and the anti-nuclear/peace groups in India." *Third World Quarterly*, 24(1):77–96.

Das, Runa (2005). "Revisiting (in)-security as the cultural production of danger: Nationalism, xenophobia and the role of religious ideology in the Indian political space." *Journal of Muslim Minority Affairs*, 25 (1):31–51.

——— (2008). "Ideology, identity, and (in)security: Competing world views of India's nuclearisation policies." *Journal of Commonwealth and Comparative Politics*, 46(1):2–28.

Datta, P.K. (1993). "Dying Hindus' production of Hindu communal common sense in early 20th century Bengal." *Economic and Political Weekly*, June 19:1305–1319.

Deccan Herald (1997). "India's nuclear options are open: Says PM." *Deccan Herald*. July 14.

——— (2004). "India-US military ties to get stronger: Rumsfeld." *Deccan Herald*. December 10. Retrieved from http://archive.deccanherald.com/Deccanherald/dec102004/i1.asp/ (last assessed November 10, 2014).

Deendayal Research Institute (1989). *How Others Look at the RSS* (New Delhi: Deendayal Research Institute).

Defense Industry Daily (2013). "India buys C-130J-30 Hercules for special forces." January 21. Retrieved from http://www.defenseindustrydaily.com/india-to-purchase-6-c130j-hercules-for-special-forces-02224/ (last assessed November 10, 2014).

Department of Defense (2010). Nuclear Posture Review Report, April 2010. Retrieved from http://www.defense.gov/npr/docs/2010%20nuclear%20posture%20review%20report.pdf (last assessed November 10, 2014).

Department of State (2002). "Transcript: Ambassador outlines the growing strength of US-India ties." November 11. Retrieved from http://www.usinfo.org/wf-archive/2002/021129/ (last assessed November 10, 2014).

Der Derian, J. and M. Shapiro (1989). *International/Intertextual Relations* (Lexington: Lexington Books).

Desai, Morarji (1986). *Selected Speeches of Morarji Desai, 1977–1979* (New Delhi: Publications Division, Ministry of Information and Broadcasting, Government of India).

Deshmukh, B.G. (1994): "The inside story." *India Today*. February 28:62.

Devare, Aparna. (2009). "Secularizing religion: Hindu extremism as a modernist discourse." *International Political Sociology*, 3(2):156–175.

Dhanda, Suresh (2010). *Nuclear Politics in South Asia* (New Delhi: Regal Publications).

Dixit, J.N. (1996). *My South Bloc Years: Memoirs of a Foreign Secretary* (New Delhi: UBS).

——— (2004). *Makers of India's Foreign Policy: Raja Ram Mohan Roy to Yashwant Sinha* (New Delhi: Harper Collins).

Dodd, Vikram (2008). "Mumbai attacks: India demands Pakistan hand over terror suspects." December 2. Retrieved from http://www.theguardian.com/world/2008/dec/02/mumbai-attack-india-pakistan/ (last assessed November 10, 2014).

Dougherty, J.E. and R.L. Pfaltzgraff (1997). *Contending Theories of International Relations: A Comprehensive Survey* (New York: Longman).

Drew, J. (1987). *India and the Romantic Imagination* (New Delhi, New York: Oxford University Press).

Dubey, Muchkund (1993). "India's foreign policy in an evolving global order." *International Studies*, 30(2):117–129.

—— (2000). "Congress and India's N-Policy-II." *The Hindu*, June 20.

Dutt, R.C. (1987). "The roots of Indian foreign policy." In P.N. Haskar (ed.). *Nehru's Vision of Peace and Security in Nuclear Age* (New Delhi: Patriot Publishers), 60–67.

Dutt, Som (1966). *India and the Bomb* (London: International Institute of Strategic Studies).

D'Souza, Shanthie Mariet (2009). "India-US relations: The need to move beyond symbolism." December 3. Retrieved from http://www.idsa.in/idsacomments/India-USRelations_smdsouza_031209/ (last assessed November 10, 2014).

Ebinger, Charles K. (1978). *International Politics of Nuclear Energy* (California: SAGE Publications).

Embassy of India (1998). "Joint press statement by DAE and DRDO." May 17. Retrieved from http://www.indianembassy.org/archives_details.php?nid=222/ (last assessed November 10, 2014).

—— (2008a). "Remarks by external foreign minister of India." March 24. Retrieved from https://www.indianembassy.org/ (archive search) (last assessed November 10, 2014).

—— (2008b). "Joint press briefing by Foreign Secretary Mr. Shyam Saran and US Under Secretary for Commerce Mr. David McCormick at the conclusion of 4th Round of Indo-US High Technology Cooperation Group." December 1. Retrieved from https://www.indianembassy.org/archives_details.php?nid=485/ (last assessed November 10, 2014).

Embree, Ainslie T. (1962). *Charles Grant and British Rule in India* (New York: Columbia University Press).

—— (ed.) (1971). *Alberuni's India* (New York: Norton).

—— (1994). "The functions of the Rashtriya Swayam Sevak Sangh to define the Hindu nation." In Martin E. Marty and Scott R. Appleby (eds). *Accounting for Fundamentalism* (Chicago: University of Chicago Press), 617–652.

Enloe, C. (1990). *Bananas, Bases, and Beaches: Making Feminist Sense of International Politics* (Berkeley: University of California Press).

Fairclough N. and Wodak, R. (1997). "Critical discourse analysis." In Tuen van Dijk (ed.). *Discourse as Social Interaction Stage* (London: SAGE Publications), 258–284.

Federation of American Scientists (1999). "Foreign Secretary's press briefing on India's nuclear doctrine, 19 August." http://www.fas.org/news/pakistan/1999/990819-pak-pr2.htm (last assessed November 10, 2014).

Feldman, Shai (1995). "Is there a proliferation debate?" *Security Studies*, 4:787–792.

Foreign Report (1984). "Shadow of an Indian H-bomb." *Foreign Report* (London). December 13:1–2.

Frey, K. (2006). *India's Nuclear Bomb and National Security* (London/New York: Routledge).

Friedman, Benjamin (2002). "India and Pakistan: War in the nuclear shadow?" *Center for Defense Information*, Washington, DC. June 18. Retrieved from https://www.cdi.org/nuclear/nuclearshadow.cfm&gt (last assessed November 10, 2014).

Gandhi, Indira (1982). *Statements on Foreign Policy, January–March, 1982* (New Delhi: External Publicity Division, Ministry of External Affairs).

————— (1983). "Mrs Gandhi reiterates India's policy of using nuclear power for peaceful purposes only." *India News*. August 1:1.

Gandhi, Mohandas (1997). *Hind Swaraj and Other Writings* (edited by Anthony J. Parel) (Cambridge: Cambridge University Press).

Gandhi, Rajiv (1987). *Rajv Gandhi: Selected Speeches and Writings, Volume I, October 31, 1984–December 31, 1984* (New Delhi: Ministry of Information and Broadcasting).

Ganguly, Sumit (1989). "The Sino-Indian border talks, 1981–1989: The view from New Delhi." *Asian Survey*, 29(12):1123–1135.

Ganguly, Sumit and P. Kapur (2007). *Nuclear Proliferation in South Asia: Crisis Behavior and the Bomb* (London: Routledge).

Ganguly, Sumit, Brian Shoup, and Andrew Scobell (2006). *US–Indian Strategic Cooperation: Into the 21st Century* (London and New York: Routledge).

Garthoff, Raymond L. (1984). *Intelligence Assessment and Policymaking: A Decision Point in the Kennedy Administration: A Staff Paper* (Washington, DC: Brookings).

Ghose, A. (1958). "New lamps for old, December 4th, 1893." In Haridas Mukherjee and Uma Mukherjee (eds). *Sri Aurobindo's Political Thought: 1893–1908* (Calcutta: Firma K.L. Mukhopadhyay), 103–110.

Ghose, Arundhati (2006). "Prospects for Indo-US cooperation in civilian nuclear energy." January 6. Retrieved from http://www.idsa.in/idsastrategiccomments/ProspectsforIndoUScooperationinciviliannuclearenergy_AGhose_060106/ (last assessed November 10, 2014).

Ghoshal, U.N. (1965). *Studies in Indian History and Culture* (New Delhi: Orient Longman).

Giacomo, Carol (1998). "Cohen: Indian tests could lead to Arms Race." *Reuters*. May 13.

Giacomo, Carol and Susan Cornwell (2007). "Biden Cool to U.S. compromise on India deal." *Reuters*. May 2. Retrieved from http://www.reuters.com/article/2007/05/03/us-india-usa-nuclear-idUSN0242817820070503/ (last assessed November 10, 2014).

Gilpatric, Roswell (1965). Committee on Nuclear Proliferation. January 7–8. Foreign Relations of the United States, 1964–1968, Volume XI (Arms Control and Disarmament). Retrieved from http://fas.org/spp/starwars/offdocs/lbj/persons.htm (last assessed November 10, 2014).

Gilpin, R. (1987). *The Political Economy of International Relations* (Princeton: Princeton University Press).

Global Security (2002). "National Strategy to Combat Weapons of Mass Destruction." December. Retrieved from http://www.globalsecurity.org/wmd/library/policy/national/wmdstrategy2002.pdf (last accessed on January 20, 2015).

———— (2006). "Annual Report to Congress: Military Power of the People's Republic of China." Retrieved from http://www.globalsecurity.org/military/library/report/2006/2006-prc-military-power.htm/ (last assessed November 10, 2014).

Goldstein, Avery (2005). *Rising to the Challenge: China's Grand Strategy and International Security* (Palo Alto: Stanford University Press).

Golwalkar, M.S. (1947). *We Or Our Nationhood Defined* (Nagpur: M.N. Kale).

———— (1980). *Bunch of Thoughts* (Bangalore: Jagarana Prakashana).

Goodenough, Patrick (2008). "US aims to help India become 'major world power.'" July 7. Retrieved from http://cnsnews.com/news/article/us-aims-help-india-become-major-world-power/ (last assessed November 10, 2014).

Gopal, Sarvepalli (1975–1884). *Jawaharlal Nehru: A Biography (Volume II)*. (New York: Oxford University Press).

Gopal, Sarvepalli and S. Bhattacharya (1986). *Situating History for Sarvepalli Gopal* (New Delhi: Oxford University Press).

Gopalakrishnan, A. (2005). "Some concerns on Indo-US Deal." *Political and Economic Weekly*, 40(35):3802–3805 (available on E-Journals).

———— (2006). "Civilian and nuclear facilities in India." January 5. Retrieved from http://www.idsa.in/idsastrategiccomments/CivilianandStrategicNuclearFacilitiesofIndia_AGopalakrishnan_050106/ (last assessed November 10, 2014).

———— (2007). "Amend US law, or reject nuclear deal." May 14. Retrieved from http://www.rediff.com/news/2007/may/14guest.htm/ (last assessed November 10, 2014).

Goradia, Prafull (1991). "Wanted a new foreign policy for India—Nonalignment obsolete." *Organiser.* January 13.

Gordon, S. (1995). *India's Rise to Power in the Twentieth Century and Beyond* (New York: St. Martin's Press).

Goshko, John M (1994). "Clinton moves to ease relationship with India." *Washington Post.* May 24:A30.

Government of India (1970). *Atomic Energy and Space Research: A Profile for the Decade 1970–1980* (Bombay: Government of India, Atomic Energy Commission).

Graham, Bob (2003). "9/11 two years later: Are we any safer." Retrieved from http://www.cfr.org/publications/6250/911 (last assessed on November 12, 2013).

Gray, Colin (1979). *The Soviet American Arms Race* (Lexington, MA: Farnborough).

———— (1981). "National style in strategy: The American example." *International Security*, 6(2):21–47.

Guha, R. (1988). "On some aspects of the historiography of colonial India." In Ranajit Guha and Gayatri Chakravorty Spivak (eds). *Selected Subaltern Studies* (New York: Oxford University Press), 27–44.

Guillem Monsonis (2009). "India's strategic autonomy dilemma and the rapprochement with the United States." March 20. Retrieved from http://www.idsa.in/event/IndiavsUS_gmonsonis_200309/ (last assessed on November 12, 2013).

Gupta, Amit (2005). *The US-India Relationship: Strategic Partnership or Complimentary Interests* (Carlisle, Pennsylvania: Strategic Studies Institute, US Army War College).

Gupta, Arvind (2013). "America's Asia strategy in Obama's second term." March 21. Retrieved from http://www.idsa.in/idsastrategiccomments/AmericasAsiaStrategyinObamasSecondTerm_agupta_210313/ (last assessed on November 12, 2013).

Gupta, Shekhar (1993). "Bills busy right now." *India Today*, July 31:38.

───── (1994). "Nawaz Shariff's bombshell." *India Today*, November 15:26.

───── (2001). "The real battle will be for the market." *Indian Express*. January 13. Retrieved from http://expressindia.indianexpress.com/ie/daily/20010115/shekhar.htm/ (last assessed on November 12, 2013).

Gupta, Shekhar and W.P.S. Sidhu (1992). "Cautious manoeuvers." *India Today*, June 30:34.

Gupta, Sisir (1966). "Indian dilemma." In Alastair Buchan (ed.). *A World of Nuclear Powers* (Upper Saddle River, New Jersey: PrenticeHall).

Guruswamy, Mohan (1996). "Age of stand-off weapons: Evil Empire called USA." *Indian Express*. December 18.

Hagerty, Devin T. (1995/1996). "Nuclear deterrence in South Asia: The 1990 Indo-Pakistani crisis." *International Security*, 20(3):79–114.

───── (2006) "Are we present at the creation? Alliance theory and the Indo-US strategic converegence." In Sumit Ganguly, Brian Shoup, and Andrew Scobell (eds). *US-Indian Strategic Cooperation: Into the 21st Century* (London and New York: Routledge), 11–37.

Haksar, P.N. (1989). *Nehru's Vision of Peace and Security in Nuclear Age* (New Delhi: Patriot Publishers).

Hammond, Grant, T. (1993). *Ploughshares into Swords: Arms Races in International Politics, 1840–1991* (Columbia, NC: University of North Carolina Press).

Han, Hua (1998). "Sino-Indian relations and nuclear arms control." In Eric Arnett (ed.). *Nuclear Weapons and Arms Control in South Asia after the Test Ban: SIPRI Research Report No. 14* (New York: Oxford University Press), 35–51.

Haniffa, Aziz (1993). "US ends push for 5-nation parley." *India Abroad*. September 24.

Haqqani, Husain (2002). "America's new alliance with Pakistan: Avoiding the traps of the past." *Carnegie Policy Brief*. October 19. Retrieved from http://carnegieendowment.org/2002/10/02/america-s-new-alliance-with-pakistan-avoiding-traps-of-past/440y/ (last accessed on November 10, 2014).

Hartung, William D. (2000). "Bush's nuclear doctrine: From MAD to nuts." *Foreign Policy in Focus.* December 1. Retrieved from http://fpif.org/bushs_nuclear_doctrine_from_mad_to_nuts/ (last accessed on November 10, 2014).

Harvard Nuclear Study Group (1983). *Living With Nuclear Weapons* (Cambridge, Massachusetts: Harvard University Press), 87, 90, 120.

Hersch, Seymour M. (1993)."On the nuclear edge." *The New Yorker.* March 29.

——— (2009). "Defending the arsenal: In an unstable Pakistan, can nuclear warheads be kept safe?" *The New Yorker.* September 16. Retrieved from http://www.newyorker.com/reporting/2009/11/16/091116fa_fact_hersh?currentPage=all/ (last accessed on November 10, 2014).

Hoffman, Steven (1990). *India and the China Crisis* (California: University of California Press).

Hoodbhoy, Pervez (2002). "Lighting the fire." *Dawn.* May 28. Retrieved from http://www.dawn.com/news/1063166/dawn-opinion-may-28-2002/ (last accessed on November 10, 2014).

Hsieh, Alice Langley (1963). "Communist China and nuclear force." Rand Corporation. Retrieved from http://www.rand.org/content/dam/rand/pubs/papers/2008/P2719-1.pdf/ (last accessed on November 10, 2014).

Hunter, W.W. (1882). *The Indian Empire: Its History, People, and Products* (London: Tubner).

IBN (2013). "India successfully test fires nuclear-capable Agni V long range missile." September 15. Retrieved from http://ibnlive.in.com/news/india-successfully-test-fires-nuclearcapable-agni-v-long-range-missile/422070-3.html/ (last accessed on November 10, 2014).

Inden, R. (1990). *Imagining India* (Cambridge, Massachusetts: Basil Blackwell).

Inderfurth, Karl (2008). "US-India relations." Retrieved from http://www.asiafoundation.com/resources/pdfs/19IndiaARA2008/ (last accessed on November 10, 2014).

India Today (1994). "Make the Most of it." *India Today*, May 31:3.

Indian Express (2001). "Business, not politics." *Indian Express.* January 11. Retrieved from http://expressindia.indianexpress.com/ie/daily/20010111/ied11033.html/ (last accessed on November 10, 2014).

Indian National Congress (2004). *Manifesto of the Indian National Congress* (New Delhi: All India Congress Party Press).

——— (2009). *Manifesto of the Indian National Congress* (New Delhi: All India Congress Party Press).

Indian Navy (2013). "Indo-US Naval exercise 'MALABAR 2013' commences." November. Retrieved from http://indiannavy.nic.in/press-release/indo-us-naval-exercise-malabar-2013-commences/ (last accessed on November 10, 2014).

International Atomic Energy Agency (2008). "Communication dated 25 July 2008 received from the Permanent Mission of India concerning a document entitled 'Implementation of the India-United States Joint Statement of July 18, 2005: India's Separation Plans.'" Retrieved from http://

www.iaea.org/Publications/Documents/Infcircs/Countries/india.shtml/ (last accessed on November 10, 2014).

International Press Center (2011). "Foreign Ministry holds a briefing for Chinese and Foreign media on President Hu Jintao's state visit to the US." *International Press Center*, January 12. Retrieved from http://www.nyconsulate. prchina.org/eng/zt/y110115/t786139.htm/ (last accessed on November 10, 2014).

Institute of Peace and Conflict Studies (2012). *India's Nuclear Doctrine: An Alternative Blueprint* (New Delhi: Institute of Peace and Conflict Studies), 1–9.

Iqbal, A. (ed.) (1987). *Writings and Speeches of Maulana Mohamed Ali* (Lahore: Islamic Book Foundation).

Irwin, H.C. (1880). *The Garden of India, or, Chapters in Oudh History and Affairs* (London: W.H. Allen).

Islamic Republic News Agency (2013). "Chinese Premier gets warm welcome as he begins Pakistan's official visit." May 22. Retrieved from http://www3. boushehr.irna.ir/en/News/80668056/Art_&_Culture/Chinese_Premier_ gets_warm_welcome_as_he_begins_Pakistan%CB%88s_official_visit/ (last accessed on November 10, 2014).

Iyengar, P.K. (2007). "U.S. needs to make changes in deal: scientists." June 18. Retrieved from http://www.thehindu.com/todays-paper/us-needs-to-make-changes-in-deal-scientists/article1857920.ece/ (last accessed on November 10, 2014).

Iyengar, P.K. and M.R. Balakrishnan (1991). *Collected Scientific Papers of Dr. P.K. Iyengar* (Bombay: Bhabha Atomic Research Center).

Jain, J.P. (1974). *Nuclear India* (Volumes I and II) (New Delhi: Radiant).

Jaipal, Rikhi (1983). *Non-Alignment* (New Delhi: Allied Press).

Jayasekara, Deepal (2013). "Tense standoff between India and Pakistan along their disputed Kashmir border continues." World Wide Socialist Web. August 31. Retrieved from http://www.wsws.org/en/articles/2013/08/31/ inpk-a31.html/ (last accessed on November 10, 2014).

Jaywant, Dipa (1980). "Bleak prospects." *India Today*. February 1–15:65.

Jinnah, M.A. (1960). *Jinnah-Nehru Correspondence* (Lahore: Lahore Book House).

Joeck, Neil (1986). *Nuclear Proliferation and National Security in India and Pakistan* (Ph.D thesis) (Los Angeles: University of California).

Johnson, Jo (2007). "Cloud over US-India nuclear accord." June 3. Retrieved from http://www.ft.com/intl/cms/s/0/99cb1422-11ed-11dc-b963-000b5df10621.html/ (last accessed on November 10, 2014).

Johnson, J.L., Kerry M. Kartchner, and Jeffrey Larson (2009). *Strategic Culture and Weapons of Mass Destruction: Culturally Based Insights into Comparative National Security Policy Making* (New York: Palgrave McMillan).

Johnston, A. (1995). "Thinking about strategic culture." *International Security*, 19(4):32–64.

——— (1998). *Cultural Realism: Strategic Culture and Grand Strategy in Chinese History* (Princeton: Princeton University Press).

Joint Press Briefing (2005). "Joint press briefing by Foreign Secretary Mr. Shyam Saran and US Under Secretary for Commerce Mr. David McCormick at the conclusion of 4th round of Indo-US High Technology Cooperation Group." November 30. Retrieved from https://www.indianembassy.org/archives_details.php?nid=485/ (last accessed on November 10, 2014).

Joint Statement (2005). "Joint Statement, India-Pakistan." April 18. Ministry of External Affairs, Government of India. Retrieved from http://www.satp.org/satporgtp/countries/india/document/papers/indo_pakApril05.htm/ (last accessed on January 10, 2013).

———— (2013). Joint statement between the People's Republic of China and Republic of India." *Outlook India*. May 20. Retrieved from http://www.outlookindia.com/article.aspx?285536/ (last accessed on November 10, 2014).

Jones, D. (1990). "Soviet strategic culture." In Carl G. Jacobsen (ed.). *Strategic Power: USA/USSR* (New York: St. Martin's Press), 35–47.

Jones, Keith (2004). "India and Pakistan to pursue composite dialogue." January 29. *World Socialist Web Site*. Retrieved from https://www.wsws.org/en/articles/2004/01/ind-j29.html/ (last accessed on November 10, 2014).

Jones, Rodney (1985), "India." In J. Goldblat (ed.). *Non-Proliferation: The Why and the Wherefore* (London: Taylor and Francis).

———— (2009). "India's strategic culture and the origins of omniscient paternalism." In J. L. Johnson, Kerry M. Kartchner, and Jeffrey Larson (eds). *Strategic Culture and Weapons of Mass Destruction: Culturally Based Insights into Comparative National Security Policy Making* (New York: Palgrave McMillan), 117–138.

Jordan, Miriam (1996). "Indian opposition party would assert nuclear capability if it gains power." *Asian Wall Street Power*. April 2:A10.

Joshi, Sharad (2008). "A pause in the Indo-US nuclear agreement." March 24. Retrieved from http://www.nti.org/analysis/articles/pause-indo-us-nuclear-agreement/ (last accessed on November 10, 2014).

Kakar, Sudhir (1996). *The Colors of Violence: Cultural Identities, Religion, and Conflict* (Chicago: University of Chicago Press).

Kamara, Kranti and Keith Jones (2007). "Indian prime minister calls Left Front's bluff over Indo-US nuclear accord." August 16. Retrieved from http://www.wsws.org/en/articles/2007/08/indi-a16.html/ (last accessed on November 10, 2014).

Kamath, P.K. (2009). *Indian Policy of No First Use of Nuclear Weapons: Relevance to Peace and Security in South Asia* (New Delhi: Anamika Publishers).

Kapur, Askok (1976). *India's Nuclear Option: Atomic Diplomacy and Decision-Making* (New York: Praeger).

———— (1979). *International Nuclear Proliferation* (New York: Praeger).

———— (1994). "India: The nuclear scientists and the state, the Nehru and the post-Nehru years." In E. Solingen (ed.). *Scientists and the State: Domestic Structures and the International Context* (Ann Arbor: University of Michigan Press), 209–229.

294 Revisiting Nuclear India

Karat, Prakash (1998). "A lethal link." *Frontline*, 15(12). Retrieved from http://www.frontline.in/static/html/fl1512/15120200.htm/ (last accessed on November 10, 2014).

Karnad, B. (1999). "A thermo-nuclear deterrent." In Amitabh Mattoo (ed.). *India's Nuclear Deterrent: Pokhran II and Beyond* (New Delhi: Harchand), 108–149.

——— (2005). *Nuclear Weapons and Indian Security: The Realist Foundations of Strategy* (New Delhi: MacMillan).

Kartha, Tara (1998). "Ballistic missiles and international security." In Jasjit Singh (ed.). *Nuclear India* (New Delhi: Knowledge World), 115–139.

Katyal, K.K. (1997). "India, Pakistan to continue talks on all issues." *The Hindu*. April 10:1.

Katzenstein, P. (1996). *The Culture of National Security* (New York: Columbia University Press).

Kegley, Charles and Gregory Raymond (1999). *How Nations Make Peace* (New York: St. Martin's Press).

Keohane, R. and J. Nye (1977). *Power and Interdependence: World Politics in Transition* (Boston: Little Brown).

Kerr, Paul K. and Mary Beth Nikitin (2013). "Pakistan's nuclear weapons: Proliferation and security issues." Congressional Research Service, March 19:1–32.

Khan, Abdul Qadir and Sreedhar (1987). *Dr. A.Q. Khan on Pakistan Bomb* (New Delhi: ABC).

Khan, Munir Ahmad (1995). "Bhutto and Pakistan's nuclear program." *Frontier Post*. April 4:1.

Khan, Rasheeduddin (1989). "Nehru's vision of Asia and the world." In P.N. Haskar (ed.). *Nehru's Vision of Peace and Security in Nuclear Age* (New Delhi: Patriot Publishers), 17–42.

Khan, S.A. (2000). *The Causes of the Indian Revolt* (Karachi: Oxford University Press).

Khan, Saira (2009). *Nuclear Weapons and Conflict Transformation: The Case of India-Pakistan* (London and New York: Routledge).

Khare, Harish (1998). "A repudiation of nuclear apartheid policy." *The Hindu*. May 12:1.

Kier, E. (1997). *Imagining War: French and British Military Doctrine between the Wars* (Princeton: University of Princeton Press).

Kinkade, W. (1990). "American national style and strategic culture." In Carl Jacobsen (ed.). *Strategic Power: USA/USSR* (New York: St. Martin's Press), 10–29.

Kissinger, Henry (2009). "Speech to the 45th Munich Security Conference." February 6. http://www.americanrhetoric.com/ (last accessed on November 10, 2014).

Klare, Michael (1995). *Rogue States and Nuclear Outlaws: America's Search for a New Foreign Policy* (New York: Hill and Wang).

Klein, B. (1988). "Hegemony and strategic culture: American power projection and alliance defense politics." *Review of International Studies*, 14(2):133–48.

Knapik, Michael and Mark Hibbs (1989). "German firm's beryllium export to India may have violated US laws." *Nucleonics Week*, Special Report, January 30.

Kochanek, S.A. (1968). *The Congress Party of India* (Princeton: Princeton University Press).

Koreshe, Shafek E. (2011). "Pakistan's third 330 MW nuclear power plant becomes operational." May 12. Retrieved from http://app.com.pk/en_/index.php?option=com_content&task=view&id=139030&Itemid=2/ (last accessed on November 10, 2014).

Kremenyuk, Victor A. (1994). "The Cold War as cooperation." In Manus I. Midlarsky, John A. Vasquez, and Peter V. Gladkov (eds). *From Rivalry to Cooperation: Russian and American Perspectives on the Post-Cold War Era* (New York: Harper Collins), 3–25.

Krepon, Michael (2003). *Cooperative Threat Reduction, Missile Defense, and the Nuclear Future* (New York: Palgrave Macmillan).

Krishna, Raj (1965). "India and the bomb." *India Quarterly*, April–June:122.

Krishna, Sankaran (1999). *Postcolonial Insecurities: India, Sri Lanka, and the Question of Nationhood* (Minneapolis, Minnesota: University of Minnesota Press).

———— (2002). "Methodical worlds: Partition, secularism, and communalism in india." *Alternatives: Global, Local, Political*, 27(2):193–217.

———— (2004). "In one innings: National identity in postcolonial times." In Geeta Chowdhry and Sheila Nair (eds). *Power, Postcolonialism, and International Relations: Reading Race, Class, and Gender* (London: Routledge), 170–183.

———— (2006). "The bomb, biography, and the Indian middle class." *Economic and Political Weekly*, 41(23):2327–2330.

Krishna, S.M. (2012). "Brown-India initiative inauguration with SM Krishna, Indian Minister of External Affairs." September 28. Retrieved from http://vimeo.com/51218205/ (last accessed on November 10, 2014).

Krishna, V.V. (1993). *Bhatnagar on Science, Technology, and Development, 1938–1954* (Delhi: Wiley Eastern).

Kronstadt, Alan K. (2004a). "Terrorism in South Asia." Congressional Research Service December 13. Retrieved from http://www.fas.org/irp/crs/RL32259.pdf/ (last accessed on November 10, 2014).

———— (2004b). "India-US relations." Congressional Research Service. Library of Congress. November 4:1–19.

———— (2005). "India-US relations." Congressional Research Service. Library of Congress. February 23:1–16.

———— (2007) "India-US. relations." Congressional Research Service Report for the Congress. June 27. Retrieved from: http://fpc.state.gov/documents/organization/80669.pdf/ (last accessed on November 10, 2014).

Kronstadt, Alan K. (2009). "India–US relations." Congressional Research Service Report for the Congress. January 30. https://www.hsdl.org/?view&did= 732863/ (last accessed on November 10, 2014).

Kronstadt, Alan K. and Sonia Pinto (2013). "US-India security relations: Strategic issues." Congressional Research Service Report for the Congress. January 24:1–52.

Kronstadt, Alan K., Paul K. Kerr, Michael F. Martin, and Bruce Vaughn (2011). "India: Domestic issues, strategic dynamics, and U.S. relations." Congressional Research Service, September 1. Retrieved from http://www.fas.org/ sgp/crs/row/RL33529.pdf/ (last accessed on November 10, 2014).

Kulakarni, R.P., Homi J. Bhabha, and V. Sarma (1969). *Homi Bhabha: Father of Nuclear Science in India* (Bombay: Popular Prakashan).

Kumar, Ajay (1986). "Getting into gear." *India Today*. January 15:137.

Kumar, Sumita (1998), "Pakistan's nuclear weapons program." In Jasjit Singh (ed.) *Nuclear India* (New Delhi: Knowledge World), 157–156.

Kumar, Sunil (2001). *Communalism and Secularism in Indian Politics: A Study of the BJP* (New Delhi: Rawat Publications).

Kumar, Vinod (2008). "India and the non-proliferation regime: Looking beyond the nuclear deal." September 12. Retrieved from http://www.idsa.in/ event/nucleardeal_avinodkumar_160908/ (last accessed on November 10, 2014).

Kux, Dennis (1985). *Estranged Democracies: India and the United States, 1941– 1991* (New Delhi: SAGE Publications).

Lal, Pyara (1981). *Nuclear Shadow Over the Sub-continent* (New Delhi: United Service Institution of India).

Latham, A. (1997). "The role of culture and identity in Indian arms control and disarmament policy." In Keith Krause (ed.). *Cross-Cultural Dimensions of Multicultural Non-proliferation and Arms Control Dialogue* (Ottawa: Non-proliferation, Arms Control, and Disarmament Division, Department of Foreign Affairs and International Trade), 103–125.

Lavoy, Peter R. (2008). "Islamabad's nuclear posture: Its premises and implementation." In Henry Sokoloski (ed.). *Pakistan's Nuclear Future: Worries Beyond War* (Carlisle, PA: Strategic Studies Institute), 129–165.

Lebow, Richard Ned (1995). "The Search for accommodation: Gorbachev in comparative perspective." In Richard Ned Lebow and Thomas Risse-Kippen (eds). *International Relations Theory and the End of the Cold War* (New York: Columbia University Press), 167–186.

Lele, Ajey (2010). "Kalam-NSS Indian-American energy initiative." November 09. Retrieved from http://www.idsa.in/idsacomments/KalamNSSIndianAmeri-canEnergyInitiative_alele_091110/ (last accessed on November 10, 2014).

Lergo, J. (1995). *Cooperation Under Fire: Anglo-German Restraint During World War II* (Ithaca: Cornell University Press).

Lifton, Robert J. and Richard Falk (1982). *Indefensible Weapons* (New York: Basic Books).

Limaye, Satu P. (2010). "India-US and India-East Asia relations." *Comparative Connections*, 11(4), January. Retrieved from http://csis.org/publication/comparative-connections-v11-n4-india-us-and-india-east-asia-relations/ (last accessed on November 10, 2014).

Ling, L.H.M. (2002). *Postcolonial International Relations: Conquest and Desire Between Asia and the West* (New York: Palgrave).

Lok Sabha (1964a). *Lok Sabha Debates*, 3rd Series, 35(6), November 23: Cols. 1280, 1301, 1309.

——— (1964b). *Lok Sabha Debates*, 3rd Series, 35(6), November 24: Cols. 1517, 1534, 1553.

——— (1964c). *Lok Sabha Debates*, 3rd Series, 35(10). November 27: Cols. 2287–2288.

——— (1966). *Lok Sabha Debates*, 3rd Series, 55(56), May 10. Col. 15714.

——— (1972a). *Lok Sabha Debates*, 5th Series, 11(5), March 17. Cols. 130–131.

——— (1984a). *Lok Sabha Debates*, 7th Series, 46(22), March 23: Cols. 337, 343–346, 356, 398, 402.

——— (1984b). *Lok Sabha Debates*, 7th Series, 46(27), March 30: Col. 398.

Lord, Carnes (1985). "American strategic culture." *Comparative Strategy*. 5(3):269–293.

Loukianova, Anya (2009). "The nuclear posture review debate." August 19. Retrieved from http://www.nti.org/analysis/articles/nuclear-posture-review-debate/ (last accessed on November 10, 2014).

Macaulay, T.B. (1952a). "Lord Clive." In G.M. Young (ed.). *Macaulay: Prose and Poetry* (Cambridge, Massachusetts: Harvard University Press), 306–373.

——— (1952b). "Indian education: Minute of the 2nd of February, 1835." In G.M. Young (ed.). *Macaulay: Prose and Poetry* (Cambridge, Massachusetts: Harvard University Press), 719–730.

Mahapatra, Chintamani (1998). "Pokhran II and after: Dark clouds over Indo-US relations." http://www.idsa-india.org/an-aug8-3.html/ (last accessed on November 10, 2014).

——— (2010). "Ups, downs and ups in Obama's approach towards India." February 5. Retrieved from http://www.idsa.in/idsacomments/UpsDownsandUpsinObamasApproachtowardsIndia_cmahapatra_050210/ (last accessed on November 10, 2014).

Mahmud, Khalid (1997). "Normalizing ties with India." *News*. March 7.

Majumdar, Bappa (2008). "India launches its first nuclear-powered submarine." *Reuters*. July 26. Retrieved from http://in.reuters.com/article/2009/07/26/idINIndia-41320820090726/ (last accessed on November 10, 2014).

Malaviya, M.M. (1919). *Speeches and Writings* (Madras: G.A. Natesan).

Malhotra, Inder (1989). *Indira Gandhi: A Political and Personal Biography* (Boston: Northeastern University Press).

Malhotra, Inder (2012). "Shastri gets his way on nuclear policy." *The Indian Express*. October 15. Retrieved from http://m.indianexpress.com/news/shastri-gets-his-way-on-nuclear-policy/1016715/ (last accessed on November 10, 2014).

Malik, Mohan (2003). "High hopes: India's response to US security policies." *Asia Pacific Center for Security Studies*. March. Retrieved from http://www. apcss.org/Publications/SAS/SASAPResponse030320/HighHopesIndiasResponsetoUSSecurityPolicies.pdf/ (last accessed on November 10, 2014).

Malik, Priyanjali (2010). *India's Nuclear Debate: Exceptionalism and the Bomb* (New Delhi: Routledge).

Malik, V.P. (2006). "Indo-US defense and military relations." In Sumit Ganguly, Brian Shoup, and Andrew Scobell (eds). *US-Indian Strategic Cooperation: Into the 21st Century* (London and New York: Routledge), 82–112.

Malik, Yogendra K. and V.B. Singh (1994). *Hindu Nationalists in India: The Rise of the Bharatiya Janata Party* (Boulder, Colorado: Westview).

Manchandani, Rita (1997). "India-Pakistan relations: Moving from animosity to curiosity." *News*. March 9.

Mani, Lata (1998). *Contentious Tradition: The Debate on Sati in Colonial India* (Berkeley, California: University of California Press).

Manning, Robert A. (1998). "India, the rogue democracy." *Los Angeles Times*. May 17. http://articles.latimes.com/1998/may/17/opinion/op-50651 (last assessed on November 20, 2013).

Mansingh, Surjit (1994). "India-China relations in the post-Cold War era." *Asian Survey*, 34(3):285–300.

Mattoo, A. (1996a). "Raison d'etat or adhocism." In Kanti Bajpai, Amitabh Mattoo, Rahul Roy Chaudhury, Varun Sahni, and Waheguru Pal Singh Sidhu (eds). *Securing India: Strategic Thought and Practice* (New Delhi: Manohar), 189–212.

——— (1996b). "India's nuclear status quo." *Survival*, 38(3):41–57.

——— (2000). "Imagining China." In Kanti Bajpai and Amitah Mattoo (eds). *The Peacock and the Dragon: India-China Relations in the Twenty-First Century* (Delhi: Harchand).

McLane, J. (1977). *Indian Nationalism and the Early Congress* (Princeton: Princeton University Press).

McMahon, Robert J. (1994). *The Cold War on the Periphery: The United States, India, and Pakistan* (New York: Columbia University Press).

Mill, J. (1975). *The History of British India* (Chicago: University of Chicago Press).

Ministry of Defense (1996–1997). *Ministry of Defense Annual Report 1996–1997* (New Delhi: Government of India, Ministry of Defense).

Ministry of External Affairs (1997). *Statements by India on Comprehensive Nuclear Test Ban Treaty (CTBT) (1993–1996)* (New Delhi: Ministry of External Affairs).

——— (2004). "Joint statement, India-Pakistan expert-level talks on nuclear CBMs." Ministry of External Affairs, Government of India. June 20:1–2.

——— (2005). "Report of the India-China Joint Study Group on comprehensive trade and economic cooperation." Ministry of External Affairs, Government of India. April 11. Retrieved from http://mea.gov.in/bilateral-documents. htm?dtl/6567/Report+of+the+IndiaChina+Joint+Study+Group+on+C omprehensive+Trade+and+Economic+Cooperation/ (last assessed on November 10, 2014).

Ministry of External Affairs (2006a). "Suo-Motu statement by Prime Minister Dr. Manmohan Singh on discussions on civil nuclear energy cooperation with the US: Implementation of India's separation plan." March 07. Retrieved from http://www.mea.gov.in/Speeches-Statements.htm?dtl/2167/SuoMo tu+Statement+by+Prime+Minister+Dr+Manmohan+Singh+on+Discussio ns+on+Civil+Nuclear+Energy+Cooperation+with+the+US+Implementat ion+of+Indias+Separation+Plan/ (last assessed on November 10, 2014).

——— (2006b). "Special media briefing by foreign secretary on India-Pakistan foreign secretary level talks." January 18. Retrieved from http://www. mea.gov.in/media-briefings.htm?dtl/2729/Special+Media+Briefing+by+F oreign+Secretary+on+IndiaPakistan+Foreign+Secretary+level+talks/ (last assessed on November 10, 2014).

——— (2012). "Transcript of media briefing by foreign secretary on prime minister's meeting with Prime Minister Wen Jiabao in Phnom Penh." Ministry of External Affairs, Government of India. November 19. Retrieved from http:// mea.gov.in/media-briefings.htm?dtl/20827/Transcript+of+Media+Briefing +by+Foreign+Secretary+on+Prime+Ministers+meeting+with+Prime+Minist er+Wen+Jiabao+in+Phnom+Penh/ (last assessed on November 10, 2014).

Mir, Amir (2011). "China seeks military bases in Pakistan." *Asia Times*. January 8. Retrieved from http://www.atimes.com/atimes/South_Asia/MJ26Df03. html/ (last assessed on November 10, 2014).

Mirchandani, G.G. (1968). *India's Nuclear Dilemma* (New Delhi: Popular Press Services).

Mishra, K.P. (1989). "Framework of Nehru's foreign policy." In Haskar (ed.). *Nehru's Vision of Peace and Security in Nuclear Age* (New Delhi: Patriot Publishers), 43–48.

Mohan, C. Raja (1995). "India's nuclear options." The *Hindu*. December 12:12.

——— (1996a). "India and the Chinese N-test." The *Hindu*. June 9.

——— (1996b). "India, China power equations changing." The *Hindu*. December 2:11.

——— (1997a). "Renewing Indo-US dialogue." The *Hindu*. January 9.

——— (1997b). "Nuclear weapons and the Gujral doctrine." The *Hindu*. September 22.

——— (2001–2002). "A paradigm shift toward South Asia?" *The Washington Quarterly*, 26(1):141–155.

——— (2004). "India and China: A shifting paradigm." The *Hindu*, July 29. Retrieved from http://www.hindu.com/2004/07/29/stories/2004072902241000.htm/ (last assessed on November 10, 2014).

——— (2006). "Will India become a global power?" Council on Foreign Relation. June 19. Retrieved from http://www.cfr.org/india/india-become-global-power-transcript-federal-news-service-inc/p11013/ (last assessed on November 10, 2014).

Mohan, C. Raja (2009). "The evolution of Sino-Indian relations: Implications for the United States." In Ayres Alyssa and C. Raja Mohan (eds). *Power Re-alignments in South Asia: China, India, and the United States* (New Delhi: SAGE Publications), 270–290.

Monsonis, Guillem (2009). "India's strategic autonomy dilemma and the rapprochement with the United States." March 20. Retrieved from http://www.idsa.in/event/IndiavsUS_gmonsonis_200309/ (last assessed on November 10, 2014).

Moon, P. (1949). *Warren Hastings and British India* (New York: Macmillan).

Moore, Molly and John Ward Anderson (1994). "Rhetoric fuels India-US rift: Perceptions of Washington vendetta threatens improved business, military ties." *Washington Post*, February 24:A.17.

Morgenthau, H. (1949). *Politics Among Nations: The Struggle For Power and Peace* (New York: Knoff).

Movement in India for Nuclear Disarmament (1998). "Preamble." Retrieved from http://www.angelfire.com/mi/MIND123/ (last assessed on November 10, 2014).

Mukherjee, Pranab (2006). "Delhi in nuke fight." *Telegraph*, June 17. Retrieved from http://www.telegraphindia.com/1060617/asp/nation/story_6364739.asp/ (last assessed on November 10, 2014).

——— (2011). "India on path for next round of growth, asserts Pranab Mukherjee." *The Times of India*. June 28. Retrieved from http://articles.timesofindia.indiatimes.com/2011-06-28/india/29711967_1_fdi-policy-structural-reforms-political-consensus/ (last assessed on November 10, 2014).

Mukherjee, S.N. (1968). *Sir William Jones: A Study of Eighteenth-Century British Attitudes to India* (London: Cambridge University Press).

Mulford, David (2005). "Reaching new heights: US-India relations in the 21st century." Retrieved from http://newdelhi.usembassy.gov/uploads/images/jjD-VelFXR3rAB0Of5Ke7dg/reach.pdf/ (last assessed on November 10, 2014).

Munir, Akram (1998). "Statement by Ambassador Munir Akram at the Plenary of the Second Session of the Conference on Disarmament." May 14. Retrieved from http://cns.miis.edu/archive/country_india/statemnt.htm/ (last assessed on November 10, 2014).

Munshi, K.M. (1962). *Foundations of Indian Culture* (Bombay: Bharatiya Vidya Bhavan).

Munton, Don and Welch, David A. (2007). *The Cuban Missile Crisis: A Concise History* (Oxford University Press).

Muppidi, H. (1999). "Postcoloniality and the production of international insecurity: The persistent puzzle of Indo-U.S. relations." In Jutta Weldes, Mark Laffey, Hugh Gusterson, and Raymond Duvall (eds). *Cultures of Insecurity: States, Communities, and the Production of Danger* (Minneapolis: University of Minnesota Press), 119–146.

Muralidhar, Reddy (2002). "We will never roll back N-program: Musharraf." *The Hindu* (Chennai), 22 February.

Myers, Steven Lee (1998). "Russia is helping India extend range of missile, U.S. aides say." April 27. Retrieved from http://www.nytimes.com/1998/04/27/world/russia-is-helping-india-extend-range-of-missile-us-aides-say.html/ (last assessed on November 10, 2014).

Nagar, P. (1977). *Lala Lajpat Rai: The Man and his Ideas* (Delhi: Manohar Book Service).

Nair, Brigadier Vijai, K. (1992). *Nuclear India* (New Delhi: Lancer).

Nalapat, M.D. (2010). "Missing: An Obama foreign policy." February 8. Retrieved from http://www.idsa.in/idsacomments/MissingAnObamaForeignPolicy_mdnalapat_080210/ (last assessed on November 10, 2014).

Namboodri, P.K.S. (1985). "Pak nuclear capability." *The Times of India*. May 11.

Narang, Vipin (2010). "Pakistan's nuclear posture: Implications for South Asian stability." January 10. Retrieved from http://belfercenter.ksg.harvard.edu/publication/19889/pakistans_nuclear_posture.html/ (last assessed on November 10, 2014).

Narula, Sunil (1996a). "Pressure tactics." *Outlook*, January 3.

———— (1996b). "In isolation ward again." *Outlook*, July 17.

Narula, Sunil, Ludwina A. Joseph, and Mariana Baabar (1998). "We'll go nuclear." *Outlook India*. February 09. Retrieved from http://www.outlookindia.com/article.aspx?205047/ (last assessed on November 10, 2014).

National Democratic Alliance (2005). "Report on reforming the security system." December 5. Retrieved from http://www.nda.gov/ (last assessed on November 10, 2014).

National Herald (1964). "Bhabha: India can make atom bomb in 18 months." *National Herald*. October 5.

National Security Strategy (2002). "Bush sends new national security strategy to Congress." September 20. Retrieved from http://www.globalsecurity.org/military/library/news/2002/09/mil-020920-usia02.htm (last assessed on November 10, 2014).

Nayan, Rajiv (2005). "The Indo-US nuclear deal has generated a lot of heat: Here's why." August 4. Retrieved from http://www.idsa.in/idsastrategiccomments/TheIndoUSnucleardeal_rnayan_040805/ (last assessed on November 10, 2014).

Nayar, Baldev Raj (1976). *American Geopolitics and India* (Columbia: University of Columbia Press).

———— (2001). *India and the Major Powers* (New Delhi: Haranand Publications).

NDTV (2010). "Full text: India-US joint statement." November 8. Retrieved from http://www.ndtv.com/article/india/full-text-india-us-joint-statement-65134/ (last assessed on November 10, 2014).

———— (2012). "Mani Shankar Aiyar & Pervez Hoodbhoy at THiNK 2011." July. Retrieved from http://www.youtube.com/watch?v=75TxKw9x0c8/ (last assessed on November 10, 2014).

Nehru, Jawaharlal (1942). *The Unity of India: Collected Writings 1937-1940* (New York: The John Day Company).

Nehru, Jawaharlal (1948). *Nehru on Gandhi* (New York: John Day Company).

———— (1950). *Independence and After: A Collection of Speeches* (New York: John Day).

———— (1961). *India's Foreign Policy; Selected Speeches, September 1946–April 1961* (New Delhi: Government of India, The Publications Divisions).

———— (1965). *The Discovery of India* (Bombay: Asia Publishing House).

———— (1989). *Discovery of India* (New Delhi: Oxford University Press).

Nehru, Jawaharlal and Sarvepalli Gopal (1980). *Jawaharlal Nehru: An Anthology* (New Delhi: Oxford University Press).

Nehru, Jawaharlal, Sarvepalli Gopal, and Uma Iyengar (2003). *The Essential Writings of Jawaharlal Nehru* (New Delhi: Oxford University Press).

News India (1987). "India should go nuke—Vajpayee." *News India.* December 11.

Nizamani, H. (2001). *The Roots of Rhetoric: Politics of Nuclear Weapons in India and Pakistan* (Westport: Praeger).

Noorani, A.G. (1967). "India's quest for a nuclear guarantee." *Asian Survey,* 7(7):490–502.

Norris, Robert and Hans Kristensen (2010). "Nuclear notebook: Indian nuclear forces, 2010." *Bulletin of the Atomic Scientists,* 66(5):76–81. Retrieved from http://bos.sagepub.com/content/66/5/76.full/ (last assessed on November 10, 2014).

Norris, Robert S., William A. Arkin, Hans M. Kristensen, and Joshua Handler (2002). "India's nuclear forces, 2002." *Bulletin of the Atomic Scientists,* 58(2), March–April. Retrieved from http://thebulletin.org/2002/march/indias-nuclear-forces-2002/ (last assessed on November 10, 2014).

Nuclear Security Summit (2010). "Highlights of national commitments Nuclear Security Summit, April 12–13, 2010." Retrieved from http://fpc.state.gov/documents/organization/140356.pdf/ (last assessed on November 10, 2014).

Ollapally, D. (2001) "Mixed motives in India's search for nuclear status." *Asian Survey,* 41 (6):925–942.

Ottaway, David B. (1989). "Bush administration debates sale of missile-testing device to India." *Washington Post,* May 28:A8.

Ozkan, Mehmet (2010). "Tenets of Indian foreign policy and Indo-US partnership." July 22. Retrieved from http://www.idsa.in/idsacomments/TenetsofIndianForeignPolicyandIndoUSPartnership_mozkan220710/ (last assessed on November 10, 2014).

Paddock, Carl (2010). *India-US Nuclear Deal: Prospects and Implications* (New Delhi: Epitome Books).

Pakistan Defense (2013). "China PM visit likely to boost bilateral trade." December 14. Retrieved from http://defence.pk/threads/china-pm-visit-likely-to-boost-bilateral-trade.84609/ (last assessed on November 10, 2014).

Pandey, Gyanendra (2006). *The Construction of Communalism in Colonial North India* (New Delhi: Oxford University Press).

Parasuram, T.V. (2004). "India, US discuss steps to reduce barriers to hi-tech trade." *The Economic Times*. November 20. Retrieved from http://articles. economictimes.indiatimes.com/2004-11-20/news/27371968_1_high-technology-cooperation-group-hi-tech-trade-high-technology-trade/ (last assessed on November 10, 2014).

Parthasarathy, Gopal (1989). "Jawaharlal Nehru and his quest for a secular identity." *Occasional Papers in History and Society* (First Series), No. XLII:1–9.

Pathak, K.K. (1980). *Nuclear Policy of India* (New Delhi: Geetanjali Prakashan).

Patriot (1987). "Minister says no current plans for Indian nuclear bomb." *Patriot*, March 14:5.

Pattanaik, Smruti, S (2003). "Indo-Pak relations and the SAARC summits." *Strategic Analysis*, 28(3):427–439.

Perkovich, George (1999). *India's Nuclear Bomb: The Impact on Global Proliferation* (Berkeley: University of California Press).

Persaud, R. and R.B.J. Walker (2001). *Race in International Relations* (Boulder: Colorado).

Phadnis, Umashankar (1997). "India to talk with Pakistan after polls, says Gujral." *Dawn*. January 25.

Pincus, Winter (2005). "Pentagon revises nuclear strike plan." September 11. Retrieved from http://www.washingtonpost.com/wp-dyn/content/article/2005/09/10/AR2005091001053.html/ (last assessed on November 10, 2014).

Poulose, T.T. (1978). *Perspectives of India's Foreign Policy* (New Delhi: Young Asia Publishers).

Powell, Colin (2003). "US secretary of state's address to the United Nations Security Council." Retrieved from http://www.theguardian.com/world/2003/feb/05/iraq.usa (last assessed on November 10, 2014).

Press Information Bureau (2006). "Joint declaration by the Republic of India and the People's Republic of China." November 21. Retrieved from http://pib.nic.in/newsite/erelease.aspx?relid=22168/ (last assessed on November 10, 2014).

Radhakrishnan, R. and C. Moore (eds). (1973). *A Sourcebook of Indian Philosophy* (Princeton, New Jersey: Princeton University Press).

Raghavan, G.N.S. (1997). *A New Era in the Indian Polity: A Study of Atal Bihari Vajpayee and the BJP* (New Delhi: Gyan Publishing House).

Raghavan, V.R. (1996). *India's Need for Strategic Balance: Security in the Post-Cold War World* (New Delhi: Delhi Policy Group).

Raghuvanshi, Vivek (1999). "India to develop extensive nuclear missile arsenal." *Defense News*, May 24:14.

Rai, Saritha (1994). "Interview with General Sundarji (retd)." *India Today*, April 30:27.

Rajagopalan, Rajesh (1999). "Neo-realist theory and the Indo-Pakistani conflict-I." *Strategic Analysis*, xxii (9):1261–1272.

Rajagopalan, Rajesh (2011). "The US-India strategic partnership after the MMRCA Deal." May 6. Retrieved from http://www.idsa.in/idsacomments/TheUSIndiaStrategicPartnershipaftertheMMRCADeal_rrajagopalan_060511/

Rajesh, Y.P. (2007). "India could dump U.S. nuclear deal: envoy." *Reuters.* January 10. Retrieved from http://www.reuters.com/article/2007/01/10/us-india-usa-nuclear-idUSDEL20300120070110/ (last assessed on November 10, 2014).

Ram, N. (1982). "India's nuclear policy." Paper delivered at the 34th Annual Meeting of the Association of Asian Studies, April 2–4, Chicago.

Ramanna, M.V. (2003). "La Trahison des Clercs: Scientists and India's nuclear bomb." In M.V. Ramanna and C. Rammanohar Reddy (eds). *Prisoners of the Nuclear Dream* (Hyderabad: Orient Longman).

Ramanna, R. (1992). *Years of Pilgrimage* (New Delhi: Penguin).

Rangarajan, L.N. (ed.). (1992). *The Arthashastra* (New Delhi: Penguin Books).

Rao, Nirupama (2009). "Keynote address at third IDSA Annual Conference on South Asia 2020: Moving towards cooperation or conflict?" November 4. Retrieved from http://www.idsa.in/node/3423/ (last assessed on November 10, 2014).

Reddy, G.K. (1985). "Nuclear option open if Pak gets the bomb." *The Hindu*, May 5.

Rediff India (2008). "Agni-III ready for induction, can reach China" May 07. Retrieved from http://www.rediff.com/news/2008/may/07agni.htm/ (last assessed on November 10, 2014).

Reiss, Mitchell (1988). *Without the Bomb: The Politics of Non-Proliferation* (Columbia: Columbia University Press).

Reuters (1987). "India announces to review of nuclear policy." *Reuters.* March 27.

Reuters Canada (2012). "Asian giants seek better ties: China's Defense Minister in India." September 2. Retrieved from http://www.reuters.com/article/2012/09/02/us-india-china-idUSBRE88100X20120902/ (last assessed on November 10, 2014).

Rice, Condoleezza (2006). "Press releases." November 17. Retrieved from https://www.indianembassy.org/India_Review/2006/Nov%2006.pdf/ (last assessed on November 10, 2014).

Robinson, F. (1975). *Separatism Among Indian Muslims: The Politics of the United Provinces' Muslims, 1860–1923* (London: Cambridge University Press).

Rondeaux, Candace (2008). "Pakistan offers to join with India in investigating Mumbai massacre." December 3. Retrieved from http://www.washingtonpost.com/wp-dyn/content/article/2008/12/02/AR2008120201120.html/ (last assessed on November 10, 2014).

Rosen, S. (1996). *Societies and Military Power: India and Its Armies* (Ithaca: Cornell University Press).

Rubinoff, Arthur (2006). "Impossible objectives and short-sighted policies: US strategies towards India." In Sumit Ganguly, Brian Shoup, and Andrew

Scobell (eds). *US-Indian Strategic Cooperation: Into the 21st Century* (London and New York: Routledge), 38–60.

Sachdeva, A.K. (2000). "Pertinence of Pakistani ballistic missiles in the Indo-Pak conflict." Paper No. 14. Institute of Defense and Strategic Analysis (New Delhi). Retrieved from http://www.idsa.in/delhipapers/ (last assessed on November 10, 2014).

Said, E. (1978). *Orientalism* (New York: Vintage).

Sandhu, Kanwar (1993). "Interview with Chief of Army Staff, General B.C. Joshi." *India Today*, July 15:50–51.

Sanger, David E. and Kurt Eichenwald (2001). "Citing India attack: US aims at attacks of groups in Pakistan." *The New York Times*, December 21. Retrieved from http://www.nytimes.com/2001/12/21/international/21PREX.html/ (last assessed on November 10, 2014).

Santhanam. V. (2002a). Director, Institute of Defense and Strategic Analysts, New Delhi (Personal Interview).

——— (2002b). "Agni-I: A short range N-missile India urgently needs." January 27. Retrieved from http://timesofindia.indiatimes.com/india/Agni-I-A-short-range-N-missile-India-urgently-needs/articleshow/427722768. cms?referral=PM/ (last accessed on November 10, 2014).

Saran, S. (2005). "Press briefing by Foreign Secretary Shyam Saran." July 18. Embassy of India (archive search). Retrieved from http://www.indianembassy.org/ (last accessed on November 10, 2014).

Savarkar, V.D. (1940). *Hindu Sanghatan: Its Ideology and Immediate Programme* (Bombay: Hindu Maha Sabha Presidential Office).

——— (1949). *Hindu Rashtra Darshan: A Collection of the Presidential Speeches delivered from the Hindu Mahasabha Platform* (Bombay: Laxman Ganesh Khare).

——— (1967). *Historic Statements* (edited by S.S. Savarkar and G.M. Joshi) (Bombay: Popular Prakashan).

——— (1971). *Six Glorious Epochs of Indian History* (translated and edited by S.T. Godbole) (Bombay: Bal Savarkar).

Sawhney, Pravin and Ghazala Wahab (2004). "Unequal music: Indo-US strategic relations." *Force*. October. Retrieved from http://www.forceindia.net/ strategic2.aspx/ (last accessed on November 10, 2014).

Seaborg, Glenn (1987). *Stemming the Tide: Arms Control in the Johnson Years* (Massachusetts: Lexington).

Sekhon, Harinder (2004). "NSSP—Are we really moving forward?" *ORF Strategic Trends*, II(43), November 1. Retrieved from http://www.orfonline.org/ cms/sites/orfonline/modules/strategictrend/StrategicTrendDetail.html?cm aid=1780&mmacmaid=1781&volumeno=II&issueno=43/ (last accessed on November 10, 2014).

Sekhon, Harinder and Cherian Samuel (2005). "Bush II presidency: Implications for Indo-US relations." *Observer Research Foundation*. February 4. Retrieved from http://www.observerindia.com/cms/sites/orfonline/modules/

policybrief/PolicyBriefDetail.html?cmaid=1133&mmacmaid=1134&volu meno=&issueno= (last accessed on November 10, 2014).

Sen, Amartya (2006). *The Argumentative Indian: Writings on Indian History, Culture, and Identity* (New York: Picador).

Sen, Ronen (2005). "India-US relations: Where are they headed?" Center for the Advanced Study of India. Occasional Paper 24 (Philadelphia, PA: University of Pennsylvania).

Sen Gupta, Bhabani (1984). *Nuclear Weapons: Policy Options for India* (New Delhi: SAGE Publications).

Seshadri, Hongasandra V. (1988). *RSS: A Vision in Action* (Bangalore: Jagarana Prakashana).

Sethi, Manpreet (1998). "The struggle for nuclear disarmament." In Jasjit Singh (ed.). *Nuclear India* (New Delhi: Knowledge World), 75–95.

Shah, A.B. (1968). *Indian Defense and Foreign Policies* (Bombay: Manaktalas).

Shahin, Sultan (2003). "US India talk nuclear technology transfer." October 7. Retrieved from http://www.asiatimes.com/atimes/South_Asia/ (last accessed on November 10, 2014).

Shambaugh, David (2009). "The evolving security order in Asia: Implications for US-India relations." In Ayres Alyssa and C. Raja Mohan (eds). *Power Re-alignments in South Asia: China, India, and the United States* (New Delhi: SAGE Publications), 137–157.

Sharif, Nawaz (1998). "We alone will decide our response, says Nawaz." *News.* May 13. Retrieved from http://www.thenews.com.pk/AdvanceSearch. aspx/ (last accessed on November 10, 2014).

Sharma, Arvind (2002). *Modern Hindu Thought: The Essential Texts* (New Delhi: Oxford University Press).

Sharma, Ashok (2013). "The US-India strategic partnership: An overview of defense and nuclear courtship." July 4. Retrieved from http://journal. georgetown.edu/2013/07/04/the-u-s-india-strategic-partnership-an-overview-of-defense-and-nuclear-courtship-by-ashok-sharma/ (last accessed on November 10, 2014).

Sharma, Dhirendra (1983). *India's Nuclear Estate* (New Delhi: Lancers).

Sharma, S.C. (2005). "Composite dialogue between India and Pakistan." In P.K. Kamath (ed). *India-Pakistan Relations: Courting Peace from the Corridors of War* (New Delhi and Chicago: Promilla and Company).

Sharma, V.V.S. (1964). "India's capability to produce nuclear weapons haunts Pakistan." *The Times of India.* November 9.

Sheth, Jagdish, N. (2008). *Chindia Rising: How China and India will Benefit Your Business* (New Delhi: Tata McGraw-Hill Publishing Company).

Shoup, Brian and Sumit Ganguly (2006). "Introduction." In Sumit Ganguly, Brian Shoup, and Andrew Scobell (eds). *US-Indian Strategic Cooperation: Into the 21st Century* (London and New York: Routledge), 1–10.

Shrivastava, V.K. (2002). Ex-Deputy Director, Institute of Defense and Strategic Analysts, New Delhi (Personal Interview).

Sibal, Kanwal (2003). "India-US partnership." Address at the Carnegie Endowment for International Peace, Washington D.C. February 4. Retrieved from http://carnegieendowment.org/2003/02/04/india-us-partnership/3jcv?reloadFlag=1/ (last accessed on November 10, 2014).

Sidhu, W.G.S. (1996). "Of oral traditions and ethnocentric judgements." In Kanti Bajpai, Amitabh Mattoo, Rahul Roy Chaudhury, Varun Sahni, and Waheguru Pal Singh Sidhu (eds). *Securing India: Strategic Thought and Practice* (New Delhi: Manohar), 174–188.

Sidhu, W.P.S. (1997). "The development of an Indian nuclear doctrine since 1980." (Ph.D Dissertation, Emmanuel College, Cambridge University).

Sidhwa, Bapsi (1991). *Cracking India* (Minneapolis, Minnesota: Milkweed Editions).

Sikri, Rajiv (2007). "Disturbing implications of 123 Agreement." August 3. Retrieved from http://www.rediff.com/news/2007/aug/03guest.htm/ (last accessed on November 10, 2014).

Simons, Lewis M. (1974). "India explodes A-device, cites peaceful use." *Washington Post*, May 19:A1.

Singh, Jasjit (1992–1993). "Trend in defense expenditure." *Asian Strategic Review*, 49:25–82.

———— (1998) *Nuclear India* (New Delhi: Knowledge World).

———— (1999). "India's nuclear and strategic policies." In Nancy Jetly (ed.). *India's Foreign Policy: Challenges and Prospects* (New Delhi: Knowledge World).

———— (2002). Ex-Director, Institute of Defense and Strategic Analysts, New Delhi (Personal Interview).

———— (2009). "Security concerns and China's military capabilities: The eagle, the dragon, and the elephant." In Ayres Alyssa and C. Raja Mohan (eds). *Power Re-alignments in South Asia: China, India, and the United States* (New Delhi: SAGE Publications), 113–136.

Singh, Jaswant (1998). "Against nuclear apartheid." *Foreign Affairs*, 77(5):47–59.

———— (1999). *Defending India* (New York: St. Martin's Press).

Singh, Manmohan (2005). Address to the Combined Commanders Conference, New Delhi. October 20. Retrieved from http://pmindia.gov.in/speech-details.php?nodeid=203/ (last accessed on November 10, 2014).

———— (2006). "Charlie Rose interviews Indian PM Manmohan Singh." February 27. Retrieved from http://www.cfr.org/india/charlie-rose-interviews-indian-pm-manmohan-singh/p9986/ (last accessed on November 10, 2014).

———— (2011). "PM Manmohan Singh's speech at the UN General Assembly." September 24. Retrieved from http://www.rediff.com/news/report/read-pm-manmohan-singhs-speech-at-un-general-assembly/20110924.htm/ (last accessed on November 10, 2014).

———— (2012). "India's economic growth issue of national security, says Manmohan Singh." *Reuters*. August 15. Retrieved from http://www.reuters.

com/article/2012/08/15/us-india-economy-idUSBRE87E06A20120815/ (last accessed on November 10, 2014).

Singh, Manvendra (1998d). "The private sector should be brought in to tap market defense technology." *Indian Express*. June 21.

Singh, Sampooran (1971). *India and the Nuclear Bomb* (New Delhi: S. Chand and Company).

Singh, Swaran (1998c). "China's nuclear weapons and doctrine." In Jasjit Singh (ed.). *Nuclear India* (New Delhi: Knowledge World), 140–156.

Singh, Gopal and Sharma, S.K. (2000). *Documents on India's Disarmament Policy, Nehru Era, Volume 1* (New Delhi: Anamika Publishers).

Sinha, Yashwant (2004). "Sinha shuts out proliferation." *The Telegraph*. February, 19. Retrieved from http://www.telegraphindia.com/1040219/asp/nation/story_2910359.asp#/ (last accessed on November 10, 2014).

Smith, Chris (1995). *India's ad hoc Arsenal: Arms Procurement in Historical Perspective* (New York: Oxford University Press).

Smith, Hedrick (1988). "A bomb ticks in Pakistan." *New York Times*. March 6:38.

Sood, Vikram (2009). "India and regional security interests." In Ayres Alyssa and C. Raja Mohan (eds). *Power Re-alignments in South Asia: China, India, and the United States* (New Delhi: SAGE Publications), 249–269.

Spear, Percival (1965). *The Oxford History of India-1740–1947* (Oxford: Clarendon Press).

Spector, Leonard and Jaqueline Smith (1990). *Nuclear Ambitions: The Spread of Nuclear Weapons 1989–1990* (Boulder: Westview).

Squassoni, Sharon (2005). "US nuclear cooperation with India: Issues for Congress." July 29. CRS Report for Congress. Congressional Research Service: The Library of Congress, Washington D.C. Retrieved from http://www.fas.org/sgp/crs/row/RL33016.pdf/ (last accessed on November 10, 2014).

Statesman (1998). "India To Go Ahead with Agni: Fernandes." *Statesman*. April 10.

Statesman Weekly (1979). "Reassurance on nuclear policy likely soon." *Statesman Weekly*. August 17:1.

———— (1985a). "China lauds PM's foreign policy." *Statesman Weekly*. August 3:6.

———— (1985b). "India can develop delivery system." *Statesman Weekly*. August 3.

Stuart, Reginald C. (1982). *War and American Thought: From the Revolution of the Monroe Doctrine* (Kent, Ohio: Kent State University Press).

Stokes, E. (1959). *The English Utilitarians and India* (Oxford: Clarendon Press).

Stubbs, M. (1983). *Discourse Analysis: The Sociolinguistic Analysis of Natural Language* (Oxford: Basil Blackwell).

Subbarao, Buddhi Kota (2006). "Indo-US nuclear deal: Some unexplored angles." March 9. Retrieved from http://www.countercurrents.org/ind-subbarao090306.htm/ (last accessed on November 10, 2014).

Subrahmanyam, K. (1968). *A Strategy for India for a Credible Posture against a Nuclear Adversary* (New Delhi: IDSA).

Subrahmanyam, K. (1970). "Options for India." *Institute for Defense and Strategic Analysis Journal.* Volume 3.

——— (1981). "A robust nuclear policy." *The Times of India*, April 26.

——— (1993). "Capping, managing, or eliminating nuclear weapons?" In Kanti K. Bajpai and Stephen P. Cohen (eds). *South Asia After the Cold War: International Perspectives* (Boulder: Westview).

——— (1995a). "Freeze on N-material was Indian plan." *The Times of India.* February 7:11.

——— (1995b). "To test or not to test." *Economic Times.* December 21.

——— (1996a). "Dealing with China." *The Times of India.* October 23.

——— (1996b). "Nuclear defense philosophy." *The Times of India.* November 8.

——— (1998a). "Indian nuclear policy, 1964–1998 (A personal recollection)." In Jasjit Singh (ed.). *Nuclear India* (New Delhi: Knowledge World).

——— (1998b). "The politics of Shakti." *The Times of India*, May 26.

——— (2005). *Shedding Shibboleths: India's Evolving Strategic Outlook* (Delhi: Wordsmiths).

——— (2010). "Beyond cold war paradigms." *Business Standard.* January, 20. Retrieved from http://www.business-standard.com/article/opinion/k-subrahmanyam-beyond-cold-war-paradigms-110111400002_1.html/ (last accessed on November 10, 2014).

——— (2010). "A robust nuclear policy." *The Times of India.* April 26.

Subramanian, T.S. (2003). "Anti-ship version of BrahMos proves its mettle." December 3. Retrieved from http://www.hindu.com/2003/12/03/stories/2003120303991300.htm/ (last accessed on November 10, 2014).

Sundarji, K. (1990). "In the nuclear trap: Wrong Assumptionsassumptions." *The Hindu*, December 11, reprinted in Pran Chopra (1993). *The Crisis of Foreign Policy* (Allahabad: Wheeler).

——— (1990). "The Nuclear nuclear Threatthreat." *India Today*, November 30:94.

——— (1993a). "Rejoinder I: In the nuclear trap: Wrong Assumptions." In Pran Chopra (ed.). *The Crisis of Foreign Policy* (Allahabad: Wheeler), 183–185.

——— (1993b). "The year of the bomb rejoinder I: In the nuclear trap: Wrong assumptions." In Pran Chopra (ed.). *The Crisis of Foreign Policy* (Allahabad: Wheeler), 186–192.

——— (1995). "Changing military equations in Asia: The role of nuclear weapons." In Francine Frankel (ed.). *Bridging the Non-Proliferation Divide* (Lanham, Maryland: University Press of America), 119–149.

——— (1996a). "Imperatives of Indian minimum nuclear deterrence." *Agni.* 2(1), May:18.

——— (1996b). "India's post-CTBT strategy." *The Hindu.* September 30.

Symonds, Peter (2008). "Tense India-Pakistan standoff continues." *World Socialist Web.* December 8. Retrieved from https://www.wsws.org/en/articles/2008/12/indi-d08.html/ (last accessed on November 10, 2014).

Synder, Jack L. (1977). *The Soviet Strategic Culture: Implications for Nuclear Options* (Santa Monica: Rand).

Talbott, Strobe (2004). *Engaging India diplomacy, democracy, and the bomb* (Washington, DC: Brookings Institute Press).

Talwar, Ashwant (1995). "BJP pledges to make nuclear arms if in power." *Indian Express.* April 4:9.

Tanham, G. (1992). *Indian Strategic Thought: An Appreciative Essay* (Santa Monica: Rand).

Tanter, Raymond (1998). *Rogue Regimes: Terrorism and Proliferation: Prospects for the 21st Century* (New York: St. Martin's Press).

Tellis, Ashley (2004). "Seeking breakthroughs: The meandering U.S.-India relationship needs a fresh impetus." *Force.* October:1–2.

———— (2005). "South Asian seesaw: A new US policy may on the sub-continent." Policy Brief No. 38, May (Washington: Carnegie Endowment for International Peace). Retrieved from http://carnegieendowment.org/files/PB38.pdf/ (last accessed on November 10, 2014).

———— (2013). "The U.S.-India strategic dialogue: Forging the next phase of cooperation." June 20. Retrieved from http://carnegieendowment.org/2013/06/20/u.s.-india-strategic-dialogue-forging-next-phase-of-cooperation/gb93/ (last accessed on November 10, 2014).

Tellis, Ashley, Andrew Marbel, and Travis Tanner (eds) (2009). *Economic Meltdown and Geopolitical Stability* (Washington, DC: National Bureau of Asian Research).

Text of Indo-US Agreement (2005). "The defense framework." June 28. Retrieved from http://rupe-india.org/41/app5.html/ (last accessed on November 10, 2014).

Thakur, Ramesh (1994). *The Politics and Economics of India's Foreign Policy* (New York: St. Martin's Press).

Thapar, R. (1966). *A History of India* (Harmondsworth: Penguin).

———— (1989). "Imagined religious communities: Ancient history and the modern search for a Hindu identity." *Modern Asian Studies*, 23(2):209–231.

The Economic Times (2003). "Agni-III to be developed." January 12. Retrieved from http://articles.economictimes.indiatimes.com/2003-01-12/news/27553858_1_agni-iii-test-fire-vk-aatre/ (last accessed on November 10, 2014).

———— (2006). "Nuke separation plan a surrender: BJP." March 6. Retrieved from http://articles.economictimes.indiatimes.com/2006-03-06/news/27446195_1_separation-plan-safeguards-fissile-material/ (last accessed on November 10, 2014).

The Financial Times (2001). "India: External sector: Emerging challenges." *The Financial Times*, November 1.

The Hindu (1964). "Nuclear race will ruin country's economy: Shastri's firm stand: many MPs. plead for change in policy." *The Hindu.* November 28.

———— (1996)."India, US to work in hi-tech areas." *The Hindu.* October 25.

The Hindu (1997a). "India to revive 'Agni' project." *The Hindu*. July 31:1.

——— (1997b). "India won't go nuclear unless forced to: PM." *The Hindu*. November 14.

——— (2006a). "Excerpts from prime minister's reply to discussion in Rajya Sabha on Civil Nuclear Energy Cooperation with the United States." August 17. Retrieved from http://www.hindu.com/nic/indousdeal.htm/ (last accessed on November 10, 2014).

——— (2006b). "Appeal to parliamentarians on nuclear deal." August 15. Retrieved from http://www.thehindu.com/todays-paper/tp-opinion/appeal-to-parliamentarians-on-nuclear-deal/article3090406.ece/(last accessed on November 10, 2014).

——— (2007a). "India-China trade touches $24.9 billion in 2006." *The Hindu*, January 31. Retrieved from http://www.thehindu.com/todays-paper/tp-national/indiachina-trade-touches-249-billion-in-2006/article1789971.ece/ (last accessed on November 10, 2014).

——— (2007b). "PM's statement in the Lok Sabha on Civil Nuclear Energy Cooperation with the United States." August 13. Retrieved from http://www.hindu.com/nic/pmnuclear.htm/ (last accessed on November 10, 2014).

——— (2012a). "Joint statement issued by India and Pakistan at Islamabad." *The Hindu*. September 8. Retrieved from http://www.thehindu.com/news/resources/joint-statement-issued-by-india-and-pakistan-at-islamabad/article3874620.ece/ (last accessed on November 10, 2014).

——— (2012b). "Navy, Air Force stage network-centric exercise." February 9. Retrieved from http://www.thehindu.com/news/national/navy-air-force-stage-networkcentric-exercise/article2872931.ece/ (last accessed on November 10, 2014).

——— (2013). "Joint statement on Manmohan Singh's summit meeting with US President Obama in Washington." September 27. Retrieved from http://www.thehindu.com/news/resources/joint-statement-on-manmohan-singhs-summit-meeting-with-us-president-obama-in-washington/article5176700.ece/ (last accessed on November 10, 2014).

The Hindustan Times (1999). "Security of the Nation." *The Hindustan Times*, September 25.

The Office of the Historians (1964). "Foreign relations of the United States, 1964–1968." Volume XXV, South Asia, July 15. 1964. Retrieved from http://history.state.gov/historicaldocuments/frus1964-68v25/d151 (last assessed November 10, 2014).

The Times of India (1985a). "India must make N-bomb: BJP." *The Times of India*. July 22.

——— (1985b). "India can meet Pak N-threat: Minister." *The Times of India*. August 8.

——— (1996). "India must declare itself nuclear state." *The Times of India*. August 10.

——— (1998). "India now needs a nuclear doctrine." *The Times of India*. May 24.

The Times of India (2006). "Not doing enough, PM will tell Musharraf." September 13. Retrieved from http://timesofindia.indiatimes.com/india/Not-doing-enough-PM-will-tell-Musharraf/articleshow/1984867.cms?/ (last accessed on November 10, 2014).

——— (2012). "Antony to seek hike in defense outlay to counter twin threats from Pakistan, China." May 9. Retrieved from http://timesofindia.indiatimes.com/india/Antony-to-seek-hike-in-defence-outlay-to-counter-twin-threats-from-Pakistan-China/articleshow/13060147.cms?referral=PM/ (last accessed on November 10, 2014).

——— (2014). "India's first nuclear submarine and ICBM will be ready for induction next year: DRDO." February 8. Retrieved from http://timesofindia.indiatimes.com/india/Indias-first-nuclear-submarine-and-ICBM-will-be-ready-for-induction-next-year-DRDO/articleshow/30019630.cms/ (last accessed on November 10, 2014).

The White House (2002). Shahin, Sultan. 2003. "US India talk nuclear technology transfer." October 7. Retrieved from http://www.asiatimes.com/atimes/South_Asia/ (last accessed on November 10, 2014).

——— (2013a). "Remarks by Vice-President Joe Biden on the US-India partnership at the Bombay Stock Exchange." July 24. Retrieved from http://www.whitehouse.gov/the-press-office/2013/07/24/remarks-vice-president-joe-biden-us-india-partnership-bombay-stock-excha/ (last accessed on November 10, 2014).

——— (2013b). "U.S.-India joint statement." September 27. Retrieved from http://www.whitehouse.gov/the-press-office/2013/09/27/us-india-joint-statement/ (last accessed on November 10, 2014).

Thomas, Mathew (2010). *In Search of Congruence: Perspectives on Indo-US Relations Under the Obama Administration* (New Delhi: Institute of Defense and Strategic Analysis).

Tomlinson, John (1991). *Cultural Imperialism: A Critical Introduction* (Baltimore: Johns Hopkins University Press).

Treaty Text (2006). "Lahore declaration." June 10. Retrieved from http://www.nti.org/treaties-and-regimes/lahore-declaration/ (last accessed on November 10, 2014).

Tripathy, Amulya and Rabi Narayan Tripathy (2008). *US Policy Towards India: A Post Cold War Study* (New Delhi: Reference Press).

Trivedi, V.C. (1965). "Statement by the Indian representative (Trivedi)." August 12. *Documents on Disarmament.* Retrieved from http://www.un.org/disarmament/publications/documents_on_disarmament/1965/DoD_1965.pdf/ (last accessed on November 10, 2014).

United Press International (2012). "India to push ahead with nuclear power." February 23. Retrieved from http://www.upi.com/Business_News/Energy-Resources/2012/02/23/India-to-push-ahead-with nuclear-power/UPI-59691330013657/ (last assessed November 10, 2014).

United States Arms Control and Disarmament Agency (1965). *Documents of Disarmament*. Retrieved from http://www.un.org/disarmament/publications/documents_on_disarmament/1965/DoD_1965.pdf/ (last accessed on November 10, 2014).

——— (1966a). "Statement by the Indian Representative (Trivedi) to the Eighteen Nation Disarmament Committee {Extract}: Nonproliferation of Nuclear Weapons." February 15. *Documents on Disarmament*. Retrieved from http://www.un.org/disarmament/publications/documents_on_disarmament/1966/DoD_1966.pdf (last accessed on November 10, 2014).

——— (1966b). "Statement by the Indian Representative (Trivedi): Nonproliferation of Nuclear Weapons." October 31. *Documents on Disarmament*. Retrieved from http://www.un.org/disarmament/publications/documents_on_disarmament/1966/DoD_1966.pdf/ (last accessed on November 10, 2014).

United States Department of Defense (2002). "Secretary Rumsfeld Joint Media Availability with Indian Defense Minister." January 17. Retrieved from http://www.defense.gov/transcripts/transcript.aspx?transcriptid=2206/ (last accessed on November 10, 2014).

——— (2011). "Report to Congress on US-India Security Cooperation." November 11. Retrieved from http://www.defense.gov/pubs/pdfs/20111101_NDAA_Report_on_US_India_Security_Cooperation.pdf, US Department of Defense. pp. 1–9.

US Department of State (1993). "Report to Congress: Progress toward regional non-proliferation in South Asia." *US State Department*. April:2.

——— (2003). "Joint Statement following US-India Defense Policy Group Meeting." August 9. Retrieved from http://www.america.gov/st/washfile-english/2003/ (last accessed on November 10, 2014).

——— (2004). "United States–India joint statement on next steps in strategic partnership." September 17. Retrieved from http://2001-2009.state.gov/r/pa/prs/ps/2004/36290.htm/ (last accessed on November 10, 2014).

US-India Friendship.net (2001). "Bush, Vajpayee Joint Press Conference." November 9. Retrieved from http://www.usindiafriensdship.net/archives/viewpints/bush-vajpayee-112001.html (last assessed November 10, 2014).

Vanaik, Achin (1995). *India in a Changing World: Problems, Limits, and Successes of its Foreign Policy* (New Delhi: Orient Longman).

Varadarajan, Siddharth (2007). "Major obstacles persist in nuclear deal." April 25. Retrieved from http://www.hindu.com/2007/04/25/stories/2007042512410100.htm/ (last accessed on November 10, 2014).

Varshney, Ashutosh (1993). "Contested meanings: India's national identity, Hindu nationalism, and the politics of anxiety." *Daedalus*, 122(3):227–261.

Venugopalan, Urmila (2011). "Sorry Pakistan, China is no sugar daddy." *Foreign Policy*. July 21. Retrieved from http://www.foreignpolicy.com/articles/2011/07/21/sorry_pakistan_china_is_no_sugar_daddy/ (last accessed on November 10, 2014).

Vishwakarma, Arun (1999). "Agni—Strategic ballistic missile." *Deccan Herald*. April, 12. Retrieved from http://archive.is/sjCke/ (last accessed on November 10, 2014).

Wallace, Terry (1998). "The May 1998 India and Pakistani nuclear tests." Retrieved from http://srl.geoscienceworld.org/content/69/5/386.extract/ (last accessed on November 10, 2014).

Waltz, K. (1979). *Theory of International Politics* (New York: McGraw-Hill).

Weiner, Tim (1998). "The World: Naiveté at the C.I.A.: Every nation's just another US." *The New York Times*, June 7. http://www.nytimes.com/1998/06/07/weekinreview/the-world-naivete-at-the-cia-every-nation-s-just-another-us.html/ (assessed November 10, 2013).

Weinraub, Bernard (1991). "Economic crisis forcing once self-reliant India to seek aid." *The New York Times*, June 29:A1, 5.

Weiss, Ann E. (1983). *The Nuclear Arms Race: Can We Survive It?* (Boston, MA: Houghton Mifflin Co).

Weissman, Steve and Herbert Krosney (1981). *The Islamic Bomb* (New York: Times Book).

Weldes, Jutta, Mark Laffey, Hugh Gusterson, and Raymond Duvall (1999). *Cultures of Insecurity: States, Communities, and the Production of Danger* (Minneapolis, MN: University of Minnesota Press).

Wendt, Alexander (1992). "Anarchy is what states make of it: The social construction of power politics." *International Organization*, 46(2):391–425.

Westad, Odd Arne (2005). *The Global Cold War: Third World Interventions and the Making of Our Times* (Cambridge: Cambridge University Press).

Wolpert, Stanley (1993). *Zulfiqar Ali Bhutto of Pakistan: His Life and Times* (New York: Oxford University Press).

Yurman, Dan (2012). "Update on India's civilian nuclear energy program." May 17. Retrieved from http://ansnuclearcafe.org/2012/05/17/update-on-indias-civilian-nuclear-energy-program/ (last accessed on November 10, 2014).

Index

123 Agreement (July 2007), India–
    United States, 222, 225, 239–244,
    262n8

Abraham, Itty, 8
Acharya, Shankar, 145
Advani, L.K., 112, 114, 130, 173,
    188, 240
Age of Consent Bill, 40
Agni missile, 123, 126
    testing of, 158, 161, 162, 164, 165,
    181, 193, 205–206, 247
Ahluwalia, Montek Singh, 145
Ahmad, Shamshad, 148
Aiyar, Mani Shankar, 219, 247
Akash surface-to-air missile, 123
Akhil Bharat Hindu Mahasabha, 45
Akram, Munir, 182
Aksai Chin, 72
al-Afghani, Jamal ad-Din, 44
Alberuni, 33
Ali, Maualana Mohamed, 44
Ambedkar, B.R., 42, 60
American myth of limited war, 13
ancient India
    culture and strategic thinking in,
        29–34
    political affairs in, 30
    statecraft and warfare in, 29–30
Anglo-Egyptian dispute, 69
Anti-Ballistic Missile Treaty (1972),
    109, 125
anti-British Swadeshi movement, 42

anticolonial struggle, in India, 47
anti-cow slaughter by-law, 40
anti-tank guided missile (ATGM),
    102–103
Antony, A.K., 248–249, 252
APSARA atomic research reactor, 84
Arab nationalism, 69
arms control treaty, 104
arms race, 68, 79, 84, 109, 113
art of warfare, 36
Arthastastra (Kautilya), 17, 20, 30,
    267
    on ancient India's political affairs,
        30
    on India's foreign policy, 31
    policy protocols of, 30
    on psychological power of the
        king, 30
    relevance in India's strategic policy
        formulations, 31
Arunachalam, V.S., 123, 150
Asian despotism, 37
Aspin, Les, 143
assimilation to civilize, doctrine of, 36
atmashakti, 42
atomic bombs, 83
    making of, 100
Atomic Energy Act (1946), 68, 89n7
Atomic Energy Commission, India,
    100, 102–103, 110, 114
Atomic Energy Commission, Pakistan,
    94, 107
Atomic Energy Committee, India, 52

atomic energy, development of, 84
  for peaceful purpose, 99
atomic fuels, 82
atomic policy discourses, 57
  collaboration with foreign
    countries, 84
  India's atomic energy plans, 82
  of state-science community, 81–86
atomic power stations
  dual-purpose, 82
  establishment of, 84
  foreign bids in constructing, 85
  at Kalpakkam, 85
  and national security, 85
  at Tarapur, 85
Atomic Research Center, India, 114
atomic science debates, emergence of
  Indian state's discourses on
    (dis)armament, 79–81
  state-science community and,
    81–86
Atoms For Peace Program (1953),
    68–69, 89n8
Aurangzeb, Emperor, 32
Australia Group, 275
Azad, Bhagwat Jha, 97

Baghdad Pact. *See* Central Treaty
  Organization (CENTO)
Baig, S.A., 70
ballistic missile development
  program, 116
Banerjee, Dipankar, 252
Banerjee, Srikumar, 256
Banerjee, Surendranath, 60
Barnes, Harry, 125
Baruch Plan (1946), 68, 88n7
Bentinck, Lord, 37
Bhabha Atomic Research Center
  (BARC), 107, 110, 114, 123, 134
Bhabha, Homi, 50, 52–53, 81–82, 86,
    99–102
Bhakti Movement, 32

Bhartiya Janata Party (BJP), 16, 119,
    127, 267, 270. *See also* Congress
  party-led UPA government
  anti-Islamic/Pakistani sentiment,
    189, 190
  concept of national integration,
    175
  Election Manifestoes (1996 and
    1998), 171, 173, 189
  Executive National Committee, 130
  Hindutva ideology, 170, 172–174,
    175–176, 187, 191, 194
  India's international relations
    under, 176–187
  India's strategic rethinking and
    (in)security imaginaries under,
    157–158, 170–171, 187–204
  on minimum nuclear doctrine,
    176, 195–198, 213n18
  national security agenda, 175–176
  nationalist agenda and projecting
    India as a Hindu rashtra,
    172–174
  neoliberal strategic security
    collaborations, 204–209
  No-First-Use doctrine, 176, 195,
    197–198
  on nuclear development in India,
    204–209
  on nuclear tests program,
    190–194
  rise of, 172–173
  testing of H-bombs/thermo-nuclear
    devices, 196
  on US neoliberal discourses with
    India, 201
  US-centric national security
    agenda, 199, 200
Bhaskar, Uday, 191
Bhutto, Benazir, 127, 147, 151, 181
Bhutto, Z.A., 94–95, 107, 111
  lobbying for nuclear weapons, 101
Bidwai, Praful, 160

Bombay Club, 63
Bose, Debendra Nath, 50
Bose, Jagadish Chandra, 50
Bose, Satyendranath, 50
BrahMos Aerospace Limited, 206
Brasstacks crisis (January 1986), 127,
    130–131, 138n13
Brihadaranyaka Upanishad, 198
British colonial administration
    discourses on India's culture and
        identity, 37–38
    discourses on the Hindu–Muslim
        riot, 39
    divide and rule policy, 40
    indology on Indian culture,
        35–37
    policies of anglicizing India's
        politics and culture, 38
    separate electorates for Hindu and
        Muslims, 40
British imperialism, 62
British industrialization, technological
    aspects of, 42
British–Indian relations, 36
Buddhism, principles of, 45
Burns, Nicholas, 223, 226
Bush, George W., 180, 199, 222
Bush, H., 128

Cariappa, K.M., 108
Carnegie Institution, Washington
    DC, 53
Carter, President, 113–114
caste practices, 38
CDC 3600 system computer, 85
Central Intelligence Agency (CIA), 69
Central Treaty Organization
    (CENTO), 70–71
Chakrvarthy, B.N., 96
Chandra, Naresh, 188
Chari, P.R., 252
Chavan, Y.B., 97
Chellaney, Brahma, 150, 162

Chenghu, Zhu, 233
Chidambaram, P., 219
Chidambaram, R., 150, 158, 160,
    166, 204
child
    marriage, 37
    worship, 38
China, 71
    border dispute with India, 117
    military implications for Indian
        security, 93
    Ministry of External Affairs, 117
    NFU status, 235
    no-first use policy of nuclear
        weapons, 116
    nuclear strength, 233
    nuclear tests, 93, 103–104, 107,
        109, 112
    posing of nuclear threat to India,
        108
    relation with United States,
        144–145, 227, 251
    rise of, 249–250
    ties with India (*See* Sino-India
        relations)
    ties with Pakistan (*See* Sino-Pakistan
        relations)
China's National Defense (2004), 233
Chisti Sufi order, 38
Chou, En Lai, 72
Christian education, 36
CIRUS spent fuel, for weapons
    production, 123
Civilian Nuclear Accord (2008), 222,
    224, 226, 242
civil–military relations, characteristics
    of, 12
Clinton, Bill, 143–145, 155, 177
Clive, Robert, 32
codes of intelligibilities, 10, 18, 265
coexistence, principles of, 65
Cohen, William, 177
Cold Start Doctrine, 253

Cold War, 42, 62, 66–67, 69, 92, 114, 268
  arms race, 68, 79, 84, 113
  military alliances, 68
  objectives of the United States, 69
  proxy wars, 68
  trends of military preparedness, 69
  US–Pakistan nexus during, 125
collective consciousness, 28
colonial Indian politics
  anti-colonial struggles, 27
  India's nation-making in, 27
  security imaginaries, 27
Combined Acceleration Vibration Climatic Test System, 126
communal identity, of Hindu–Muslims in India, 39
communal riots, 38–40
Communist Party of India, 104
Comprehensive Test Ban Treaty (CTBT), 141, 143, 168n7, 196, 275
  anti-Western discourse against, 155–156
  entry-into-force clause, 143–144
  immunity to India from signing, 178
  United States' stance on, 144
computer technology and software, 125
Congress party-led UPA government, 215. *See also* Bhartiya Janata Party (BJP)
  Civilian Nuclear Accord (2008), 222, 224, 226, 242
  "India–China–US" trio, strategic balancing factor in, 227
  India–Pakistan relations, 228–233
  on India's international relations, 221–237
  India–US relations, 221–228
  Manifestoes of 2004 and 2009, 218, 220
  neoliberal nationalist agenda of, 217–220

post-2004 nuclear security affairs under, 237–256
  strategic collaborations and nuclear/missile development, 256–259
Cornwallis, Lord, 37
Council of Scientific and Industrial Research (CSIR), 86
Cray supercomputer, 125–126
Cuban missile crisis, 68
cultural identity of India, 48
  religious/anti-Muslim component of, 49
cultural integration, policy of, 32
cultural plurality, notions of, 43
cultural thinking
  in ancient India, 29–34
  in colonial India, 34–41
  interpretations of, 34–41
  in medieval India, 29–34

Dalai Lama, 72
Dean Acheson Plan (1946), 68
decision-making, strategic, 12
defense planning system, in India, 119
Defense Research and Development Organization (DRDO), 102, 122, 125, 134
  Integrated Guided Missile Development Program (IGMDP), 123, 134
"defenselessness" of India's strategic culture, 151–152
Department of Atomic Energy, India, 134
Department of Research and Defense Organization (DRDO), 142, 205–207
Desai, Ashok, 145
Desai, Morarji, 99, 104, 113
dharma, 27–31, 267
  moral aspects of, 34
  significance of, 34
Dhruva (R-5) nuclear reactor, 123

Director of Arms Control and Disarmament Agency, USA, 104
disarmament, in post-independent India, 79–81
definition of, 80
domestic bureaucratic institutional politics, 6
dual-use technology transfer, issue of, 276
Dubey, Muchkund, 160
Dutt, R.C., 64

Eighteen Nation Disarmament Committee in Geneva (July 1965), 96, 104
Eisenhower Doctrine, 70, 89n9
Eisenhower, President, 68–69, 71
energy resources, securing of, 275
English, as official language of India, 37
Enlightenment, 36–37
Enterprise, USS (US aircraft carrier), 107, 119
equality and mutual benefit, principles of, 106
European laws and judicial systems, 37

Fast Breeder Reactor, Kalpakkam, 123
Fernandes, George, 181, 184, 185, 188, 194, 197, 200
Fissile Material Cut-Off Treaty, 143, 146, 157, 168n3, 225, 231, 256, 275
fissile materials, 83, 95, 122
Foreign Assistance Act (1976), USA, 111, 127
foreign policy of India. *See also* nuclear policy of India
making of, 64–67
cultural politics of, 13

Gandhi, Indira, 92, 105, 114, 122, 136, 171, 269
India's strategic culture under, 104

nuclear policies under, 103, 111, 114–124
Gandhi, Mahatma, 43–44, 60, 100, 120, 131, 272
Gandhi, Rajiv, 91, 127, 141, 151, 255, 269
nuclear policy of India under, 124–135
penchant for computer software and technology, 124
visit to China, 129
Gandhi, Sonia, 234
Gandhian idealism, 58
Ghauri missile system, testing of, 176, 181, 190
Ghose, Arundhati, 156, 160
Ghoshal, U.N., 32
Gillani, Syed Yousuf Raza, 231
Gilpatric Committee, 95
Glenn Amendment Act (1994), 143, 148
global disarmament, 106, 113, 117, 121
Godbole, Madhav, 197
Gopalakrishnan, A., 241
Gorbachev, 125, 129
Govindacharya, K.N., 158
Gowda, Deva, 140, 160, 161, 166, 204
Graham, Bob, 201
Grant, Charles, 36
Gujral Doctrine, 148, 149, 169n11
Gujral, I.K., 140, 148, 149, 160–161, 162
gunboat diplomacy, 108
Gupta, Sisir, 104
Guruswamy, Mohan, 162

Haider, Salman, 148
Hank Brown Amendment (1995), 141, 148
Hastings, Warren, 37
high-level technology cooperation, US–India, 125
Hind Swaraj, 43

Hindu civilization/culture, 175–176
Hindu India, concept of, 49
Hindu kingdoms
   defense structure of, 32–33
   failure to resist foreign invasions,
      33
   lack of scientific spirit in, 33
   organizational skill of, 32
Hindu Mahasabha, 41, 45–47
Hindu nationalists, discourses of,
   45–49
Hindu *rashtra,* 46
Hindu Sanghatanist economic policy,
   concept of, 47, 56n8
Hindudharma, 46
Hinduised political program, 47
Hindu–Muslim
   consciousness, 32
   riots (*See* communal riots)
   unity, 44
History of British India, The (1817),
   35–36
Hoodbhoy, Pervez, 247
Hu, Jintao, 234
Hussain, Mushahid, 182
Hydaspes, Battle of, 29–30
Hyde Act (2006), USA, 222, 240,
   242
hydrogen bombs, 101

imagined communities, 17
India
   nationalism, ideological vision of,
      61
   political institutions,
      Europeanization of, 37
   politics and culture, British policies
      of anglicizing, 38
India–China relations. *See* Sino–India
   relations
Indian National Congress (INC), 41,
   42–45, 65. *See also* Congress party-
   led UPA government
Indian Parliament attack (2001), 183
Indian philosophy, principles of, 63

India–Pakistan relations, 71, 147–148
   under Bhartiya Janata Party,
      181–184, 189–190, 201–203
   bilateral ties, 148
   border clash incidents (2013),
      232–233
   confidence building measures, 127
   Congress party-led UPA
      government years, 228–233
   disputes affecting, 71
   impact of US–Pakistan military
      alliance on, 69–71
   Kashmir issue, 128, 179, 182, 185,
      190, 208, 228, 232, 248
   Operation Gibraltar (September
      1965), 95
   post-9/11, 183–184, 201–203
   Rann of Kutch incident (April
      1965), 94–95
   role of nuclear weapons in, 127
   terrorist incidents and, 229
India–Pakistan war
   in 1965, 95
   in 1971, 94, 107–108
India–Pakistan–Iran gas pipeline,
   275, 276
India's nuclear policy options/choices
   post-Cold War nuclear politics,
      140–141
   developments, 164–166
India's strategic culture, 64–67
   approaches to, 26
   British interpretations of, 26
   characteristic of, 28
   colonial discourses on, 37–38
   communalizing, 38–41
   definition of, 64
   discursive reconstructions of, 19
   Eurocentric degradation of, 36
   evolution of, 27, 31
   foundations of, 26, 28–29
   Hindu nationalists, discourses of,
      45–49
   Indian National Congress, views
      of, 42–45

nationalist discourses of, 41–49
and nuclear security, 15–17, 21
reconstruction of, 72–79, 96–99,
  105–109
religiocentric observations on, 34
religion-based assumption
  regarding, 34
social construction of, 21, 58, 67
source of, 28
tenets of Hinduism and, 20
Vedas and, 28–29
India's strategic rethinking and
  (in)security imaginaries
anti-CTBT status, 156–161
under Bhartiya Janata Party,
  157–158, 170–171, 178,
  187–204
China and, 203–204
following US-led international
  nuclear racism, 159
ideological and discursive
  orientations, 163
Indo-Pak nuclear debate,
  151–152
Pakistan-centric nuclear insecurity,
  182, 194–195
post-9/11, 199–204
post-2004, 237–256
in terms of anti-US nuclear
  hierarchy and robustness, 164
in terms of defense budget,
  153–154
thermonuclear tests, 161
US nonproliferation pressures, 155,
  160
US pressure on India's nuclear
  weapons program, 154–155
Western/racial focus of, 155
India–US relations, 141, 154–155
123 Agreement, 222, 225, 240,
  241, 242, 243–244, 262n8
Agreed Minutes of Defense
  Relations, 146
arms deal and defense cooperation,
  257

under Bhartiya Janata Party, 177,
  178–181
Bush–Rao meeting on regional
  nuclear restrains, 142–143
China factor and, 227
civil nuclear cooperation, 225, 239,
  240
Civilian Nuclear Accord, 222
during Clinton era, 143
Commonwealth links, 66
Congress party-led UPA
  government years, 221–228
in context of Pakistan, 147
context of Warsaw Guidelines
  (1992), 142
Cooperation in High Technology
  Transfer (MoU), 125
counter-terrorism cooperation,
  179–180, 221, 224, 229,
  246–247, 258
Cray supercomputer, 125–126
criticisms of India–US nuclear
  initiative, 241–242
CTBT agenda, 143–144
defense pact (2005), 257
defense research and cooperation,
  146
exchange visits, 145, 168n8
on exports of computer and
  technology, 126
flow of dual-use technology,
  244–245
on global disarmament, 113
Hyde Act (2006), 240, 241
impact of Cold War on, 71
impact of US–Pakistan relation
  on, 70
on India's insecurities from United
  States, 144, 146–147
Indo-American security
  cooperation, 142
Maritime Security Cooperation
  Agreement, 257–258
Medium Multi-Role Combat
  Aircraft (MMRCA) deal, 245

Memorandum of Understanding, 120, 125
on military and defense collaboration, 118
military collaborations since 2002, 200, 208, 209, 226–227, 256–259
neoliberal nuclear security, 222–223
New Framework for the US–India Defense Relationship (June 2005), 257–258
Next Steps in Strategic Partnership (NSSP) Program, 181
nonproliferation of weapons of mass destruction, 155, 160
Nuclear Accord (2008), 226, 230
on nuclear security, 53, 113
collaborations on, 245–246
on nuclear technology orientation, 121
nuclear technology/strategic security developments, 179, 181, 225–226
during Obama era, 223–228
post-9/11 alliance, 179, 199–201
proliferation-related irks/ insecurities in, 143
rethinking of super powers and, 141–142
on security cooperation, 125
strategic partnerships, 275
trade and investment, 145–146
Indira Doctrine (1983), 118, 138n11
Indo-Aryan synthesis, of cultural renaissance, 28
Indo-Soviet relations, 66
on nuclear and missile technology development, 123
on purchase of military equipment, 123
Industrial Policy Resolution (1948), 88
industrial revolution, 60

Integrated Guided Missile Development Program (IGMDP), 123, 142
"intellectual colonialism," of the nonproliferation regime, 111
International Atomic Energy Agency (IAEA), 69, 88n7, 110–111
International Conference on Peaceful Uses of Atomic Energy, First (August 1955), 83
international relations (IR), 1, 26, 57, 265
with China, Pakistan, and United States, 67–72, 104–105
under Indira Gandhi, 103, 111, 114–124
interpretation of, 67–72, 104–105, 124–129
nuclear policy of India and, 115–117
nuclear weapons policy debates, 99–103
under Prime Minister Shastri, 92–96
under Rajiv Gandhi, 124–135
strategic culture and security imaginary, 105–109
strategy-making, 11–15, 96–99
theoretical approaches to security in, 6–9
Western narratives of, 7
interstate interdependence, concept of, 266
interstate security relations, 5
invasions faced by India, 30–32
Islamic invasions, 34
Turkish–Afghan invasions, 32
Irwin, H.C., 40
"Islamic bomb", 107
Islamic universalism, ideals of, 42
Israeli–Arab conflict, 69
itihasas (historical event), 28
Iyengar, P.K., 131, 134, 152, 154, 241

Jammu and Kashmir, 94
Jana Sangh, 85, 98, 100, 108
Janata Government, nuclear policy
    under, 112–114
Jha, L.K., 106
Jiang, Zemin, 149, 169n12
Jinnah, Muhammad Ali, 44
Johnston, A., 14–15, 18
Joint State Defense Working Group,
    69
Jones, D., 12
Joshi, B.C., 154

Kahuta centrifuge plant, Pakistan,
    114, 117
Kakodkar, Anil, 204
Kalam, A.P.J. Abdul, 123, 134, 154,
    158–159, 161–162, 166, 191, 204,
    242
Kamath, H.V., 104
Kamtekar, D.S., 197
Karamat, Jehangir, 181
Karat, Prakash, 240
Kashmir crisis, 71, 128
Kaul, S.K., 158
Kautilya, 17, 26, 30–31, 219, 266
Kerry, John, 224
Khampa rebellion, Tibet, 72
Khan, A.Q., 111, 116, 119, 147, 152,
    181, 242
Khan, Ayub, 94–95
Khan, Munir Ahmad, 107
Khan, Riaz Mohammad, 231
Khan, Shaharyar, 147, 148, 152
Khar, Hina Rabbani, 232
Khursheed, Salman, 154, 224
Kidwai, Khalid, 182, 231
Kissinger, Henry, 107, 226
Kolar Gold Fields, 85
Kripalani, Acharya, 66
Krishna, Raj, 104
Krishna, S.M., 232, 256
Kumar, S. Krishna, 151

Light Combat Aircraft (LCA), 125
liquid-fuel rocket engines, 102
Look East policy, India, 276

McMahon Line, 72
Madras Atomic Power Station-I and
    II, 123
Mahabharata, 28–29
Mahmud of Ghazni, Sultan, 34
Malkani, K.R., 157
Manhattan Project, 53
Manila Conference (July 1954), 70
Markey, Ed, 201
Mathur, Harish Chandra, 97
meaning-fixing, politics of, 9–11
medieval India, culture and strategic
    thinking in, 29–34
Medium Multi-Role Combat Aircraft
    (MMRCA) deal, 245
Menon, Krishna, 99, 104
Menon, Shivshankar, 238
Middle Eastern Defense Organization,
    70
militarized India, notion of, 47
Mishra, Brajesh, 162, 178, 185, 188,
    194
missile development, in India, 102,
    123–124
Missile Technology Control Regime
    (MTCR), 126, 128, 275
Mohan, C. Raja, 162
Mughal Empire, 32
Muhammadan culture, elements of, 44
Mukherjee, Pranab, 153, 192, 219,
    222, 223, 232, 238, 246, 247
Mukherjee, S.B., 200
Mulford, David, 223
Muni, S.D., 248
Munshi, K.M., 28
Muppidi, H., 10
Musharraf, Pervez, 182, 184, 201
    post-9/11 strategic cultural shifts
        toward India, 202

Muslim League, 45
Muslim struggle in India, 45
Mutual Defense Assistance
    Agreement, 70

Nag antitank guided missile, 123
Nambiar, Satish, 148
Naqshbandi Sufi order, 38
Narayanasamy, V., 256
national cultures, sociocultural
    characteristics of, 2
national defense planning, India, 16
national development of India,
    Western technology and science
    for, 55
National Security Council, India, 69,
    119
national security of India, 64–67
    China's military implications for,
        93
    Nehru's idea of, 65
nationalist identities, 27
nation-building
    military dimensions of, 47
    strategic culture and discourses of,
        60–64
Nayyar, K.K., 162
Nehru, Jawaharlal, 51, 57, 84, 86,
    100, 103
    on Chinese suzerainty over Tibet,
        72
    idea of national security, 65
    nonviolence and nonalignment,
        concept of, 111
    Panchsheel, theory of, 65
    perception of US–Pak alliances, 70
    on relation with China, 72
"new world order," evolution of, 80
Next Steps in Strategic Partnership
    (NSSP) Program, 181, 221
Nixon, President, 107
Nonaligned Movement (NAM), 65
    Articles I, II, and III of, 106
Non-Aligned Summit, New Delhi, 122

nonalignment, India's concept of, 98
nonnuclear weapon states (NNWS),
    96, 156
northern tier state alliance, 70
nuclear apartheid, 109
nuclear deterrence, 85, 100
nuclear disarmament, 106–107
nuclear hierarchy, trends of, 103,
    105, 112
nuclear liability bill, 277
nuclear nonproliferation, 95, 105
    international safeguards against,
        113
Nuclear Non-Proliferation Act
    (NNPA, 1978), USA, 113, 121
Nuclear Non-Proliferation Treaty
    (NPT), 103, 106, 143, 275
    India's rejection of, 110
nuclear nonviolence, 96
    Gandhi–Nehru's notions of, 5
    India's philosophy of, 112
nuclear policy of India
    debates on, 99–103
    development of nuclear weapons,
        109–112, 122–124
    Gandhian nuclear nonviolence and,
        112
    under Indira Gandhi, 103, 111,
        114–124
    international relations and, 115–117
    under Janata Government, 112–114
    on nuclear technology
        developments, 133–135
    peaceful nuclear explosion and,
        109–112
    politico-diplomatic-military
        strategy for, 112
    under Prime Minister Shastri,
        92–96
    pro-nuclear shift in, 112
    under Rajiv Gandhi, 124–135
    strategic culture and security
        imaginary, 105–109, 117–122,
        129–133

Nuclear Posture Review (NPR), 143,
168*n*5, 180, 211*n*6, 224
nuclear power, 82–83
military applications of, 100
Nehru–Tito–Nasser Joint Statement
on, 83–84
for peaceful purposes, 83
nuclear power stations. *See* atomic
power stations
nuclear reactors, 82, 84
APSARA, 84
Dhruva (R-5), 123
Fast Breeder Reactor, 123
Purnima, 110
RAPS II, 110
nuclear revolution in India, 82
nuclear security
in Indian context, 15–17
policy making for, 1–2
nuclear self-reliance, India's goal of,
131
nuclear sovereignty, concept of, 105
nuclear strategy, 11
in international affairs, 266
Nuclear Suppliers Group (NSG), 111,
142, 225, 275
nuclear test
by China, 93, 103–104, 107, 109,
112
by India, 103, 123
by Pakistan, 121
for peaceful purpose, 103,
109–112
nuclear weaponization of India, 103
nuclear weapons
abhorrence of, 79
acquisition of, 93, 99
atomic bombs, 83
comprehensive test ban treaty, 95
development of, 109–112
domestic and international
inhibitions in, 101
Gilpatric Committee for preventing
spread of, 95

Hiroshima and Nagasaki tragedy,
79–80
India's strategic discourses in
support of, 107
making of, 100
mechanisms to check the spread
of, 68
no-first use policy of, 116
nonproliferation policy, 68
policy debates, 99–103
policy of India, 268
program for, 272
and trends of military
preparedness, 69
nuclear weapons states (NWS), 96,
144
nuclear-based defense installations, in
India, 99

Obama, Barack, 223–228, 244, 245,
254
Operation Checkerboard (1987), 129
Operation Gibraltar (1965), 95
Oriental blackies, 157
Oriental despotism, idea of, 35
Outer Space Treaty (1967), 115

Pakistan. *See also* India–Pakistan
relations; Sino-Pakistan relations;
US–Pakistan relations
ballistic missiles programs, 128,
147–148
as failed state, 277
India-specific nuclear doctrinal
stand, 229–230
Kahuta centrifuge plant, 114, 117
Kargil crisis, 182–183
Kashmir issue, 182–183
missile development by, 116
nuclear capability, 117
nuclear explosion, 121
nuclear missile programs, 118,
121, 147–148, 162, 165, 176,
181, 229–231

nuclear technology expansion, 111
nuclear weapons program, 118, 121
posture of minimum nuclear
deterrence, 230
testing of nonnuclear triggering
package, 129
panchsheel, 65, 268
Pandey, Gyanendra, 38
Panipat, Battle of (1757), 32
partition of Bengal (1905), 40, 42
peaceful coexistence, principles of, 129
peaceful nuclear explosion (PNE),
103, 109–112, 138n9
nuclear weapons policies leading
to, 112
Peaceful Nuclear Explosive (1974),
171
Peng, Li, 149
Perry, William, 143
Plassey, Battle of (1757), 32
political institutionalization,
European notions of, 45
Ponappa, Leela, 252
postcolonial India, nationalist identity
for, 41
Poulose, T.T., 79
Praja Socialist Party, 97, 99, 104
Prasad, A.L., 241
Pressler Amendment, 124, 127–128,
147
Principles and Objectives for
Nuclear Non-Proliferation and
Disarmament, 155
Prithvi series missile system, 123,
148, 154, 160, 164, 206
Program Analysis Group, 110
public-sector industrialization, 50
puranas, 28
Purnima reactor, 110

Qureshi, Shah Mahmood, 229

Radhakrishnan, Sarvepalli, 42, 60
Raghavan, V.R., 153

Raghunath, K., 178, 188
Rai, Vijai, 153
Rajagopalachari, C., 63
Ram, Jagjivan, 108
Ram Janambhoomi Babri Masjid
incident, 153
Ramanna, Raja, 106, 110, 123,
130–131, 134, 152, 161
Ramayana, 28–29
Rann of Kutch incident (April 1965),
95
Rao, Nirupama, 250
Rao, P.V. Narasimha, 122, 145, 148,
149, 152, 155, 159
Rashtriya Swayam Sevak (RSS), 46,
48, 174, 267
Reagan, President, 115, 120, 125
Republican nationalism, ideology
of, 13
Rice, Condoleezza, 223, 227
Richardson, Bill, 181
Rithambara, Sadhvi, 174
Rohini-560 satellite, 110, 123
Roychowdhury, Shankar, 229
Rumsfeld, Donald, 200, 221

Saha, Meghnad, 50–51
Said, Edward, 7
SALT II negotiations, 113–115
Santhanam, K., 165, 191, 204
Sarabhai Profile, 110
Sarabhai, Vikram, 103, 109–110
Saran, Shyam, 219, 221, 238
sati, social-cultural evil of, 38
Savarkar, Veer, 45–46, 49, 174
conception of India as a Hindu
nation, 46
Schunker, M.R., 119
science in colonial India, discourses
of, 49–54
security community, 24n1
security imaginary, concept of, 9–11,
24n2, 26, 96–99, 105–109
Sen, Ronen, 219, 223, 246

Separation Plan, 222, 239, 241, 243, 262n7
Sethna, H.N., 241
Shanghai Initiative (1995), 146
Sharif, Nawaz, 147, 148, 152, 181, 183, 232–233
Sharma, Krishna Lal, 153
Shastri, Lal Bahadur, 92–96, 103
  defense-oriented pragmatic realism, 135
Shekhar, Chandra, 140, 148
Singh, Charan, 114
Singh, Jasjit, 153, 191, 250
Singh, Jaswant, 16, 151, 160, 175, 177, 178, 188, 240
Singh, Manmohan, 145, 219–220, 222, 224, 232, 234, 238, 243
Singh, Swaran, 94, 96
Singh, V.P., 140, 150, 151, 166
Sinha, Yashwant, 201
Sino-India relations, 148–149, 169n12. *See also* China; Sino-Pakistan relations
  after 9/11, 186–187, 203–204
  Agreement on the Actual Line of Control, 185
  on Arunachal Pradesh, 128
  under Bhartiya Janata Party, 184–187
  border issues, 149, 250–251
  under Congress party-led UPA government, 233–237
  Declaration on Cooperation, 185
  diplomatic interactions between 1991 and 1997, 149
  factors affecting, 72
  on India's thermonuclear tests, 161–162
  on Kashmir issue, 149, 235
  mutual agreements on bilateral trade and cooperation, 234
  on nuclear issue, 150
  Operation Checkerboard (1987), 129

post-2004, 249
Sino-Indian dialogue (1998), 185
strategic thinking on, 129
on supply of low-enriched uranium, 149–150
war of 1962, 59, 67, 85, 97
Sino-India war (1962), 59, 67, 85, 97
Sino-Pakistan relations, 235–236, 251–252
on development of nuclear weapons technology, 117, 128, 271
military alliances and transactions, 132
military assistance to Pakistan, 128
nuclear collusion against India, 252
Sino-Soviet conflict, 129
Six Glorious Epochs (Savarkar), 45
Six-Nation Five-Continent Appeal (May 22, 1984), 122
SLV3 satellite launch vehicle, 123
social construction, 9–11, 20
social insecurities, 1
social institutions, evolution of, 29
social regeneration, 43
social-cultural evils, in India, 37
South East Asia Treaty Organization (SEATO), 70–71, 89n10
Soviet Union, 66–67, 71, 91, 96, 121, 134
conflict with China, 129
invasion of Afghanistan, 114
relations with India (*See* Indo–Soviet relations)
Treaty of Friendship and Cooperation with India, 107
Space and Upper Atmospheric Research Commission, Karachi, 94
Srinivasan, M.R., 241
Star Wars program, 115
Space Command (1987), 125
state sovereignty, notion of, 7
Strategic Arms Limitations Talks I, 109

strategic cultures
  critique of, 17–19
  definition of, 11
  in Indian context (*See* India's strategic culture)
  methodology for study of, 21–22
  notions of, 3
  research on, 19–21
  scholarships, 17
  and security, 17–19
  strategy-making in international politics, 11–15
strategic thinking of India
  in ancient times, 29–34
  during colonial period, 34–41, 64
  interpretations of, 34–41
  in medieval India, 29–34
  and position of nuclear restrain, 270
  post-Cold War, 140–141
strategy-making, in international politics, 11–15
Sub-Nuclear Explosion Project, 105
Subrahmanyam, K., 104, 108, 119–120, 130, 150, 153–154, 157, 158, 160, 161, 223, 247, 251, 272
Subterranean Nuclear Explosion Project, 102
Sundarji, K., 119, 127, 129, 153, 161, 190
Swaraj, Sushma, 174
Swatantra Party, 93, 97, 100
Symington Amendment, 111, 115, 138n8

Talbott, Strobe, 177, 226
Tanham, G., 15
Tarapur Nuclear plant, 120
  US supply of fuels to, 121
Tata Institute of Fundamental Research, Bombay, 52, 84–86
territoriality, notion of, 48
time, Hindu concept of, 16
Treaty of Friendship and Cooperation, India–Soviet Union, 107

Trishul surface-to-air missile, 123
Trivedi, V.C., 96, 98, 105–106
Tryst With Destiny (Nehru), 60
Turkish–Afghan invasions, in India, 32

UNESCO, 80
United Kingdom, 66, 70
United Nations, 95
  Commission on Disarmament, 96
  Disarmament Commission, 80
  General Assembly an Action Plan, 131
United States. *See also* India–US relations
  "Af–Pak" strategy, 224
  Arms Control and Disarmament Agency, 95
  under Barack Obama, 223–228
  Bilateral Defense Policy Group, 147
  under Bill Clinton, 143–145
  CTBT agenda, 143–144
  nonproliferation policy, 112
  post-9/11 security discourses with India, 179, 199–201
  South Asian agenda, 145, 155, 159
  Space Command (1987), 125
Upanishads, 55n1, 267
uranium enrichment, 113, 116, 126
uranium plant, Jaduguda, 84
USAID, 85
US–China relations, 144–145, 227, 251
US–Pakistan relations
  Cold War nexus, 125
  India's concerns on, 70
  military aid against India, 94–95, 116, 125, 127
  military pacts, 69–71, 86–87, 132
  on nuclear weapons program, 118, 127, 271
  post-9/11 proximity, 275–276
  Pressler Amendment and, 124, 127

US–Soviet Union relations
  Anti-Ballistic Missile Treaty, 125
  arms control measures, 95
  comprehensive test ban treaty, 95
  on nonproliferation of nuclear
    weapons, 81
  SALT agreement, 113–115

Vajpayee, Atal Behari, 114, 126, 154,
  157, 185, 189, 194, 199, 200, 202,
  240
Vanaik, Achin, 160
vasudhaiva kutumbakam, 29
Vedas, 28–29, 267
Venkataraman, R., 122

Wassenaar Arrangement, 244–245,
  275
Wen, Jiabao, 185, 234
Westphalian notions of India, 65

Yadav, Mulayam Singh, 162
Yeltsin, Boris, 141, 178

Zangger Committee, 111, 137n5
Zardari, Asif, 232
Zero Energy Reactors for Lattice
  Investigations and Neutron Assay
  (ZERLINA), 85
Zia-ul-Haq, President, 112, 116, 127,
  138n12

About the Author

Runa Das is an Associate Professor in the Department of Political Science, University of Minnesota Duluth, USA. Prior to this she was a Visiting Lecturer at Wayne State University, Michigan, USA.